Designing and Assessing Courses and Curricula

A Practical Guide

THIRD EDITION

ROBERT M. DIAMOND

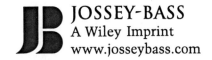

JOSSEY-BASS
A Wiley Imprint
www.josseybass.com

Library of Congress Cataloging-in-Publication Data

Diamond, Robert M.
    Designing and assessing courses and curricula: a practical guide/Robert M. Diamond.—3rd ed.
        p.   cm.—(Jossey-Bass higher and adult education series)
    Includes bibliographical references and index.
        ISBN 978-0-470-26134-7 (pbk.)
    1. Universities and colleges—Curricula—United States.   2. Curriculum planning—United States.   3. Curriculum evaluation—United States.   I. Title.
    LB2361.5.D5   2008
    378.1'9'0973—dc22
                                                                          2008014793

THIRD EDITION
PB Printing   10 9 8 7 6 5 4 3

CONTENTS

The Present State of Higher Education: Some Perspectives

Despite some notable progress on the frontiers of reform since the 1960s and 1970s, higher education's core practices remain largely unchanged, rending the enterprise less than it should be in today's environment. Many of the items heading the agenda for change in 1970 continue today. Critics regularly question the learning exhibited by college graduates. Moreover, achievement gaps in higher education persist between students of lower and higher socio-economic status and across ethnic and racial groups. . . . Also, while everyone agrees that improving educational performance entails more concerted interactions with primary and secondary schools, the linkages between them remain weak.

—National Center for Postsecondary Improvement

Change is urgently needed. Even as college attendance is rising, the performance of too many students is faltering. Public policies have focused on getting students into a college, but not on what they are expected to accomplish once there. The result is that the college experience is a revolving door for millions of students, while the college years are poorly spent by many others.

—The Association of American Colleges and Universities

Student success in college cannot be documented—as it usually is—only in terms of enrollment, persistence, and degree attainment. These widely used metrics, while important, miss entirely the question of whether students who have placed their hopes for the future in higher education are actually achieving the kind of learning they need for a complex and volatile world . . .

—The National Leadership Council for Liberal
Education & America's Promise

In a 2006 article I made the following observation: "Significant changes will never occur in any institution until the forces for change are greater in combination than the forces preserving the status quo." If not there yet, higher education is extremely close to that tipping point.

The years following the publication of the Second Edition of *Designing and Assessing Courses and Curricula* have not been good ones for American colleges and universities. Business and industry leaders increasingly call for graduates who can speak and write effectively, have high-quality interpersonal and creative thinking skills, have some understanding of the rest of the world, and can work effectively with individuals from different cultures and backgrounds. In addition, state and federal funding for higher education has either diminished or failed to keep up with need, and one of the major forces for innovation in colleges and universities for decades, the American Association for Higher Education, has folded. At the same time that the calls for major improvements in the quality of academic programs and for institutional accountability have risen in both quantity and intensity, major foundations long known for their support of colleges and universities shifted their funding priorities to other areas. While there may be some disagreement as to accuracy of some of the statistics used to support the need for reform (Attewell and Lavin, 2007), there is little disagreement both inside and outside of the academy that colleges and universities must pay greater attention to the quality of the education they provide to students.

These concerns about quality and accountability are not new—they have been around for years. In the Preface to the 1998 edition was a quote from Roy Romer, then chair of a task force for the Education Commission of the United States: "For all its rich history, there are too many signs that higher education is not taking seriously its responsibility to maintain a strong commitment to undergraduate learning; to be accountable for products that are relevant, effective and of demonstrable quality; and to provide society with the full range of benefits from investments in research and public service" (Romer, 1995, p. 1). The demand for increased accountability articulated in the observations by Romer is directly related to one of the major recommendations of the 2006 Department of Education's Commission report on the Future of Higher Education. Ernest Boyer's observation that there is a "disturbing gap between colleges and the larger world" (1987, p. 6) is as true today as it was over twenty years ago.

Further complicating the challenges to colleges and universities are the significant changes that have taken place in our students over the last two decades. Our student population has not only grown substantially but has become more diverse in terms of age, gender, and cultural background. Today only 16 percent of the student population can be described as "traditional" (aged eighteen to twenty-two, attending college full-time, and living on campus), a growing percentage are the first generation in their family to attend college, and over fifty percent of all students are women (Smith, MacGregor, Matthews, and Gabelnick, 2004). In addition, many entering students are lacking in important prerequisites and effective study habits.

There are two other factors contributing to the pressure to change felt by those in leadership positions at American universities.

- *The impact of globalization.* William Tierney has identified five trends and challenges that globalization has created for higher education.

  1. Education no longer has any borders, students are able to take classes virtually anywhere in the world—in person or online.
  2. A college or university is less of a physical place today and more of an interaction that may occur anywhere, on the Internet or in any one of a number of emergent virtual realties.
  3. In a globalized world competition increases: students have more choices about the kind of institution they will attend and the kind of training they desire.
  4. Globalization has weakened the social welfare state and increased the importance of privatization. As state funding support has decreased, state institutions have been required to raise more and more money from private sources. As a result the difference between state and private institutions is becoming increasingly blurred.
  5. Colleges and universities are becoming more decentralized and decisions are being made closer to where the action takes place. State planning or centralized decision-making is taking a backseat to entrepreneurial activity at the local level [2007, pp. 1–2].

- *The significant role played by accreditation agencies in fostering change by requiring statements of learning outcomes and evidence that instructional goals are being met.* As more and more political and professional leaders perceive accreditation as a major lever for change, there are increased pressures on the agencies and associations who determine criteria to focus on learning outcomes and institutional accountability. New demands for specificity, for academic quality, and for extensive documentation have taken accreditation from being an activity dealt with by small numbers of administrators to a process that will involve every faculty member and academic administrator.

Why Institutions Are So Hard to Change _____

Although the pressures for change intensify and are no longer possible to ignore, the reactions to these pressures by many colleges and universities has been modest, to say the least. On many campuses, the rhetoric may have changed, but there have been few significant attempts to address the issues directly. Procedures, structures, and priorities have tended to remain constant. The reasons for this are many.

People usually find that it is far less risky to do nothing than to try to change and, in higher education, tradition is a most powerful force. Trustees and administrators often do not see their role as change agents, and many in these positions are selected on criteria that have little to do with leadership or their understanding of the forces now impacting higher education. With competition between institutions, programs, and faculty the norm, it is extremely difficult to get the cooperation that is required to successfully address institutionwide issues, and with faculty often more committed to their discipline or department than to the institution, this type of cooperation becomes even more difficult to attain. In addition, the reward and recognition system for individual units, faculty, and administrators usually tends to support the status quo. On most campuses there is simply no reward for participating in the activities that are desperately needed. For more on the forces resisting change, and actions that can be taken to overcome them, see "Changing Higher Education: Realistic Goal or Wishful Thinking?" (Diamond, 2006).

Not discussed in the article are three other factors that add to the challenges faced by anyone attempting to implement major reform at a college or university.

The impact of technology on teaching and learning. Technology significantly increases the instructional options available to faculty, but also has a negative impact on two other areas that rarely receive the attention they deserve: institutional budgets and the ways in which students study and learn. As institutions attempt to implement a wide range of administrative applications of technology and to provide students with the computer support that they demand, an increasing percentage of the total budget is devoted to supporting the purchase of equipment and the required maintenance and technical support. In a number of instances these monies have been generated by an increase in internal charges for a wide range of services that were at one time provided at no cost to individual units. In this approach, individual units are charged directly for a portion of the total costs to the institution. In periods of flat budgets, departments are then forced to redirect the funds that they have available to support faculty and the improvement of instruction. On a number of campuses one of the areas directly affected by these cuts has been the academic support center—at the very time that more faculty are requesting their assistance. The second area where technology has an impact is on the way students approach the entire learning experience. Faculty are reporting decreasing attendance in classes, more students multitasking during lectures, and difficulty in getting students to devote to their assignments the amount of effort and time required for quality work.

The increase in the number of part-time or adjunct faculty. One unintended outcome of the movement away from tenured faculty at colleges and universities is the impact this change has on the entire academic enterprise. Individuals in these positions, although often dedicated and talented, are usually not expected to serve as advisors to students or to participate in the course and curriculum design efforts that are so urgently needed. As a result, with nearly 50 percent of all faculty in these untenured or part-time positions, the remaining faculty find themselves asked to do more with little compensation and no additional support.

The dominance of the U.S. News & World Report rankings. The *U.S. News* rankings have been described as "the nation's *de facto* accountability system—evaluating colleges and universities on a common scale and creating strong incentives for institutions to do things that raise their ratings" (Carey, 2006, p. 1). Emphasizing three factors—fame, wealth, and exclusivity—this approach to the use of data has had a significant affect on the priorities of many institutional leaders, in that the quality of the education their institutions provide becomes less important than the percentage of applicants turned down or the money received in grants and donations.

Our challenges are complex, but we do have a solid base to build on. We know how to improve the quality of our teaching, how to help under-prepared students succeed, how to improve retention, and how to prepare our graduates to be more productive and successful citizens. There are projects in colleges and universities in the United States and throughout the world that have been successful in addressing all the issues and concerns being raised. Unfortunately, too few academic leaders or faculty know the research, and even fewer politicians have the political will to play their key role in changing the state and national priorities so that these issues can be successfully addressed. Until the faculty reward system is modified to strike a proper balance between teaching, research, and service, and until alumni and political leaders pay more attention to the quality of the education students receive than they do to the success of an institution's athletic teams and to national rankings, which have little to do with the actual effectiveness of an institution's academic program, little will change. Fortunately we may be reaching a point in the United States where the entire system of higher education will have no option but to change. The nation is getting close to demanding such change.

Designing and Assessing Courses and Curricula

When taken together, these challenges present a clear call for imaginative planning, with faculty and administrators working together toward change. There is a need for academic programs to take full advantage of the abilities of faculty, of technological developments, and of creative new forms of teaching and learning. Although the various reports and studies call for changes in content and pedagogy, they do not describe how these changes might be made.

Institutions, departments, or faculty often recognize significant problems in the content and design of their curricula or courses, but their efforts to change are hampered by uncertainty about how to make orderly changes, where to begin, what outcomes to target, and what roles faculty, curriculum committees, and administrators should play. This book provides a model for change that answers these questions.

Attempts to change curricula are not new. Major projects in developing core curricula were undertaken in the 1920s and again in the 1940s. But each of these efforts foundered as it attempted to build in more flexibility and greater student choice. This trend was even more in evidence in the early 1970s, when requirements, structure, and sequence of programs and courses almost disappeared from many campuses. The key, as Joan Stark and Lisa Lattuca pointed out in their review of curriculum innovation, is "to find the balance that will provide choice while preserving culture, one that will provide exposure to alternative perspectives while avoiding fragmentation" (1997, pp. 354–355). No easy challenge.

Although the problems we face are significant, this is also an exciting time to be a faculty member at the many colleges and universities where increased attention is being paid to teaching and learning. These institutions are rethinking their goals and priorities, their curricula, and the way learning takes place. Numerous examples will be found throughout these pages. The promotion and tenure system is also beginning to undergo major transformation, and many of the disciplinary associations are actively facilitating the change by providing their members with creative new instructional materials and by expanding the scope of activities they consider scholarly.

We also have available to us technological innovations that open up opportunities to significantly increase faculty access to course and curricular information as well as to improve the quality and scope of our students' learning experience.

Purpose of the Book

Designing and Assessing Courses and Curricula responds to the questions of faculty and administrators who recognize a need for change but are unsure of how to reach their goals. The chapters focus on an approach that has been used at institutions with very different profiles—private and public, large and small—and with varying budgets. It offers a practical approach to systemic change and perhaps even more important, it is one of the few change models that focuses on the crucial relationship between courses and the curriculum of which they are a part. The book shows how to move from concept to actualization, from theory to practice. Case studies illustrate the model's adaptability to broad curricular change and to course and program design; it works with equal success in both areas.

In their study of the contextual influences on faculty as they design their courses, Stark and Lattuca observed that less than one-third of those teaching general education courses reported that books and articles on teaching and learning were an influence in their course planning (1997, pp. 224–225). To successfully revise a course or curriculum, you need up-to-date knowledge about learning and the various ways to facilitate it. Without this knowledge, efforts to improve student learning are unlikely to succeed.

As one of our goals is to direct you to more detailed information on topics of specific interest to you as you move through the design process, most chapters include an annotated additional resources section as well as resources discussed in the body of the material. When applicable, we have also identified those materials that are available over the Internet.

The process we will follow has remained constant over the years, but this book represents a major revision from the second edition. Based on feedback from previous users, the book has been totally restructured to make it easier to use. Many chapters have been shortened, with most case studies and resources being relocated in separate sections in the back of the book. This has permitted the case studies to be expanded and allows you to locate more easily the specific materials that will be of greatest use to you.

You will find new chapters on accreditation, distance learning, and teaching adult students, and many existing chapters have been significantly updated or rewritten. The chapters on diversity, technology, and selecting instructional options have been expanded, and several chapters from the second edition have been divided into separate chapters to provide you with more detailed information on specific topics.

Several factors make this model particularly relevant. Programs that have been developed using the model successfully meet the goals identified in the major reports on educational change, as well as the requirements of all the new accreditation standards (including clearly stated goals, learning outcomes, assessment, and continuous improvement). Compared with other approaches, this model is cost-effective, as it provides visible results in the shortest possible time.

Finally, and equally important, although this approach requires hard work, you will find it exciting, challenging, and rewarding, and administrators will remark on its efficiency and effectiveness.

Purposes and Audiences

Many excellent books have been written about teaching and learning. But that is not the focus of this book. This is a practical, descriptive handbook for faculty and administrators involved in the improvement of teaching and learning. It provides you with an effective model for designing, implementing, and evaluating courses and curricula. It suggests design options that are available to help you meet the diverse needs of your students, and offers guidelines for those you invite to help you in the design process. Finally, it helps to move the focus of course design from content coverage to student learning, keeping in mind the role that the course has in meeting the overarching goals of the curricula.

Although based on sound theory, this book is not a theoretical discourse; rather, it is a practical guide for faculty and administrators, showing how to approach and implement the redesign of courses and curricula—the structures in which learning takes place.

The suggestions are derived from my own experience and that of many associates in various institutions and other creative faculty throughout the United States. Although many case studies are drawn from the records of Syracuse University's Center for Instructional Development, others are from large and small public and private colleges and universities that represent the broad spectrum of American higher education. The book shares the strategies that have worked well in making constructive, planned change of the sort higher education is presently challenged to initiate.

Overview of the Book _____

To assist you through the design, implementation, and assessment process the chapters of the book are divided into four distinct parts.

Part 1: A Frame of Reference

The six chapters in this section are designed to lay the groundwork for the work that will follow. After an overview of the rationale behind the process and its many benefits, you will find in Chapter 2 an in-depth look at the changes that are under way in accreditation and the impact that these changes will have on institutions, programs, faculty, and administrators. In Chapter 3 you will find specific recommendations on some relatively easy actions you can take to keep yourself up-to-date on the newest research on teaching and learning and on issues impacting higher education. Because the work that you will do on courses and curricula has all the characteristics of true scholarship, Chapter 4 offers a discussion of faculty rewards and how this work can be more appropriately recognized in the tenure and promotion process. Chapter 5 introduces the specific steps in the model and discusses in more detail the characteristics that have made this approach so effective. Included is a discussion of the types of individuals you may want to get involved in your project and their respective roles. In Chapter 6 we describe an extremely effective technique that you may wish to use as you develop the design of your course or curriculum.

Part 2: The Process

This, the most structured section of the book, follows sequentially the model of course and curriculum design that we will be using. Each chapter will walk you through the process step-by-step. To save you a great deal of time and effort we have included a number of resources that you should find helpful. These range from checklists and lists of questions to numerous case studies from different fields of study. Because experience has shown us that one of the most common causes of failure is beginning a project that should never have been undertaken in the first place, Chapter 7 focuses on the questions you should ask even before you begin. Different guidelines are provided for projects focusing on a single course and for those designing an entire curriculum. The three chapters that follow discuss how to get a project under way, the significant and often overlooked interrelationship between goals, courses, and curricula, and collecting and using the data you will require to make quality design decisions. One of the strong points of the approach that we use is that the initial design step is to think in the "ideal." If you had the best possible program or course, what would it look like? Only after this stage is complete will you be able to determine how close you can come to the ideal when you consider resources, time, and so on. This two-stage process is described in Chapters 11 and 12. Chapter 13 addresses the basic issue of stating your learning goals in outcome terms and provides suggestions on how to craft clear statements in less stressful ways. The final chapters in this section focus on designing and implementing an assessment plan that meets your needs and those of your institution. After an overview of a number of assessment issues, the chapters focus first on curriculum projects and then on assessment in the context of an individual course. Included is some very important advice on what to consider when you are exploring the use of commercially prepared instruments and protocols.

Part 3: Designing, Implementing, and Assessing the Learning Experience

With an emphasis on the crucial interrelationship between courses and curricula, this section focuses more directly on designing and assessing the courses themselves. The seven chapters in this section are structured specifically to assist you in making the best possible instructional design decisions for your students. In the chapters on the research on teaching and learning, you will find the most recent and practical information on the various available approaches to teaching. Recognizing the changes that have taken place in students themselves, we have included chapters on meeting the needs of adult learners as well as those of a diverse student body. These topics are explored from two perspectives: from the perspective of a faculty member dealing with a class composed of men and women from diverse backgrounds and cultures; and from the perspective of higher education's goal to develop in our students the ability to work with and respect people with different perspectives and priorities. This section concludes with a chapter on developing a syllabus that provides your students with all the information that they need to be successful in your course.

Part 4: Your Next Steps

Chapter 23 addresses the final step in the design process, using the data you collect to revise your course or curriculum. We discuss the various uses for the information you collect—from establishing benchmarks to identifying areas where work still needs to be done. In the final chapter we review some of the major forces that will impact higher education in the years ahead, review the characteristics of a quality curriculum, and conclude with some of the lessons we've learned along the way about successful innovation and change.

Some Important Suggestions

Two very useful parts of the book are the Resources and Case Study sections. The items included in these sections have been carefully selected to help you through the design, implementation, and assessment process. They are practical and have the potential to significantly improve the quality of your final product. In addition, these examples should prove helpful to you long after the specific project you are working on has been completed. In some cases we've made the titles a little longer to provide you with a better ideas of what's included. In the Case Studies section, don't focus only on those courses that relate to your own discipline. In many instances the problems the faculty faced and the actions they took to resolve them relate to courses in almost any field of study. Taking a few minutes to scan these two sections before you get very far into the design process may prove to be an extremely good use of your time.

This book is dedicated to the many faculty, administrators, and staff members at colleges and universities throughout the United States who care about the quality of teaching and learning, and to my wife, Dolores, who has supported me throughout my career. I couldn't have done it without her.

ACKNOWLEDGMENTS

First and foremost, I would like to thank the many talented and dedicated faculty and administrators whose work is represented in these pages, and extend my gratitude to my former colleagues at Syracuse University who played an active role in the development of many of the case studies and resources that we have included. I would also like to express my special thanks to Lion Gardiner, Wally Hannum, Roger Sell, and Trudy Banta for the outstanding new materials that they have contributed to these pages; to Martha Gaurdern and Julie Mills for their graphic assistance; to Ruth Corbett for her clerical support; and to Elizabeth Murphy, Lion Gardiner, and Roger Sell for their excellent advice that kept me on track as the manuscript progressed.

Robert M. Diamond
St. Petersburg, Florida

Robert M. Diamond, 1930–2007

Bob Diamond was a bright star in the constellation of higher education improvement, and shed his powerful light on many key issues in the field. It is hard to believe that this tireless contributor and friend will no longer be with us in person, but his example will continue to inspire us, as his writing will continue to help our efforts to improve the vital work of higher education.

Although Bob's contributions to Jossey-Bass publications began before my own work with the Higher and Adult Education series, I had the good fortune to work with him on more than one book, and to benefit from his judgment as a reviewer and all-around source of good advice as well. Thus I was pleased but not surprised to receive numerous offers from Bob's colleagues letting me know that they would be glad to help complete this book. They all knew Bob's work was needed, and that the best way to honor their friend's memory was to help get his work out to those who need it. Thanks to all of you for that very fitting tribute to Bob's commitment and devotion to his work. I also want to extend special thanks to Bronwyn Adam for her kind assistance during the production process.

David Brightman
Senior Editor
Higher and Adult Education

Artwork by Bob Diamond

ABOUT THE AUTHORS

Robert M. Diamond was president of the National Academy for Academic Leadership and emeritus professor at Syracuse University. At Syracuse he was research professor and director of the Institute for Change in Higher Education and, prior to this, assistant vice chancellor and director of the Center for Instructional Development. He received his Ph.D. and M.A. from New York University and his B.A. from Union College. Dr. Diamond held administrative and faculty positions at SUNY Fredonia, the University of Miami, and San Jose State University. A Senior Fulbright Lecturer in India, he was president of the Division for Instructional Development, Association for Educational Communication & Technology. He also was an affiliated scholar with the Center for the Advancement of Engineering Education at the National Academy of Engineering.

Dr. Diamond authored numerous articles and books, including *Designing and Improving Courses and Curricula in Higher Education: A Systematic Approach*; *Instructional Development for Individualized Learning in Higher Education*; and the chapter on "Instructional Design: The Systems Approach" for the *International Encyclopedia of Education*. Dr. Diamond also authored *Aligning Faculty Rewards with Institutional Mission*, *Preparing for Promotion and Tenure and Annual Review*, "What It Takes to Lead a Department" in *The Chronicle of Higher Education*, "Changing Higher Education: Realistic Goal or Wishful Thinking?" in *Trusteeship*, and *The Disciplines Speak: Rewarding the Scholarly, Professional and Creative Work of Faculty* and contributed to the *Field Guide to Academic Leadership*.

In 1989, Dr. Diamond received the Division of Instructional Development Association for Educational Communication and Technology Award for outstanding practice in Instructional Development and in 1997 was cited by the American Association for Higher Education for his leadership in innovation and change. The Center for Instructional Development was the recipient of the 1996 Theodore M. Hesburgh Award for Faculty Development to Enhance Undergraduate Learning.

Dr. Diamond coauthored the 1987 and the 1997 National Studies of Teaching Assistants, the 1992 National Study of Research Universities on the Balance Between Research and Undergraduate

Teaching, and the 1997 study, Changing Priorities at Research Universities: 1991–1996. He was also responsible for the design and implementation of Syracuse University's award-winning high school–college transition program, Project Advance. He served as director of the National Project on Institutional Priorities and Faculty Rewards. He was a consultant to the Ohio Board of Regents and to colleges and universities and disciplinary associations in the United States and overseas.

Wallace Hannum is associate director of technology for the National Research Center on Rural Education Support and a member of the faculty of the School of Education at the University of North Carolina at Chapel Hill. Dr. Hannum teaches graduate-level courses on the use of technology in education, learning theories, and instructional design. Dr. Hannum's research focuses on instructional uses of technology, especially distance education. He created a statewide online program for professional development of teachers and routinely uses a variety of technologies in his teaching. Dr. Hannum has consulted on the use of technology for professional development with many organizations, both public and private. He has participated in the design and implementation of numerous technology-based programs and projects. He has created standards and guidelines for technology use as well as taught numerous workshops to enable organizations to make effective use of technology for instructional purposes. He has worked extensively on education projects in Africa, Asia, and Latin America. Dr. Hannum is author of five books and numerous articles on topics related to technology and instructional design.

G. Roger Sell is currently professor and director of the Academic Development Center at Missouri State University, a position he has held since 2002. Prior to that time, he was director of instructional development and evaluation at The Ohio State University (1980–1988), senior program director of the Center for Teaching Excellence also at Ohio State (1988–1993), and director of the Center for the Enhancement of Teaching at the University of Northern Iowa (1993–2002). Following the completion of his Ph.D. at the University of California-Santa Barbara in educational administration, he worked in the research and development of adult learning programs at the University of Mid-America and the National Center for Higher Education Management Systems. He has taught in undergraduate, graduate, and continuing professional education. Dr. Sell's most recent work focuses on student success, the scholarship of teaching and learning, the evaluation of teaching, and the assessment of student learning. He served as president of the Professional and Organizational Development Network in Higher Education in 2002 and over his career has been a consultant to dozens of colleges and universities in the United States and other countries.

PART ONE

A Frame of Reference

CHAPTER 1

A Learning-Centered Approach to Course and Curriculum Design

Too many Americans just aren't getting the education that they need—and deserve.

United States Department of Education, 2006, vii.

As a faculty member, you can undertake very few activities that will have a greater impact on students than your active involvement in the design of a course or curriculum. As a direct result of these efforts, learning can be facilitated, your students' attitudes toward their own abilities can be significantly enhanced and, if you're successful, students will leave better prepared for the challenges they will face after graduation. In addition, because major course and curriculum designs tend to remain in place for years after the project has been completed, your efforts will impact far more students than you may anticipate at first.

The Curriculum Is Not Always Equal to or More Than the Sum of Its Parts

A growing number of authors report that too many of our students simply do not receive the quality of education that society expects and that the country needs for the years ahead. The educational experience of our college students has been described as disjointed, unstructured, and often outdated. Courses often have little relationship to the curriculum that is in place and may overlook the critical skills that students need to acquire.

The observations identified in the Association of American Colleges and Universities' report, *Integrity in the College Curriculum: A Report to the Academic Community* (1985), are even more appropriate today than they were over twenty years ago: "As for what passes as a college curriculum, almost anything goes. We have reached a point at which we are more confident about the length of a college education than its content and purpose. Indeed, the major in most colleges is little more than a gathering of courses taken in one department, lacking structure and depth, as is often the case in the humanities and social sciences, or emphasizing content to the neglect of the essential style of inquiry on which the content is based, as is too frequently true in the natural and physical sciences." The report continued, "The curriculum has given way to a marketplace philosophy; it is a supermarket where students are shoppers and professors are merchants of learning. Fads and fashions, the demands of popularity and success, enter where wisdom and experience should prevail. Does it make sense for a college to offer a thousand courses to a student who will only take thirty-six?" (p. 2).

The research, too, suggests that in many cases college and university curricula do not produce the results we intend. Curricula that are not focused by clear statements of intended outcomes often permit naive students broad choices among courses resulting in markedly different outcomes from those originally imagined: by graduation most students have come to understand that their degrees have more to do with the successful accumulation of credits than with the purposeful pursuit of knowledge (Gardiner, 1996, p. 34). In his 2006 essay on the status of innovation in American colleges and universities, Ted Marchese, former vice president of the Association for Higher Education and editor of *Change* magazine, made the following observation:

> What's at stake? Does this matter? Does it matter that university completion rates are 44 percent and slipping? That just 10 percent from the lowest economic quartile attain a degree? That figures released this past winter show huge chunks of our graduates who cannot comprehend a *New York Times* editorial or their own checkbook? That frustrated public officials edge closer and closer to imposing a standardized test of college outcomes? Does it matter that we look to our publics like an enterprise more eager for status and funding than self-inquiry and improvement? [2006].

Although his comments are certainly discomforting, they are accurate. Despite the efforts of many dedicated faculty and administrators and the support of numerous foundations, we are still not doing a particularly good job of educating our students. Too many of our graduates leave underprepared to be effective and productive citizens, and far too many students who enter college never graduate. As a result, America is losing out in many areas. Fewer and fewer citizens vote, we are perceived as an isolated country with little understanding of other cultures and of the world in general, and numerous other nations' educators are doing a far better job of developing in their citizens the competence that will be required in the years ahead.

In the additional resources section at the end of this chapter you will find several publications that discuss in more detail the challenges that colleges and universities face.

In short, we have reached a point where we educators, in addition to becoming more efficient and effective, have to rethink at a basic level what we teach and how we teach. We must rethink our roles as faculty, how we can most effectively use the time and talents of our students, and how we can fully utilize the expanding capabilities of technology. The approach that we will use in this book is designed to help you do all of these things.

The Challenges of Curriculum and Course Design

Designing a quality course or curriculum is always difficult, time-consuming, and challenging. It requires thinking about the specific goals you have for your students, the demands of accreditation agencies, and about how you, as a teacher, can facilitate the learning process. This demanding task will force you to face issues that you may have avoided in the past, to test long-held assumptions with which you are very comfortable, and to investigate areas of research that may be unfamiliar to you. At times you may become tired and frustrated and wish to end the entire project. Just keep in mind how important this work is and press on. Despite the work involved most faculty who have used this model report that they found the process of design and implementation challenging, frequently exciting, and when completed, most rewarding.

Unfortunately, as important as these activities are, we faculty are seldom prepared to carry them out. Although you may have been fortunate enough to have participated in a strong, well-conceived program for teaching assistants, few faculty have had the opportunity to explore the process of course and curriculum design or to read the research that provides a solid base for these initiatives. This book is designed to help you go through the design, implementation, and evaluation processes. It will provide you with a practical, step-by-step approach supported by case studies, a review of the significant literature, and introduce you to materials that you should find extremely useful.

Figure 1.1.
From Goals to Outcomes to Assessment

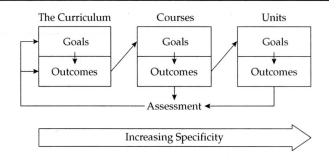

An Important Relationship

As you follow through the steps of designing or revising a course or curriculum, it is extremely important to keep in mind the important relationship between goals, outcomes, and assessment. It is a relationship that remains a constant whether you are focusing on a curriculum, a course, or a unit or element within a course.

1. The outcome statements that are produced for the curriculum will be the basis on which the primary goals of each course within that curriculum are determined.

2. The outcome statements that are produced at the course level will be the basis on which the primary goals of each unit or element within that course are determined.

3. As you move from the curriculum to the courses within it, and to the individual units or elements within each course, the goal and outcome statements become more specific.

4. The success of your effort will be determined by how well your students meet the criteria for success as defined in the outcome statements at the course and unit or course element level. (See Figure 1.1.)

Getting Assistance

Although curriculum development is always a team activity, course design often is not. In both instances, however, the process can be facilitated and the end result improved if others are involved. These may include specialists in assessment or technology, other faculty or experts in the community, and although often overlooked, the registrar. In addition, we have found that having someone from outside your content area serve as a facilitator can be extremely useful. This individual may be a faculty member from another department or a staff member from the Academic Support Center on your campus. The facilitator, who has no vested content interest in the project, can help you explore options, ask key questions by challenging your assumptions, and get the important but often overlooked issues out in the open. Simply by not being in your discipline, facilitators can also put themselves in the position of your students and raise questions about assumptions and sequence. The importance of this role cannot be overstated. In Chapter 5 we discuss this function in some detail.

Course Design and the Delivery of Instruction

The best curriculum or course design in the world will be ineffective if we do not pay appropriate attention at the course level to how we teach and how students learn. Although faculty, employers, and governmental leaders agree that graduates need critical-thinking, complex problem-solving, communication, and interpersonal skills, research shows that the lecture is still the predominant method of instruction in U.S. higher education (Gardiner, 1996, pp. 38–39).

To ensure that students develop the higher-level competencies that you believe to be essential will require thinking about how you and your students spend time both inside and outside the classroom, what the responsibilities of your students should be, and how you will assess them during and at the end of courses, and at the conclusion of their total learning experience. It may also require rethinking your role as a faculty member. The chapters in this book on the design and delivery of instruction will describe the many options available to you, as well as the research on teaching and learning that can help inform your decisions.

Accountability

A major problem that all institutions face is the perception of business and governmental leaders, and of the public at large, that we have enthusiastically avoided stating clearly what competencies graduates should have and that, as a result, colleges and universities have provided little evidence that they are successful at what they are expected to do. Unfortunately, these perceptions are not far from the truth. The public demands for assessment of programs and institutions have, for the most part, fallen on deaf ears, and as a result of this inattention, higher education in general receives increasingly less support from the public and private sectors. While tuition has increased significantly, the quality of our product has not.

As governors and other public leaders have made extremely clear, this problem of accountability needs to be addressed if support is to increase.

This demand for more information on the quality of learning at colleges and universities has led to many of the changes that are under way in accreditation, and to the increased attention being paid to learning outcomes and assessment by numerous national associations and institutions (see Chapter 2). As a result, collecting data and reporting results must be major elements in the process of course and curriculum design and implementation. One of the underlying assumptions in the work you will be doing is that the instructional goals you develop, and the assessment of your students' success in reaching them, will be made public. Only this level of specificity can answer higher education's severest critics. For this reason, as we move along we will discuss in some detail the development and assessment of both broad instructional goals and specific learning outcomes.

Institutionwide Initiatives

Recognizing both the need for quality information and the demands for increased institutional accountability, a growing number of colleges and universities have been developing a campuswide approach to assessment of the quality of their academic programs that can provide faculty and administrators with extremely useful information as they attempt to improve both courses and curricula. An early first step should be for you to find out what data already exists on your campus or is in the process of being collected.

The University of Indiana, Bloomington, and Monmouth University are two of the institutions that moved in this direction early on. One of the first major campuswide initiatives to develop a culture of assessment took place at Truman State University (formerly Northeast Missouri State University). In Case Study 1 you will find a detailed description of what actions were taken and the long-term impact of these initiatives. The case study clearly shows the importance of quality leadership and faculty involvement in the institutional process of change.

A Brief Introduction to the Model

This book focuses on an approach that has been used successfully at institutions with very different profiles: private and public, large and small, and with varying budgets. It shows how to move from concept to actualization, from theory to practice. The model is designed to facilitate significant and long-lasting change. Case studies will illustrate the model's adaptability with examples ranging from major curricular redesign to developing individual courses and programs.

Benefits of This Approach:

- The model is easy to use, sequential, and cost-effective; it will save you both time and effort by significantly reducing the time needed for implementation.
- It can be used for the design or redesign of courses, curricula, workshops, and seminars in every subject area and in every instructional setting—traditional and nontraditional.
- The programs you develop will meet accreditation agencies' demands for clear statements of learning outcomes with an associated high-quality student assessment process.
- It is politically sensitive, protecting you from decisions by others that could jeopardize implementation.
- It will ensure that all important questions are asked and all options are explored before key decisions are made.

Several factors make this model particularly relevant. As the case studies illustrate, programs that have been developed using the model meet the goals identified in major reports on educational change. Faculty who have used the model, and the administrators to whom they report, have a sense of ownership of the courses and programs that are developed, ensuring that these programs and projects will become an integral part of the existing system and thus survive.

Since the model was first used in the mid-1960s, changes incorporated as a result of experience working with it, and comments from faculty and staff, have made it less complex and easier to use, reducing the time needed for implementation. Program assessment is a part of the process and places outcome measures of a course or curriculum within the context of national, state, and regional goals.

This approach has several additional characteristics that significantly affect its success. By using a person who is not a content expert to facilitate the design process, this model allows you and other faculty to focus on content and structure while ensuring that assumptions are questioned and alternatives are explored. The model also allows you to focus first on what an ideal program would look like, eliminating perceived limitations—many of which turn out to be more imagined than real. Furthermore, this approach is data driven, using information from a wide range of sources to help determine scope, content, effectiveness, and efficiency. Equally important, although this process requires hard work, faculty, as mentioned before, find it exciting, challenging, and rewarding, and administrators remark on its efficiency and effectiveness.

One additional benefit should be mentioned. In the process we will follow, specific approaches or solutions are not determined until goals are identified and all options are explored. All too often in education we find advocates of a particular approach starting with the answers before they have even identified the problems that need to be addressed.

The model follows a specific sequence that begins with an assessment of need and a statement of goals (moving from the general to the specific), which is followed by the design, implementation, assessment, and revision of your course or curriculum (Figure 1.2). This sequence assures a meshing of goals, instruction, and assessment.

Under an external mandate to assess the quality of their academic programs, departments, schools, colleges, and universities are finding that no matter where you begin in the process, you will need to go back to the statement of need before you can develop a statement of goals on which assessment must be based (Figure 1.3). For example, to assess your program you will first need to know where you are trying to go, and then, based on this information, you will need to develop an assessment program that can help determine whether you are successful.

Those responsible for assessment initiatives are reporting a number of common problems that we will address as we move through the design process.

Figure 1.2.
Basic Design Sequence

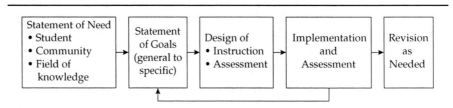

Figure 1.3.
Assessment Sequence

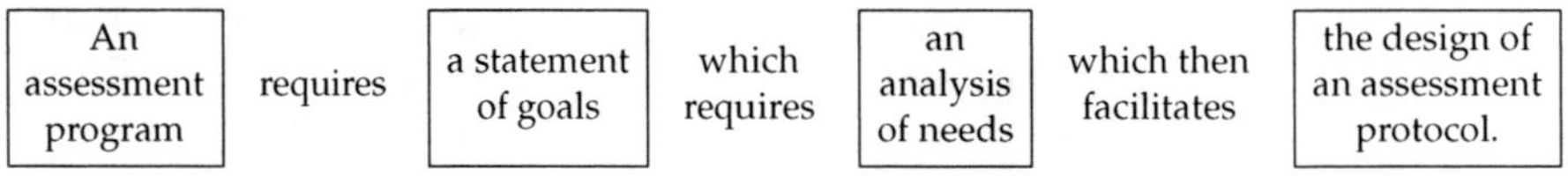

- Statements of outcomes do not exist for many curricula and many courses.
- When outcome statements do exist, there is often a gap between stated performance goals and assessment (assessment tends to focus on recall and recognition, whereas more important and complex goals are never assessed).
- When outcome statements do exist, there is often a gap between stated goals and what is taught.
- When outcome statements do exist, they often focus on content rather than on critical thinking and learning skills.

In other words, in course and curriculum design it is best to resist the pressure that many of us feel to discuss assessment before we have agreed on the goals for the program or course we will be reviewing. Obviously, we need to identify goals before we can have a meaningful conversation about assessment, or about content and structure. Furthermore, when the focus is on assessment, we often feel threatened, which can undermine the sense of common purpose that any such effort needs. By starting with a consideration of how to facilitate effective learning, we will establish a rapport among everyone involved that makes for a successful team effort. This process reduces stress because it helps us get where we want to go in far less time and with significantly less of the frustration that is common in course and curriculum efforts.

The Question of Time

One question that always comes up is, "How long is this process going to take?" Our goal is to help you design and implement the best possible course or program in the shortest time possible. Under ideal circumstances with maximum support, we've been able to design a course during the spring semester, produce the new materials needed in summer (using a small grant to pay for summer employment of the faculty) and implement the new course in the fall. However, this time line is the exception rather than the rule. There will always be surprises and delays and in many cases you will be doing this in addition to your full-time teaching assignment. So be conservative and give yourself additional time.

For curriculum projects, a year or more of design work is not unusual. However, with a quality facilitator, teams can often meet formally once a week and accomplish a great deal of work. Because most new or redesigned curricula will require several levels of approval—by department, school, and institution—additional delays can be anticipated. Keep in mind, however, that once the overall curriculum design is completed, work can begin on individual courses even before formal approval is obtained. In most instances, when a total curriculum is involved, some courses will be able to be utilized with very few, if any, major changes. In more than one instance we began offering an important new curriculum before completing the design of the courses that were to follow.

In the chapters that follow we will discuss how a systematic approach ensures the most efficient use of your time and effort and that of your colleagues as you work together to improve your program.

Additional Resources

Lederman, D. "Fixing Higher Ed, Legislator-Style." *Inside Higher Ed*, Nov. 28, 2006. Available at http://www.insidehighered.com/news/2006/11/28/ncsl.

> This excellent review of the 2006 National Conference of State Legislators includes background and major recommendations, and places it in a national context. Focuses on the role of state legislators in helping to address the issues faced by colleges and universities. Includes links to other important reports.

Marchese, T. J. "Whatever Happened to Undergraduate Reform?" *Carnegie Perspectives, No. 26*, Stanford, Calif., 2006. Available at http://ctll.stanford.edu/tomprof/index.shtml.

> An excellent overview of over two decades of innovations in higher education. Well worth the time.

National Academy of Engineering. *The Engineer of 2020: Visions of Engineering in the New Century.* Washington, D.C.: National Academies Press, 2004.

> This small volume by the National Academy of Engineering is must reading for anyone in the sciences and engineering. It not only addresses the challenges being faced by schools and colleges of engineering in the United States but describes, in some detail, the competencies that will be required by engineers in the future. Has implications for faculty and administrators in all the arts and sciences.

Newman, F., Couturier, L., and Scurry, J. *The Future of Higher Education: Rhetoric, Reality, and the Risks of Market.* San Francisco: Jossey-Bass, 2004.

Discusses the changes that will occur in higher education in the years ahead, the forces behind them, and the ways in which colleges and universities will need to respond.

Project Kaleidoscope. *Recommendations for Urgent Action: Transforming America's Scientific and Technological Infrastructure.* Project Kaleidoscope. Washington, D.C., 2006.

Reviews the recommendations (and the rationale behind them) of nearly twenty recent reports addressing America's capacity as a world leader in addressing societal problems through scientific and technological innovation. Must reading for anyone involved in the design of courses and curricula in business, engineering, and science.

Schemo, D. J. "At 2-Year Colleges, Students Eager but Unready." *The New York Times*, Sept. 2, 2006. Available at www.nytimes.com/2006/09/02college.html.

Discusses the challenges being faced by community colleges as they attempt to provide support to under-prepared students. Raises major questions concerning the K–12/Higher Ed interface and describes the challenges faced by both students and institutions when remediation is not addressed.

CHAPTER 2

The Expanding Role of Faculty in Accreditation and Accountability

One of the principal means of providing accountability is accreditation, the most critical part of quality assurance in higher education. Like higher education itself, accreditation is a complex, heterogeneous system that involves regional, national, and specialized accrediting agencies, all of which have different roles and missions. The particular strength of accreditation is its independence from both government and the institutions it accredits. All accreditors now make student learning outcomes a central component in the accreditation reviews, and this will continue. But we must expand our efforts to ensure the public that accreditation is a strong, meaningful assurance of academic quality.

"Addressing the Challenges Facing American Undergraduate Education: A Letter to Our Members," 2006

Institutions and academic programs have been externally reviewed by accreditation agencies, state offices, and professorial associations for some time. However, although under the radar of most faculty, the changes that are now taking place—in the questions being asked and in the criteria being used to judge quality—have the potential to be the most significant force toward change to impact higher education in the last fifty years. Keep in mind that accreditation and most program reviews are the certification that your institution or program meets the requirements for academic excellence, curriculum, faculty, and so on. Without accreditation, recognized degrees cannot be awarded, state and federal support is unavailable, and degrees earned by your students will not be accepted by most other institutions or recognized by potential employers.

For many years, most of us thought of these reviews as something that came about every five years or so, had little to do with us personally, was handled by a small group of administrators located somewhere in the deans' offices and central administration, and rarely required any major activity on our part. Although changes have been slow in coming, and the discussions regarding the role of the government are often contentious, there is little question that in the future, faculty will play a much more central role in the preparation of their institution's response. These changes will directly impact our teaching, how we evaluate our students, and our responsibilities as faculty and administrators.

External reviews of an institution or individual programs occur regularly, but the changes in requirements are not only significant in the scope of the questions that must be addressed but in the much faster pace at which these changes are occurring. In years past, an institution could simply dust off its previous documents, make a few modest modifications, and be finished, but this is simply no longer possible.

Although individual reviewing offices revise their criteria and standards independently, the major changes are generally consistent and, in almost every instance, becoming far more demanding and increasingly detailed. More significantly, most of the major revisions focus on academic programs and will, as a result, require a great deal of time and effort on your part and on the part of the entire academic community. It is, therefore, imperative that you begin planning today for the documentation that you will be required to provide tomorrow.

The Questions Accreditors Ask

Although there are differences in the specific requirements of the various reviewing bodies, there are a number of commonalities among them. The wording may vary, as may the specific materials that an institution will be asked to provide; however, the basic questions asked of the academic side of the institution are fairly consistent.

- Does the institution have a clearly defined academic mission and vision?
- Are the educational goals of each academic program consistent with the stated priorities of the institution?
- Are procedures in place to evaluate the extent to which these goals are being achieved?
- Are procedures in place to evaluate educational effectiveness?

- Does the evaluation of academic programs and individual courses include the gathering and analyzing of both quantitative and qualitative data to demonstrate student achievement?
- Is student achievement in a course or program determined by how well that student meets the specific instructional goals (outcomes) that have been identified?
- Is each curriculum designed in such a manner that every student has the opportunity to reach the specific level of achievement that has been identified?
- Can the institution demonstrate that that all graduates are capable in the basic core competencies that have been identified (reading, writing, oral communications, mathematics, statistics, interpersonal skills, problem solving, computer skills, and so on)?

In short, more than ever before, the review process is focusing on (1) clearly stated learning outcomes; (2) the quality of teaching and learning; (3) the evaluation process; and (4) institutional accountability.

Most significantly, the process we use will assist you in designing courses and curricula that will meet, and often exceed, these newer and more detailed requirements.

Timing

For years accreditation was, for most institutions, a once-every-ten-years occurrence. In the last few years, however, the expanding number of for-profit institutions and the huge growth in off-campus and nontraditional courses have, along with a growing number of complaints about poor quality programs, prompted reviewing bodies to pay far greater attention to quality assurance than ever before. One result of these pressures has been the demand for increasing the frequency of reviews. Recognizing that institutions are faced with numerous reviews and that faculty and staff resources are limited, the various reviewing offices tend to work more closely with one another to ensure that, whenever possible, they request the same basic information and define quality the same way. As cooperation has not been the case in the past and some "turf wars" can be expected, these changes will be gradual. However, they are coming. Along with modifications in specific requirements, we are beginning to see changes in the timing cycle as agencies move toward a continuous improvement process where reviews are scheduled more frequently or, in some cases, as part of an annual process.

The Structure of Accreditation

As you work on the design of a course or curriculum you will be directly impacted by the reviewing criteria established by at least two and possibly three different offices or associations, which include:

• *The Regional Associations.* The United States is divided into six basic regions, each with its own set of criteria and procedures: the Middle States Association Commission on Higher Education, the New England Association of Colleges and Schools Commission on Institutions of Higher Education, the North Central Association of Colleges and Schools, the Higher Learning Commission, the Northwest Commission on Colleges and Universities, the Southern Association of Colleges and Schools, and the Western Association of Schools and Colleges. These are voluntary, nongovernmental agencies that are unique to the United States. In most countries the maintenance of educational standards is a governmental function.

• *State Departments of Education or Boards of Regents.* As there are major structural differences among the states, it will be important for you to determine which specific state agency accredits your own institution or program. For example, Departments of Education in some states accredit only public institutions, but in others the Boards of Regents will accredit both public and private colleges and universities.

• *Professional or Specialized Accreditation Associations.* These agencies accredit discipline- and field-specific programs such as architecture, business, engineering, nursing, law, medicine, and physical therapy. Most cover both undergraduate and graduate degrees. It should also be mentioned that a number of health care–related programs in community and junior colleges receive their professional approval through professional boards where the standards are often designed following the criteria established by the appropriate national professional accrediting association.

• *National Accreditation Agencies.* These agencies most commonly accredit proprietary institutions or nonprofit educational entities associated with museums.

• *Institutional Accreditation Agencies.* These agencies accredit single-mission institutions such as theology, art and design, and music.

For most of us, the regional and state accreditation agencies will provide the guidelines to follow. However, if you teach in a professional or specialized program, the discipline-specific association will give you a detailed description of the minimum skills and knowledge required of all graduates. In a number of these fields a formal examination of your graduates is also required.

The office of the chief academic officer at your institution should know which accreditation standards will be appropriate for you and should have copies of their guidelines available. One of your initial steps *before* you get under way with any course or curriculum program design is to get your hands on the most recent set of guidelines for the accreditation offices that your department and programs must satisfy. As guidelines are changing rather rapidly, make sure you have the most recent version. Most are available on the agency association's Web sites. Pay particular attention to:

- Their specific requirements regarding learning outcomes and assessment

- The programs and resources available to assist you in both areas; many agencies have exceptionally solid support programs and materials on both topics designed specifically for faculty members

Summary

Changes in criteria and standards are the way of life in accreditation, but some of the more important trends will continue regardless of the results of the ongoing negotiations between the for-profit and nonprofit institutions, the Department of Education, and the voluntary regional and state accrediting agencies.

- Institutions will increasingly be held accountable for the learning of their students.

- Institutions will be required to identify the knowledge and skills required of all students receiving a degree and to determine in advance the level of student performance that will be acceptable.

- To meet these goals there will be increased pressure on academic programs to state, in measurable terms, the academic goals of their students and to track their success in meeting these standards.

- There will be increased pressure on academic programs to ensure that the curricula they offer provide all students with the opportunity to reach the established goals.

- Faculty will have the primary responsibility of ensuring that these mandated requirements are met.

- Finally, it can be anticipated that the requirements will not only be modified on a continual basis but, if the present trend continues, each change will be more specific in requirements than the one that preceded it.

You can anticipate that, sooner or later, the end product of the work you do in course or curriculum design will be required to address the specific demands of accreditation. Dealing with these standards now as you move through the design, implementation, and evaluation process will, in the long run, save you and your academic department a great deal of time and effort. You'll be glad you did.

Resources

In the Resources section you will find a number of representative statements and guidelines from different accrediting groups. You will note that as you move from regional to state to disciplinary-specific accrediting agencies the statements tend to become far more specific as to what is required. As noted previously, many of these agencies also offer excellent workshops, programs, and written materials designed to assist you in preparing for a review. One example, from the North Central Association, is also included.

Resource A: Achieving Educational Objectives: Teaching and Learning (Western Association of Schools and Colleges)

Resource B: Student Learning, Assessment, and Accreditation (The Higher Learning Commission of the North Central Association)

Resource C: The Proposal Templates (Ohio Board of Regents)

Resource D: Criteria for Accrediting Engineering Programs (Accreditation Board for Engineering and Technology)

Resource E: Providing Institutional Support (The Academy for Assessment of Student Learning of the Higher Learning Commission of the North Central Association)

CHAPTER 3

Staying Informed

Although the model that we use to design, evaluate, and revise courses and curriculum, and the questions that you should ask, have remained generally constant over the last twenty years or so, the same cannot be said for the research on teaching and learning, the field of assessment, the instructional options available to you, and the knowledge, skills, interests, and demographics of your students. One of the greatest challenges you face as a faculty member or administrator will be in keeping up-to-date so that the teaching-related decisions you make are (1) based on the latest research on teaching and learning, (2) take full advantage of the resources and options that are available to you, and (3) are sensitive to important issues that impact your program, your discipline, and your institution.

To assist you in keeping informed we will, in the chapters that follow, highlight the best resources and information that are now available. As new materials and resources are always becoming available, in this chapter we will discuss a number of actions that you can take on your own to keep up-to-date on most recent developments in higher education that directly relate to course and curriculum design. Many of these are free and all are direct and to the point. We will also suggest a small number of basic publications that you should have available in your own office to serve as a primary resources in key areas.

In addition, you should always follow the programs and publications of the appropriate disciplinary, accrediting, and professional academic associations in your academic area.

Free and Highly Recommended: General

There are two multitopic national newsletters that you should follow regularly. The time you will need to scan them for significant information is brief but the potential benefits can be substantial.

- Inside Higher Ed

Inside Higher Ed is a daily, electronic newsletter that focuses on the latest news in higher education. Not every topic will be of interest to you, but the reports are well written and objective. Both the reports and essays include direct links to all major citations and to other related reports on the subject and are usually followed by comments from other readers that are sometimes heated and often interesting. Some of the topics are related to teaching and assessment and others will be of interest to you personally. To enroll, visit their Web site: http://insidehighered.com.

- Tomorrow's Professor

This weekly newsletter, sponsored by the Stanford University Center for Teaching and Learning, provides you with chapters, major segments, or entire essays from the latest books, reports, and studies that focus on teaching and learning. The staff does an excellent job of identifying what faculty will find most useful; it's a great way to see what's available, and the material provides you with a sense of the focus and writing style of books you might be interested in purchasing. A list of past postings is available at http://ctl/stanford.edu/tomprof/postings.html. To subscribe go to: http://mailman.stanford.edu/mailman/listinfo/tomorrows-professor.

The following Web sites contain a range of materials that could be useful to you as you move through the design, implementation, and evaluation of a course or curriculum.

- Carnegie Perspectives (http://carnegiefoundation.org/perspectives/index)

This monthly publication from the Carnegie Foundation for the Advancement of Teaching includes essays focused on educational issues that relate directly to teaching and learning. The above link to their archives is the best place to start.

- National Academy for Academic Leadership (http://thenationalacademy.org)

This Web site, which is updated regularly, contains separate sections devoted to resources in such areas as teaching and learning, assessment, technology, course and curriculum design, leadership and change, and faculty rewards.

- Educational Research Information Clearinghouse (www.eric.ed.gov/ERICWebPortal?home.portal)

This federally supported site contains most of the recent research on teaching, learning, and assessment. It covers all levels of education, and the easy-to-use retrieval systems will get you to the topics you are looking for rather quickly. The more specific you are in selecting your key search words, the better your results will be.

Free and Recommended: Specific Subjects

The following recommended Web sites are from national projects and centers and are devoted to a single topic or initiative. Additional specialized sites will be noted in a number of chapters.

Assessment

• Internet Resources for Higher Education Outcomes Assessment (www2.acs.ncsu.edu/UPA/assmt/resource.htm#gen)

This site contains links to a comprehensive array of international assessment resources, including discussion lists; accrediting agencies; glossaries; the Bloom Taxonomy; journals; assessment rubrics; survey data; assessment pages of individual colleges, universities, and organizations, including their assessment handbooks; student assessment and evaluation of courses and faculty members; and assessment in student affairs.

• Internet Resources for Institutional Research (http://airweb.org/links/)

Sponsored by the Association for Institutional Research, this site provides institutional researchers with useful resources. In addition to numerous assessment links, the site also has links relating to administration, data, publications, government, institutional research, quality improvement, student affairs, teaching and research, and technology.

Teaching and Learning

• The Scholarship of Teaching and Learning in Higher Education (http://carnegiefoundation.org/elibrary/docs/bibliography)

Sponsored by the Carnegie Foundation for the Advancement of Teaching, this excellent bibliography offers annotated links to numerous case studies and projects in various disciplines at many institutions. While on the foundation site, check their most recent publications.

• The National Survey of Student Engagement (www.nsse.iub.edu)

This Web site from the Institute for Effective Educational Practice provides detailed information on the survey and on the lessons learned from the information collected. Also includes links to a number of useful tools.

Technology

• Innovate (http://innovateonline.info)

An open-access, bimonthly, peer-reviewed online periodical, this source focuses on the creative use of technology to improve teaching. As an added feature, each article includes an interactive "webcast" which allows you to connect with the author and other readers to discuss the material. The site also includes a direct link to other articles on related topics.

• The TLT Group (www.tltgroup.org)

The TLT Group is an extremely active, high-quality site focusing on the use of technology in higher education. Originally established under a grant to the American Association of Higher Education this group provides you with the opportunity to be as actively involved as you would like.

Items to Have on Your Bookshelf_____

Every faculty member has, in his or her office, a least one bookshelf devoted to favorite and most often used publications in the discipline. We suggest that you add to it a small but important section devoted to teaching, learning, and assessment.

You may already have such a collection, but there are a few publications that we suggest you have available as your begin your work on course and curriculum design. As many of these titles have multiple editions, make sure you are ordering the most recent.

Association of American Colleges and Universities. *College Learning for the New Global Century.* Washington, D.C.: Association of American Colleges and Universities, 2007.

> This report from the National Leadership Council for Liberal Education and America's Promise is relevant to every faculty member. Directly addressing the essential aims, learning outcomes, and principles for a quality twenty-first century education, the report is loaded with examples and quality references, and is available at www.aacu.org.

Diamond, R. M. *Preparing for Promotion, Tenure, and Annual Review: A Faculty Guide.* (2nd ed.) San Francisco: Anker/Jossey-Bass, 2004.

> The questions to ask, the information you should provide. Inexpensive but extremely useful. Includes numerous

examples of how to document scholarly activity in a number of situations.

Gardiner, L. F. *Redesigning Higher Education: Producing Dramatic Gains in Student Learning ASHE Higher Education Report, 23(7).* San Francisco: Jossey-Bass. 1996.

Still the best publication for a quick overview of the most important research on teaching and learning.

Grunert-O'Brien, J., Millis, B., and Cohen, M. *The Course Syllabus: A Learning Centered Approach.* (2nd ed.) San Francisco: Jossey-Bass, 2008.

How to improve learning by providing students with quality information. What to include with numerous examples.

McKeachie, W., and Svinicki, M. *McKeachie's Teaching Tips: Strategies, Research and Theory for College and University Teaching.* (12th ed.) Boston: Houghton Mifflin, 2006.

Practical chapters on just about every topic on teaching you might hope to find. Each chapter includes excellent references for additional information. A great place to start.

Palomba, C. A., and Banta, T. W. *Assessment Essentials: Planning, Implementing, and Improving Assessment in Higher Education.* San Francisco: Jossey-Bass, 1999.

Provides an excellent introduction to the process of assessment and to the various approaches and their applications.

Publisher Mailing Lists

There are two primary publishers that focus on teaching, learning, and assessment and other topics relevant to higher education faculty and administrators. To keep up with the newest publications, we suggest that you get on their mailing lists. Your campus library and academic support center library will most likely include most of their publications in their collections.

Jossey-Bass, a Wiley imprint (www.josseybass.com). Jossey-Bass has recently purchased Anker Publishing, another major source of higher education materials. All Anker materials are available through this Web site.

Stylus Publishing (http://styluspub.com). In addition to their books, the series *Effective Practices for Academic Leader* regularly includes issues on such topics as assessment, technology, and scholarship.

Academic Support Centers

Today, most colleges and universities have an academic or faculty support center with the primary function of assisting faculty in the improvement of teaching. In addition, most will have a resource library on teaching, learning, and assessment that is available for your use, with a staff member there to help you find what you are looking for. If you are unfamiliar with your center and the help they can provide, we suggest that you take an hour or so to visit. There is an excellent chance that you will find a collection of materials and a range of talents that can prove invaluable as you move through the design, implementation, and evaluation stages of your project. In the chapters that follow we will suggest a number of specific ways in which the staff of such a center might be of help to you as you move along.

CHAPTER 4

Scholarship and Faculty Rewards

Faculty members who take on a major role in curriculum development or in the major design of a new course often do so at their own risk. These time-consuming projects take faculty away from those activities that for many years have been the most highly valued in promotion, tenure, and merit-pay decisions: research and publication. As a result, many untenured faculty tend to avoid such activities. The message has been extremely clear on many campuses: if you wish to advance your career, these are not activities on which you should spend your time and energy.

Fortunately, the climate is slowly changing. More and more institutions are recognizing the importance of these activities. Further, a number of initiatives by disciplinary associations, individual colleges and universities, and national projects have begun to place greater priority on teaching and learning, and, as part of these efforts have formally recognized that, under certain conditions, working on course and curriculum initiatives is true scholarship.

Some Background

In 1990, Ernest Boyer, building on the work of Eugene Rice, proposed that colleges and universities move beyond the debate of teaching versus research, and that the definition of scholarship be expanded to include not only original research but also the synthesis and reintegration of knowledge, professional practice, and the transformation of knowledge through teaching. At the same time, projects began at Syracuse University that involved over thirty disciplinary associations in an effort to describe the range of faculty work in their fields and to conduct a series of national studies to determine the perceptions of faculty and administrators of the balance between teaching and research. When completed, these studies included data from over 50,000 faculty and administrators at over 150 institutions (Gray, Froh, and Diamond, 1992; Gray, Diamond, and Adam, 1996). In the years that followed, the American Association for Higher Education established its highly successful Forum on Faculty Roles and Rewards and supported a number of related initiatives.

Unfortunately, despite the active involvement of academic leaders and faculty at institutions throughout the country, many of the problems identified over a decade ago still prevail today. On many campuses there still exists a significant disconnect between what institutions say is important and what they reward. Research and publication remain the primary criteria used in promotion and tenure decisions, with far less importance still given to teaching and community service activities. (For a useful overview of the perceptions of Chief Academic Officers see the Appendix in *Faculty Priorities Reconsidered: Rewarding Multiple Forms of Scholarship* (2005) by KerryAnn O'Meara and Eugene Rice.) In addition, many faculty are still caught between the definition of appropriate scholarship used in their academic unit and the definition used by faculty from other disciplines who serve on campuswide tenure and promotion committees.

Although the work of Ernest Boyer has been instrumental in bringing the issues of faculty rewards and scholarship to the agendas of many institutions, using his approach as the structure for change can create implementation problems. From our work with the disciplines, one major finding has been generally overlooked. Although faculty from different disciplines cannot agree on terminology, in large measure they do agree on those characteristics that combine to make an activity scholarly. Therefore, once you have a campus consensus that your faculty reward system requires major revision, if you focus your efforts on identifying those common characteristics and processes that are needed for any activity to be considered scholarship, you can effectively eliminate or reduce many of the problems that you would otherwise encounter. That is, where the scholarship takes place, or the nature of the work itself, are no longer issues. Scholarship can take place in the laboratory, the classroom, the community, or elsewhere. The focus is now on quality, significance, and process.

This approach has a number of additional advantages:

- Individual academic units can be given the responsibility of determining if a specific activity falls within the work of the discipline and the priorities of the institution, school or college, and department.

- All-campus review committees can now focus on whether or not the activity actually meets the agreed-upon criteria for scholarly or creative work. It is not the role of a committee external to the academic area to determine *if* the activity is appropriate for the discipline.

- The criteria can be relatively clear, easy to understand, and consistent across all disciplines. Although some discipline-specific characteristics may be added at the school or college level, a single basic statement serves the entire institution.

- This approach can facilitate the goals of a number of national projects that focus on expanding the scope of scholarship (such as *The Scholarship of Teaching and Learning* and the *Community-Campus Partnership for Health* initiatives) by applying the same standards for scholarship to all disciplines throughout the institution, thus placing these efforts on a par with research in any other academic area.

- The system is fair and recognizes individual and disciplinary differences. No one academic perspective or group of disciplines determines what scholarship should be for another.

- By focusing in depth on candidates' most significant scholarly efforts the process actively discourages equating scholarship with the number of publications.

- The process is cost-effective. Faculty preparing for review know what is expected of them and of the required documentation. The role of faculty review committees is clarified, focusing on the quality of the product and the process, not on whether or not the activity itself is scholarly.

- This approach can easily be incorporated into the descriptions of scholarly work developed by Boyer, Rice, Hutchings, and Shulman.

- The process will be relatively easy to implement without many of the hassles and frustrations common to efforts in this area.

Recognizing Course and Curriculum Design as Scholarly Work

To do this we build on two previous publications. The first, *Recognizing Faculty Work,* by Robert Diamond and Bronwyn Adam (1993), identifies six characteristics that typify scholarly work:

- The activity requires a high level of discipline expertise.
- The activity breaks new ground or is innovative.
- The activity can be replicated and elaborated.

- The work and its results can be documented.
- The work and its results can be peer reviewed.
- The activity has significance or impact.

In the second, *Scholarship Assessed*, Charles Glassick, Mary Taylor Huber, and Gene Maeroff (1997), building on the earlier work of Ernest Boyer and Eugene Rice, suggest that six qualitative standards can be applied to scholarly work:

- Clear goals
- Adequate preparation
- Appropriate methods
- Significant results
- Effective presentation
- Reflective critique

There is some overlap between the two, but the Glassick, Huber, and Maeroff work tends to focus on the *process* of scholarship, whereas *Recognizing Faculty Work* describes more the *product* of scholarly, professional, or creative faculty work. A combination of these two aspects, process and product, provides you with a framework on which you can start your effort to develop for your institution a practical and functional way of describing the scholarly work of faculty.

What Makes It Scholarship?

An activity will be considered scholarly if it meets the following criteria (Diamond, 2002):

1. The activity or work requires a high level of discipline-related expertise.
2. The activity or work is conducted in a scholarly manner with
    - Clear goals
    - Adequate preparation
    - Appropriate methodology
3. The activity or work and its results are appropriately documented and disseminated. This reporting should include a reflective component that addresses the significance of the work, the process that was followed, and the outcomes of the research, inquiry, or activity.
4. The activity or work has significance beyond the individual context. It

- Breaks new ground
- Can be replicated or elaborated

5. The activity or work, both process and product or results, is reviewed and judged to be meritorious and significant by a panel of the candidate's peers.

It will be the responsibility of the candidate's academic unit to determine if the activity or work itself falls within the priorities of the department, school/college, discipline, and institution. It will be the candidate's responsibility to prove substantiation of the significance and quality of his or her work.

This approach makes it possible for you to document your work for use in tenure and promotion decisions and for your annual review. Your challenge will be to document your work to meet these criteria. Here again, the resources listed below are available to help you.

Important

- Before you begin any course or curriculum project make sure that you collect any data (student learning, enrollment, retention, attitude toward the subject, job placement, and so on) that you can use later as base-line data to show improvement and impact.

- If you are an untenured faculty member, or are coming up for promotion, and you are appointed to or asked to serve on a curriculum committee, or asked to develop a new course, remember that this activity, if done well, has the potential of being extremely time-consuming and demanding. For this reason, get the assignment in writing and, prior to accepting, negotiate the tenure or promotion ramifications. Also, if possible, get a formal statement from your chair or dean that this work can be considered scholarly at the time of your review.

- If you are not yet tenured and on a tenure track and are asked to participate in a major curriculum revision, this will also be the time for you to explore the potential of stopping your tenure clock during the period of the assignment.

Resources

Arreola, R. A. *Developing a Comprehensive Faculty Evaluation System.* (2nd ed.) San Francisco: Anker/Jossey-Bass, 2002.

Describes practical approaches to faculty evaluation and to collecting the wide range of information that review committees should require. Includes protocols, worksheets, and assessment instruments. One of the basic resources on faculty evaluation.

Bernstein, D., Burnett, A. N., Goodburn, A., and Savory, P. *Making Teaching and Learning Visible: Course Portfolios and the Peer View of Teaching.* San Francisco: Anker/Jossey-Bass, 2006.

Provides excellent advice for faculty on how to document the quality of their teaching and how to use peer review and a course portfolio to improve the quality of their work and to provide documentation for external review. Numerous portfolio examples are included.

Diamond, R. M. *Aligning Faculty Rewards with Institutional Mission: Statements, Policies, and Guidelines.* San Francisco: Anker/Jossey-Bass, 1999.

A practical guide to what should be included in institutional, school, college, and departmental promotion and tenure guidelines and in union contracts. Addresses the issues of institutional mission and vision statements. Examples from numerous institutions throughout.

Diamond, R. M. *Preparing for Promotion, Tenure, and Annual Review: A Faculty Guide.* (2nd ed.) San Francisco: Anker/Jossey-Bass, 2004.

Designed to help faculty prepare for promotion, tenure and annual review. Also provides specific suggestions on how your work in curriculum and course design can be documented (see Table 2). Discusses the questions to ask and recommends the materials that should be provided to the review committee. Includes a number of illustrative examples on preparing documentation for differing roles and instructional approaches.

Diamond, R. M., and Adam, B. E. (eds.). *The Disciplines Speak: Rewarding the Scholarly, Professional and Creative Work of Faculty.* Vol. I. Washington, D.C.: American Association for Higher Education, 1995. Available from: Stylus Publishing (1-800-223-0023).

Diamond, R. M., and Adam, B. E. (eds.). *The Disciplines Speak: More Statements Regarding the Scholarly, Professional and Creative Work of Faculty.* Vol. II. Washington, D.C.: The American Association for Higher Education, 2000. Available from: Stylus Publishing (1-800-223-0023).

An overview of the effort to describe the work of faculty in a disciplinary context is followed by over twenty-five statements from national disciplinary associations in which they describe the range of scholarly and professional work appropriate for their field. The introduction to Volume II includes a discussion of the lessons learned along the way and commonalities and differences among the disciplines.

Glassick, C. E., Huber, M. T., and Maeroff, G. I. *Scholarship Assessed: Evaluating the Professoriate.* San Francisco: Jossey-Bass, 1997.

The follow-up to Ernest Boyer's *Scholarship Reconsidered* focuses on definitions and documentation of scholarship. Includes results from the 1994 survey on institutional changes in the faculty reward system.

Hutchings, P., Bjork, C., Babb, M. (eds.). *An Annotated Bibliography of the Scholarship of Teaching and Learning in Higher Education.* The Carnegie Foundation, 2002. Available from http://www.carnegiefoundation.org/programs/sub.asp?key=21&subkey=72&topkey=21

An extensive, highly annotated bibliography with an excellent introduction by Pat Hutchings. Includes annotated links to numerous case studies and projects in various disciplines and institutions participating in the Scholarship of Teaching and Learning Project supported by the Foundation.

Katz, S. N. "What Has Happened to the Professoriate?" *The Chronicle of Higher Education.*, Oct. 6, 2006.

This excellent essay describes the complex, diverse, and changing roles of faculty and how these changes have impacted the challenges faced by faculty and the priorities placed on teaching. Raises a number of crucial issues.

Licata, C. M., and Morreale, J. C. *Post-Tenure Faculty Review III: Outcomes and Impact.* Bolton, Mass.: Anker, 2006.

This, the third and final book in the comprehensive series on post-tenure review, provides academic leaders with a comprehensive review of the goals, impact, and lessons learned from the post-tenure review initiatives from institutions throughout the United States. (For more background information on the subject, see Volumes I and II.)

Morreale, J. C., and Licata, C. M. *Post-Tenure Review: A Guide Book for Academic Administrators of Colleges and Schools of Business.*

St. Louis, Mo.: The International Association for Management Education, 1997.

> Although, as the name implies, this work focuses on schools of business and management, much of its contents would be useful to any institution developing a post-tenure review system.

O'Meara, K. A., and Rice, R. E. (eds.), *Faculty Priorities Reconsidered: Rewarding Multiple Forms of Scholarship.* San Francisco: Jossey-Bass, 2005.

> After a review of the work of Eugene Rice and Ernest Boyer in redefining scholarship, this comprehensive volume includes chapters dealing with implementation issues and nearly a dozen case studies. The detailed findings of a 2001 national survey on changes in the faculty reward systems and the perceived impact of these changes is also included.

Seldin, P. *The Teaching Portfolio: A Practical Guide to Improved Performance and Promotion/Tenure Decisions.* (3rd ed.) San Francisco: Anker/Jossey-Bass, 2004.

> This latest edition of the primary work on teaching portfolios includes, in addition to the solid advice provided in the earlier editions, information on Web-based teaching portfolios, seven institutional case studies, and numerous sample portfolios from various disciples.

Seldin, P., and Associates. *Evaluating Faculty Performance.* Bolton, Mass.: Anker Publishing, 2006.

> A practical update on current evaluation practices and methods. Common problems are addressed. Includes numerous checklists and forms. A good place to start in developing a faculty evaluation system.

Syracuse University. *Self Study: Report 1—Faculty Roles.* Available from http://syracuse.edu/selfstudy/report1/facultyroles.html. Retrieved Jan. 24, 2000.

> Syracuse University was the first research institution in the country that totally revised its mission and faculty reward system to reflect a balance between research and teaching. Report 1 identifies topics addressed in the action plans required from all schools and colleges and provides interesting reports on how different populations (faculty, chairs of promotion and tenure committees, department chairs, and deans) perceived the impact of these initiatives.

Tierney, W. G., and Rhoads, R. A. "Enhancing Promotion, Tenure, and Beyond: Faculty Socialization as a Cultural Process." *ASHE Higher Education Report*, 6. Washington, D.C.: George Washington University, 1993.

Discusses how faculty values are shaped and how these values are reflected in faculty roles. Discusses promotion and tenure as part of a socialization process.

Tomorrow's Professor

Published one hundred times a year and free to subscribers, this newsletter highlights a single publication in each issue. Each issue, approximately four to six pages, may include an entire essay but more often is all or part of a carefully selected chapter of a recent publication, an article in a newsletter, or a research report. It is an excellent way for you to get a sense of the focus and writing style of books before purchasing. Below are specific issues that address the focus of this resource section. They may be retrieved by number through the following link: http://ctl.stanford.edu/Tomprof/postings.html. Issues are posted two weeks after publication. On this site you can also find a complete list of all past publications in the series.

#599: Preparing for Promotion, Tenure, and Annual Review—Planning Ahead. R. M. Diamond

#602: Post-Tenure Review Practices: Context and Framework. C. M. Licata, and B. E. Brown

#726: The Scholarship of Engagement: What Is It? D. M. Cox

#737: Preparing Future Faculty and Multiple Forms of Scholarship. J. G. Gaff

CHAPTER 5

An Introduction to the Model and Its Benefits

National studies may call for changes; states and national accrediting agencies may require institutions to redefine their goals and to determine whether they achieve them; and students, faculty, and staff may proclaim that improvements are needed. However, it is what happens in the classroom that will determine whether these improvements actually take place. Ernest Boyer, in *College: The Undergraduate Experience in America* (1987), pointed out that there is a major disconnect between what is and what should be. "The undergraduate college, the very heart of higher learning, is a troubled institution. In a society that makes different and contrary demands upon higher education, many of the nation's colleges are more successful in credentialing than in providing a quality education for their students. . . . We found divisions on the campus, conflicting priorities and competing interests that diminish the intellectual and social quality of the undergraduate experience and restrict the capacity of the college effectively to serve its students" (p. 2). Unfortunately, most, if not all, of these concerns are as valid today as they were twenty years ago.

Traditionally, course improvement has been the responsibility of individual faculty, and efforts to redesign curricula have usually been assigned to departmental committees established specifically for this purpose. Although the faculty involved devote a great deal of time and energy to these activities, they often receive little recognition for their efforts, no matter how successful they have been. In other cases, successful projects, often with outstanding merit, receive little departmental, administrative, or collegial support, and because of this will wither on the vine. For significant academic improvements to occur and be retained, several conditions are essential:

- We faculty must have ownership in the process, retaining responsibility for teaching and academic content.
- The academic administration of the institution must support these activities and provide the resources necessary for success.
- Priorities must be established, projects selected, and resources allocated accordingly.
- Assessment must be an integral part of the process, and the success of all instructionally related projects must be measured primarily on the basis of improvement in student performance and attitudes.
- As needed, others should be available to assist us in the production of instructional materials and in assessment.
- The procedures that we follow must allow us to provide the most effective program we can with the time and resources we have available to us.

Although the focus here is on courses and curriculum, keep in mind that what goes on in the classroom or within distance education settings is only a part of our students' total instructional experience. No matter how effective we are as teachers and how well-designed our courses and curricula are, we will not be successful if our libraries and residence halls are not conducive to studying, if student advisers and counselors provide our students with little personal support, if few opportunities for group discussions exist, and if we, as faculty, are rarely available to meet with students outside of the classroom, laboratory, or studio. Keep in mind that although face-to-face interaction is preferred, this is often no longer possible in settings where technology must provide us with direct links to our students. In addition, some of the most crucial goals can be accomplished only by having students participate in activities that take place outside of the formal classroom, such as internships, practicums, and community projects. Optimum learning requires a rich social, cultural, and physical environment. When feasible, a total educational program must be nurtured and planned, often by involving the staff from the offices of student affairs and residential life, business leaders from the community, and others both on and off campus.

A Note About Community Colleges

The model we describe is as appropriate to two-year institutions as it is to four-year and graduate colleges and universities. Keep in mind that some of the most creative and innovative approaches to teaching are now taking place at community colleges. If you are addressing the needs of under-prepared students or involved in programs where your students have different goals, or represent various cultures and age groups, you should take some time to review the growing literature on innovation and change coming from community colleges and two-year institutions. All too often the exciting and important work being done at these institutions passes under the radar of faculty and academic administrators who have spent their careers at four-year and graduate institutions. For one example of what higher education can learn from community colleges, see "Learning About Student Learning from Community Colleges" (2006) by Lee Shulman and Pat Hutchings. A Carnegie Foundation Perspective, this brief essay focuses on improving the working relationship between the information needs of academic programs and institutional research offices.

Need for an Effective Approach

The needs for instructional improvement are too great and our resources too limited to allow us to be inefficient or ineffective in the way we address our curricular problems. We cannot afford to leave things to chance, hoping that the right questions will be asked, the key people will be involved, and all the appropriate options will be explored. The approach we use is structured to help you design the best possible program in the shortest possible time.

Following a specific effective model for course or curriculum design provides several advantages. It

- Identifies the key factors that you should consider in a sequential order.
- Serves as a procedural guide.
- Allows you to understand where you are in the process and, if others are involved, their roles.
- Improves your efficiency by reducing duplication of effort and ensuring that critical questions are asked and alternative solutions explored.

Applying Systems Theory to Instructional Design

Systems Theory is basically a detailed process designed to solve complex problems. The concept, developed initially by the military during World War II to hunt for submarines in the Atlantic, was applied following the war by a number of fields to address new and extremely complex problems. It wasn't until the early 1960s that this approach began to be applied to address educational issues, with most projects focusing on individual courses, on individual units within a course, or on specific techniques of teaching.

In their analysis of instructional system designs, Hannum and Briggs (1980) found seven common elements:

- Planning, development, delivery, and evaluation of instruction were based on systems theory.

- Goals were based on an analysis of the environment of the system. For example, a two-year college must have goals different from those of a university.

- Instructional objectives were stated in terms of student performance.

- The design of the program was sensitive to the entering competencies of the students and to their short- and long-term academic goals.

- Considerable attention was paid to planning instructional strategies and selecting media.

- Evaluation was part of the design and revision process.

- Students were measured and graded on their ability to achieve desired standards and criteria rather than by comparing one student with another.

While successful in doing what they claimed to do, these early approaches tended to have one or more important limitations:

- They did not question what was being taught but focused primarily on improving the delivery and effectiveness of instruction.

- They were more suitable for use in a single course than in curriculum projects or other efforts that are larger in scope.

- They tended to narrow, rather than broaden, the focus of those who use them.

- They rarely addressed the political concerns of project implementation and survival.

In his more recent approach to course design, L. Dee Fink (2003) provides a far more comprehensive approach than many of the earlier models. The approach that we will use not only addresses some of the same concerns but has a number of additional advantages. It

- Can be used for both course and curriculum design

- Forces you to think "outside the box"

- Identifies the key factors that you should consider in a sequential order
- Serves as a procedural guide
- Allows you to understand where you are in the process and, if others are involved, their roles
- Improves your efficiency by reducing duplication of effort and ensuring that critical questions are asked and alternative solutions explored
- Is data driven

As you begin to consider your project, remember that the process of designing, implementing, and evaluating a course or curriculum is complex. The process requires that you

- Be sensitive to the academic setting of your project
- Be aware of the capabilities, interests, and priorities of the students the program is designed to serve
- Have knowledge and appreciation of the discipline
- Understand the resources and options available to you
- Articulate those instructional goals that all students must meet regardless of their majors and long-term personal goals
- Have a working knowledge of the research on teaching, learning, and assessment

The model we will use (Figure 5.1), which was first developed at the University of Miami in the early 1960s, has undergone a number of significant revisions, but its basic structure has remained. Faculty and support staff at many institutions have used it to design a broad range of courses and curricula. Users report that it is easily understood, efficient, and effective. The model is less complicated than most of its type and requires less time between inception and implementation than others. In addition, as will be shown through a number of examples, it can be used to design and implement courses, curricula, and other instructionally related projects such as workshops and seminars.

The model has two basic phases: (1) project selection and design and (2) production, implementation, and evaluation. Like most models, it is generally sequential, requiring that certain steps be completed before others begin. However, the linear nature of the process is somewhat deceptive. Ideally, some actions must precede others, and certain decisions should not be made until all relevant facts are known. But in practice all the data may not be available when an initial decision is required; information collected later may contradict earlier data, suggesting a different decision;

Figure 5.1.
Process for the Development of Educational Programs

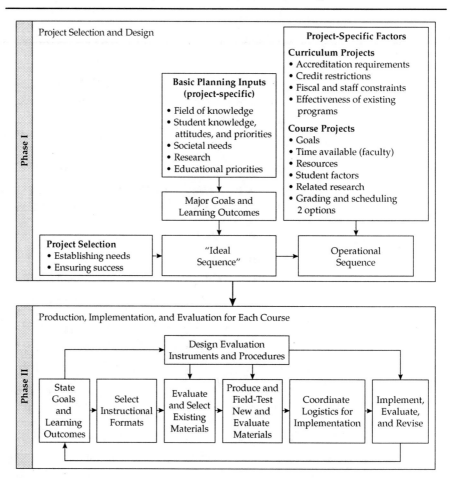

Figure 5.2.
Work Flow by Time

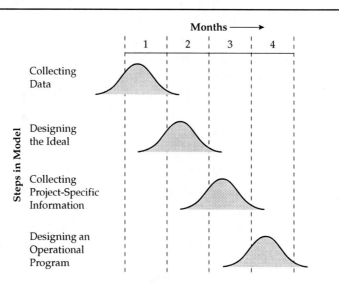

or those involved may, for a number of reasons, wish to focus on an issue that is somewhat out of sequence. This model allows such flexibility. Although the overall flow of the model is generally followed, the steps in the model may overlap (see Figure 5.2).

Characteristics of the Model

In addition to its simplicity, the model has five other characteristics that, when combined, differentiate it from most others.

- Forces those using it to think in ideal terms
- Encourages the use of diagrams to show structure and content
- Relies heavily on the use of data
- Encourages a team approach
- Is politically sensitive

Thinking in the Ideal

The initial goal of the design phase is to develop the "ideal" course or curriculum. When completed, the diagram that is developed represents the best possible instructional sequence for meeting the specific goals that you have established for the course or curriculum. We have found it most efficient to start with the ideal and then modify it according to the specific administrative, material, and human constraints that exist. Limiting the original design to meet anticipated constraints unnecessarily limits the creativity and openness of the process and thus results in an inferior product. Another reason to try to develop an optimum design is that anticipated limitations or constraints are often more perceived than real. How do you know you cannot do something until you try? The final design evolves slowly with many revisions as new data are provided and various viewpoints are discussed.

Even though working toward the ideal is an exciting part of the design process, it is not always easy. Many faculty find it extremely difficult to imagine abandoning the time frames, credit structures, course syllabi, and textbooks that they are accustomed to using. Comments from faculty who have been through the process of thinking in the ideal, however, have been generally positive:

> It forced us to "stretch" for the ultimate rather than starting out settling for those things that we thought were possible.

I was initially resistant to the "ideal" approach because I tend to be a pragmatic person who works and plans on the basis of resources available. However, once I got past the typical mentality, the freedom afforded in the ideal mode brought forward a number of surprising, imaginative, and positive ideas.

Initially, the question was a challenge to abandon traditional assumptions about how the college classroom "should" look or work. That created the opportunity to consider faculty roles other than lecturer/demonstrator. I had great reservations about changing my role in the classroom. However, when I realized that in the ideal I could cover more materials in greater depth with adequate and better comprehension on the part of the students, I got very excited.

There was no threat of failure in working with the ideal.

Thinking in the ideal is an exciting and intellectually rewarding experience that allows the planners to test assumptions about content; about the students, their goals, abilities, and priorities; and about structure and methodology.

Use of Data

Decision making in each of the phases of the model relies heavily on the collection and use of data. Whether data help clarify the problems that have been identified, provide information about the students or the professional field, or measure student performance, their accuracy is essential if the course or curriculum developed is to be successful. As different steps are discussed, you will see that data play a major role in both the design and implementation stages. In our model, data will be used to

- Confirm and clarify the problem being addressed
- Provide information essential to the design of the program
- During the field testing of the program, provide evidence that is essential for revision (data on learning, logistics, effectiveness, and so on)
- Provide information for the final evaluation of the program and for use in reporting the results of the project to external publics, such as funding agencies and administrators

Team Approach

For a project to be successful, a number of talents are needed. Ideally, the primary design team will be composed of faculty who are responsible for the content of the program or course, a process person, and, as needed, experts in assessment and technology and, if major changes in grading, time frames, and credits are expected, the registrar. Although it is often overlooked, the college or university registrar's office can play a vital role in helping you by developing new support systems that may be required to implement your project.

Faculty The faculty are obviously the key to any design project. Whether working individually or as a group, faculty members must have the necessary experience, content expertise, and the willingness to devote the time and energy that will be required. In curriculum projects, each major academic area must also be represented. The selection of the participants is often crucial in determining a project's success. If you are working on your own course, particularly an introductory course, it would be wise to involve other faculty. Doing so will increase the content knowledge base and provide backup in case you or another faculty member working on the design is no longer teaching the course. It ensures that all your hard work will not disappear if something unexpected happens.

Facilitators Surprising as it may seem at first, one of the most useful people on your project may be someone with teaching or professional experience outside the content area involved. At a growing number of institutions this person may be a staff member from the academic-support unit established to assist faculty in teaching. Ideally, this person will have experience in the design process, an understanding of both teaching and evaluation, an awareness of the most recent developments in teaching and learning, an understanding of the use of technology, and, most important, the ability to work well in a supportive role. Units called instructional or faculty-development centers, or centers on teaching and learning, now exist on hundreds of campuses in the United States and often have staff who are trained to assist you in this way. If such a center does not exist, we suggest that you find a faculty member outside of your academic area who is willing to help, who understands teaching and learning, has the process skills necessary to serve in this capacity, and is enjoyable to work with. Before you begin, this individual must clearly understand the role that he or she will play and the approach you will use.

By coming to the project without the discipline's vocabulary and without the traditional viewpoints of your field, the individual in the facilitator role is also ideally suited to test your assumptions. Without being a threat to you, he or she can question what is being done and why. For example, if the content or language of a project is unclear to this person, it may well be unclear to the students. In a sense, facilitators are surrogate students. They also might suggest new options and raise questions that you may not have considered.

Individuals who can serve effectively in this role are not always easy to find. They need to have a range of human-relations skills and a firm knowledge of education and teaching—and they must be willing to work in support of a project that is not theirs but belongs to the faculty they are assisting. They are also people who are at home with new ideas and supportive of innovation. One experienced faculty member commented at the completion of a project where she served in this capacity: "While I understood that my role was to facilitate the design, I was, admittedly, skeptical that I could effectively do so with little to no knowledge of the subject matter. In the end, however, it was my objective perspective, background in education, and experience with undergraduates that proved most beneficial."

Ideally, the facilitator chairs meetings when several faculty are involved, brings other resource people to these meetings as appropriate, ensures that the model is followed, and equally important, keeps the project moving.

A Note to Facilitators: As the process person on the project, your basic function is to help the faculty with whom you are working to define and reach their goals for their courses or curriculum. As your experience is outside the discipline, you can raise issues that otherwise might go unaddressed, and you can challenge assumptions. The primary way you will do this is by asking key questions and exploring with your colleagues instructional options and various assessment techniques. At times you will find it helpful to put yourself in the role of the student. Are the instructor's spoken or written statements expressed as clearly as possible, so that all your questions are answered and you have all the information necessary to do what is expected of you?

To assist you in this role, we have included in the following chapters checklists of the questions that should be addressed as well as additional references that may prove helpful. Many of these reference materials are in your library or in the faculty, instruction, or learning center on your campus. As you move through the process, list those questions that you feel will be most appropriate to address.

When meeting with faculty during the design phase, you will find it helpful to talk through the sequence of the course or curriculum and, using the chalkboard, to develop the flow of instruction. After each design meeting copy the material from the board, edit it to make the sequence clearer, and then send it to the faculty so that they can review it and make changes before the next meeting. Make sure before everyone leaves that the next meeting is scheduled and that all are clear about what they are to do prior to that time.

Always keep in mind that there will be surprises, some good and some frustrating, and that there will be times when ideal sequences will not be followed. We have found this role to be challenging, engaging (it is always an education learning about another field), rewarding, and enjoyable. It is worth the effort.

Evaluators You may also need some assistance in designing survey instruments and assessment protocols. Although you or another faculty member can collect some data, sometimes specialized skills and objectivity are essential.

Evaluators must have a firm understanding of how different types of data can be collected, and they will be most helpful to you if they can communicate effectively with those outside the field. Evaluation assistance can often be found in the academic/teaching-support unit on your campus. If an evaluator is not available through this source, try the department of psychology, school of education, or your institutional research office. If such a person is not available, you can make use of the wide range of sample instruments and techniques that we provide in later chapters and in the Resources section.

Support Staff You may also need secretarial assistance and the services of specialists in computer graphics and media production. Individuals with these skills are usually available in your department or through the instructional-media unit of most institutions. Don't be embarrassed to ask for help if you need it.

Political Sensitivity

If there is one attribute that determines the success of a project, it is ownership. Many projects, often effective ones, fail as the result of neglect or antagonism on the part of administrators, other faculty, or key academic committees. By involving these various groups from the beginning, this model helps generate the political support and ownership that you will need for implementation and approval. If faculty colleagues who feel they should be consulted are not, if administrators who will have to provide resources for implementation know little about the project, or if the steps that must be followed for formal approval are not taken, the new program—no matter how good it is—will probably not survive. This model will help you ensure that the appropriate faculty and administrators are involved and supportive and that a climate for success exists.

A Key to Success: Start at the Beginning and Explore the Resources You Have Available_____

All too often we begin a course redesign with a mental idea of what the program will look like—in effect picking the solution before we have defined our problem. In this model such decisions are delayed until all factors are considered. Throughout this book we will discuss options that you should explore as you develop a course or curriculum. We will identify questions you should ask and issues you should consider. Although the questions are consistent, the answers will vary from project to project.

One of the factors that will help determine the options available to you is the institution in which you work. Although many design and instructional options are available to everyone, some may exist on one campus and not another. A large institution, for example, may have more specialists available to support your work, whereas a faculty member in a smaller institution may find that the existing support is limited, but more accessible and easier to find.

In later chapters we will discuss how such factors as class size, age and homogeneity of students, location of the campus, space available, distance learning options, and whether the campus is commuting or residential have a direct bearing on the ways learning can be facilitated. Although we explore many options, it will be up to you to determine which is most appropriate for you and your students. Unless all options are explored, however, it is impossible for you to identify the best possible course or curriculum. Large or small, urban, suburban, or rural, each location has unique advantages, and each challenges you to make the most of what is available to you.

Summary _____

The systems model we use in subsequent chapters is not a traditional one. More comprehensive than most, it forces us to think in the ideal and ask a facilitator from another discipline to direct us through the process. Relying on flow diagrams to show content and structure and using quality information throughout, the model is both effective and efficient. Although it may seem complex at first, faculty find this approach comfortable. In the chapters that follow, we will provide you with an approach to diagramming your courses or curricula that will save you a great deal of time and effort, along with a number of case studies to illustrate how to use each step of the model in developing courses and curricula.

Additional Resources

Fink, L. D. *Creating Significant Learning Experiences: An Integrated Approach to Designing College Courses.* San Francisco: Jossey-Bass, 2003.

> Introduces a design model that maximizes the quality of learning by utilizing resources both within and outside of the classroom. Loaded with practical suggestions. Ties in nicely with the learning outcomes and assessment initiatives.

Saroyan, A., and Amundsen, C. *Rethinking Teaching in Higher Education.* Sterling, Va.: Stylus Publishers, 2004.

> This book is useful whether you are rethinking an existing course or designing a new one. Covers the analysis of course content, conceptions of learning, selecting teaching strategies, and both student and teaching evaluation.

CHAPTER 6

Diagramming

Simple diagrams are an excellent method for visualizing an entire course or curriculum and for showing relationships and sequence. You will also find that diagrams will significantly speed up your design and implementation process and serve as an excellent tool for describing your program to others. For these reasons, we use diagrams in this book to help illustrate the process of course and curriculum design. The diagrams that we include were used in courses and curricula that have been developed using this model.

Using boxes and arrows in such diagrams can be confusing at first, but the technique for diagramming has, nevertheless, proven to be an extremely helpful communication device. A diagram showing the elements of a program in their proper sequence can clarify the scope of the project; help identify gaps, overlaps, and sequencing problems; facilitate modifications; and perhaps most important, clarify communication among those working on a project and later, when the program is offered, between faculty and students. Experience has shown that using such terms as "in any order," "as required," or "as selected" to explain the connections in a flow chart can substantially reduce its complexity. Although at first you may not be comfortable with this technique, your feeling should change once its practicality becomes obvious.

> My first reaction was that all "those people" were addicted to rectangles and arrows, probably since the first grade. Over time, I appreciated the help of "visual" memory in rethinking and reconstructing course projects.

> It enables "time" to be visualized as well as relating subject matter and ideas to each other.

> I first thought it was too simplistic to capture the overlap built into a course, but with use I grew to see its merits rather than limitations.

> What a help; why didn't I think of it?

The early diagram for a course or curriculum will identify each of the major instructional components and the sequence in which they occur. During this stage the focus is on topics and elements of the program, not on how instruction will take place. Figure 6.1 is an example of this type of preliminary outline.

By the time the design phase is completed, the diagram will include (as appropriate to the specific course or curriculum) the following information:

- The step-by-step flow chart of the course content or, in the case of curriculum design, the overall sequence of courses

- When, in the total sequence, orientation and diagnostic testing sessions are scheduled

- The elements of the program that are essential and required of all students—that is, the instructional "core" (particularly important in curriculum projects)

- The specific remedial units that are available for the students and when they should be completed in relation to the other elements of the program

- Options and optional topics (and, if possible, which options may be used for additional credit)

- When seminars, faculty conferences, large-group sessions, in-class and out-of-class group activities, and independent study assignments are essential or recommended

- The separate tracks for specialization

- When and where exemptions are possible, based on the data on entry levels of competence

- For courses, times for evaluations

The amount of detail in a particular diagram is directly related to how far along the design process is and to the scope of the program being developed: the farther along the project is and the broader the scope of the program, the more detailed the diagram will be.

Figure 6.1.

Preliminary Diagram: International Relations

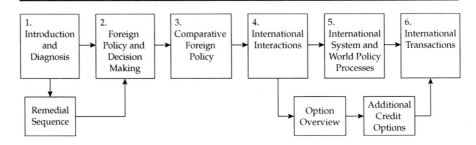

Each of the larger elements in a diagram is broken down into a more detailed unit outline. For example, Figure 6.2 is a detailed description of one of the sections in the diagram for the course in international relations (Module 5, International Interactions). (Note that in the later version of the diagram the number of this

Figure 6.2.
Unit Outline for Module 5: International Interactions

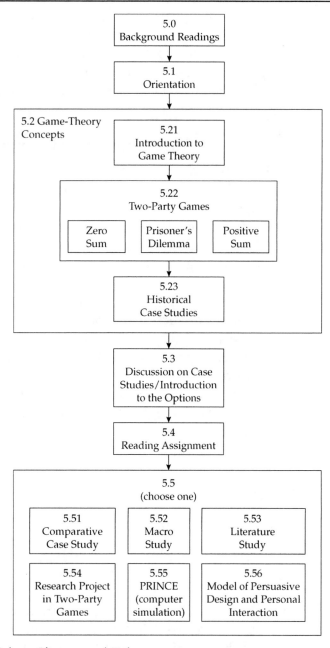

Source: Cohen, O'Leary, and Eickmann.

unit has changed.) A single course may consist of four, five, or even more of these unit outlines. Usually, for convenience and clarity, each of these outlines represents a self-contained unit of the course, covering several weeks of study, with its own set of objectives, options, and evaluation. In Figure 6.2, the unit outline identifies the five major segments of this module.

You will note in later examples that in curriculum design, each course or major component of instruction is represented in the same way as individual units are in a diagram of a course.

Although these diagrams should be as specific as possible, they should not be considered final or static. Diagrams may undergo constant and sometimes extensive modification as the preliminary (ideal) design is put into operation and is field tested. However, the more specific and detailed the design, the clearer the goals and the easier and more rapid the transition from design to implementation.

Some Specific Suggestions

The early diagram should focus on the overall sequence, but should not as yet be tied to a specific time frame. Specifically, the diagram should identify each of the major instructional components and the sequence in which they fall.

Before discussing specific examples, it will be helpful to look at some diagramming techniques that we have found to be most helpful.

We will use a box □ as the basic symbol for a component. In course projects a component is an instructional unit or module designed for a major topic area. In a curriculum project, the major component would be a course or a key activity that stands on its own.

A basic time sequence can be illustrated by a series of boxes (or circles or triangles; the specific symbols used are arbitrary) connected by arrows:

Figure 6.3

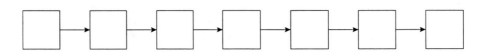

As noted earlier, while a horizontal (left to right) diagram is usually preferred in the development state, final drawings are often in a vertical format (top to bottom). The vertical format has proven to be a more efficient use of space and thus more practical for reports. In an actual diagram, each element would identify the specific topic as option or assignment being offered.

If a test is used with assignments based on the test results, you could illustrate this as follows (in this example, the remedial sequence, if assigned, is required prior to the instruction unit):

Figure 6.4

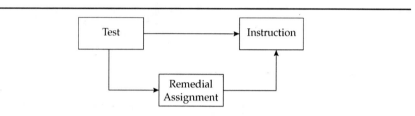

If there are student options at a given point in the program, you could diagram it in several different ways:

Figure 6.5

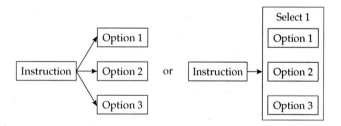

Enclosing two or more components in a larger box indicates that, taken together, they form a larger instructional unit. Typically the objectives of the enclosed modules will be closely related. Options, followed by seminars and then a large group or evaluation session might look like this:

Figure 6.6

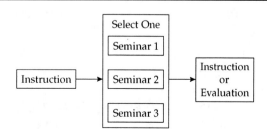

If a series of units is to be included where the order of completion is not important, you could diagram the sequence as follows:

Figure 6.7

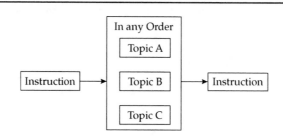

There are, of course many variations. As many specifics are still unknown at this stage of the development process, a program including both exemptions and remedial units might appear, as follows (notice how the diagram indicates the time by which the remedial unit must be completed):

Figure 6.8

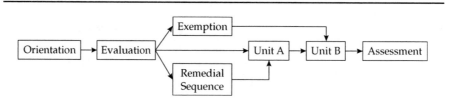

The specificity of a particular element in an outline will be directly related to the scope of your project. If an entire curriculum is involved, one diagram will be used to emphasize the interrelationship of major components or courses, as in Figure 6.1. In the case of a single course, the first diagram will emphasize main topic areas and their basic sequence.

Again, the key is to show the reader the structure of a program or course and how the various components interrelate. The fewer lines that cross over one another, the better. Arrows crossing each other can be extremely confusing to the reader.

A Short Exercise in Diagramming

In Resource F you will find a brief description of an introductory course. Before turning to the second page of the Resource, try your hand at diagramming the overall design of the course. If you're working as a member of a team, it's sometimes interesting to do this in teams of two or three. When working as a team, using a chalkboard or large newsprint pad will facilitate your discussion. You'll find this experience most helpful later in your work and it should only take you ten to twenty minutes to complete your diagram. On the second page, you'll find one possible way to illustrate the instructional flow of the course. Just remember, the fewer boxes and arrows and the simpler the diagram, the better.

PART TWO

The Process

CHAPTER 7

Making the Decision to Go Ahead

Figure 7.1.
The Model

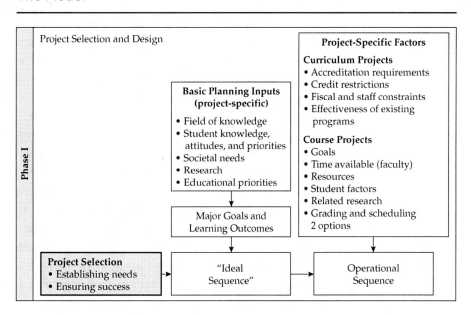

Before you begin any course or curriculum design project, two major questions must be answered: First, is there a need for the project? Second, if there is, are the resources available to ensure the success of the project? A decision to create or redesign a course or curriculum should not be taken lightly, because it will require you and everyone else involved to commit a great deal of time and effort. In addition, entering into this activity can have a direct impact on your professional career and the careers of other faculty involved. If you are an untenured faculty member at a research university, there may even be, as noted earlier, an element of risk involved in devoting time to this activity

Projects begin after a person or group has concluded that a problem or need exists. After that conclusion has been reached, a systematic needs assessment can accomplish two purposes: it can specifically define the problem, and it can generate information that you will need later, in the design phase. Before you undertake such a formal needs assessment, however, be sure that the support necessary for success exists. Without this commitment, engaging in a course or curriculum development project is a waste of your time and your institution's resources. It is extremely frustrating to begin a project only to find out later on that you don't have the resources or support that you need to finish.

Why Projects Begin

Faculty members become involved in course or curriculum projects for a variety of reasons. For example, you may be convinced that the content of your course is outdated; you may be concerned about a high failure or dropout rate; or graduates may be telling you, informally or through formal assessment, that they left the institution unprepared for their career choices. You and others may have become increasingly concerned about your students' attitudes, a diminishing number of majors entering the field, or a perceived decline in the quality of your students. In some instances you may have simply become bored with the course as you are presently teaching it—the academic seven-year itch. Some course or curricular projects begin when faculty find that they are no longer covering all that they wish to and thus conclude that changes must be made. Other projects are undertaken as a direct response to concerns expressed by employers, the fiscal need for larger enrollments, or a strong desire on the part of the entire department to update or improve program quality. A project may begin when a faculty member becomes intrigued with a new instructional approach or technology and finds that to use it well he or she must first address some basic issues that have been ignored for years. Some projects begin because faculty views of their roles in the classroom change. In short, there are many reasons for rethinking your course or your department's curriculum.

Questions to Consider

Whether the identification of a problem is based on hard data, hunches, vague feelings of frustration, or the desire to engage in a challenging and perhaps even enjoyable exercise, several questions should be asked before work begins. These questions constitute the evaluation component at the project-selection step of the design phase. Most often, these informal evaluation activities are performed by those most directly involved in deciding whether to begin a project.

How important is the project to the department, to you, to other faculty, to the chairperson, to the dean? If there is little support for what you are proposing, if few see the need or perceive the stated problem, or if there are other problems that they feel are more important, beginning the project at this time may be a major mistake. You would find little support or assistance for your effort, and later on you could have difficulty getting needed approval from key committees and administrative offices. Although the lack of such support will not be a problem if you are revising an existing course, external approval is essential for curriculum revisions or new courses.

How will this effort be recognized in the faculty reward system? If you or other key faculty are coming up for tenure in the next several years, consider the impact a major project might have on the tenure decision. On some campuses a significant and successful commitment to course and program improvement is viewed positively. On others it may be perceived by the tenure committee as detracting from what you should be doing; teaching, conducting research, and publishing. As noted earlier, this is the time to negotiate the weight this activity will have in decisions about promotion, tenure, and merit pay. For example, if you are taking on a major project, can your tenure clock be stopped during the period of this activity?

Are there others who can help and should be involved? Other faculty who teach the same course or who are directly responsible for the curriculum in which the course is offered should be involved or, at least, informed of what you are proposing. Are other faculty willing to assist—faculty who teach the follow-up course, faculty who send students to your course from other departments, faculty with special expertise that could be useful? Also, don't forget others, both on and off campus, who may have knowledge and skills that would be helpful as you move along.

Do you and the others who will be involved have enough time? The answer to this question will determine not only whether you should begin but how long the project might take. Sometimes limitations in time and money have necessitated phasing in a new program rather than introducing it all at one. On many campuses you also have the ability to negotiate released time or summer employment with your dean or department chair.

It is often best to use the academic year for design activities and summer for the production of materials (if salaries for summer work are available) for several reasons. First, the design phase can usually be completed during the academic year because it does not require an extensive number of hours each week. It takes time to collect, analyze, and interpret data, and others will want time to react to the draft designs, so scheduling meetings once a week or twice a month is fairly common. This schedule provides you with the necessary time to mull over what has been done and to make revisions between meetings. Second, released-time arrangements during the academic year rarely provide sufficient time to work on the project. If you are given released time, you will often also have other committee and advising assignments that take up the time set aside for the project. In institutions where summer employment is an option, you can schedule blocks of time for writing the new materials and preparing assignments and exams with no interruptions for other responsibilities. Third, during the summer, support and production people will usually be more accessible than they are during the school year.

Establishing Academic Priorities: Collecting the Information Needed

One of the paradoxes of academic innovation is that those projects most easily undertaken often have little to do with the established goals or needs of the academic department; support and investment are therefore highly unlikely. Although most significant in curriculum-related initiatives, priorities outside your specific department or content area can affect the success of a course-focused project as well.

Realistic priorities are established from data collected from the community (alumni, employers, parents), students, the instructional staff, and the administration. Such data collection can answer important questions. What programs should be emphasized and improved? Where do problems exist? What changes are needed, and can they be made under the existing structure? Can and should fundamental restructuring be encouraged?

In establishing priorities, all those who are or should be concerned ought to be involved. Their participation is particularly important at the community level, where specific subgroups are often overlooked. The decision to revise a course that you teach can certainly be made by you alone. Determination of its importance, however, will often be made by others.

Students

Students can provide valuable information about the value and effectiveness of academic programs. Unfortunately, structured attempts to gather these data are the exception. In many instances only the more politically active, highly capable student is heard. Nevertheless, you should seek input from all segments of the student population, including minority, international, and departing students. Often the students' immediate needs as they see them must be met before efforts can be undertaken to meet their long-term and more significant needs. Asking specific questions can help you identify problem areas: Are dropout or failure rates higher in certain courses? Are the stronger students leaving certain programs?

The characteristics of your students can also make a significant difference. Different groups may require different objectives, procedures, and instructional elements. Designing the academic program for a highly transient student population poses a particular challenge. Junior colleges located near military establishments and in urban centers, for example, have a highly mobile student population. Such problems must be identified because they have a direct effect on the priorities of the program and on its design.

The Job Market

What are the needs of the society in which your educational program exists? These needs may be on a national or local level, or specific to the particular population that a professional program is designed to serve.

You must also consider the future needs of employers. For example, we must anticipate the skills that will be required by the time today's first-year students graduate and look for employment. All too often we have designed our curricula and programs to meet immediate needs without giving enough attention to long-range requirements. A study by one professional group, which chose not to publish its findings for political reasons, concluded that the faculty in the field had "lost touch" with what was happening in the workplace. As a result, many graduates were unprepared for the jobs for which they were applying.

With sufficient effort relevant trends can be identified. The large number of teachers and administrators retiring in the next decade, at all levels from elementary school to college, will certainly have a direct effect on the job market. In addition, for the next several decades the need for graduates in all fields with competencies in technology, information systems, and computers can only be expected to rise. Increasingly, graduates have available to them job openings in a far wider range of fields than ever before as employers recognize the need for diversity in the competencies of their employees. It is imperative that we continue to monitor the occupational outcomes of our graduates. Significant changes in job opportunities are not the exception. More specifics on the changing competencies required of our graduates will be found in the chapters that follow.

Some effort has been made on a few campuses to establish a close working relationship between the academic departments and those who hire their graduates. At Syracuse University, for example, boards of visitors have been established for professional schools to provide input and resources. Advisory groups for design projects in the professional areas can help to identify a need for the revision of existing programs and also provide excellent suggestions regarding content that should be consulted when programs are being designed. In addition, those serving on these advisory groups are often willing to make student internships and other resources available to the programs.

Other Faculty

When content problems exist in courses or curricula, the faculty are usually aware of them. Major discoveries, new theories, and discipline modifications all have an impact on priorities. It is often helpful to involve faculty from other schools or departments. Management specialists, for example, can provide insight on academic programs in school administration or political science, psychologists can be helpful in evaluating programs in mass communication, and law faculty can assess the usefulness of a course in leadership and in dealing with the rights of employees. In some instances faculty already have courses available that meet the needs of another department.

Contacting your disciplinary or professional association can often provide useful information for determining society's priorities. For example, William Laidlaw of the American Assembly of Collegiate Schools of Business states:

> The customers of business schools, the companies who hire their graduates, tell [us] that business schools do a fine job providing a technical education, teaching analytical skills, and developing decision-making abilities. They criticize business schools for not teaching people management skills such as leadership, teamwork, and effective communication, and they feel business schools should do a better job of teaching ethics, technology management, and an international perspective. Without diminishing the knowledge currently imparted, companies want business schools to strengthen additional qualities and knowledge areas without lengthening the program or increasing the cost. Now the challenge is to figure how to meet customer demand [Laidlaw, letter to the author].

Administrators

A central administration that is sensitive to the concerns of parents, alumni, students, and faculty, and that is aware of both budget and resource limitations, can also help to identify the specific academic programs that need the most attention. Administrators (as well as faculty) also have to keep the broad goals of higher education in mind. Because significant demographic changes are usually prominent and readily identified, they are likely to generate easily articulated goals. But there is a danger that new job-related objectives will displace the broader, less easily defined "liberal" goals of education. Administrators (and others) can prevent this from happening by ensuring that basic long-range needs are addressed; the need for these competencies will not change. Quality employees will always need communication, interpersonal, problem-solving, and critical-thinking competencies regardless of their fields and their roles within them. Those responsible for the curriculum must keep these basic goals in view as more discipline-related goals receive much greater attention.

Deciding to Begin Curriculum Projects

Two elements must exist before you begin a major curriculum revision. First, a solid base of instructional talent must be available in all the appropriate academic areas; every key department must be supportive and must be represented by faculty members who command the respect of their peers. (And because these talented faculty members often receive other job offers and leave, it is best to involve more than one faculty member from each academic area to ensure continuity.) Involving a quality teaching staff with classroom experience and expertise in their disciplines ensures that the project is academically respectable and that it will be durable. Outside expertise can be used, but consultants cannot provide the required specific teaching skills, knowledge of content, and political base.

Second, there must be institutional stability. Beginning a curriculum project is unwise if the school or department faces changes in administration—for example, if the chair or dean is to be replaced shortly. Under such circumstances any decision about curriculum redesign made today may lack support tomorrow. A new department chairperson, interested in establishing his or her own program, can eliminate a successful program by administrative fiat without extensive research into why it was undertaken and what effects it has had.

Exhibits 7.1 and 7.2 are checklists of the factors you should consider in deciding whether to undertake curriculum projects.

Exhibit 7.1.

Establishing the Need for Curriculum Design Projects

	Yes	No	Need More Data
External Factors			
1. The existing program meets the present and long-term needs of your students.			
Alumni feedback	☐	☐	☐
Employer feedback	☐	☐	☐
Recruiter feedback	☐	☐	☐
2. Graduates of your program are successful in finding a job or being accepted into graduate school.	☐	☐	☐
3. The curriculum meets accreditation standards (if appropriate).	☐	☐	☐
4. The curriculum is up-to-date and sensitive to changing needs in the field.	☐	☐	☐
Internal Factors			
5. Attrition rate is acceptable.	☐	☐	☐
6. Enrollment is stable or increasing.	☐	☐	☐
7. Quality of students is stable or increasing.	☐	☐	☐
8. More students are transferring in than transferring out.	☐	☐	☐
9. Faculty like the sequence and content of the existing program.	☐	☐	☐
10. Students are pleased with the existing program.	☐	☐	☐
11. Core learning outcomes are clearly stated for all students.	☐	☐	☐
12. Discipline-specific learning outcomes are clearly stated for majors and required courses.	☐	☐	☐
13. Students are assessed on their ability to meet these goals.	☐	☐	☐
14. Tests and other evaluation protocols emphasize higher-order competencies.	☐	☐	☐
15. Every student has the opportunity to receive the instruction and reinforcement necessary to meet these goals.	☐	☐	☐
16. There is a "capstone" or comprehensive assessment at the end of the program.	☐	☐	☐

Exhibit 7.2.

Indicators of Potential Success for Curriculum Design Projects

	Yes	No	Not Sure
1. There is administrative support for the project.			
Provost	☐	☐	☐
Dean	☐	☐	☐
Chair(s)	☐	☐	☐
2. The individuals in key positions will be in place for the duration of the project.	☐	☐	☐
3. Strong faculty representing each discipline/ department that will be affected are willing to participate.	☐	☐	☐
4. Faculty who will be serving on the design team are willing to follow the model selected.	☐	☐	☐
5. Someone from the institution's academic-support center or a faculty member from another discipline is willing to serve as facilitator.	☐	☐	☐
6. The institution is willing to provide the resources needed for planning and implementation (travel, summer employment, released time).	☐	☐	☐
7. Necessary provisions have been made regarding promotion, tenure, or merit pay for those faculty who will be donating extensive time to the project.	☐	☐	☐
8. These commitments are in writing.	☐	☐	☐

Realistically, curriculum projects take a year or more to complete. Everyone involved should plan accordingly, keeping in mind that the end result will usually be the need for new courses, the redesign of existing ones, and the development of a range of other programs and elements.

Deciding to Begin Course Projects

Although you will ask a number of the same questions for a course project as for a curriculum project, there are, as you might expect, major differences between beginning a large, often multidepartmental curriculum project and in beginning a course project over which the faculty member teaching the course has significant control. There will also be some modest but important differences between redesigning an existing course and designing a new one that must be approved not only at the departmental level but at the school, college, or institutional level as well.

Designing New Courses

The primary justification for any new course is to fill a gap in the present list of offerings. However, before you begin to design a new course, make certain that your chair and dean are in total support of this initiative. It is also crucial that other faculty who may have an interest or competencies in the area either be involved in your design effort or be given the opportunity to participate. The least you should have is their approval to proceed. Although it may be frustrating at times, making changes is often a political activity. Without the support of other faculty and their agreement that there is a need for the new course, getting approval will be difficult no matter how good your course idea may be. In some instances you may find that faculty members will be offering a course much like yours in another school, college, or program. If there is a possibility of overlap, you will need to explain the differences between what you propose and what exists, and communicate how your new course meets presently unmet needs. If the amount of overlap is significant, you might wish to work together with faculty from the other department to explore a joint offering with options that meet both your needs.

Early in the process, you should be sure that you know the procedures that must be followed for the approval of new courses on your campus, including what information you will need to provide to the various department, school, and curriculum committees.

Many programs have "experimental" course numbers that can be assigned to a course while it is in the developmental or field-testing stage. Usually limited in use to one or two semesters, such numbers allow you the freedom to try new approaches and give you time to develop a comprehensive description of the course and to include some hard data in the documentation that will be needed by the review committees. The more detail you can provide, the greater your chance of approval.

Redesigning Existing Courses

Whereas new course initiatives focus on gaps in the present offerings, the justification for redesigning an existing course may be to address omissions or to improve the effectiveness or efficiency of the present offering. If an existing course is not going well, you know it, other faculty know it, your students certainly know it, as will your chair and dean. Your task is to determine exactly what the problems are. Resource G presents an approach you may want to consider for evaluating a course that you now teach. Focusing on the kinds of questions it includes can help you determine whether major problems exist and what they are, information essential to deciding whether to begin. Exhibits 7.3 and 7.4 are checklists of factors you should consider in making your final decision.

Exhibit 7.3.

Establishing the Need for Course Design Projects

	Yes	No	Need More Data
New Course			
1. Meets need not met by existing courses.	☐	☐	☐
2. Will permit the elimination of courses or will reduce duplication.	☐	☐	☐
3. Will introduce a new area of content with a new or expanded set of learning goals.	☐	☐	☐
Existing Course			
1. Is not successful.	☐	☐	☐
2. Is outdated; new content must be added.	☐	☐	☐
3. Has no clear statement of goals.	☐	☐	☐
4. Does not measure student attainment of complex goals.	☐	☐	☐
5. Has a high failure or dropout rate.	☐	☐	☐
6. Does not prepare students for next course in sequence (if appropriate).	☐	☐	☐
7. Depends primarily on lecture when other techniques may be more appropriate.	☐	☐	☐
8. Elicits negative student response.	☐	☐	☐
9. Uses resources inefficiently.	☐	☐	☐

Exhibit 7.4.

Indicators of Potential Success for Course Design Projects

	Yes	No	Not Sure
1. There is top administrative support for the project (chair and dean).	☐	☐	☐
2. The administrators supporting the project will be in place for the next two years.	☐	☐	☐
3. If the course is to be taught by more than one faculty member, everyone involved is willing to participate in the project.	☐	☐	☐
4. Faculty working on the project will be given enough time (released time, summer employment).	☐	☐	☐
5. If extensive time will be required, adjustments will be made in the promotion and tenure criteria/time line as appropriate, and agreement is in writing.	☐	☐	☐
6. Participants in the project are willing to follow the model selected.	☐	☐	☐
7. Someone from the institution's academic-support center or a faculty member from another discipline is willing to serve as facilitator.	☐	☐	☐
8. Administrators are willing to allow sufficient time for design, field testing, and revision of the course that is developed.	☐	☐	☐
9. No major curriculum revisions are under way or planned that would affect the goals and content of the course.	☐	☐	☐
10. The course will be required, or the pool of students is sufficient.	☐	☐	☐
11. If resources are needed, they will be provided.	☐	☐	☐
12. Space for offering the course will be available.	☐	☐	☐

Summary

Before you begin you must clearly identify and understand the need for the course or curriculum effort you are proposing and be confident that all the elements are in place to ensure success. Not doing so will place the project at risk and result in wasted time—and could have negative professional implications. In addition, the information you collect to show that a need exists will be invaluable to you later in the project as you develop the program. These base data can also be used to show the changes that have occurred as a result of your work. All too often this essential information is never collected and, as a result, claims of significant impact are difficult, if not impossible, to make. Finally, the more accurate the information you begin with, the greater chance you will have of developing a highly effective course or curriculum.

CHAPTER 8

Getting Started

Figure 8.1.
The Model

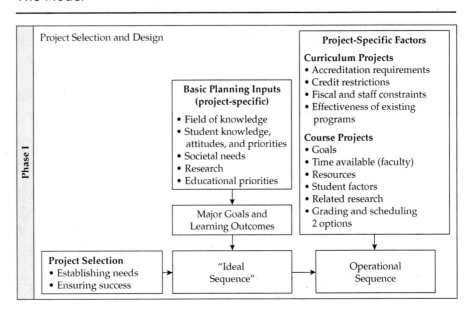

In this chapter we focus on getting your project under way, with particular emphasis on the crucial first meeting of everyone involved. If your project is to redesign a course that you will be teaching, the meeting will be between you and the process person. If your project is a curricular one, the meeting might include several faculty besides yourself, your facilitator, and other individuals who may be essential to the success of the project.

Although a number of informal conversations must take place prior to the start of your work, the first formal meeting of those who will actively participate in the project is extremely important. At this meeting you will discuss the overall goals of the project and articulate the basic instructional philosophy. You will describe the development process, define the roles of all the participants, and lay out the fundamental groundwork for the project. This will also be a time to review basic institutional procedures and guidelines.

Who Should Be Involved

The initial design meeting should include the facilitator (serving as chair) and all the faculty who will be working directly on the project. A team of faculty, when possible, is preferred because it provides a strong academic base. If a particular course is the focus of your project, make an effort to include all faculty who teach it. In curriculum projects, the team should consist of carefully selected representatives from each of the major academic programs or departments involved.

For a curriculum project, one faculty member should be identified as the key content expert and coordinator. This academic team leader should have the ability and the content expertise needed to coordinate the efforts of other faculty members.

The team leader may be a department chair or a dean who wishes to be actively involved in the design process. In addition to directing activities that take place within the academic departments, the team leader acts as chair when the facilitator is not available.

If the group is large (over eight or so), appointing a small steering committee will increase efficiency. Everyone on the steering committee is expected to participate actively in the development process, and other members will not have such an active role. In some instances administrators (deans or department chairpersons) will wish to become members of the steering committee, and they should be encouraged to do so. This committee is absolutely essential for the success of large projects, and therefore the selection of its members should be given careful thought.

Students

Graduate or undergraduate students may be members of a development team in order to provide support and bring to the table issues from the student's perspective that faculty or administrators might miss, but they should not play a major role in determining the goals, structure, and content of programs. Delegating content decisions to students is likely to elicit a negative response when the final design is presented to faculty for adoption.

However, students can often provide a most useful perspective to any initiative and can also play a big role in program implementation. In her discussion of the value of student participation to the design and implementation of a first-year program for entering students, Mary Stuart Hunter (2006) made the following observation: "Perhaps the most overlooked and underappreciated resource available to us are the students themselves. It is far too common for campus officials to spend an inordinate amount of time and energy developing strategies to improve the first college year without ever asking for student involvement. Not only can students provide valuable information to inform our work, but they can also be highly effective partners in the delivery of programs and services."

Evaluation Specialist

Because data about the students and, when appropriate, the professional field are often presented at this initial meeting, it can be helpful to include a person who can handle the collection and interpretation of this information. Including an evaluation specialist (if available) in this meeting provides an additional range of expertise, gives this evaluator a better understanding of your project from the beginning, and gives everyone who will work together on the project the opportunity to get to know one another.

The Registrar

Although the need for the involvement of the registrar or a member from his or her office may not be immediately apparent, adding this member to your team may be extremely important as you move ahead and you start to explore new structures, time lines, and grading options.

Experts in technology, assessment, teaching methodology, and course and program design are sometimes made available to faculty and academic offices, but the registrar is, unfortunately, rarely involved in these discussions from the earliest stages. As Diamond and DeBlois observed:

> Such an omission can be costly because the registrar can often be a critical component in academic transformation. No matter which of the many possible outcomes of the accountability movement we are talking about: whether a national unit record system; new metrics for gauging academic progress and graduation rates; adaptable information systems for new forms of instructional design; discipline-specific measures of learning outcomes; mission-, demographic-, and Carnegie class-specific success standards outcomes, assessment and grading criteria, in each instance new support systems and policy changes will often be required and in each instance the registrar is a key agent for any changes that may be required. . . . The registrar can play a vital

role in academic innovation by providing invaluable policy counsel and advice about the degree to which information systems can be customized and, ultimately, can grease the tracks of academic innovation [2007].

Pre-Project Meetings

Before the first formal design meeting of the whole team, meetings must be held with key faculty and administrators. These meetings help you to establish priorities, determine the scope and goals of your project, and identify others who should be involved, the resources available, and the procedures that will be followed. These pre-project meetings can also help to develop the commitment that will be required of the department and other faculty. In some instances you may find that there is little support for what you have in mind, and as a result, you may decide not to begin. Also at this time, any unresolved tenure and promotion considerations should be addressed, and participants should be told whether summer employment or released time will be made available.

Goals of First Formal Meeting

To be successful, the initial formal design meeting must achieve several important objectives:

- The goals and scope of the project and the anticipated time line should be reviewed and agreed on. Those participating must be comfortable with the plans for the process and project.

- There should be a clear understanding of everyone's responsibilities.

- The role of the facilitator should be clearly defined. Stress the point that the facilitator is a process person who will help the participating faculty by asking questions, playing devil's advocate, and offering suggestions. The goals and content of the course or curriculum must always remain the responsibility of the faculty.

- A commitment must be made to getting the development process under way so that everyone feels that progress has been made.

- An operational instructional philosophy for the course or program should be established.

It is also sometimes possible in the first meeting to begin to discuss what the overall goal of the project should be and what an ideal program might look like. At the end of this initial meeting the facilitator should review what has been accomplished and then send the summary to participants for comments and reaction. In addition, other basics should be covered, such as meeting times and upcoming deadlines. If you are unable to locate someone to act as facilitator, you or one of the other faculty involved may need to serve in this role. It is not the best approach but sometimes you have no other option available.

Developing an Instructional Philosophy

Throughout this book we will describe what it means for a course or a curriculum to be learning- or student-centered. For some faculty this will mean a shift from focusing on what they will cover to what their students will learn, directly affecting how they perceive their roles as faculty. It will determine the structure and nature of instruction, how goals are articulated, how students are assessed, and where and how learning takes place.

Lee Allen (1996), building on the work of Robert Barr and John Tagg, included the following in a list of features that promote student-centered learning:

- Students learn how to find knowledge, they do not wait for faculty to provide it.
- Ongoing student and course assessments show faculty where teaching is effective and ineffective.
- Students' performance on activities and assignments is assessed by more people than a single instructor.
- Students construct the questions they need to ask, rather than expecting their teachers to choose the facts students ought to know.
- Students become active and participatory learners; they are not just audiences for teacher lecturers.
- Students have opportunities to learn through teamwork and to be rewarded for group efforts, not just for their own activities.
- Academic effort is measured by how much students learn, not how many hours faculty teach.
- Faculty guide students, helping them formulate fruitful problems and questions and uncover effective ways to learn answers.

As Allen reports, those involved need to develop an understanding of assessment, learning styles, motivation, and various instructional methods and technologies—an understanding not often required in the past, when the focus was primarily on content and presentation.

Before you begin, everyone involved needs to agree about the instructional philosophy that will underlie the course or the curriculum. If indeed it is to be student- and learning-centered, every major decision made in the design process will need to be framed in that context.

In addition to the questions that you will address as part of the decision to go ahead (Chapter 7), important questions will be raised as you begin to focus on the goals, priorities, and content of your course or curriculum. Some of these will be specific to the institution or program, but many will be based on regional or national needs or on issues directly related to your particular discipline.

For example, in 2005 the National Academy of Sciences published *The Engineer of 2020: Visions of Engineering in the New Century.* After a review of the present state of engineering education in the country, the authors of the report—representing schools of engineering and national leaders in business and industry—described the immediate and long-term needs of the country and the role they envisioned for engineering, and then presented a list of specific recommendations and competencies that they believed engineers would require in the future. The significance of that report to schools and colleges of engineering was obvious. It also raised a number of specific questions that faculty involved in course or curriculum projects should be addressing as they design and implement redesigned or new programs (see Resource H).

Case Study: Getting the Right People Involved in Designing an Orientation Program for Teaching Assistants_____

In the summer of 1986, Syracuse University's vice president for undergraduate studies, Ronald Cavanagh, and the vice president for research and graduate affairs, Karen Hiiemae, decided to explore the possibility of implementing a required orientation program for all new teaching assistants. This would be one of the first programs of its kind in the United States. The first step was to establish a steering committee and appoint to this committee those individuals who would be essential for designing, implementing, and supporting any program that might be proposed. Because this project would involve faculty, administrators, and graduate students, the committee included the following members (in addition to the two vice presidents, who served as co-chairs):

- The director of the graduate school
- Two faculty representatives who were responsible for the training and supervision of teaching assistants in their departments. (Faculty from English and mathematics, the departments with the largest number of teaching assistants, were selected. These departments had already developed support programs for their teaching assistants, and it was imperative that this initiative not be perceived as a threat to the programs already in place.)
- Two graduate students, including the president of the graduate student organization.
- A faculty representative from the graduate council, a university-wide body that supervised graduate education.
- The director of the academic support center, who would be responsible for the overall design of the program and would serve as facilitator.

Once a decision was made to implement the proposed program, the steering committee was expanded to include a representative from the unit that provided support to international students and also the two individuals who would manage the program. Several additional support staff attended all meetings.

The planning that went into the selection of this key group was not wasted. Every committee member played an essential role in the successful design and implementation of the program. Two of the faculty members assumed responsibility for important elements of the program. In this project the graduate students played major roles in both the design and the implementation of training and social activities, and the graduate school developed administrative procedures that were essential for a smoothly running program. By selecting these key individuals to play an active role in the design of the program, ownership was ensured, the quality of the final program was enhanced, and a number of potential "turf" problems were eliminated. In addition, it allowed those departments already actively involved in the training of their graduate students to determine which elements of the new program they would like to utilize and which activities of their existing program they would like to retain.

Summary

Care must be taken in identifying individuals to be involved from the beginning of your project and, for curricular and other projects involving several courses, in establishing the committees and task forces that will carry out the project once a decision to move ahead is made. The following participants should be included (as appropriate):

- Faculty: for course projects—those with major teaching or administrative responsibilities (maximum, four to six); for curriculum projects—representatives of all major academic areas
- Administrator(s): dean or department chair (optional)
- Facilitator (chairs meetings, essential)
- Evaluator (optional)
- Graduate assistants (staff role only)

The initial design meeting should help all involved to understand what they are being asked to do and how much time will most likely be required. The following topics should be covered:

- Need for and general goals of project (review)
- Instructional philosophy (for example, will the course or program be student- and learning-centered) and its implications
- Review of design model
- Roles of participants (including time commitment)
- Available resources (including stipends for faculty)
- Anticipated time lines
- Significant institutional policies and procedures
- Schedule for future meetings
- Initial work on design of program

CHAPTER 9

Linking Goals, Courses, and Curricula

As we teach our courses, we tend to lose sight of the fact that each course is but one element in a learning sequence defined as a curriculum. The closer the relationships are among courses, curriculum, and planned out-of-class activities, the more effective the learning experience will be for our students. So, whether you are working on the design of a single course or of a curriculum, it is imperative that you keep in mind the relationship between the two. A quality education does not happen by chance; it requires careful planning, skilled teaching, and an overall structure that ensures that every student has the opportunity to reach the goals of the program in which he or she is enrolled. A quality education requires a level of orchestration seldom found at colleges and universities as well as the active involvement of a faculty that is paying a great deal of attention to structure, content, and process. It requires hard work.

Goals of a Curriculum

In general the goals of a curriculum evolve from the total of the instructional outcomes associated with three elements (see Figure 9.1).

- The basic survival competencies that *all* students should have upon graduation
- The discipline-specific core competencies related to the core requirements (usually the humanities, social sciences, and natural sciences)

Figure 9.1.
The Underpinnings of a Curriculum

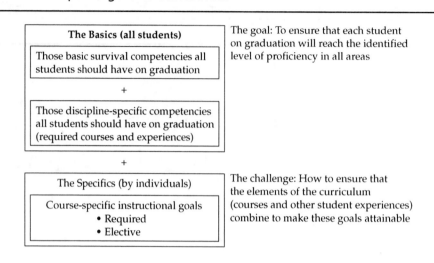

To ensure that every student has the opportunity to reach the required level of proficiency in each area that has been identified, several major tasks must be accomplished:

- A list of the basic competencies for all students must be developed and approved by the institution.

- These competencies must be described in terms that are measurable and demonstrable.

- A comprehensive plan must be developed to make sure that the basic competencies are learned and reinforced throughout the entire time a student is enrolled.

- Each disciplinary area responsible for a portion of the core curriculum must describe and include in the goals of each of their courses the appropriate learning outcomes that it will introduce or reinforce.

- For these courses a common set of assessment techniques and instruments must be developed.

Developing a Cohesive Curriculum

A curriculum must be developed sequentially, beginning with an institutional statement of goals and ending with the assessment of each student before and after graduation. As you move through the design process, from defining general goals to developing course goals and then unit-by-unit objectives, the statements become increasingly specific. The design of each course, the selection of instructional methods, and student assessment will be based on these statements.

The process of moving from a statement of goals to deciding on and implementing a program and relating individual courses to the curriculum requires careful planning. If, for example, speaking skills are identified as a basic competency that every student must have by graduation, public speaking must be initially taught and then reinforced, and *no student should be able to graduate without receiving appropriate instruction and practice in this skill.* Courses must be analyzed to identify where this skill is introduced and then reinforced, and the curriculum must be structured so that every student has the opportunity to acquire speaking skills. In the case of developing competencies in speaking, the required courses will most likely be those with smaller enrollment, or lecture courses that have discussion sessions associated with them.

Once all key competencies are determined, a curriculum committee might use a basic competency checklist to facilitate this task (see Figure 9.2). This checklist could be used to assign specific competencies to individual courses or other formal learning experiences and to describe the level at which the competency will be taught, indicating in which courses the competency will be introduced, used, further developed, and assessed. We have found that the following matrix can be extremely helpful not only in ensuring that each goal is met but also that students will be unable to complete the curriculum without the necessary instruction.

Keep in mind that many of these basic core competencies can be taught within regular, discipline-based courses. If you are responsible

Figure 9.2.
The Underpinnings of a Curriculum: A Checklist

Key

| A: Introduced |
| B: Used |
| C: Further developed |
| D: Comprehensive assessment |

Course Number

The Basic Competencies (institution-specific)																			
Communication																			
Writing																			
Speaking, etc.																			

for one of the required courses in your program, one of your major responsibilities will be determining which of the basic competencies can be taught or reinforced within it. Developing and using interpersonal skills (teamwork), problem solving, critical thinking, basic statistics, and so on are widely listed core objectives and can be an integral part of most courses. Most important, NO student should be able to pass through your curriculum without having the opportunity to learn and use each of the identified core competencies.

The Basic Core Competencies

There is far more agreement about basic competencies than one might at first expect. When faculty are asked, "What basic competencies or skills should every college student have upon graduation?" we have found that responses are remarkably consistent.

The Core Competencies

On most lists

Communicating skills

Listening

Reading

Speaking

Writing

Interpersonal skills

Working on a team

Leadership

Willingness to take risk

Mathematics including

Basic statistics

Interpretation of charts and graphs

Problem solving

Resource utilization

Recent Additions

Conflict resolution

Ethics

Interviewing skills

Lifelong learning

Participatory citizenship

Time management

Understanding and respecting diverse cultures

Developing Your Own List of Core Competencies _____

Fortunately, although each institution, school, college, and academic program must develop its own unique set of core competencies, you do not have to start from scratch. There are many excellent resources now available that specifically address the issue of what competencies each student should have upon graduation. The challenge will be in getting a majority of your faculty to agree on (1) the specific list for your institution or program and (2) how each of these competencies will be described and then measured.

It is a major mistake to take any published list of basic skills or competencies and accept it in its entirety for use on your campus or in your program. Not only will the specific items on such a list vary from institution to institution but the definition of each item will vary as well. The final list of competencies, their definitions, and how they should be assessed must evolve on each campus and in each program. Faculty ownership in the process is an essential element for successful use of the material that is developed.

A 2005 report from the Association of American Colleges and Universities found "a remarkable consensus on a few key outcomes that all students, regardless of major or academic background, should achieve during undergraduate study" (p. 3). See Exhibit 9.1. This report also includes a list of *Principles of Excellence,* which provides you and members of your team with a practical frame of reference to use as you move through the design, implementation, and evolution stages of your project (see Exhibit 9.2).

A number of institutions have been using reports such as these as the framework for restructuring their academic program. One excellent example is the work that has been done at Ocean County College in Toms River, New Jersey. The Academic Master Plan that evolved followed the goals advocated in these reports and also spelled out in detail the specific steps that would be required to reach them and specific areas of responsibility. The entire Master Plan is available on their Web site.

Always keep in mind that although certain instructional goals are long range and focused on performance well after graduation, it is possible within an undergraduate program to identify the skills, attitudes, and understandings that are the underpinnings of these long-range goals.

Exhibit 9.1.

The Essential Learning Outcomes

Beginning in school, and continuing at successfully higher levels across their college studies, students should prepare for the challenges of the twenty-first century by gaining:

KNOWLEDGE OF HUMAN CULTURES AND THE PHYSICAL AND NATURAL WORLD

- Through study in the sciences and mathematics, social sciences, humanities, histories, languages, and the arts

Focused by engagement with big questions, both contemporary and enduring

INTELLECTUAL AND PRACTICAL SKILLS, INCLUDING

- Inquiry and analysis
- Critical and creative thinking
- Written and oral communication
- Quantitative literacy
- Information literacy
- Teamwork and problem solving

Practiced extensively, across the curriculum, in the context of progressively more challenging problems, projects, and standards for performance

PERSONAL AND SOCIAL RESPONSIBILITY, INCLUDING

- Civic knowledge and engagement—local and global
- Intercultural knowledge and competence
- Ethical reasoning and action
- Foundations and skills for lifelong learning

Anchored through active involvement with diverse communities and real-world challenges

INTEGRATIVE LEARNING, INCLUDING

- Synthesis and advanced accomplishment across general and specialized studies

Demonstrated through the application of knowledge, skills, and responsibilities to new settings and complex problems

Source: **College Learning for the New Global Century**, A Report from the National Leadership Council for Liberal Education and America's Promise, 2007, p. 12. Reprinted with permission.

Exhibit 9.2.
The Principles of Excellence

PRINCIPLE ONE

- Aim High—and Make Excellence Inclusive

Make the essential learning outcomes a framework for the entire
educational experience, connecting school, college, work, and life

PRINCIPLE TWO

- Give Students a Compass

Focus each student's plan of study on achieving the essential learning
outcomes—and assess progress

PRINCIPLE THREE

- Teach the Arts of Inquiry and Innovation

Immerse all students in analysis, discovery, problem solving, and
communication, beginning in school and advancing in college

PRINCIPLE FOUR

- Engage the Big Questions

Teach through the curriculum to far-reaching issues—contemporary and
enduring—in science and society, cultures and values, global interdependence, the changing economy, and human dignity and freedom

PRINCIPLE FIVE

- Connect Knowledge with Choices and Action

Prepare students for citizenship and work through engaged and guided
learning on "real-world" problems

PRINCIPLE SIX

- Foster Civic, Intercultural, and Ethical Learning

Emphasize personal and social responsibility, in every field of study

PRINCIPLE SEVEN

- Assess Students' Ability to Apply Learning to Complex Problems

Use assessment to deepen learning and to establish a culture of shared
purpose and continuous improvement

*Source: **College Learning for the New Global Century**, A Report from the National
Leadership Council for Liberal Education and America's Promise, 2007, p. 26. Reprinted
with permission.

Resources

Regardless of your academic discipline, you should take a few minutes to review the materials in the following Resource Sections and Case Studies.

- The competencies discussed and the rationale for including them in a list of required core competencies may be relevant to your own discipline.

- Many of the competencies will be needed by every student you teach.

- Building on this information from other fields will allow you to make linkages between what you are teaching and the specific interests of students with different majors and priorities.

- You may find some of the approaches used by other institutions useful on your own campus.

In Resource D, "Criteria for Accrediting Engineering Programs," you will find a detailed list of learning outcomes required for all programs approved by the Accreditation Board for Engineering and Technology (ABET). Like many professional accrediting groups, ABET has become increasingly specific in their requirements for program approval.

Resource I. "Multicultural Competencies for Counselors" from the American Counseling Association is another example from a professional association. This section of the full report focuses on a single competency that is becoming increasingly important to this and many other professions.

Resource J. "Ethics," from the 2006 Report of the Commission on Public Relations Education, is another example of a disciplinary group addressing a competency that appears in most of the newer lists.

Resource K. "Mathematics, Prerequisites, and Students Success in Introductory Courses" includes two statements from the fields of management and business.

Case Studies

A growing number of institutions are developing comprehensive statements that provide detailed information on the learning goals for all of their students. These statements are not only emphasized in the materials used to describe the character and goals of the institution but serve as the basic foundation behind the curriculum initiatives that followed their development. You will notice that although structurally different, each statement includes specific outcomes and also addresses issues of assessment. Notice how different the formats are in Case Studies Two and Three even though both institutions are from the same state system.

Case Study 2: Alverno College

Case Study 3: Southeast Missouri State University

Case Study 4: Missouri State University

Summary

In every institution, the final determinant of the quality of the academic program is the performance of its graduates. The degree of success will depend on how well the curriculum is delivered through its courses and other learning experiences provided to students. Every student must have the opportunity to reach and demonstrate every stated basic competency. Carefully articulated learning outcomes must be the basis on which instructional methods are chosen and the criteria by which competency must be measured. The effectiveness of an institution or program and of individual faculty members is then determined by the ability of students to meet these goals. At the same time it must be recognized that not all students will reach these goals, because their attitudes, willingness to work, and ability also play an important role in determining success. Our responsibility is to do all we can to facilitate the learning that is required and to give each student a fair opportunity to succeed.

In the past we have tended not to track the total experience of our students, to assess their growth, or to evaluate the success of individual academic programs. We have rarely been willing to describe our instructional goals or to determine our effectiveness in helping our students attain them. Although not technically accurate, some faculty members perceive any approach that requires defining and measuring learning outcomes or structuring a curriculum as infringing on their rights as teachers. With active involvement on their part in the statement of goals and in course and curriculum design, these concerns can usually be overcome.

We really no longer have an option. Unless we relate our curriculum, our courses, and our teaching to clearly articulated goals, we will not have the effective educational system that parents, students, our communities, and accrediting bodies and review offices demand—and that we ourselves desire. Fortunately, since the mid-1980s much has been done to assist us in this task. New instructional approaches have been identified that can help us develop the more advanced competencies that appear on most lists of intended outcomes, and the field of assessment can provide us with the tools and techniques necessary to evaluate how successful our students are. Both of these areas will be described in detail in later chapters.

Additional Resources

Association of American Colleges and Universities. *College Learning for the New Global Century. A Report from the National Leadership Council for Liberal Education and America's Promise.* Washington, D.C.: Association of American Colleges and Universities, 2007.

> Included in this report, in addition to the two appearing in this chapter, are summarized data from surveys of business and governmental leaders, faculty, and students as well as data on student achievement. You may find these to be extremely useful as you develop a list of required core competencies for your own program.

Association of American Colleges and Universities. *Liberal Education Outcomes: A Preliminary Report on Student Achievement in College.* Washington, D.C.: Association of American Colleges and Universities, 2005. Available at www.aacw.org/publications/index.cfm.

> This brief sixteen-page report is loaded with useful information. Includes a suggested list of core competencies for all undergraduate students and backup materials from numerous studies. The Reference section is outstanding and full of useful quotes.

Modern Language Association. *Foreign Languages and Higher Education: New Structures for a Changed World.* Washington, D.C.: Modern Language Association, 2007. Also available at www.mla.org/mlaissuesmajor.

> An outstanding report that places the teaching of foreign languages in the context of a changing world dynamic. Up-to-date, it offers a number of specific recommendations. Should be read by anyone involved in developing a list of required core competencies.

Price, T. L. "How to Teach Business Ethics." *Inside Higher Ed,* June 4, 2007. Available at http://insidehighered.com/views/2007/06/04/price.

> Provides useful guidelines for faculty in business and industry.

Wince-Smith, D. L. "The Creative Imperative: A National Perspective." *Peer Review, 2006, 8*(2). Available from http://ctl.stanford.edu/tomprof/index.shtml (TP Msg. #723).

> Discusses the relationship between creativity and national prosperity and challenges universities and colleges to graduate students with an expanding range of needs, skills, and competencies.

CHAPTER 10

Gathering and Analyzing Essential Data

Figure 10.1.
From Goals to Outcomes to Assessment

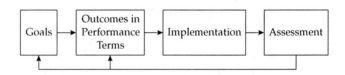

This chapter presents a review of those questions that should be asked and the data that should be collected as work begins on the design of a course or curriculum.

Once the decision has been made to begin a specific project, basic data must be collected in five areas:

- The characteristics of the students—their backgrounds, abilities, and priorities
- The desires and needs of society
- The educational priorities of the institution, school, or department
- The requirements of the appropriate field of knowledge, including the academic requirements of accrediting agencies
- The results of related research

Surveys and achievement tests, as well as informal discussion sessions held to identify specific needs and outcomes, may be used at this point to gather information. The data collected in these five areas are extremely important because they help you to define the required and optional elements of your program, to determine whether remedial units or exemptions are appropriate, and to form the basis for selecting the basic content of instruction. In addition, faculty often find that the results of these surveys are not only surprising but at times may run counter to long-held beliefs and assumptions.

This information is also essential in developing the primary goals and learning outcomes for your course or curriculum. As you move through design, implementation, and evaluation, each of these goals will be fleshed out in detail (see Figure 10.1).

Student Characteristics

An important source of data that is often overlooked is the student. If you are going to be successful, it is imperative that you have, right from the beginning, good information about your students.

Entry-Level Knowledge of Subject

Surprising as it may seem, few faculty members are aware of what their entering students already know about the subject, and as a consequence they cannot be sure that the assumptions they make about their students are accurate. We more commonly overestimate skills, prior knowledge, and competencies than underestimate them. For example, studies by Pervin and Rubin (1967) and Dresser (1987) have suggested that insensitivity to students' backgrounds, interests, and needs is a primary reason many students feel dissatisfied with or leave their institutions. We tend to assume that our students have the prerequisites that our courses require. This gap between what we expect and what exists has proven especially critical in the areas of reading, writing, basic mathematics, and specialized science vocabularies. Some students fail science because they cannot handle simple mathematical problems. Others have difficulty in history and the social sciences because their vocabularies are not as advanced as assigned reading presumes, and their writing, listening, and problem-solving skills are not up to the level anticipated by the instructor. The vocabulary level of many textbooks is, unfortunately, often inappropriate for many students. And in fact, the standard texts used in many introductory courses have been becoming more difficult and complex with each new edition (Burstyn and Santa, 1977).

In one series of studies we found that some students who can pass calculus tests have problems at the eighth-grade level with multiplication and division of fractions, decimals and percents, tables and charts, or word problems. An in-depth analysis of eight large-enrollment introductory courses in the natural and social sciences revealed that all faculty members required and assumed competencies in performing operations with fractions, decimals, percents, ratios, and proportions (see Resource K). In addition, the textbooks in seven of the eight courses assumed that the students had a working knowledge of probability, basic statistics, graphs, and tables. A follow-up study in five of these courses showed a direct correlation between student success in the course and competency in the basic mathematics skills that were assumed in the texts (Hardin, 1992). The approach taken here and the matrix that we used (as shown in Resource K) can easily be adapted for use with any entry-level course.

Attrition, failure rates, and other useful information. There is also a wide variety of useful information that will most likely be available in your institution's student record system from your registrar. Programs with histories of large numbers of students transferring out, and courses with high failure or drop rates can often signal major course or curriculum problems. Miami Dade College, for example, in an effort to reduce attrition, conducted a study in 2003 to identify high enrollment courses with low pass rates. These "high-risk" courses were determined to be an important factor in preventing entering students from completing their degrees. Of the fifteen large-enrollment (over 300 students) high-risk (pass rate below 60 percent) courses that were identified, eight were in mathematics, including the four with the largest enrollments. These four courses alone had a combined enrollment of over 17,000 students in a single semester with well over 6,500 receiving a failing grade. In an attempt to remedy this situation, the institution supported a number of faculty-driven initiatives to improve student success in these courses. Actions included more testing, increased advisement, supplemental instruction, additional student support, faculty development, the incorporation of more mathematics into other disciplines, and launching a formal four-year institution-wide Quality Enhancement Plan (QEP). Once this plan is fully implemented (2008) it is anticipated that it will impact approximately 45,000 students per year. For more on the program and its impact, contact Rene Barrientos at (305) 237-0982, or rbarrien@mdc.edu.

At another institution, one department, after reviewing the data, found that it was their better students who were transferring to other majors after their second year in the program. This led to a process where all students requesting to transfer were interviewed to determine the reasons behind their decision. This information became the basis for a number of major changes which, in time, successfully reduced the number of students leaving the program.

In other instances some of your students will know far more about a subject than you anticipate. Work experiences, familiarity and comfort with technology, taking college courses in high school, hobbies, and special interests all combine to make this a fairly common occurrence in almost every introductory course and in a growing number of advanced ones.

It is not unusual to find college-level courses taught in high school or high school material taught in junior high school. One survey found that approximately 20 percent of the students in an introductory psychology course had had formal instruction in the subject while in high school. An additional 2 percent had been able to take college psychology courses at a nearby institution while still in the eleventh or twelfth grade.

The problem of addressing entry-level prerequisites becomes even more complex when we not only have to deal with knowledge and skill deficiencies but with process deficiencies as well. McGonigal addressed this issue directly when she observed:

> Instructors from all fields face this challenge. In the sciences and mathematics, it is common for students to have learned an oversimplified definition or approach in high school. Students making the shift from classical to modern physics, for example, cannot simply layer new information onto old understanding. In the humanities, students may, for the first time, be asked to develop original interpretations of texts or to consider conflicting interpretations of texts instead of seeking the one, instructor-approved, "correct" interpretation. This new approach must replace the approach that students have learned, practiced, and been rewarded for. In the social sciences, instructors often have the difficult job of helping students unlearn common sense beliefs that may be common but unjustified. In all these cases, students' previous knowledge must be completely revised, not merely augmented [2005].

The immediate problem created by such variance in the academic levels of entering students can be significant: we may underestimate the competencies of some students, while overestimating the abilities of others. Older students who have been away from the classroom for some time or students with specific learning disabilities add further dimensions to the mix.

The student who brings to your course advanced knowledge of the subject or relevant work experience can actually be an invaluable asset to your class when you use these competencies in small-group activities or when you have these students assist less-qualified students.

Data describing students' academic levels are also useful for estimating the number of students who will need remedial and review assignments as well as the number who enter a program with some of the objectives already met (and thus warrant exemptions or options or both, perhaps for additional credit).

Attitudes

The attitudes that students have toward a particular course or field of study can influence what they learn. If they are initially hostile to a subject, it is vital that we take these attitudes into account when we design a course or modify a program by incorporating new materials or adding new options. Students who enroll in science courses for non-science majors, for example, may dislike the science even before they begin the course. If such attitudes are kept in mind when the course is designed, and steps are taken to change attitudes, a positive view of science can be developed in many students. Your enthusiasm for the subject can also lead students to develop more positive attitudes.

Unfortunately, in some instances, entering students may see little value in the knowledge and skills taught in a course. To produce the attitude necessary to improve student performance, we can relate the content of our course to their interests, or take the time to explain why the course is important to them, or provide them with work experiences that can show them the importance of specific competencies in a direct way.

A study at one institution, which shall remain anonymous for obvious reasons, showed that before its redesign, one physics course had been having a definite effect on the attitudes of students. Students usually entered the course with a somewhat neutral attitude toward the discipline, but by the time they completed the course, their attitude had become completely hostile! In this instance the faculty had assumed the students were highly motivated science majors, but in fact they were liberal arts students who wanted a science course that met Mondays, Wednesdays, and Fridays at 10 AM—and this was the only one available when they registered.

Priorities and Expectations

What do the students expect from your course, and what are their priorities as they relate to the area of study? If the students' expectations and priorities do not fit well with initial content, new units added early in the program can modify their expectations, or new content can be built into the program that meets or modifies their priorities and expectations. Data on student expectations can often be enlightening to a teacher. For example, a survey in an American history course showed that the students were far more interested in the American Revolution and in Native Americans than had been anticipated. Assignments in these areas were easily expanded without changing the overall goals of the course. This survey identified excellent topics for optional assignments and required papers.

Long-Range Goals

An analysis of the long-range goals of your students and their major fields of interest helps to identify special seminars, options, and projects that might be included in a course. Such an analysis also can help you to relate the course content to areas and topics that particularly interest students. The interrelationship of separate disciplines can have a direct and positive effect on the attitudes of students toward a course that might otherwise be perceived as unrelated and uninteresting.

A general mathematics course, for example, can have seminars or special projects relating to history (the role of mathematics in history), modern music (new mathematics-based notation techniques), and business (use of statistics). The opera portion of a general music course with a large enrollment of history and political science majors could include a discussion of the role of opera in history and politics, and the more general areas of art, history, music, religion, and literature can often be interrelated. For example, what determines the form and content of the music, art, or literature of a given period? This question cannot be answered without studying the politics, religion, and history of the period and the place.

Older Students

As previously noted, the increasing numbers of older students in our classrooms bring with them a wide variety of experiences, which often are an invaluable asset. At the same time, these students present a number of challenges, as they often having distinctly different goals from those of the more traditional students, and they may also have been away from the classroom for some time. Rusty in some of the basic skills that we may expect our students to have (using the library, understanding the format of a research paper, being computer literate), these students may need time to adjust and additional assistance, particularly when they first return to the classroom. One element of a survey filled out by students on the first day of class can be questions about whether they are returning students and, if so, what experiences they have had since leaving school. You will find more specific information on this topic in Chapter 20.

Gathering the Information

Surveys that you design for the purpose, studies conducted by other faculty or by professional or disciplinary groups, publications in the field, and interviews that you conduct on your own can all help you to collect important information about students as you explore the design of your course or program. As described in Chapter 2, some of the most detailed information on learning outcomes available in professional areas will be found within the published accreditation criteria of most accrediting agencies.

Data from Outside Academe

The second major area of data collection is outside the institution: alumni, employers, recruiters, and published reports and research. Although most data of this type are related to and collected for specific programs, the information can be more generalized and have a direct bearing on several programs.

Two excellent examples of this type of material are:

> For all projects: *College Learning for the New Global Century* (2007).

> For projects in science, mathematics, and engineering: *Rising Above the Gathering Storm: Energizing and Employing America for a Brighter Economic Future* (2007).

The perceptions of those on and off campus may be quite different. The weight given to each basic competency and the perception of the effectiveness of higher education in helping students to reach these goals can vary considerably. Business and community leaders tend to be more pragmatic and focused on current job needs than those within the academy (Exhibit 10.1). Although the various populations within an external community may agree, when there is disagreement you, as the faculty responsible for developing the program, will have to make the final decision.

Exhibit 10.1 below is based on a series of focused conversations conducted by the Education Commission of the States in 1994 with support from the Johnson Foundation and the Pew Charitable Trusts and in cooperation with the National Policy Board for Higher Education Institutional Accreditation, the National Governors' Association, and the National Conference of State Legislators. It is important to remember that such analyses reflect the views of a particular set of respondents at a particular point in time. Your views about student outcomes may be quite different from those represented here.

Exhibit 10.1.
Desirable Student Outcomes: Different Roles, Different Perspectives

	BUSINESS AND GOVERNMENT LEADERS	ACADEMIC LEADERS
1. Higher-order: applied problem-solving abilities	Possess and use these skills in complex real-world settings; creativity and resourcefulness.	Emphasis on technical skills or knowledge in discipline.
2. Enthusiasm for continuous learning	Flexibility and adaptability to change on the job and in one's life. Ability to access new information and learn how to do new things.	Few agree that preparing for continuous learning is an outcome that college can and should provide.
3. Interpersonal skills, communication, and collaboration	Oral communication a premium, needed for teamwork and communication with non-specialists. Listening.	Valued but assume that these outcomes result from presumed "collegial" environment.
4. Strong sense of responsibility for personal and community action	Personal integrity, and ethical and civil behavior, honesty.	Although shared as values, not often articulated as necessary college outcomes.
5. Ability to bridge cultural and linguistic barriers.	An awareness of and respect for ethnic and national differences—foreign or second languages skills for intercultural communication. Practice oriented. Actual experience.	
6. Sense of "professionalism"	High level of emphasis—include self-discipline and ability to work through an organizational structure and get things done. "Civility."	Not a high priority.

Source: Reported in Romer, 1995, pp. 17–19 (reprinted in AAHE Bulletin, Apr. 1996, pp. 5–8).

In addition to the material you can collect yourself from external communities, a host of other useful resources address the issues of goals and student outcomes. Pay particular attention to recent publications from national groups such as the American Association of State Colleges and Land Grant Universities, and the Association of American Colleges and Universities.

Although some of the data collected from external sources are general, many are specific to particular careers. For example, in a project that redesigned a music education program, most of the graduates said that at some time in their careers they were required to design an auditorium or a classroom for teaching and playing music—a task for which they felt they were totally unprepared. As a result, a unit on facilities design and equipment selection was added to the curriculum. In another survey retailers identified specific math skills as a major problem and indicated a demand for computer skills in the field. These data had a direct effect on the retailing curriculum that was developed.

Such career-specific information will be informative as you develop the goals of your course or curriculum in order to keep the program focused on the needs of the professional community. To facilitate this process, we suggest two specific actions on your part.

- For curriculum projects, establish an extensive advisory committee composed of key individuals of the major employees of your graduates and key alumni from the program who are working in the field. This group can provide you with excellent input and by having "ownership" in your new program, they may be willing to assist you in a number of valuable ways—internships, resources, and other collaborations for both your students and faculty.

- Spend time with the recruiters of your students. Conversations with recruiters who know your program and interview your students can provide you with an expert outsider's detailed perspective of your program that you can get from no other source.

It should also be noted that discipline-specific materials quite often are an excellent source of information on changes under way in the field. For example, the 2006 report *The Professional Bond—Public Relations Education and the Practice* (Turk, 2006) of the Commission on Public Relations Education contains detailed information on what the authors believe should be included in both undergraduate and graduate programs in the field, as well as excellent sections on a wide range of topics including ethics, diversity, technology, and distance learning. (See Resources J for their section on ethics.) The full report is available online at www.commpred.org/report.

A good example of what you can find is a 1984 study conducted by the Radio-Television News Directors Association, in which radio and television news directors and faculty in related professional programs were asked to identify the skills needed by on-air professionals and then to evaluate recent graduates on these skills.

For on-air people in television, five qualities were identified by 112 news directors as being particularly important: writing skills, the ability to communicate well on the air, the ability to think clearly, the ability to work under tight deadlines, and interviewing skills.

When the study compared the competencies needed with the qualities of those who were applying for positions, serious problems were identified. Recent graduates were rated low on each of the twelve categories of the survey, including the five qualities considered most important (Table 10.1).

University professors tended to be far more generous in the assessment of their graduates than were the professionals in the field. The majority of faculty, for example, stated that entry-level people could write very well and had the ability to work under tight deadlines.

The findings of this report are not unique. Recruiters and employers have consistently reported that although the college graduates they interview or hire know the content of their respective disciplines, they are less competent in writing, speaking, and other important skills that they seek. At times, the information and suggestions you receive from external communities will run counter to your own conclusions and be quite eye-opening. Not only can community sources identify competencies required for success in a field but they can also provide insight into how well your instructional goals are being met. One professional group commissioned an external agency to review the

Table 10.1. News Directors' Ratings of Various Skills for On-Air Television People

		Evaluation of Recent Graduates		
	Very Important (%)	*Rate Very Well (%)*	*Somewhat (%)*	*Not Very (%)*
Writing skills	96.4	2.0	29.3	68.7
Ability to communicate well on the air	96.4	1.0	46.0	52.0
Ability to think clearly	96.4	5.0	67.0	26.0
Ability to work under tight deadlines	92.0	3.0	40.4	53.5
Interviewing skills	83.9	2.0	50.0	46.9

Source: Radio-Television News Directors Association, 1984, p. 39.

discipline, the curriculum, and the needs of the field as described by employers and professionals. The final report, which created such discomfort for the board of directors that it was never distributed to the field, stated that the faculty had become isolated from the profession and that as a result the curriculum and the content of many courses within it were outdated and, therefore, its graduates were poorly prepared for the profession. Usually the differences between the perceptions of faculty and those outside the academy are less dramatic.

Questionnaires can be extremely effective tools for collecting career-specific information. A survey designed for faculty and alumni can be structured to serve two distinct purposes: to provide general information and to provide career-specific data focusing on particular programs and majors. Although the general questions can be developed jointly by a steering committee, the career-specific sections can be the product of extensive conversations with the faculty of each major division of a school or college, focusing on the information that faculty believe would be most useful in helping them evaluate and improve their programs.

To address both immediate and long-term needs, we suggest that the instruments be divided into four sections:

1. Professional skills and personal traits.
2. For each field, specific topics and practical experiences that should be included in an undergraduate program and criteria for entry-level job candidates.
3. View of the future.
4. Individual background information.

The information gleaned from these questionnaires not only helps set major priorities but can also be used in a number of course and curriculum projects.

Establishing an employer and alumni advisory committee for projects in professional schools has proven extremely beneficial both in terms of the important feedback they provide and the resources they can bring to the project.

The final curriculum or course objectives must include both general societal goals as well as the goals of the specific community that the institution or program serves.

Educational Priorities of the Institution

In collecting data it is important to identify the specific community your program serves. In some instances it is the local area or a particular section of the state; in others, as in the survey of the Radio-Television News Directors Association, it may be a national or international body of professionals, or the specific accrediting agency for the profession. In other cases, the unique characteristics of the institution influence or determine many of the goals of a curriculum. For example, metropolitan institutions such as the University of Memphis and Portland State University have revised their missions and many of their programs to focus on their communities and to build close relationships between the goals of academic programs and the needs of their constituents. New courses have been added that actively involve students in the community as a formal part of their educational experience.

On both the curriculum and course levels, however, don't overlook the portion of the college community that is closest and thus easiest to ignore—the faculty in related departments and in your own. If the course is a prerequisite for other courses, find out what the faculty teaching those courses expect. Quite often we find a gap, never discussed, between what faculty in an upper-level course expect from students and what faculty teaching a prerequisite course believe is possible. When these gaps occur, it may require changes in both courses to improve this transition.

Problems may also occur for political reasons. Projects have failed when a group of faculty opposed the effort for reasons that could have been avoided—for example, when faculty have not been consulted and could have provided important input in the design process. Overlooking such groups can be a particular problem in larger institutions, where departments within a single school or college may work independently or compete with one another for both students and financial support.

Institutional priorities provide useful information and should be identified because these priorities may directly affect the design of a curriculum and courses. Such priorities are often shaped by financial and material constraints and by specific campuswide initiatives (ranging from an urban emphasis to a commitment to commuter or distance education) that encourage focusing on one particular area or type of program and discourage focusing on another. These priorities may determine the source and type of your students. Enrollment and financial considerations, combined with the history of a given institution, influence the programs that the institution offers. For example, church-supported institutions may have unique objectives, as the case of Alverno College described in Case Study 2. Likewise, we should not necessarily expect an institution located in a metropolitan area to have the same priorities or programs as one located in a rural setting. As needs differ, priorities also differ, and so should the characteristics and content of our academic programs. Pay particular attention to your institution's mission and vision. These statements change on a regular basis, sometimes becoming more focused or specific in response to environmental conditions.

Whenever possible, try to relate your project to the priorities of your institution and your school or college. For example, if a principal aim of a lower-division course is to generate majors, this goal should be stated and understood. Unfortunately, this important objective is rarely acknowledged or discussed. There is nothing improper about trying to attract students to a discipline. If the objective of attracting more students is stated, emphasis can be placed on educating students about the discipline, the faculty, the department, the profession, the potential for jobs, and on building in your students a positive attitude toward the overall discipline.

Field of Knowledge

Content modification should be a continual process. As discoveries are made, as theories are modified, and as new areas evolve, the adjustment of the educational content should begin immediately. Therefore, you need to ensure that the content of any program you are designing is as contemporary and as academically sound as possible and that the instructional process allows for continual updating of the overall design. Major journals and a review of the topics covered in national conferences, along with conversations with professionals in the field, are all excellent sources for identifying trends and content changes in the discipline. For example, to study the field of music education, the faculty involved with designing their curriculum undertook a range of activities:

- Reading and studying music and music-education books, especially the most current ones
- Reading and analyzing articles, advertisements, and other information in the major professional journals in the discipline for the last ten years to identify general trends in music education
- Reviewing the research literature for the past fifteen years related to the teaching of music
- Reviewing and evaluating graduate research related to the teaching of music as reported in *Dissertation Abstracts* during the last fifteen years
- Examining curriculum guidelines published by major professional groups
- Surveying and studying the undergraduate music-education programs of all competitive colleges and universities

- Examining and analyzing the competency-based certification guidelines and recommendations made by the state and national accrediting bodies
- Reading and studying the literature about competency-based teacher education, a national trend affecting teacher-education programs in many states

As we have stressed many times, if you are working in a professional field requiring formal accreditation, it is also crucial to make sure your program meets the specific criteria for accreditation. Unfortunately, for many years these associations focused more on what was to be covered than on what was to be learned, often severely restricting the design options of faculty in these fields. In some disciplinary areas the accreditation process leaves the development of specific goals up to the individual department or program, focusing instead on how successful students are in achieving the performance goals that are agreed on as essential indicators of competence.

Research

Specific studies may be relevant to the project. These studies generally fall into three areas: the content of the discipline, the future direction of the profession, and pedagogy.

Content of the Discipline

In most professions formal studies are conducted to determine what content is appropriate for the field. In some instances, such as industrial design, these studies may be sponsored by the national professional organization. In other instances they may be undertaken by a few faculty working independently on a course or curriculum project. Journals in the discipline that include articles on teaching and curriculum can often be an excellent source of information on recent studies related to course and program content. Many examples will be described in some detail in the chapter that follows.

Future Directions of the Discipline

The future direction of the profession or of the content and research component of the discipline should not be overlooked. Not only does reviewing the direction these areas may be taking ensure up-to-date content, but it also provides a basis for decisions regarding new content and objectives. Any new program, if it is to be successful, must be future oriented and based on the thinking of the outstanding practitioners and researchers in the field. Usually the best materials will come from your national association and a small number of publishers that focus on your particular field of study.

Pedagogy

Ongoing research examines how students think, how they learn, and how they can effectively be taught. Although the findings about teaching and learning are most useful during the production and implementation stage, this information can affect the overall structure of a program. For example, a decision to implement mastery learning, or to use the Perry research (1970) on how the thinking of students changes with maturity, could determine the structure of the course and the sequence in which content is presented, as could the more recent work on experiential and transformation learning and application of technology.

An excellent source of basic research on pedagogy as it applies to higher education is the federally sponsored National Center for Research to Improve Postsecondary Teaching and Learning at Stanford University. A most useful publication that should be in every faculty research library is Lion F. Gardiner's *Redesigning Higher Education: Producing Dramatic Gains in Student Learning* (1996) where you will find an excellent review of the research on student development, the curriculum, teaching, and assessment. Concise, with excellent citations, it can save you a great deal of time and energy. In Chapter 3, Staying Informed, and in the chapters that follow, you will find references to publications and to Web sites that will provide you with the latest information on the extensive studies that are now under way on teaching and learning at the college level.

Time and Space

Two factors about which you need to gather information from both your registrar and other faculty are time (the structure of your academic calendar, whether you have the option of using weekends, out-of-class hours, and time outside the semester) and space (on- and off-campus locations and their spatial options). Distance education will often have an extremely different range of options and limitations.

If you are working on a curriculum, keep in mind that you often have far more structural options than are apparent at first. For example, curricula may be structured around disciplines, themes, problems, issues, or processes. Gathering this information at the beginning of your project will enable you to keep in view the compelling educational ideal, vision, and mission that underlie your effort.

Summary _____

This chapter has covered the various questions that should be asked and the data that should be collected for use in the initial design phase. Remember that the quality of the data helps determine the success or failure of your project. To ensure that sufficient information is available for sound decision making, data should be collected in the following areas:

- Students

  Entering level of competence

  Ability to meet assumed prerequisites

  Goals, priorities, and major

  Reasons for enrolling and background

  Attitudes about discipline, area, and so on

  Assumptions about course or program

- Data from outside academe (employers, recruiters, alumni, community leaders)

  Basic competencies all students should have by graduation

  Career-specific requirements

  Existing gaps between required competencies and abilities of graduates

- Educational priorities

  Mission of institution, program, department

  General goals of the program (course)

- Field of knowledge

  Required and essential content

  Future trends in discipline or area of focus

  Accreditation requirements (professional programs, state)

  New content areas

- Research

  Discipline-related

  Pedagogy (teaching and learning)

- Time and space

  Options and limitations

In the next chapter we describe in more detail how this information can be effectively used in the design of new courses and curricula.

CHAPTER 11

Thinking in the Ideal

Figure 11.1.
The Model

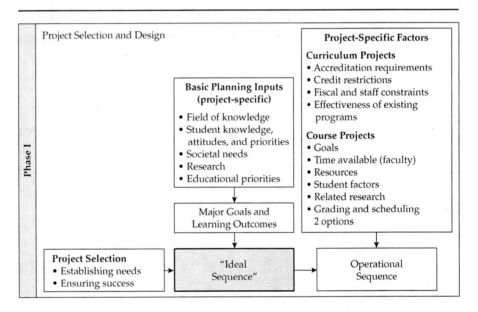

As actual design work begins on a course or curriculum, those involved use all the data that have been collected, their experiences, and their creativity to decide what an "ideal" program would look like. Because not all the data will be available immediately, this is a period of revision and a time for contemplation and discussion in curriculum projects. Formal meetings are usually held no more than once a week, and semi-monthly meetings are not uncommon.

Different faculty teaching in different disciplines often address the same general problems in significantly different ways. In this chapter, we will use several case studies to describe this initial design phase. These and the additional Case Studies in the Resources section have been selected from a number of disciplines and address a wide range of academic problems. Because we use the same approach at this stage of the process to discuss both course and curriculum design, this chapter contains examples and case studies from both areas.

Focusing on Structure and Sequence

At this point in the process our focus is on the major elements in your instructional program and how they should be sequenced to facilitate the learning you desire. This, as you might expect, is a rather complex process. You not only will have to take into account your general goals but will also have to consider how they interrelate and how they can be reached within your course or program of study.

Important

Because this chapter focuses primarily on developing the ideal flow of your course or curriculum, the case studies we have selected are intended to show a variety of structures, or to demonstrate the changes that can take place from one draft to another. The specific content of the case study is not as important as the rationale behind the design itself.

As you begin this most exciting and challenging phase of your project, it is crucial that you keep an open mind: brainstorm new ideas, explore all options, and listen carefully to everyone else who is involved in the project. Now is the time to reflect on what has worked in the past and what has not, and what you have heard from students and employers. Keep the discussion open and ensure that all ideas are heard.

Although fine tuning continues throughout the design and implementation process, few significant changes in sequence or content occur between the final ideal conceptualization and the actual course, with most modifications resulting from time or resource limitations.

However, during the effort to reach for the ideal, the changes that take place in the design of a course or curriculum from one meeting to the next can be substantial. For example, Figures 11.2 and 11.3 are the first and third drafts of the design for the first semester of a two-semester course in communications design.

Figure 11.2.
Draft 1: Communications Design, First Semester

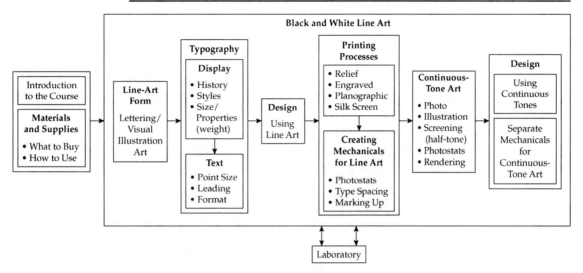

Source: Toni Toland.

Figure 11.3.
Draft 3: Communications Design, First Semester

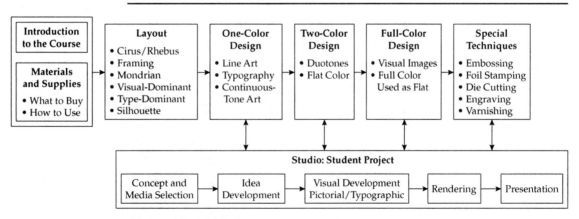

Source: Toni Toland.

Notice how the original idea of focusing on black-and-white line art in the first semester and color in the second was changed by the faculty member to an entirely different approach, with the color options available to the designer now serving as the theme for each unit. In addition, the laboratory portion of the course has begun, by the third draft, to take shape in both content and sequence. Major changes of this type often evolve as the faculty member continues to think about the course and answers questions posed by the instructional developer or other faculty. At other times, changes result directly from comments from other faculty or professionals in the field, or may be based on additional data that have been collected. During this stage, modification is both facilitated and encouraged.

Blended Curricula and Blended Course

As you move through the design process, keep in mind that curricula and individual courses are not limited to a single instructional approach. For example, we are seeing a growing number of on-campus courses that incorporate distance education approaches, and distance education programs that include face-to-face or residency components. The key is to select the combination of instructional approaches that will give your students the best possible learning experience, working within the time and resources available to you. In later chapters we will discuss in some detail the wide range of structural and procedural options that are now available.

For an excellent example of a blended curriculum, take a look at Antioch University's Ph.D. program in leadership, which combines short-term intensive residencies and self-paced learning with electronic interactions among students and faculty. The library support system for this program is also outstanding and can be viewed at www.phd.antioch.edu.

Using the Research on Teaching and Learning

This also might be the ideal time for you to take a few minutes to review the potential of flexible credit and continuous registration systems (see Case Study 5). After you've read the material, check with your registrar to see if either or both of the options are or could be available at your institution for your use. We have found these systems ideal for use in courses or curricula where you have to deal with prerequisite issues or when you'd like to provide students with a range of options. You'll notice that a number of the case studies in this chapter and in the Resources section use one or more of these systems.

A number of studies and summary reports on teaching and learning can be helpful as you address these issues and as you move into designing the actual learning experience. Romer (1995) listed twelve characteristics of good teaching practice which are as valid today as they were when the list was first published. Notice the number of items that focus on how the sequence of instruction should reinforce what students are learning.

Research Findings on Good Teaching Practice

Quality begins with an organizational culture that values:

1. High expectations. Students learn more effectively when expectations for learning are placed on high but attainable levels and when these expectations are communicated clearly from the outset (see Exhibit 11.1).

2. Respect diverse talents and learning styles. Good practice demands careful design of curricula and instructional efforts to meet diverse backgrounds and learning styles.

3. Emphasis on the early years of study. The first years of undergraduate study—particularly the freshman year—are critical for student success.

A quality undergraduate curriculum requires:

4. Coherence. Students succeed best in developing higher-order skills (critical thinking, written and oral communication, and problem solving) when such skills are reinforced throughout their educational program.

5. Synthesizing experiences. Students also learn best when they are required to synthesize knowledge and skills learned in different places in the context of a single problem or setting.

6. Ongoing practice of learned skills. Unpracticed skills atrophy quickly, particularly core skills such as computation and writing.

7. Integration of education and experience. Classroom learning is both augmented and reinforced by multiple opportunities to apply what is learned.

Quality undergraduate instruction builds in:

8. Active learning. At all levels students learn best when they are given multiple opportunities to actively exercise and demonstrate skills.

9. Assessment and prompt feedback. Frequent feedback to students on their performance also is a major contributor to learning.

10. Collaboration. Students learn better when engaged in a team effort rather than working on their own.

11. Adequate time on task. Research also confirms that the more time devoted to learning, the greater the payoffs in terms of what and how much is learned.

12. Out-of-class contact with faculty. Frequency of academic, out-of-class contact between faculty members and students is a strong determinant of both program completion and learning. [Romer, 1995]

Reviewing the research on curriculum design is essential as you think through the design of your course or curriculum. This research provides a base on which you can make a number of your design decisions.

Research Findings on Curriculum Design

• Most curricula are unfocused, do not include clear statements of intended outcomes, and do not produce the intended results. There's a notable absence of structure and coherence.

• A number of conditions foster the development of college-level competencies, including challenging courses, a supportive environment, active involvement in learning, high expectations, clearly defined and attainable goals with frequent assessment and prompt feedback. The goals must be challenging and communicated to the student.

• Providing a wide range of options to fulfill general education requirements tends to be counterproductive. The most effective curricula tend to have a carefully structured core program with few electives.

• An effective curriculum provides multiple opportunities to apply and practice what is learned. [Primarily from Gardiner, 1996]

As you structure your program, keep in mind the specific population of students that will be enrolling. Adult students are significantly different from those who enter directly out of high school. If you have commuting students in your class, how can you provide them with the same range of crucial interactions available

Exhibit 11.1.
Research Findings on Helping Students Meet High Expectations

- The higher the quality of instruction, the less relevant to achievement are a student's entering abilities.
- Although some faculty believe many students simply lack the intellectual equipment required to learn, understanding the background and developmental and contextual reasons why students behave as they do can greatly enhance our ability to help them develop.
- Intelligence is made up of learnable skills.
- Most students can learn higher mental processes if these processes are made central to instruction.
- Cooperative learning with high standards and goals can significantly improve the success rate of high-risk students.

Source: Adapted from Gardiner, 1996.

to students living on campus? For more on these and other related issues, see Chapter 17.

Ernest Pascarella and Patrick Terenzini, coauthors of two of the most comprehensive volumes on higher education, *How College Affects Students* (1991, 2005), stress the importance of thinking about the entire learning experience of your students and not just about what goes on within the classroom. Consider how you might build in community activities or internships or how you might combine what you are doing with the residential life of the on-campus students in a living-learning center or a campus activity. Considering such possibilities can only improve the quality of the students' educational experience. "*Real* college impact is likely to come not from pulling any grand, specific (and probably expensive) policy or programmatic lever, but rather from pulling a number of smaller, *interrelated* academic and social levers more often. If a college's effects are varied and cumulative, then its approaches to enhancing those effects must be varied and coordinated" (Pascarella and Terenzini, 1991, p. 32).

Dealing with a Lack of Prerequisite Skills

As we mentioned in the previous chapter, one of the most prevalent problems in course and curriculum design is the tendency of faculty to make false assumptions about the knowledge and skills that students bring to their courses. These incorrect assumptions lead to failure for the students who are ill prepared, boredom for their classmates who are often more than adequately prepared, and frustration for the faculty. The case study that follows in Freshman English describes a program designed to accommodate a wide range of entry levels for students in a required first-year course.

Case Study: Freshman English

Few courses generate as much reaction on any campus as the introductory course in writing. Student proficiency in writing varies considerably, and even the weakest writers believe that they are more proficient than they are. Faculty outside the composition field have a variety of concerns about student writing and may have misconceptions about the teaching of writing. The first-year composition course presents a series of major design problems to anyone attempting to develop an effective offering:

- The course usually enrolls large numbers of students and to be effective must be taught in relatively small sections. This becomes a staffing challenge, particularly on many large campuses where the freshman writing course is delegated to graduate students with little background or interest in teaching writing.

- Students enter the program with an extremely wide range of writing skills. Although a small number have an excellent background in writing, most do not. Students who have learned English as a second or third language are often particularly weak in written language usage.

The problem facing the English faculty who designed this program was therefore not unique: how, with the resources available, to structure an introductory course that would develop the necessary writing skills in all students and also be sensitive to the extreme range of entering competencies.

The design team decided to totally rethink not only what was taught but how it was taught. In the process a number of major issues were addressed.

Content

In the past the course used literature and poetry as the basis for student writing. The faculty concluded that a major problem with this approach was that it forced students who were having basic writing problems to write about subjects that not only were new to them but were at times hard to understand. As a result, the faculty often found it difficult to separate confusion about the subject from problems with the technical aspects of writing. The faculty therefore concluded that they would focus on the writing by giving students the opportunity to write about subjects that were familiar to them until they developed basic skills in structuring and organizing their essays.

Structure and Time

Recognizing that students entered the course with a wide range of writing skills, the faculty explored a number of structural options for dealing with this diversity. Two questions raised by the instructional developer helped the faculty develop solutions. First, because students entered the course with such a wide range of writing skills, did they have to begin at the same place? Second, because students learn at different rates, was it necessary for all to take the same amount of time to reach an acceptable level of writing performance? When the decision was made that both the beginning point and time could indeed be flexible, an entirely new approach to the design of the course became possible. Not only could students begin at different levels based on their entering competencies but they also could move through the course at their own pace. (See Figure 11.4.)

Standardization Between Sections

Because the course relied heavily on teaching assistants, many of whom had little previous experience teaching composition, it became obvious early in the design process that the final structure would have to facilitate standardization in grading. The criteria used for evaluating writing would have to be taught to and understood by each of the teaching assistants and by the students, and grading standards would have to be consistent across all sections. To address this issue, all new teaching assistants were required to take a formal course in pedagogy, in which they would learn the grading protocol developed for the course.

Evaluation and Placement

If students were to begin at different levels according to entry writing skills, the problem of assessment also had to be addressed. The faculty felt that existing tests could be used for this purpose and proposed a combination of a commercially produced diagnostic test and a written essay. After several years the commercial test was replaced by one developed locally that was more suited to the specific needs of the course.

Figure 11.4.

Instructional Sequence for Freshman English

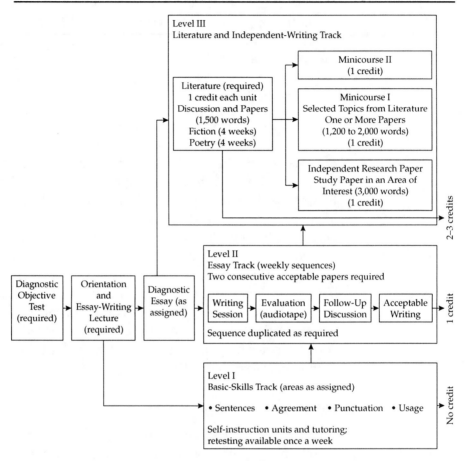

Note: Several changes in this format were made after testing. Levels I and II were combined, placing greater emphasis on individual counseling. In addition, the essay test replaced the objective instrument as the basis for placement. Based on performance on the diagnostic test, students were placed in Level I (remedial, no credit) or in Level II (1 credit) of English 101. When performance on the Criterion Tests indicate they have reached the required level of competence, students in Level I join the Level II class in writing weekly in-class essays arguing a position on a topic discussed in class. Two consecutive passing papers qualify the student to move to Fiction (1 credit) or Poetry (1 credit), each unit requiring at least two formal papers totaling 1,500 words. These two literature units completed English 101. English 102 consisted of an independent research paper (1 credit) and one 2-credit minicourse, or two 1-credit mini-courses. The independent research paper was at least 3,000 words (12 pages), and the mini-courses each required at least two papers equaling 1,500 words for each credit. Students were allowed three semesters to complete the program, and a few were able to complete it in less than two semesters.

Source: Randall Brune.

Remediation

One of the most difficult problems the faculty had to address was remediation—how to deal with those students who entered the course with writing problems at the basic level—problems with punctuation, usage, agreement, and so on. The problem was even more complex because most of the teaching assistants had little training or interest in teaching basic grammar and usage. The decision was made, therefore, to combine independent study using programmed texts with tutoring. Furthermore, this tutoring would be done not by the teaching assistants but by part-time instructors experienced in teaching basic writing and hired specifically for this purpose.

The selection of the specific programmed texts that were to be used turned out to be far more difficult than was at first imagined. After identifying the specific skills they wished to have taught (approximately twenty) the faculty began a review of every programmed text on the market to identify those pages or frames that dealt effectively with specific topics. Although over thirty texts were available, the majority were found to be poorly written and to contain unacceptable treatments of some topics. In addition, one of the most effective publications was no longer available. After several years a number of texts with logical sequences were identified and used.

Other Applications of This Approach

As we mentioned previously, this approach can be used for the design workshops, seminars, and orientation programs as well as for final courses and curriculum. For example, the most successful teaching assistant program at Syracuse University was developed using this model.

Case Study: The Orientation Program for New Teaching Assistants

This project, undertaken at Syracuse University, also indicates the importance of collecting base data before an important new program is implemented. The orientation program was a major departure from the way the university trained and supported its teaching assistants and would involve a major commitment of financial and other resources if it were continued after pilot testing. Data collection was imperative to show the impact of the program on the participants and the institution.

To provide this information, a survey instrument was developed and administered to all teaching assistants at the university the semester before the new program was to begin. The questions on the survey pertained to the needs of teaching assistants and the support they were receiving. The same instrument was administered again the spring following the first offering of this program, which provided a comparison of the replies from first-year teaching assistants and indicated how participants in the program differed from their counterparts from the year before.

In addition to interviewing the participants during the program and the experienced teaching assistants who served as group leaders, the university collected data in a number of other ways. Mid-program and end-of-program questionnaires were administered, deans and faculty who supervised teaching assistants were interviewed during the fall semester following the program, and data on the effectiveness of the teaching assistants as teachers were collected in several large-enrollment courses.

The data collected proved invaluable in ensuring the continuation and institutionalization of the program and in identifying areas that needed improvement. Although the first offering of the program was highly successful, some areas needed change. When offered the next summer, the program incorporated these changes: more time was set aside for the students to find housing, international students who had studied previously in the United States could be excused from the international program, the amount of time spent in small groups was increased, and the number of large-group lectures was substantially reduced. The length of the program was also slightly reduced, and a number of other scheduling changes were instituted. The evaluation protocol was repeated once again to measure and identify the impact of these modifications.

Based on additional data from the teaching assistants and their departments, the program is now a part of the Graduate School and now provides an expanded year-round support system for the teaching assistants with increased participation by the academic units. Results have been positive. Although the scope and intensity of the evaluation effort has been reduced somewhat from its early years of operation, the program will always include an evaluation component.

For more information, visit www. gradschpdprograms.syr.edu.

Some Suggestions

For many faculty this stage is the most creative, intellectually stimulating, and enjoyable of the entire design process. It is the time to think outside of the box, to think creatively, to test assumptions, and to think in the ideal. The questions that should be on your mind during this phase are basic ones: If you had the best possible curriculum or course, what would it look like? If you were successful what skills, knowledge, and attitudes would your students have at the end of the experience?

During this stage of thinking in the ideal you can expect your design to go through a number of evolutionary stages, major components will be added and dropped, and the structure of the sequence itself will change as you think through the logic of developing new competencies and reinforcing others. In our experience working with faculty in a numbers of disciplines, we have found certain approaches to be effective in facilitating the design process during this stage:

- Meet in a comfortable room with a large number of white or chalkboard surfaces. Large pads of newsprint can work, but you'll find that they are not particularly easy to use when you are constantly adding, deleting, and modifying what you are working on. In addition, having the entire flow diagram visible as you work along allows the entire team to see the whole instructional sequence at all times, and this is extremely important as the sequence evolves.

- Have the time flow run from left to right, as you have far more space in this direction. Later in the project, when the overall sequence is complete, you may wish to present the sequence vertically to save space. You'll see a number of our case studies using both approaches.

- Have one member of the team, often the facilitator, responsible for drafting the latest version of the flow diagram at the end of each meeting and then distributing the material well before the next scheduled meeting.

- Meeting once a week or every other week during this stage works well as it gives participants time to review what has been done and to think through changes they might want to suggest.

- During the design meetings make sure that everyone has the opportunity to provide input; don't allow one individual to dominate the conversation.

- If you find that you could use the assistance or advice of other faculty, specialists in assessment or technology, or have questions for the registrar, don't hesitate to ask for help. Most of these people will be pleased to be involved in your project, and the earlier the better.

- The leader of your team should be responsible for keeping all key administrators and chairs informed as you move ahead. There has been more than one occasion where a chair or dean identified potential problems or opportunities that the design team had overlooked. In addition, there are times when administrators can help you find resources or open doors that you could not do on your own.

- If you are involved in the redesign of an existing course or curriculum, don't focus on what now exists. Focus on what ideally "should" be. When you do, you'll find that content that has been in place for years will be eliminated, new content will be added, and new instructional patterns will emerge. The last thing you need are individuals fighting to maintain the status quo regardless of pressure for change.

- And finally, don't assume anything. All too often we make assumptions of what we can and cannot do before we test the system. At Syracuse University we would never have developed our continuous and flexible credit systems if we had never asked the registrar if it was possible for us to do what we felt was necessary. You will find that the final program that you implement will be closer to the "ideal" than you ever felt possible.

Additional Case Studies

Before you get under way, take a few minutes to review the following examples in the Case Studies section of this book. Pay particular attention to the specific challenge the faculty faced and how they resolved it. Many of the approaches that you will find are applicable to every field of study. Don't let the subject matter itself get in the way of your benefiting from the example.

The following case studies will be most helpful to you at this time:

Dealing with Prerequisite Problems

- Case Study 6—Addressing Math Deficiencies and Collecting Student Data: Introductory Economics
- Case Study 7—Expanding the Course Time Frame to Compensate for a Lack of Prerequisites: General Chemistry
- Case Study 8—Expanding the Course Time Frame to Compensate for a Lack of Prerequisites: Introductory Calculus
- Case Study 9—Dealing with Prerequisites at the Graduate Level: A Course in Cost-Effectiveness

Designing the Ideal Course or Curriculum: Collecting and Using Data

- Case Study 10—Using Data from Students: Introductory Course in Religion
- Case Study 11—Designing an Ideal Curriculum: Music/Music Industry

- Case Study 12—Design an Ideal Curriculum: Surveying Alumni: Master's Program in Management
- Case Study 13—Ensuring the Acquisition of Basic Core Competencies in an Introductory Course: Introduction to Business and Management
- Case Study 14—Distance Learning: The Lessons Learned
- Case Study 15—Revising an Existing Course: Music for the Non-Major

Summary

This chapter has described the exciting and challenging process of designing an ideal program. The case studies illustrate how each course or curriculum is unique. No single, all-purpose design fits all cases. As students, faculty, institutions, resources, and disciplines vary, so must the course or curriculum that is developed. Notice that although we have discussed content and structure, we have, for the most part, not explored instructional formats or instructional objectives. These activities take place much later in the process. The next chapter describes how, through analysis of resources and options, field tests, and so on, this idealized version is modified, eventually becoming the program that is offered.

CHAPTER 12

Adjusting from the Ideal to the Possible

Figure 12.1.
The Model

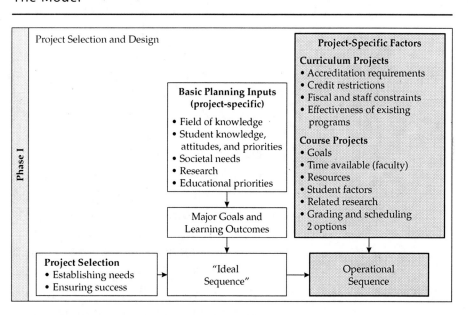

At some point in the development process the preliminary, or "ideal," design phase is completed and modification begins in order to meet the practical limitations of the real world. This transition from the ideal to the possible is gradual. You cannot identify a specific point at which one stage ends and another begins. The separation is described here more to clarify the transition than to indicate a specific transition in the process.

Throughout the process you will use information you have gathered from a number of sources, but you will rely on your own insights and experiences as you decide which modifications are necessary for your design to be implemented. This is in effect the time for a reality check, the point at which you decide, based on the resources and constraints you have, how close to the ideal your new course or curriculum will be. As we mentioned in the last chapter, you will probably find that your final design is far closer to your ideal than you originally thought it would be.

An Important Frame of Reference

The key is that in the end, your curriculum ensures that each student has the opportunity of reaching the goals and outcomes that you have established. This goal will require a level of detail that does not exist in most programs. For this reason, whether you are working on a course or curriculum project, there are several essential elements you should keep in mind as you move from your ideal design to the one you will implement.

- Goals will become more specific as you move from the overall curriculum to the courses within it and then to the elements within each course.

- As a result, the outcome statements designed to meet these goals will also become more specific, with the most detailed statements being at the individual lesson or activity level.

- It will be the responsibility of those designing the curricula to (1) determine the overarching goals and describe the associated learning outcomes, (2) to assign, with the involvement of the faculty responsible for each course, primary goals to required and elective courses, and (3) to ensure that the goals that are established are met.

- It will be the responsibility of faculty teaching each course to ensure that the goals assigned are met and that the course outcome statements and assessment procedures support these goals.

Increasing Specificity

Before you move ahead with your design, it is important that you read Chapter 13 on writing outcome statements. There you will find a number of useful and time-saving suggestions on writing the type of outcome statement that will meet your immediate needs and will support successful teaching, learning, and assessment.

The Steps That Follow

At the conclusion of this phase you will have completed the basic design of your curriculum or course. The steps that follow will be significantly different for curriculum or course projects. While the design stage of curriculum projects will now be complete and your primary focus will be on getting the new program approved, course projects move on to Phase II, Production, Implementation, and Evaluation (Figure 12.2).

Curriculum Projects

Once the overall curriculum has been designed, you will have four additional responsibilities:

1. Identifying which courses or other major program elements are new, requiring major redesign, or can be used as they are, with only minor revision.

2. Preparing the materials required as the new curriculum begins its move through the school, college, and institutional review and state and regional accreditation approval process. In some professional disciplines additional approval, by a national body, will also be required.

3. Assigning, with the involvement of the faculty, specific learning outcomes to individual courses.

4. Identifying the procedures that you will use to determine the success of the new curriculum once it is implemented.

A major advantage of this model is that the documents you have produced during Phase I will meet most, if not all, of the requirements of the various review committees.

Figure 12.2.
Development Process

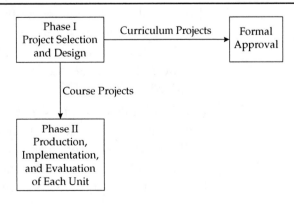

In Resource O you will find a useful list of the questions you should ask when the phase is completed. This list can also be used as a structure to develop your assessment plan for use after the curriculum has been implemented.

Course Projects

- Work on new courses or on those requiring major revision will begin from the beginning on Phase I, focusing on the goals and outcomes that have been assigned to each.
- Existing courses that have been included in the new curriculum must be reviewed in light of assigned goals and the identified nondisciplinary core competencies.

A note of caution: Major course design efforts should not be undertaken if the required courses that precede it are scheduled for design or revision. Significant changes in one course always will impact the content, structure, and design of the course that follows.

Curriculum Projects: Factors to Consider

In moving from the ideal to the possible, or operational, curriculum, several major factors must be considered—factors that are, in some instances, outside your control. Among these are the following:

- *Accreditation requirements.* Does the proposed curriculum include those academic areas, credits, and courses required by the institution or by external professional agencies? These requirements may range from a basic liberal arts core to specialized technical or professional courses.
- *Credit restrictions.* Can the proposed program fit within the number of credit hours required for the major or minor? State departments of education, individual institutions and the schools and colleges within them, and often external certification agencies specify the minimum and maximum number of credits a student can be required to take within and outside a single academic area or discipline. Are these standards being met?
- *Fiscal and staff constraints.* Is the proposed curriculum financially feasible? Can it be staffed? If new positions and new facilities are required, can the needed fiscal resources be found? If class size is to be reduced to permit oral presentations or group projects, are there sufficient instructors

available? If students require access to laptops, specialized software, or other technologies, how can they be made available at minimal cost to the student?

- *Effectiveness of existing courses and programs.* If some elements of an existing curriculum are to be used, are they effective and do they meet the needs for which they have been selected? Will all students have the needed prerequisites? If not, how will this gap be addressed? What other changes in existing courses will be required?

To answer some of these questions, you must involve the dean of the school or college, other faculty, and in some instances, the academic vice president or associate provost as well. Even though they may not be active participants, involving these individuals with the project from the beginning ensures that they have early knowledge of what is being proposed and why.

Case Study: Retailing Major

Figure 12.3 is the third draft of the idealized version of an undergraduate curriculum in retailing. Figure 12.4 is the operational version of the same program.

Although the general content stayed the same over the ten-month period between these two versions, there were important changes in a number of areas. These modifications were made for three main reasons. First, an analysis of existing faculty resources and of the total number of credits that could be required during a single semester or over the entire four-year program showed that several of the original ideas could not be implemented as planned. As a result, the proposed one-credit skill track was combined with the existing one-credit Job Seeking and Placement course into a three-credit course that students were required to take prior to their field experience. The new computer-applications unit, rather than standing alone as an upper-division requirement, was moved into the three-credit Advanced Retailing Mathematics course.

The second major reason for modifications was the effectiveness of some of the courses. Data showed that the single Retailing Mathematics course was not successful, mostly because passing the diagnostic math test, although encouraged, was not required. Consequently, students who had avoided mathematics throughout their academic careers entered this important course inadequately prepared. In the revised program, students were required to pass a diagnostic test of mathematics skills in order to continue in the retailing program. A Basic Mathematics Skills Laboratory was added to support students identified by the test as needing additional

Figure 12.3.
Ideal Curriculum for Retailing Major

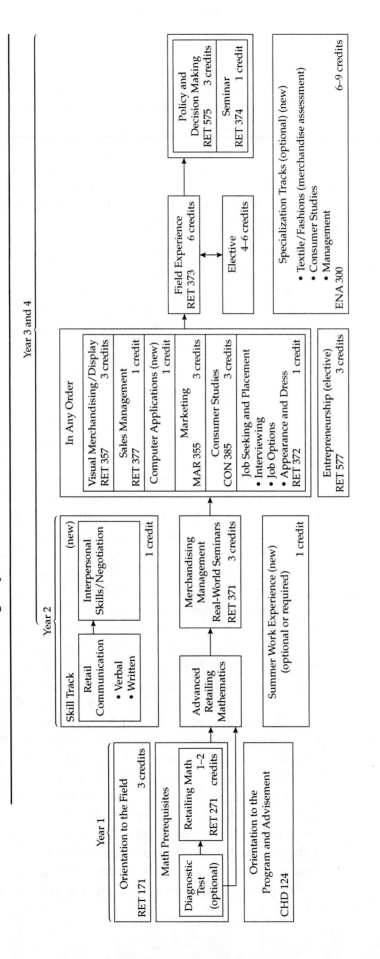

Figure 12.4.
Operational Curriculum for Retailing Major

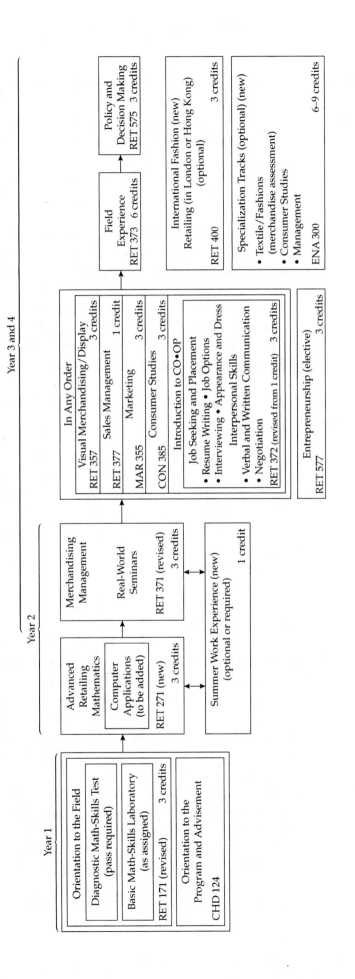

help in meeting this requirement. As a result, student attitudes and achievement improved.

The final reason for changes in the structure of the curriculum was the support found outside the department for cooperative programs. For example, with the support of the university's study abroad program, retailing-related course offerings were developed in both London and Hong Kong as part of the semester-abroad experience.

Information collected during interviews with recruiters, employers, and alumni also had a direct impact on the computer-applications unit, the communications area, and the interpersonal skills area, and strongly supported the increased emphasis on basic mathematics.

In the final version of this program only one of the required courses was new. However, three others, while retaining their course names and numbers, underwent major revision. In two of these, changes in credit were also made.

Course Projects: Factors to Consider

In course projects you will have enough detailed information at the end of this phase so that Phase II, which includes production, implementation, evaluation, and revision can begin (Figure 12.2). In course projects, the amount of time spent on developing the operational design (the last step in the design phase) is as great or greater than that required for production, implementation, and evaluation of the new course.

When the operational diagram is completed for a course, each instructional component or unit has been specified (options, remedial units, seminars, large-group meetings, term activities, and topics for independent study or special projects), and the overall sequence of these units has been determined. In addition, all elements of the program are placed in a realistic time frame. Although modification continues throughout the entire developmental process, the changes beyond this point are usually relatively minor, with little effect on the overall design. As a result, it should be possible at the completion of the operational diagram for you to assign the development of specific units to other faculty, if more than one faculty member is involved, and to schedule implementation or field testing. It is often a good idea to complete Phase I (design) by the end of the spring semester so that the summer can be used (if time and funding are available) to select and produce instructional materials, design syllabi, and construct tests to meet the goal of fall implementation.

The entire instructional program is based on the decisions that you will now be making. The modification from ideal to operational design is based on several factors, each of which will directly impact the final design of your course. Attention at this time to all these factors is essential.

Goals

Individual lessons or class objectives are dealt with in the production phase of a project, but the major instructional approaches of a course must be decided here. If the major focus of the course is on information dissemination, lectures and independent study become the obvious instructional modes. If the major emphasis is on problem solving, critical thinking, and other more sophisticated goals, instruction will be built around laboratories, small-group activities, and practical experiences. If speaking skills are to be developed, the time necessary for presentations must be built into the instructional sequence. The development of interpersonal skills requires time for group meetings and planning. At this point the consequences of having instruction be content-focused or learning-centered become apparent. Each objective for the course suggests a variety of instructional approaches. In Chapter 15 we will get into the process of selecting the appropriate instructional approaches for goals in some detail.

Time

How many hours a week are students available for instruction, and when are they available? Is the schedule flexible? Can the period be extended? Is there time for independent study and teamwork? The question of student availability is even more complex for distance learning and independent study. Be careful in the assumptions you are making about your students' time commitments.

At first, implementing individualized instruction and flexible scheduling may create havoc for a registrar, but administrative policies must serve the academic needs of the program. Flexible-credit and continuous-registration options (Case Study 5) can often improve the quality of your course or program. Unfortunately, this flexibility is sometimes difficult to develop, especially in state systems where central-office controls may severely limit local administrative flexibility.

You must also take into consideration the time students have to complete assignments outside of class and the number of days students have between classes. Whether the institution is on a semester, trimester, or quarter system has a direct effect on the design of a course. In some scheduling systems, the decreased time between class sessions severely limits the amount of work students can be expected to do outside the classroom.

At this point you must also directly address the needs of adult and commuting students. In one project, the faculty found that combining four three-credit courses into two six-credit courses meeting six hours a week produced more flexibility and more time for small-group work within the class. In this format, classes could meet as a group for one hour or so and then break into teams for project work and special assignments during regular class time, thus ensuring that commuting students could participate in these important activities.

Resources

Several kinds of resources should also be considered as you design your course.

Human Resources As faculty, we have a wide range of human resources available to us as we explore the best possible way of promoting learning; these resources are often overlooked and under-utilized. At this point in the process you should explore the range of options available to you.

Within your institution, faculty inside or outside your department may be willing to teach the course jointly with you or to be available as guest lecturers or panel members in their area of specialization. In addition, the course you are developing may be far stronger if it is jointly offered by several departments. Or you may decide to develop a link between two courses that are interrelated. These ventures could range from combining students from several courses into project teams (where the specialization from each course is essential for success) to formal coordination between writing and speech courses and a disciplinary course. In this kind of coordination, the paper is written or the speech is delivered in a content-focused course but is a formal assignment in both courses. Each paper or presentation is evaluated by *both* the content expert and the specialist in communication, with each focusing on his or her area of expertise. For the student, the importance of speaking or writing within a discipline is reinforced, and the final result is far better than if the courses remain totally isolated from one another.

On many campuses, highly talented teaching assistants can play a variety of roles from handling laboratory sections and assisting with logistics to being responsible for entire sections or areas of instruction. Increasingly, faculty are also using upper-division students as tutors, small-group discussion leaders, or project advisers in lower-division courses. These peer tutors not only improve the quality of the course but benefit from the learning experience. Although such students are often paid, others volunteer as part of an assignment in another course or for credit.

A host of human resources are also available to you off campus. Although there are budgetary implications, part-timers or faculty from other institutions in your area may fill a gap or meet a need. The wide range of experts in the community can also be an invaluable resource. Business and government leaders and other practitioners, many of whom may be alumni, can bring to your classroom "real-world" expertise. Native speakers of other languages who live in the community can contribute to foreign-language courses. Also, don't forget to explore the use of retired people from your community. They can be an invaluable resource based on their work and experience. How to best involve these people will be determined by your needs and their availability. For more on the use of retired people in your community see "Utilizing America's Most Useful Resource" by Diamond and Allshouse.

Involving others in your project is, however, never easy. It takes time to locate them and requires careful planning and the coordination of schedules. For example, although team teaching can bring significant new dimensions into your program, it has disadvantages (see Exhibit 12.1). You will have to decide when the results are worth the effort. Select the combination of talents that can provide for your students the most effective learning opportunity without creating an impossible logistical problem for you.

Do not assume that other people will not want to be involved. Individuals often provide their services because they enjoy doing so. Other departments may be willing to make resources available because it introduces them to a new group of students, or they may help you with the understanding that you can reciprocate with services for them. A dean or provost may have funds specifically set aside to support innovation and academic improvements. Upper-classmen and graduate students often elect to earn experience credit through their academic unit if the project relates to their field of study. You will be surprised how easily you can involve others when you have solid justification for doing so and you ask the right people.

Computers and Other Technical Resources Several additional resources may be extremely important as you determine the structure of your course. On the top of the list is computer availability. What percentage of your students have their own computers? On a growing number of campuses, purchasing a computer is a requirement. While most students now have their own computers, you must make sure that their computers have the capabilities—including software applications—that your assignments require. Are well-equipped computer clusters available on campus, and what is their availability? Will you need to request the use of specific classrooms or laboratories? How do you handle these questions in off-campus or online courses? The answers to these questions will determine whether you can use e-mail for networking among students or between yourself and your students, whether you can use resources such as course management software in your plan, and the type of assignments you can give your students. See Chapters 18 and 19 for further discussion of this topic.

Exhibit 12.1.
Team Teaching: Advantages and Disadvantages

Advantages

- Enthusiastically supported by students, when it works well.
- Enthusiastically supported by faculty as a means of professional development and collegiality.
- Can be an inexpensive way for a faculty member to prepare to teach in a new subject area of discipline.
- Demonstrates commitment of institution to teaching and to lively interchange of ideas between faculty members; excellent marketing tool.
- Wonderful vehicle for interdisciplinary education (for both the students and participating faculty members).

Disadvantages

- Requires unique skills and attitudes among participating faculty members to be successful.
- Expensive for institution (if participating instructors receive full-credit for teaching the course) or faculty member (if participating faculty receive partial credit but are expected to or want to attend all class sessions).
- Tendency for faculty not to attend all class sessions especially if they have heavy teaching loads; thus the course becomes sequentially taught rather than team taught.
- Often requires extensive preparation; faculty members generally are used to working alone and are unfamiliar with subject matter outside their specialty.
- Often produces fragmented presentations due to limited preparation time.
- The larger the team, the more often there tends to be discontinuity or lack of integration between individual faculty presentations.
- As team size increases, faculty attendance tends to drop off, sense of responsibility for the course decreases.
- Tendency of faculty to treat teammates' specialty areas as sacrosanct produces shared classroom situation, rather than true team teaching situation.

Community Resources Other resources such as museums and art galleries in your community should be examined for possible use in your course. In such areas as music, art, literature, and history, there may be related exhibits, concerts, and plays available in your community or from a national source. What resources do local libraries contain? How can you use them?

Instructional Materials Existing instructional materials should be examined before new materials are developed. Are there commercial series or packages of materials that you can use? Commercially available computer simulation, review materials, and demonstrations, if well done and designed for the specific population involved, are ideal for remedial work.

Space

Space limitations may also force major changes in the design and content of your program. How large are the lecture halls, and can media be used effectively in them? It may be necessary to modify the course design substantially if there are not enough seminar rooms available for group work or if the rooms are not available at key times. Similarly, in a science course, the availability of laboratory stations and equipment is an important consideration. Creative use of the space available, however, is also an option. Some faculty are finding that even in a fixed-seat auditorium their students can work together for five to ten minutes at a time simply by turning in their seats.

Funding

How much money is available for development and implementation? Are there funds to support your work over the summer or to permit your release from other assignments? Does your college or university have a small grant program that can fund innovations in teaching or course design? A growing number of institutions have such programs, and the ways in which available funds can be used are often flexible. If disposable materials must be used, or if students frequently use equipment that must be replaced or repaired regularly, can a course fee be instituted? Can some of the new materials be sold to the students, reducing the cost to the department? You are always operating with fiscal constraints, which may require you to design one course to handle more students for the same amount, a second course to cut costs, and a third to make better use of existing resources.

Your final course design will, moreover, be affected not only by the total funds available for development and implementation but also on occasion by restrictions on how money can be spent. Most funding sources, particularly the federal government, specifically limit how and where grant money can be spent. For example, certain grant dollars may be available only for staffing and personnel, whereas other funds must be used only for the purchase of equipment and materials. The ideal is to have maximum flexibility in developing the instructional design.

In addition, you must keep in mind what resources will be available once your program becomes operational. If a grant supports development and pilot testing, make sure the course can continue after these funds are used up. All too many innovative programs developed with foundation or governmental support have died soon after their subsidies were withdrawn. Interdisciplinary courses, too, can be a particular problem if faculty are not rewarded for their participation. In such cases, explore ways in which the involvement can become part of their formal teaching load. The excitement of being involved in an innovative project is brief.

Students

The data you collected earlier on the students now play a major role in the design of your course. How many students do you anticipate will enroll, and who and where are they? What learning experiences have they had? Will additional orientation be required to smooth course implementation? Are there students with identifiable attitudes, problems, backgrounds, or strengths who should be separated at certain times for specialized instruction? How many commuting students do you have? If you have an adult population, what experiences will they bring to your classroom? Should special units be included to build on students' interests? How many students can be expected to select certain options? How many will probably have to be assigned to remedial units? Do some students have related experiences that suggest they should be given exemptions or that they could be used as resource persons? Can more students be accommodated by identifying the most capable and exempting them from modules they have already mastered? If you have adult students, do they need some review? A brief survey given to your students on the first day of class can tell you a lot about their interests and backgrounds. By including review questions in this survey, you can also assess whether students have the necessary prerequisite knowledge and skills.

The location of the students and the times they are available can also affect your plans. Full-time students allow design options that are not possible when a class has many part-time students who are available for only a few hours a week. A course that relies primarily on independent learning, team activities, internships, or off-campus assignments must be designed far differently from the standard class. This factor is becoming increasingly important as a growing number of institutions explore the potential of distance education.

For more on meeting the needs of adult students see Chapter 20. In Chapter 21 you will find materials on meeting the needs of students from diverse cultures and backgrounds.

Instructional Options

Which approaches and techniques work and which do not? What instructional options do you have? What has been tried elsewhere, and what happened when it was? If an approach did not work, why didn't it? Are some of your projects the same as those being undertaken at other institutions, and how are they different? For example, research on the use of courseware like Blackboard or WebCT for grading papers can have immediate significance for distance learning, as well as for first-year composition courses and others that require a great deal of writing. Another source you should check is the faculty-support unit on your campus. Many of these centers or offices have comprehensive libraries on teaching and learning that will make your work even easier.

A modest warning. Unfortunately, approaches that are not successful are tried again and again by those who regard their efforts and skills as unique and who consider past results irrelevant. Use existing materials, and learn from the experience of others. Although many failures are not reported in detail, it is wise to study related projects at other institutions. A phone call or letter to those working on a similar project often proves extremely helpful, and if travel funds are available, a visit to see such a project can also be useful. Unfortunately, national recognition does not necessarily correlate with either quality or replicability. In many instances, the recognition a project receives may result more directly from its support by particular external agencies or foundations than from the quality and practicality of the project itself.

Can a successful project be replicated, or is the success the result of a single outstanding faculty member or unique circumstances? Are there both positive and negative features of a particular technique, and what are they? What have been the experiences, for example, at Michigan State, MIT, Maricopa Technical Community College, Phoenix, Carnegie-Mellon, RPI, Brigham Young, San Jose State University, and Miami-Dade Community College, where courses have been developed to include major instructional-technology applications? Which applications have the faculty found most useful, and what suggestions do they have for implementation?

If you are exploring *service learning,* you will be interested in the experiences of Portland State University, Indiana University-Purdue University at Indianapolis, Drexel University, Bentley College, Evergreen State College, LaGuardia Community College, and the University of Colorado at Boulder, which have tried to interrelate the classroom and the community. If you are dealing with students who must travel long distances or who live in isolated areas, check the creative applications of technology that have been implemented at the University of Miami, the University of Hawaii, the University of Guelph, Empire State College in New York, University College at the University of Maryland, the British Open University, the University of South Africa, and Sydney Technical College in Australia. Each of these institutions serves large numbers of off-campus students by using various approaches to distance learning. Faculty at these campuses can provide you with examples of successful (and unsuccessful) efforts to bring discussion and interaction into this nontraditional setting.

How useful and cost-effective are the interactive video units developed at University College (University of Maryland), the Medical School of the University of Arizona in Tempe, and Utah State University? Is the evaluation approach that is used successfully at Alverno College transferable to larger campuses with a wider range of programs and more heterogeneous student populations? Whether it be the use of the case method in business courses at Harvard University or the use of journal assignments in the writing-across-the-curriculum program at Miami University, much useful information is available from other institutions.

Capitalize on the successes and failures of other institutions, and use existing materials whenever they meet your needs. Not to do so is a waste of your time, talent, and resources. You will also find useful information in the books and periodicals, many of them noted throughout this book, that focus on various instructional and assessment techniques. Time spent now in exploring options and what others have learned will significantly reduce the problems you face later on.

Grading and Scheduling Options

Your grading system may also have to be revised if new credit structures and time frames are introduced—an additional problem for the registrar and, if it is used, for the computer center. Mini-courses and credit options require an administrative system that allows additional credits to be earned and easily recorded. One way to maximize schedule flexibility is to block-schedule a course, as was done in the introductory course in religion described in Case Study 10. A subject may traditionally be taught three hours a week, but scheduling sessions twice weekly for two hours greatly increases the options because every student can meet during any of those four hours. This schedule, for example, permits the use of two-hour classes or two one-hour sessions running back to back. When nontraditional scheduling is planned, it is important to explain to students that although the course may be scheduled four or five hours a week, they will not be required to attend all these sessions. The amount of time allocated to all the instructional units must equal the total time allotted for the semester. If a continuous-registration system, flexible credit, or the flexible use of space makes sense for the project, get the registrar involved early. When such decision makers have some ownership in the project, they can often be helpful.

As all of these factors are explored, you will be able to outline the course as it will be implemented. At this stage expect most changes to be modest. During the preliminary design period, major additions, deletions, and changes in content are common; as you move from the ideal to the possible, fine-tuning will be more usual.

Some minor modifications may occur in the design of a course or curriculum during the production stage that follows, but most of the remaining changes take place after field testing or initial implementation. These later adjustments are based on the data collected during the initial offering of the new or revised program.

Case Study: Introductory Philosophy Course

Figures 12.5 and 12.6 diagram an introductory philosophy course, Writing and Philosophical Analysis. This course was developed specifically to permit students to meet the writing-intensive course requirement in Arts and Sciences Core Curriculum. Notice how the writing emphasis has been built into the entire fabric of the course. The two drafts represent the changes that took place in a single design meeting. In Units II, III, and IV the instructional sequence became more clearly defined, and one section in Unit III was eliminated to reduce the grading load on the instructor. In addition, although the number of papers increased, the length of many was reduced, and the types of essays required was also more clearly defined.

Figure 12.5.
Ideal Design for Introductory Philosophy Course

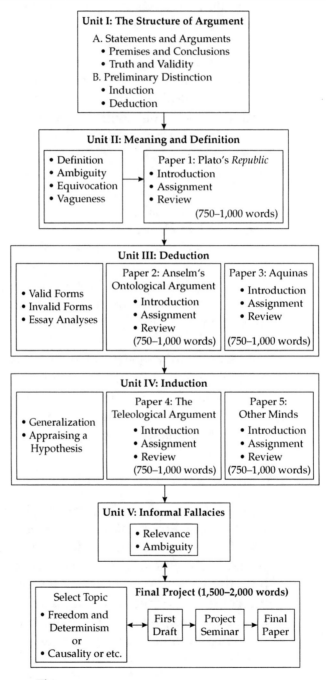

Source: Stewart Thau.

Figure 12.6.
Operational Design for Introductory Philosophy Course

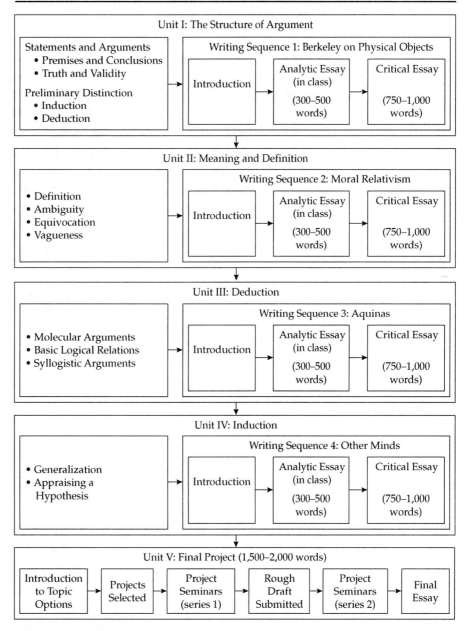

Source: Stewart Thau.

Summary

This chapter discussed moving from the ideal to an operational curriculum or course. This and the preceding chapters have examined some courses and curricula that are traditional in design and others that are unusual in their concept and structure. Although these courses vary substantially in design and sequencing, each was produced using the same model and development.

After the operational sequence is complete, production, implementation, and evaluation can begin at the course level. A major advantage of this approach is that once the operational elements of the instructional sequence are identified, many of the specific units can be developed simultaneously (if more than one faculty member is involved) because each unit has its own list of learning outcomes already determined, a time frame, and a clear relationship to the other components. The number of units that can be undertaken at one time and the time that can be saved are limited only by the availability of faculty. The following chapters discuss in detail the development of outcome statements and the instructional design and technology options available to you as you implement the course that you have designed.

CHAPTER 13

Clarifying Instructional Goals and Learning Outcomes

Figure 13.1.

Production, Implementation, and Evaluation for Each Course

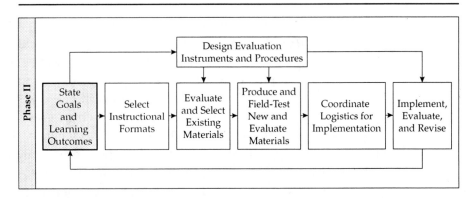

Robert Mager (1975) tells the story of a sea horse who, with money in hand, swims off to seek his fortune. After purchasing flippers and a jet-propelled scooter to speed up his travels, he comes across a shark. The shark informs the sea horse that if he swims into the shark's mouth, he will find his fortune. The sea horse follows this advice and is never heard from again. The moral of this fable is that if you are not sure where you are going, you are likely to end up someplace you do not want to be.

The call for stating the goals of instruction in measurable terms is not new. What is new is the demand that institutions become more accountable for the learning of their students and

147

that they be able to document the quality and effectiveness of their academic programs. For the first time, institutions are now required by accreditation agencies and state offices to state their instructional goals in outcome terms and to document their effectiveness in reaching these goals through appropriate assessment of student learning.

In previous chapters, we described the importance of developing a clear statement of instructional goals for your course, stated in terms of student performance. These statements will serve as your starting point as you consider how learning should occur and how students should be assessed. In this chapter, we will describe the qualities of well-written objectives and provide you with an approach to developing them that faculty have found to be efficient and effective. In the chapters that follow, we will discuss in detail the relationship between your instructional goals and your evaluation of students' performance, and show how these data can be used to improve your course.

The Relationship Between Goals, Outcomes, and Assessment

The most important concept in bringing quality to any curriculum or course is the fundamental relationship that must exist between goals, outcomes, and assessment. The closer this relationship is, the more effective the teaching and learning experience will be. Unfortunately, in too many instances there is a significant disconnect among the three. What we say is important is often not what we teach, and the focus of our testing and other assessments often has little in common with either. It is essential that our learning outcomes describe in detail what we mean by our goals and that students are then judged by how well they can meet these criteria.

Goals are usually short statements or even single words that describe the major objectives of the instructional experience. Statements of goals can be found at all levels of the instructional program, curriculum, courses, and units within courses. Although goals can sometimes be listed in broad outcome terms as seen in Resource D, they are usually described in more detail in most of the statements developed by individual institutions or programs (see Case Studies 1, 2, and 3.)

Figure 13.2

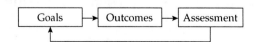

Learning outcomes are detailed descriptions of what a student must be able to do to reach a goal under the specific conditions that have been established. However, before outcome statements can be developed, you must identify those specific skills and attitudes that are required to reach a goal.

The basic sequence you will follow moves from goals to outcomes to assessment (see Figure 13.2).

From Goals to Outcomes: Your First Step

For students to reach a specific goal, they will usually need to possess a range of skills, a basic knowledge base, and, in many instances, certain attitudes as well. Your first step before writing your learning outcomes will be to identify these specific contributing requirements.

A Case Study: Critical Thinking

Although "critical thinking" appears on most lists of core competencies, it is a goal that that is not clearly defined in the minds of most faculty. When you ask a group of faculty to describe what it means to be a critical thinker you will often get as many different responses as you have participants. Fortunately, over the last few years there has been a growing body of research that describes in some detail what it means to be a "critical thinker."

In his outstanding review of the literature, Peter Facione (2007) provides us with an important first step in identifying those elements that combine to make up the process of being a critical thinker. He describes it as a process that requires both "cognitive" skills (interpretation, analysis, evaluation, inference, explanation, and self-regulation), and "disposition" (a willingness to apply this approach as a way of life). He then goes on to define each of these terms in some detail. Building on this base of information it now becomes possible for you to write a series of outcome statements that, when taken together, describe "critical thinking."

However, this is not the time to get hung up on specific definitions. What is important is that when you are finished writing your outcome statements for your course or curriculum, no one (other faculty, professionals in the field, or your students) will have doubts about what you mean and what will be required of the students to be successful.

In Resource L by Lion Gardiner you will find three excellent examples showing the relationship between goal statements and learning outcomes. The first two examples address common core competencies, critical thinking and ethics, and the third focuses on a goal that is discipline-specific, the principles and concepts of ecology.

In reading these examples, notice the care that has been taken to be as specific and concise as possible. Statements that are loosely worded can create major problems later on when different readers reach different interpretations.

The Importance of Stating Outcomes

Based on numerous projects, both successes and failures, we can now identify those characteristics that are common in successful programs. Six factors that appear to be essential are:

- High-quality outcomes stated in performance terms
- The translation of these goals into course-specific goals
- The match between goals and assessment
- The match between objectives and the instructional method selected
- The ownership of the initiative by participating faculty and the academic unit

If we are to determine whether academic programs are successful, we must initially determine the goals of courses and curricula. We must state in specific terms what we expect our students to be able to do, and then design evaluation instruments and procedures that adequately assess whether students meet these criteria at the end of the instructional program.

In addition to forming the base on which assessment programs must be designed, clearly stated outcomes offer important advantages at the course and program levels:

- Fairness in both testing and grading is facilitated.
- The goals of the course, its content, and the evaluation procedures are both consistent and interrelated.
- The outcome statements will allow you to determine which practices and materials are effective and which are not.
- The emphasis is changed from what faculty members must cover to what a student should be able to do as a consequence of instruction.
- A logical instructional structure is communicated by identifying a sequence of outcomes and thus content—that is, the student must be able to do *a* before he or she can do *b*.
- Communication among faculty, between faculty and support staff, and between faculty and students is improved.
- Self-evaluation by the students is encouraged because they know what is expected of them.

- Efficient student learning is facilitated and anxiety is reduced, because the students are provided with direction and they know what the instructional priorities are.

- Students understand how the course relates to other courses and to the overall goals of the curriculum.

Misconceptions About Outcomes: A Brief History

A major obstacle for the assessment movement has been and continues to be the necessity of stating outcomes in performance terms. In their report on over eighty course and curriculum projects, Bergquist and Armstrong (1986) noted that stating goals in performance terms was the first major problem. "While viewed by the architects of Project QUE (Quality Undergraduate Education) as the foundation of academic planning, the outcomes approach was one of the more controversial elements of the project. The crux of the challenge was aptly described by one campus coordinator (who chose to remain anonymous): 'The major shift to describing program goals in terms of student outcomes required effort on the part of faculty, most of whom had conceptualized their teaching in terms of their content area rather than with reference to student outcomes'" (p. 82).

The authors concluded, however, that although focusing on the results of learning did not gain total acceptance among the several hundred faculty and administrators who were involved, at the end of the project the majority viewed the approach as both practical and essential.

Unfortunately, the use of the term *behavioral objectives* has been a second major hurdle to overcome. In the early days of behavioral objectives, they were defined in terms of minutiae, leading to long lists of steps toward limited goals. The result was frustration on the part of the faculty who were most open to experimentation and change. In *On College Teaching* (1978), Ohmer Milton, reviewing Robert M. Barry's early and excellent chapter on clarifying objectives in the same book, writes: "In my judgment the weakest area of classroom instruction is that of specifying course objectives. He [Barry] quite properly avoids the unwarranted simplicity of much that is written about college course objectives—a simplicity especially true of many treatises about 'behavioral objectives.' All too often this concept has been carried to ridiculous extremes and has earned a resulting contempt among senior faculty who are now in leadership roles" (p. 3).

No wonder that as it developed its statewide assessment program, New Jersey (State of New Jersey College Outcomes Evaluation Program Advisory Committee, 1987) diligently avoided using the term *behavioral objectives*, focusing instead on college *outcomes*, which soon became another name for behavioral objectives.

Learning outcomes need not be low-level cognitive skills. Many faculty have come to equate a learning outcome with a multiple-choice, true-false, or similar selected-response format. This misconception is unfortunate as well as incorrect. Outcomes legitimately can include changes in attitude and in high-level performance skills. The students' abilities to relate philosophies to concepts and to defend their answers, to relate history to current events, to design a structure or write an article that meets prestated criteria, and to perform cooperatively within a small group are examples of valid higher-order learning outcomes that can be measured.

The way the assessment approach was described to faculty often deterred its acceptance. Because many of the early advocates of stating goals in performance terms focused on minutiae and on complex classification systems, they alienated the very people they were hoping to convert. Horror stories from these early efforts still abound and some of these approaches continue to surface as demands for greater accountability increase.

From Broad Statements to Specifics

Broad course and curricular goals are your starting point. Next you need to develop statements that are useful to you and to your students—outcomes that are clear, concise, and can be measured within the framework of the instructional unit.

Before you develop your course-specific outcomes, you should refer to other, more general statements created by the college, university, state, or discipline. Because individual courses are the vehicles for developing many of these general competencies, faculty are responsible for including within their statements course outcomes that are content- and discipline-specific and appropriate objectives from the broader list. Goal statements must become increasingly specific as they move from the national and state levels to the college or university, to the school, to the department curriculum, and finally to the course. In most instances the more specific goals are also more easily measured.

In addition to the broad goals you may address in your course that are not discipline-specific, there may be others that together constitute a complex goal that will be reached later in a student's academic program. For example, the Task Force on the Student Experience at Rutgers University compiled a list of the competencies they believe describe the "qualities of the liberally educated person" (1986). The qualities, characteristics, abilities, and competencies in this list were described in observable and measurable terms. However, as the following examples demonstrate, these characteristics still require additional specification before student performance can be assessed.

These are two of the Task Force's competency statements (1986) in the category of "scientific reasoning":

1. [The student] demonstrates an understanding of the scientific method of inquiry, including accurate measurement based on observation and the use of controlled experiment.

2. [The student] identifies the assumptions and limitations of the scientific method of inquiry and distinguishes the extent to which this method is applicable in various situations and contexts in all disciplines and fields of inquiry.

The faculty would have to adapt these statements, rewriting them to apply to their specific courses. They would have to describe how the student will demonstrate "an understanding of the scientific method of inquiry" or how the student will identify "the assumptions and limitations of the scientific method" in an applied context.

This problem of moving from general program goals to outcomes at the course level is one that all faculty members face. Such statements as "make sound, responsible judgments on the ethical policy issues involved" and "apply an historical perspective to the role of science and technology" are not unusual. The challenge for you is how to move from these broad statements to specific learning outcomes—that is, what the students have to do to show that they can apply a "historical perspective" and "make sound, responsible judgments." Quite often, statements from national associations on other campuses can be most helpful as you move along. Resource I on Multicultural Competencies for Counselors and Resource J on Ethics are examples of two such statements.

In the end, you, as the faculty member responsible for the course, must write your own outcome statements. Although a course may fulfill the requirements of others (professional agencies, the board of trustees, the university, the department), the outcome statement must be developed to satisfy your needs as the individual responsible for instruction.

Writing Outcomes

To be useful, objectives should contain three basic elements:

- A verb that describes an observable action.
- A description of the conditions under which the action takes place ("when given x, you will be able to . . .").
- The acceptable performance level—that is, what percentage of correct answers will be considered acceptable, how many

errors will be permitted, how many and which examples must be included, and so on.

In addition, before you begin this task, the student for whom the material is designed should be described, and the prerequisites should be identified. Problems often are the result of a mismatch between the students for whom we have designed the course and the abilities and experiences of those who have or will enroll.

Use clear, concise words to describe student behavior in these objectives, words not open to misinterpretation. Mager (1975) provides the following suggestions for terms to avoid and terms to use:

Words Open to Many Interpretations	Words Open to Fewer Interpretations
To know	To write
To understand	To recite
To really understand	To identify
To appreciate	To sort
To fully appreciate	To solve
To grasp the significance of	To construct
To enjoy	To build
To believe	To compare
To have faith in	To contract

Categorizing Outcomes

Although there are almost as many ways of categorizing outcome statements as there are authors of textbooks on the subject, the use of such a system at the course level is questionable (although it may be helpful to categorize goals when you are reporting them outside your institution). In Resource M, you will find one of the more widely used approaches to categorizing the outcomes for your courses. It will be up to you to organize your objectives in the way that you find most comfortable. However, it is rarely cost-effective for you to spend a great deal of time analyzing the type or level of your outcome statements. It is far more essential to ensure that useful statements are written, that they include all the elements that should be addressed, that they are measurable within your course, and that when students reach the end of the course, you can be confident that the goals you established have indeed been met.

Process Outcomes

In some instances an outcome focuses more on the process than on the students' ability to solve a problem or come up with the right answer. Such an outcome might, for example, be conceptualizing a value. In their discussion of how to test the conceptualization of a value, Krathwohl, Bloom, and Masia (1964, p. 157) write, "The process of conceptualization is largely cognitive, involving abstraction and generalization . . . the emphasis is less on the *quality* of the cognitive process[es] than on the fact that they are being used."

In testing the conceptualization of a value, you might use examples in which there are no right or wrong answers and ask the student to express a point of view. Here, you are more interested in the process the student uses to reach the point of view than in the specific conclusion. For evaluation purposes, focus is then on the process used, the alternatives explored, and the student's justification for the conclusion. Or you might ask your students to list a number of alternative solutions to a problem and then to defend the solution selected.

An Almost Painless Way to Specify Outcomes

When we faculty are asked point-blank to state our instructional outcomes, we have several reactions. First, we tend to resent the question; second, we often produce far more objectives than could ever be used; and third, many of these outcome statements are at a trivial level because they are the easiest to write. This process has a tendency to disenchant many faculty, as it is time-consuming, often boring, and usually frustrating.

As an alternative to writing objectives in the abstract, a facilitator can help you to develop strong, clear objectives by playing the role of the student and asking you, "*If I'm your student, what do I have to do to convince you that I'm where you want me to be at the end of this lesson, unit, or course?*" Out of this discussion will emerge outcome statements that are measurable and that tend to be far more important and at a higher level than you would produce otherwise. This process, while difficult at times, is generally comfortable and efficient, and produces the specific statements that are needed for the development of projects. Most important, it works.

Specifying Grading Criteria and a Word About Grade Inflation

As a final step for evaluation purposes you need to establish a standard of performance that will explain the basis for your grades. In some instances, a grade may cover a number of outcomes combined within a broad level of performance. You will also have to select among grading options—for example, pass-fail or the mastery approach, where performing at a high level is the only way to pass, or the more traditional letter grades, A, B, and so forth. Waiting until you see how well your students have done on a test before you determine grades is a disservice to you, your course, and your students. It is *not* grade inflation if more of your students perform at a level that you and the other faculty involved have determined is A-level work. It is only grade inflation when your original standards are lowered. In well-designed courses you should expect to see more students earning higher grades.

Representative Samples of Outcome Statements

A sampling of objectives from various courses follows. Note that each is written directly to the students, tells them what they must do to be successful, and identifies what they must be given before they are evaluated.

- *Government.* When given a major decision made by a governmental leader, you will be able to identify the major factors that the leader had to consider and discuss why the action was taken and what apparent trade-offs were made.

- *Economics.* Demonstrate graphically and explain how a change in expectations will affect the *loanable funds market.* (Begin with an appropriately labeled graph that represents the initial equilibrium.)

- *Management.* Identify (based on readings, case studies, or personal experiences) those activities that are most likely to distinguish effective, well-managed technology development programs from ineffective programs.

- *Statistics.* When given two events, you will be able to determine whether they are independent or whether there is a relationship between them (that is, one event affects the probability of the other). On the basis of this determination, you will be able to select and use the appropriate rules of conditional probability to determine the probability that a certain event will occur.

- *Religion.* When given a definition of the term *religion*, you will be able to identify which of the following characteristics is emphasized: feeling, ritual activity, belief, monotheism, the solitary individual, social valuation, illusion, ultimate reality, and value.

- *Music.* On hearing musical selections, you will be able to identify those that are examples of chamber music and be able to identify the form, texture, and makeup of the ensemble.

- *Art.* When shown a print, you will be able to identify whether it is a woodcut, an etching, or a lithograph, and you will be able to list the characteristics on which this identification was based.

- *Psychology.* When given a case study, you will be able to identify whether it describes a case of schizophrenia, and if it does, which of the following schizophrenic reactions are involved: hebephrenic, catatonic, or paranoid.

Another excellent and useful approach to describing the behavior expected of critical thinkers will be found in Resource N. Note how the specific skill is described and then shown in a behavioral or outcomes context. An additional step would be required for the range of skills to be in outcome terms (see Facione, 2007).

Although many objectives lend themselves to this format, for others you may find this approach awkward and confining. Such broad goals as critical thinking, effective speaking and writing, interpersonal skills, leadership, and the development of a positive attitude toward a particular subject need to be described to your students in somewhat different terms. For example, if you want your students to develop the ability to manage change, one of your goals for the students at the end of the sequence might be to "identify sources of conflict between yourself and others and take steps to eliminate this disharmony." In demonstrating competence in writing, one skill for which you might hold students responsible is to "be able to incorporate information from various sources to support the hypothesis that you are developing."

Limitations of Outcome Statements

As you establish outcomes for your course, keep in mind the limitations of outcomes. Some broad objectives or goals cannot be measured because of time and program limitations. In art and music, for example, a secondary goal may be to develop in the student viewing and listening habits that will last throughout a lifetime. This goal cannot be measured after a single course or even after a four-year program. In these instances you need to select as outcomes the skills, knowledge, and attitudes that you believe will result in the desired behavior. Evaluation must focus on the objectives that fit within the scope of the course. Later, in alumni surveys, you can determine if your graduates do show the desired behaviors.

When overused, the detailed learning outcomes can limit creativity and reduce instructional excitement. As noted earlier, outcome statements are a key ingredient in selecting your instructional methodology and evaluating student performance. The process of developing and testing for specific outcomes is important, but it should not preclude flexibility and, as opportunities arise, adding new elements. In addition, the larger goals of a course must always be kept in view. For example, although it will never appear on a quiz or your final examination, a primary goal of a course may be to excite the students about a subject area or field of study. You would certainly be collecting and using enrollment data, but this is not a goal that would be publicly stated in most of your documents. This is not to suggest that we should eliminate long-term performance-based outcomes but rather to emphasize that although they may be important, these outcomes have inherent limitations that must be recognized as one develops and uses them.

Additional References

As a first step you should review the most recent publications of the disciplinary associations in your discipline. With the recent emphasis on the need for quality statements of learning outcomes and associated assessment procedures, a growing number of these groups are publishing materials on outcomes and assessment directly related to their specific field of study. In addition, as seen in Resources I and J, these publications often include excellent justifications on why certain learning outcomes are crucial to their particular discipline.

Because quality student assessment requires well-defined learning outcomes, you will find that almost every new book on assessment or instructional design will include useful material on writing and assessing learning outcomes. In many instances this will include examples of quality outcome statements. The following publications are excellent examples of what you can expect to find.

Allen, M. J. *Assessing Academic Programs in Higher Education.* San Francisco: Anker/Jossey-Bass, 2004.

> Designing and assessing courses and curricula. Includes practical suggestions on identifying learning outcomes, assessing performance, and setting standards.

Banta, T. W. *Assessing Student Achievement in General Education.* San Francisco: Jossey-Bass, 2004.

> As the title implies, this book focuses directly on the basic core competencies, writing, speaking, interpersonal relations, critical thinking, and so forth. Highly practical.

Comeaux, P. (ed.). *Assessing Online Learning*. San Francisco: Anker/Jossey-Bass, 2005.

> Addresses the challenges of assessing students enrolled in online courses. Includes strategies for student self-assessment and approaches to evaluating critical thinking and writing skills using technology.

Driscoll, A., and Wood, S. *Developing Outcomes-Based Assessment for Learner-Centered Education*. Sterling, Va.: Stylus, 2007.

> Articulating learning outcomes to provide evidence of learning that are appropriate for your course. Numerous case studies with concrete examples of what worked and what didn't.

Wehlburg, C. M. *Meaningful Course Revision: Enhancing Academic Engagement Using Student Learning Data*. San Francisco: Jossey-Bass, 2007.

> Focusing on using multiple, direct measures of student learning to improve the quality of courses. Addresses the need for continual assessment and course revision.

Phase II

Once the outline of a course is complete (Phase I), the production, implementation, and evaluation activities begin (Phase II). During this phase several activities take place:

- Course goals are finalized.
- Learning outcomes are specified.
- Evaluation procedures and instruments are developed.
- Methods or strategies of instruction are chosen.
- Instructional materials are selected or developed (or both).
- When possible, new materials are field tested.
- The program is implemented, evaluated, and when needed, revised.

During Phase II you should anticipate that you will continue to make changes in the design of your course. Although these modifications are usually minor, they can sometimes determine the overall success of your project. Changes usually take place in two areas: time and content. If it becomes clear that the specified objectives cannot be reached in the time allotted, some outcomes may be modified or moved to other courses so that certain units are given more time. Even after implementation most courses undergo fine-tuning as problems are identified and addressed, changes occur in the discipline, adjustments are made in the content, or other faculty with different strengths and backgrounds enter the program. This chapter focuses on the first step of this phase: stating your learning outcomes. Later chapters will cover the other steps in Phase II.

As you move through this first step, take care to build the appropriate and broader, more general goals of the curriculum into the objectives of your course, As we noted previously, these non-discipline-specific core outcomes exist in every course; they include those skills and competencies that every student needs after graduation—the abilities to write and speak effectively, to work well with others, to engage in critical thinking, and so on. One of your challenges will be to identify those basic goals that fit appropriately within your course.

Summary

No matter which specific form you use, statements of learning outcomes should do the following:

- Describe your goals in performance terms
- Communicate to your students your expectations and how the students will be assessed
- Serve as the basis for selecting instructional methods
- Serve as the basis for your assessment of student achievement

Keep in mind that the clearer your outcome statements, the easier it will be for you to design your course and assess your students' success in reaching the goals established for your academic programs. In the next chapter we will focus on designing your assessment plan for both curricula and courses.

CHAPTER 14

Designing and Implementing Your Assessment Plan

Overview and Assessing a Curriculum

Assess (v): to examine carefully.

Assessment is a process that focuses on student learning, a process that includes reviewing and reflecting on practice as academics have always done, but in a more planned and careful way.

—Palomba and Banta (1999, p. 1)

Previous chapters emphasized the direct relationship between goals, learning outcomes, and student assessment. This chapter focuses in depth on this relationship and on the crucial importance of collecting and using quality information.

Throughout the design process thus far, you have collected, analyzed, and used information. Before you even began, you collected data to determine need and to identify the problem. You used a wide variety of information to help design the "ideal" program and then to modify the design so that it could be implemented with the resources available.

In this stage, you will design your assessment plan, identifying the information that you need to know and determining how best to collect it. Because data are so important, it is essential that all of your assessment instruments be ready before you begin implementation so that you will be able to collect essential information at the ideal time.

Keep in mind that the assessment of student performance has two different but overlapping purposes. First, to provide you with the key information you need as the designer of the course or curriculum and, second, to provide you with a basis for evaluating each student. As a result, much of the data that you collect will often be used in more than one way.

You should also remember that some of the data collected during the implementation and revision stage of a course will be most appropriate for inclusion in reports that focus on the assessment of the curriculum of which it is a part.

The Structure of This Chapter and the Next

Designing your assessment plan for a curriculum and for a course have much in common; however, they also have significant differences in focus and in purpose. For this reason we have divided our discussion on assessment into two parts. This chapter, which contains basic information on assessment and then an overview of assessing a curriculum, is followed by Chapter 15, which looks at assessing a course. Whatever your focus, we strongly recommended that you read both chapters, because what happens in a course impacts the total curriculum, and what happens in a curriculum has impact on the course as well.

A Basic Reference

Before we move on, we would like to recommend that you get a copy of *Assessment Essentials: Planning, Implementing, and Improving Assessment in Higher Education* by Catherine Palomba and Trudy Banta (1999). It is one of the best books available on the subject and includes useful information on a host of assessment techniques. Details are provided on a number of approaches, and perhaps even more useful is their list of references and individuals to contact for more information. Not to be overlooked, the approach used by the authors meshes perfectly with the model we have been using to get to this stage in the design process.

Evaluation Assistance

Whether you are working on a new course or an entire curriculum, now is the time, if at all possible, to involve an expert in evaluation. This person may be from an academic support agency, the institutional research office, or from the School of Education or the Department of Psychology. Not only can they assist you in developing and field testing your own assessment plans, but they can also help you locate other materials that may be of use. In addition, if data analysis and number crunching is needed, an evaluator will usually have the skills and the support staff needed to provide these services.

Using Before-and-After Comparisons

Pre- and post-comparison can be extremely powerful in determining the impact of your effort. If your curriculum or course is replacing an existing program, curriculum, or course, you have an excellent opportunity to collect data that show the specific changes that have occurred as a result of what you have done. This type of information is both useful and powerful. In deciding to begin your project, you identified a need, justified the project as important, and collected data about what was and was not working with the existing program. You may have also collected data about attrition, student attitudes toward the course or program, and job or grad school placements.

As you plan your assessment, whether it be at the course or curriculum level, an effort should be made to see whether these problems have been resolved. Some of the more common questions for before-and-after comparisons include:

- If instructional elements were missing from the original program, have they been included?
- If there were attendance problems, have they been reduced or eliminated?
- If job placement was a problem, are employers now actively seeking your graduates?
- If student attitudes were negative, have they improved?
- If attrition was high, has it been reduced?
- If few students were majoring in your field, has the number of majors increased?
- If faculty teaching follow-up courses complained about the quality of student preparation, have their needs been met?
- If the line of students wishing to drop the course went around the block, has it been reduced or eliminated?
- If students were constantly complaining about the course or program, have these complaints been reduced or eliminated?
- Has the number of students failing a course been reduced?
- How do the new and old programs compare in instructional costs?

Information of this type can be extremely powerful and most useful to you as the instructor, to administrators, to alumni, and to outside funding agencies. For this reason, before you begin, collect as much information as you can about the course or program that your new design will be replacing. Pay particular attention to student learning, retention, attitudes, and instructional costs.

Unanticipated Assessment Results

Every project will have results that you do not anticipate. In many instances these surprises are positive as well as negative. Perhaps your students are performing far beyond your expectations or have attitude changes you could only have hoped for. Perhaps you are spending instructional time more efficiently. These outcomes may become apparent as the program progresses, or may come to the surface from data collected on students' perceptions at the end, or from comments made later by students, their parents, other faculty, administrators, or employers. Be sensitive to this feedback; it may provide you with important information that you can use to improve your course or program and other courses as well.

Different Audiences: Different Reports

Before you even start collecting data, you should keep in mind that the information you will collect and report will, before you are done, most likely have a number of audiences, each with its own interests and priorities. As a result you should expect to produce a number of reports that, although based on the same data, will be significantly different from one another in both purpose and content.

- *Internal.* The most detailed and comprehensive of all reports will be the one you prepare for your own use and for others who have been involved in the design and implementation process. The data will provide you with the information you need to determine what worked, what did not work, and where important changes need to be made.

- *For department chairs, deans, and other administrators.* This is an overview of the project, designed to keep key campus leaders informed of your progress. Highlighting successes and impact (improvements in learning, attitudes, increases in retention, and so on) and identifying major problem areas, this report is designed to inform the reader about the next steps that will be undertaken to address concerns, collect more information and, if appropriate, to expand the program to include more students.

- *Campus reports.* Brief, informational reports to the campus community about your initiative and its impact. These can appear in student newspapers or in campus publications, and can be used to provide updated information to your board of trustees.

- *External reports.* Special reports designed for audiences with specific interests, these can range from brief reports or articles for public-relations purposes to extensive documents prepared for accreditation site teams or other national or state offices. These more comprehensive reports will often include details on goals, outcomes, and assessment as well as examples of course syllabi and newly developed instructional materials. In many instances materials from the project will also be used by you or other members of your design team as the focus of professional articles and presentations.

Fortunately, you will usually have a good idea, even before you begin a project, of what type of reports you will be expected to write and of what other uses you may have for the data. By structuring the data you collect in usable forms from the very beginning, you can substantially reduce the work that will be required to provide various publics with the information that they will require. The more you plan ahead, the easier the task will be.

For an interesting take on the significance of having different audiences, see Jeremy Penny's essay "Assessment for Us and Assessment for Them."

Using Assessment Instruments Developed Elsewhere

It is extremely time-consuming and often difficult to develop your own assessment tools—perhaps unnecessarily so, if there are existing tools that do the job well and are available to you. Although you will also want to develop your own materials to meet the unique needs of your curriculum or course, you should always be on the lookout for effective tools and techniques that have been developed elsewhere and can be adapted for your use.

The key will be asking the right questions as you evaluate the potential usefulness of existing instruments. Be particularly careful with test instruments being sold nationally by various testing companies. Quite often the claims are not founded on quality data, and it is extremely important that there be a match between your assessment questions and your outcome statements. Many times your goals will be far more sophisticated than those measured on standardized tests.

Exhibit 14.1. does an excellent job of listing the questions you should ask before you adopt any instrument from an external source. Use it—you will save a great deal of time and often a significant amount of money.

Exhibit 14.1.

Selecting Assessment Instruments

Before selecting an assessment instrument, it is helpful to consider the following questions:

1. What outcome are we seeking? What will a student know or be able to do when this outcome is achieved?

2. In what settings, inside or outside the classroom, will the student have an opportunity to learn the knowledge and skills we consider important?

3. What assessment instruments will give us information about the extent to which students are mastering the knowledge/skills we consider important?

4. What assessment findings do our instruments yield?

5. What use can we make of the assessment findings? What changes can we make in methods of instruction, course content, curricular structure, student services such as advising, and/or the college experience more broadly to ensure that more students will develop the knowledge and skills we seek and at deeper levels?

If the knowledge and skills identified in response to the first question are stated using action verbs, such as think critically or write . . . , it will be easier to identify the type of assessment needed to complete the response to item #3. Do we need a test of generic skills like writing and critical thinking, a specialized test in the major, an attitude inventory, a questionnaire that asks about students' perceptions of the college environment?

The *Mental Measurements Yearbook* and Web sites such as www2.acs. ncsu.edu/UPA/assmt/resource.htm provide information about assessment instruments. The first thing to look for in any instrument is face validity— when faculty and students look at the items and response formats, does it appear that the instrument is measuring the outcome(s) of interest?

Instrument reliability is a necessary, but not sufficient, criterion for judging the technical quality of a test or other measure. First see if the test developer has provided a measure of internal consistency, which is often reported as a type of correlation between the two halves of the instrument. Equally important is test-retest reliability; that is, would a student respond in the same way on a second administration of the test at a later time?

Once you have developed confidence in the test's reliability, several additional aspects of instrument validity should be investigated. Is the instrument actually measuring the construct of interest? For critical thinking, e.g., is there evidence of significant correlations with other valid measures of critical thinking? Does each of the scales or components of the test measure what is intended? Is there evidence in the literature that the measure predicts the outcome(s) you seek, by itself or in combination with other measures?

One of the advantages of using a commercially available instrument is that it provides the possibility of comparing one's own students' scores with national, regional, or peer group norms. If these comparisons are important, it will be essential to obtain a list of institutions represented in the norm group to ascertain that institutions similar to one's own are represented there. Also important, especially if a test is to be used in making decisions about institutional or program quality, is to find out how the students who took the test on other campuses were chosen—for example, was it administered to all sophomores or all seniors, or was it given only to a sample of students who volunteered to take it?

If you seek a test of generic abilities, such as critical thinking, writing, speaking, is there evidence that students who go to college develop these skills to a greater extent than students of similar ability who did not go to college?

Finally, does the instrument provide information that is helpful in your context—do the findings the instrument yields actually help you answer question #5 above? If the instrument provides direction for making changes that will increase student learning of the outcome(s) sought, then the test has validity for use in your context.

Source: T. F. Banta, 2007. Reprinted with permission.

Developing a Plan for Assessing a Curriculum

Developing a high-quality and comprehensive assessment plan for an entire curriculum is an extremely complex task. Unfortunately, higher education does not have a tradition of doing this very well. There are a number of factors that make this task particularly challenging:

- A large number of faculty and courses are involved.
- It must take place over an extended period of time.
- The information that must be collected is extremely varied, requiring an array of approaches that focus on a variety of topics.
- Needed revisions are usually at the course level and are sometimes resisted by faculty.
- The student population is increasingly diverse.
- Instruction may take place simultaneously on campus, off campus, and in a variety of distance-learning venues.

A Red Flag

In some instances a curriculum may include two or more programs with majors that have little in common other than the place in which they are housed. When this occurs, it is usually the result of administrative decisions based more on saving costs than on any instructional justification. In instances where there is significant disagreement among faculty on goals, major outcomes, and material of the programs, it may make more sense to consider each program as an independent curriculum for design and assessment purposes. It will make everyone's job much easier.

Timing

With the exception of single-year graduate programs, new or revised curricula must be phased in sequentially, year by year. There are a number of significant advantages to this approach.

- Most courses are designed to be sequential. Course design and implementation should follow this sequence. This is extremely important, as changing the content and goals of one course will always impact the courses that follow.

- By implementing the new curriculum one year at a time, the work on the second-year courses can be sequenced accordingly. This spreads out the work and the introduction of the new program over the full four years of the sequence.

- When needed, work on the revision of one year's courses can be undertaken while work is completed on the following year's courses. As the outcomes rarely change as a result of revision, this pattern usually works well.

- It is unfair to students already enrolled in a program to make changes in existing requirements or major changes in the courses themselves if they have not been totally prepared for these changes.

Figure 14.1.

The Data Collection Sequence—Undergraduate Curriculum

| | Data Source | | | | |
	Fresh.	Soph.	Jr.	Sr.	Alumni Employers
Pre-Implementation				✓	✓
Year 1	✓				
Year 2	✓	✓			
Year 3	✓	✓	✓		
Year 4	✓	✓	✓	✓	✓
Revision (as needed)	✓	✓	✓	✓	✓

Figure 14.1 describes the ideal data-collection sequence for a traditional four-year undergraduate curriculum. Pay particular attention to several details. First, data collection begins *before* the implementation of the new program; second, information is collected from students enrolled in the program and from alumni and employers; and third, revision based on data is an ongoing activity that will impact all courses for the entire life of the program.

A Curriculum: The Sum of Its Parts

You cannot design a quality assessment program of a curriculum without paying a great deal of attention to the quality and effectiveness of each course in the curriculum. It will be the sum of all this information that will determine whether or not your new program is successful. For this reason it is important that the school or department in which the curriculum is offered make sure that each course successfully meets the instructional goals that have been assigned to it. One of the most problematic areas is those core competencies that, although vital to the curriculum, are not the primary focus of one or more courses. In this list we would find such competencies as critical thinking, team building, ethical behavior, and speaking effectively. It was for this reason that early on, we suggested that you develop a checklist to identify which of these core requirements were to be introduced, reinforced, and further developed in which specific courses. Only with this type of structure will you be able to pinpoint the specific location of the problem when students are found to be performing below a certain competency by the end of their program. It will also be essential for your assessment plan to ensure that these competencies are not only taught along the way but that all other important goals are addressed specifically in the assessments taking place at the course level.

Your First Steps

Your initial step in evaluating any curriculum is to determine the questions you should ask. There are two resources in this book that will give you a framework for deciding on the focus of your investigation as well as an extensive list of possible questions. In addition, because you will have already collected important information in the process of determining whether or not to pursue your project, you will have available key data to use as a benchmark for comparison purposes. As we mentioned before, all too often crucial information is not collected before a project begins, making it impossible to determine and report actual impact. Review the following:

- Exhibit 7.1 in Chapter 7: Establishing the Need for Curriculum Design Projects
- Resource O: Curriculum Review: The Questions to Ask

From these materials you should be able to draft a rather comprehensive list of key questions.

There is one specific recommendation we would like to make as you plan to implement your new curriculum: Consider participating in one of the major institutional database projects now growing in popularity. They will provide you with extremely useful information that you can use to determine the overall impact of your new program. Participation in these programs, even before you begin to implement your new curriculum, will give you an ideal benchmark for comparison purposes. Two of the more comprehensive ones are:

- The National Survey of Student Engagement (NSSE)

  Reports data on the degree of academic challenge of your program, student-faculty interaction, the characteristics of your campus environment, and other important educational experiences

- The Collegiate Learning Assessment (CLA)

  Rates institutions on their success in teaching higher-order thinking and communication skills

Comparing changes in these reports with data you collect on student performance in capstone courses, retention figures, and surveys of employers and graduates can provide you with a comprehensive and powerful picture of how the quality of your academic program has changed with implementation of the new curriculum.

For an overview of these and other new initiatives see Kevin Carey's *College Ranking Reformed: The Case for a New Order in Higher Education* (2006). This report from the *Education Sector,* funded by the Lumina Foundation, takes direct aim at the ranking approach used by *U.S. News and World Report.* It discusses the focus of these surveys and includes examples of the information these instruments provide.

For more detailed information on the National Survey of Student Engagement and the Inventory for Student Engagement and Success, see *Assessing Conditions to Enhance Educational Effectiveness* (2005), by George Kuh, Jillian Kinzie, John Schuh, and Elizabeth Whitt; also visit the following Web site: www.nsse.iub.edu.

Another resource that will be helpful for you at this time is *Assessment in Practice: Putting Principles to Work on College Campuses* (1996), by Trudy Banta, Jon Lund, Karen Black, and Frances Oblander, which discusses a wide variety of assessment techniques with case studies from over 160 institutions. Focuses on the approaches that have been found to be most effective.

Resources

As you move from basic recall and recognition goals to focusing more on process and complex behaviors, assessment becomes increasingly difficult. In addition to the help you can obtain from other faculty, particularly the experts in learning and assessment found in schools or departments of education, there is an ever-expanding list of excellent publications that will provide you specific information on selecting, designing, and interpreting various approaches to assessment.

Allen, M. J. *Assessing General Education Programs.* San Francisco: Anker/Jossey-Bass, 2006.

> General education and core programs are a key component of most academic programs. They are also one of the most difficult areas to assess. Using numerous case studies, this book provides a usable process for addressing this most complex issue.

Banta, T. W., and Associates. *Building Scholarship in Assessment.* San Francisco: Jossey-Bass, 2002.

> Provides an overview of assessment and what has been learned about the process.

Bresciani, M. J. *Outcomes-Based Academic and Co-curricular Program Review: A Compilation of Good Practices.* Sterling, Va.: Stylus, 2006.

> Practical suggestions with examples from over forty institutions. What approaches were used and why.

Bresciani, M. J. (ed.). *Assessing Student Learning in General Education: Good Practice Case Studies.* San Francisco: Anker/Jossey-Bass, 2007.

> Case studies from thirteen institutions with a focus on the core competencies. Addresses how different institutions use different approaches and how the culture of the institution impacts the approach used.

Collegiate Assessment of Academic Proficiency (CAAP). Available at www.act.org/caap.

> Designed by ACT to help post-secondary institutions "assess, evaluate, and enhance the outcomes of their general education program."

The Collegiate Learning Assessment Project. Available at www.sae.org/content/procolleg.at.htm.

> Designed to assess an institution's contribution to student learning. Focuses on reasoning and communications skills.

Driscoll, A., and Wood, S. *Developing Outcomes-Based Assessment for Learner-Centered Education.* Sterling, Va.: Stylus, 2007.

> Loaded with practical examples, both successes and failures.

Kuh, G. D., Kinzie, J., Schuh J. H., and Whitt, E. *Student Engagement and Success.* San Francisco: Jossey-Bass, 2005.

> Presents a self-guided framework for conducting a comprehensive, systematic, institution-wide analysis that can also be used at the school, college, division, or department level. Describes policies and programs from over twenty institutions. The approach can be used for accreditation self-studies, and for professional and strategic planning.

Maki, P. L. *Assessing for Learning: Building a Sustainable Commitment Across an Institution.* Sterling, Va.: Stylus, 2004.

> Sets the assessment of learning within the context of both the level of a program, department, division, or school within an institution and the level of the institution based on the mission, educational philosophy, and educational objectives. Defines assessment as the ability to determine the match between what we expect of our students and their actual performance. Provides case studies, resources, and exercises. Will assist institutions in responding to the calls for increased accountability and the use of learning outcomes. Published in association with AAHE.

Measure of Academic Proficiency and Progress (MAPP). Available at www.ets.org/patal/site/ets/menuitum.

> The ETS approach to measuring academic proficiency and progress.

Palomba, C. A., and Banta, T. W. *Assessment Essentials: Planning, Implementing, and Improving Assessment in Higher Education.* San Francisco: Jossey-Bass, 1999, 2007.

A widely ranging practical handbook on the application of assessment in higher education. Among its many topics are monitoring quality in learning, monitoring campus environments, specifying outcomes, and using results.

Serban, A., and Friedlander, J. (eds.). *Developing and Implementing Assessment of Student Learning Outcomes.* San Francisco: Jossey-Bass, 2004.

Focusing on community college examples, the book describes approaches in a number of disciplines.

CHAPTER 15

Designing and Implementing Your Assessment Plan

Assessing a Course

Figure 15.1.

Production, Implementation, and Evaluation for Each Course

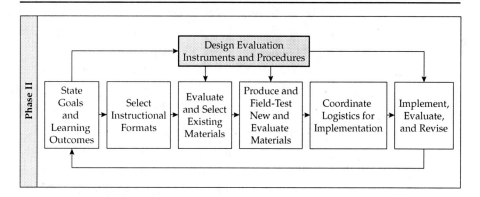

By this point in the design process you should have stated all major instructional outcomes for your course and for each instructional unit within it. You can now begin work simultaneously in two areas: the selection and design of the evaluation procedures and instruments that are necessary, and the design and production of the instructional units themselves.

As you think through the design and implementation of your course, keep in mind that assessment at the course level provides data both on individual student performance for grading purposes, and on the overall effectiveness of instruction for identifying those areas that may require improvement. Another function, of course, is that it helps the student to assess his or her own progress in meeting course goals.

As you develop your approach to assessment, make sure it includes the more complex goals of your course and that you build in data collection throughout the semester. The ongoing collection of good information will give you a clear sense of what is and is not working, and thus you'll have the opportunity to make adjustments immediately as problems occur.

Collecting Useful Information

Like most faculty members, you are not unfamiliar with the process of assessment. You do it all the time in assessing the quality of your students' work and in using information to improve the quality of your courses. What may be new is the care that you will be taking to ensure that data you collect measures how well your students reach the specific goals and outcomes that you have established. Although evaluation specialists may help you develop certain assessment instruments and protocols, it is imperative that you play an active role in the process. As John Muffo (1996, p. 1) has observed, we as faculty will most readily accept the results of studies if we gather the data ourselves. Only when we can trust the data will we do what they imply is necessary to improve a course.

Based on the objectives that you have developed and the overall structure of the course, it is now possible to design procedures and instruments that serve four distinct purposes:

- *Identifying students for remediation and exemption.* Such identification requires specifying anticipated prerequisites and designing a diagnostic instrument or procedure that tests for the prerequisite abilities. Tests of this type must be very specific to permit remedial assignments to be made on the basis of individual need. Most tests used for course placement are too general for this purpose; we have seen this approach in a number of the case studies that we have discussed.

- *Determining whether the learning outcomes (of individual units and entire courses) are being met by measuring student performance.* This includes the measurement of newly acquired skills, knowledge, and attitudes. There must be a perfect fit between the stated outcomes, the content of the course, and the student evaluation instruments that will be used. As mentioned earlier, all too often the learning outcome statements that are given to students have little in common with either the content of the course or the questions that are asked on tests and examinations. Unless all three elements are closely interrelated, significant problems will develop, and the students will become frustrated and antagonistic.

- *Determining whether and how students' attitudes toward the course and the discipline or field have changed.* Some courses have, as an unstated objective, the goal of improving the attitude of the student toward the field or profession. For comparison purposes, questions focusing on attitudes can be built into course orientation activities or prerequisite tests and then into end-of-course evaluations.

- *Determining whether the overall course design and the materials and procedures are efficient and effective.* Survey instruments used at the end of a specific unit or entire course can collect useful data on pacing, interest, structure, and overall design.

Unfortunately our assessment of student performance is one of the areas where American education is most vulnerable. As the research indicates (Exhibit 15.1), assessment practices have generally focused on the low-level skills of recognition and recall. As a result, there are significant gaps between what we as faculty say our major goals are and the way we evaluate the competencies of our students. Research also indicates that the tests we use are often unreliable or of questionable validity, which should certainly make us uncomfortable about the way in which grades are assigned and interpreted.

Exhibit 15.1.
Research Findings on Testing and Grading

- Most tests now in use ask for factual recognition or recall.
- Although faculty desire students to develop higher-order cognitive skills, the tests that are used rarely measure these competencies.
- When essays are used, faculty tend to emphasize knowledge of facts, and students write essays to meet this expectation.
- A small proportion of faculty (less than 20 percent) report using "problem-solving" items on essay tests.
- Grades are used primarily for external reporting and not to give feedback to students.
- The low level of classroom assessment and the lack of attention to validity and reliability call into question the results of most tests and the grades that are given.
- Publisher-provided test items tend to focus primarily on recall items.
- Nearly 50 percent of students report never or rarely having to write an essay examination.

Source: Primarily from Gardiner, 1996, pp. 66–68.

Although much is yet to be learned about student assessment and how we can document a student's overall performance, we can do a much better job than we have in the past of allowing our students to demonstrate what they have learned. A number of institutions and associations are leading the way in exploring how this can be done. As you move through the process of developing an assessment plan for your course, a review of the literature on this subject will reduce your work and result in a well-understood and fair assessment program for your students. You will also find that certain assessment techniques are particularly effective for specific types of learning objectives. A list of excellent references and resources, in addition to the *Assessment Essentials* by Palomba and Banta (1999) mentioned earlier, is at the end of this chapter.

Assessing Group Work

In some instances the assessment technique you use can also facilitate the learning you hope to accomplish. For example, one of the most common learning goals of core programs is the ability of the student to work effectively as a member of a team. As more and more of us integrate group work into our courses, we find that to do so successfully requires careful orchestration. The goals of the exercise have to be clear; students must understand their responsibilities; and assessment must be designed to accurately reflect the work of the group and the work of the individual.

Charles Walker developed a classroom assessment technique (CAT) to help faculty members monitor student groups and detect problems early on. He identified the following essential steps for constructing team assignments:

> (1) pick a task that is worthwhile, feasible, and best done by, or only done by, a group; (2) set task goals for the group that are specific and concrete and that allow unambiguous feedback on their accomplishment; (3) discuss and select strategies and procedures that will help the group achieve its goals within the time limits that have been set; (4) define and assign roles and duties that are exclusively faithful to the goals and procedures of the group; and (5) acquire the resources (human effort and expertise, financial, informational, institutional, and time) that are necessary for the group to accomplish its goals [Walker, 1995, pp. 4–5].

As part of the model he has also developed a team response form that he finds not only helps students learn the social and organizational skills necessary but places on the group itself the responsibility for dealing with conflict and other inter-personal problems (Exhibit 15.2). Being task-focused, this approach also

Exhibit 15.2.
Group Assessment Form

Course_____

Section_____

Instructor_____   Date

_____

Name (optional)_____   Group

_____

1. Is the work of your group worthwhile and challenging?
2. Does your group have specific goals and objectives? List the specific goals of your group on the back of this form.
3. Do the members of your group agree on the goals? Do you have consensus on the priority of these goals?
4. Has your group discussed strategies and procedures for attaining your goals? Have you identified any effective procedures?
5. Does each member of your group have a role, that is, unique responsibilities to help your group do its work? On the back, list the name of each group member and his or her specific responsibilities.
6. Does your group have the resources (member skills and knowledge, time, and other essentials) that it needs to achieve its goals?

Source: Walker, 1995, pp. 4–5.

helps to steer faculty and students around sensitive personal and interpersonal matters that can often create major problems.

There are a variety of instruments available for use in developing your own teaching priorities. For example, a number of years ago Elizabeth Jones, under a grant from the U.S. Department of Education, developed a useful *Writing Goals Inventory* (1994). By filling out the first three of the eight pages of this inventory, you can determine which criteria you will emphasize in assessing writing assignments (Resource P).

Simulations

Simulation, which can be used for almost every skill or real-life situation, assesses the students' ability to perform in lifelike situations. Games, role playing, and computer simulations all fall under this broad category. Although time-consuming and labor-intensive to set up, simulations permit you to project how your students might perform in real-world situations. You might use several of these instruments and procedures, alone or in combination, as appropriate during the teaching of your course and also during the field testing of specific instructional activities and materials.

Pilot Testing New Materials and Instructional Techniques

Obviously, if existing materials are not usable, new units must be designed, produced, and evaluated. The specific format and approach selected should be the easiest to use given the constraints of time and budget. The emphasis should be on the instructional goals rather than on a specific approach or equipment system. Under-used and over-technological lecture halls and many language laboratories, television production systems, and off-brand computers in storage on many campuses are mute testimony to instances in which the glamour of the hardware systems overshadowed rational decisions regarding their purchase and use.

To assist in this process, a short questionnaire called the MINI-QUEST can be used to evaluate a single unit, lesson, or sequence (Exhibit 15.3). Much useful data can be obtained from such a simple instrument. Student answers to the open-ended question also prove to be invaluable.

Exhibit 15.3.
MINI-QUEST Questionnaire for Student Evaluation of a Unit.
(For new instructional material, change "unit" to "material")

Date_____Unit Title_____

Course Title_____

Instructor_____

Please circle the most appropriate alternative.

1. Interest
The unit was
1) Very uninteresting
2) Uninteresting
3) Interesting
4) Very interesting

2. Pace
The unit was:
1) Much too fast
2) A little too fast
3) Just right
4) A little too slow
5) Much too slow

3. Amount Learned
I learned:
1) Nothing
2) Very little
3) A fair amount
4) A great deal

4. Clarity
The unit was:
1) Very unclear
2) Unclear
3) Clear
4) Very clear

5. Importance
What I learned was:
1) Very unimportant
2) Unimportant
3) Important
4) Very important

6. General
Generally, the material was:
1) Poor
2) Fair
3) Good
4) Excellent

7. Please indicate any questions raised by the unit.
8. Please write at least one specific comment here about the unit. (Use the back if necessary.)

Where to Start

Your first step will always be to identify the most important questions on which you want to focus your assessment. Fortunately, you have already addressed your primary focus when developing your statements of learning outcomes. As you move through the design process, you will be even more specific as you describe the exact behavior or attitudes that you require of your students if they are to be successful in meeting these goals.

We have also discussed two other resources that should prove to be extremely helpful as you establish your assessment priorities:

- Review Exhibit 7.1 in Chapter 7: Establishing the Need for Curriculum Design Projects.
- Resource O: Curriculum Review. The Questions to Ask.

Keep in mind that this information led you to redesigning an existing course or designing a new one in the first place. Also, make sure you pay attention to those non-discipline-specific core competencies that you have included in your statement of intended outcomes.

Keeping Students Informed: An Important Lesson

Don't be surprised if the general student reaction to the new course or procedure is not at first as positive as you might have hoped. Recent studies have shown that it is not unusual for student response to be more negative during the first run of a new or revised course, even when their achievement has improved significantly. This negative reaction tends to disappear during the semesters that follow. You can also reduce this reaction by keeping students informed of what you are trying to do and of what you have learned as you move along.

At times, particularly during the initial trial of a program, it is essential that the students involved in the experimental or pilot group be kept informed of what is happening and what you are learning. Providing information to the students during this period serves several purposes. First, it gives the program credibility. Students know that you are listening to them and that you care. Second, as a result, they are willing to tolerate the intrusion of evaluation and may improve the quality of the information they provide. And third, if problems occur, they tend to forgive and to be far more positive toward the whole experience than they might otherwise be. In one new project, the students were willing to overlook an unrealistically heavy workload when they were informed that as a result of their feedback, the assignments and time schedule were being changed for the next semester. A memorandum sent to students involved in the pilot run of the music course described in Case Study 15 not only covered test results by level and described the student attitudes toward the test and individual units but also discussed the changes that were being made based on their input. Finally, the memorandum stressed the importance of the information that the students had provided to the development team and thanked them for their assistance.

The "one-minute paper" is an excellent technique for collecting data and reporting to students. In this approach you ask your students, near the end of the class, to write a brief paper listing what they learned from the day's activities and what they did not understand. You then begin the next class by referring to their comments, answering questions, and addressing concerns. Remember, a course may not always proceed as you had hoped, and your students are the ones most affected by any problems.

A Final Word on Assessment

In the long run, your success as a faculty member will be determined by the performance of your students. The more successful they are in reaching the goals that you have established, the more successful you will have been as a teacher. As basic as this relationship is between student performance and teaching success, it is not unusual to find significant problems resulting from a major disconnect between what we say is important and the criteria we use to judge our students. As noted earlier, although our goals include higher-order reasoning abilities, the most frequently used assessment techniques tend to focus on recall and recognition.

The collection and use of data are essential to the success of this model. Clear and concise outcome statements, combined with an assessment program that measures how well your students reach these goals and that collects information on your course or program's individual elements, on student attitudes toward the program, and, if appropriate, on job placement and success after graduation, are essential to a quality education system. This process will ensure that your program will continually improve as new approaches and materials are implemented.

Without planned information collection and evaluation, the courses described in this book would not have reached the level of effectiveness that they have. Although some of the evaluation focuses on structure, other questions focus on the effectiveness of a single lesson, on the materials used, or on the content and goals of the course. In every project a wide range of questions can be asked, but limited time and resources require that you focus on the essentials. You and your colleagues are responsible for identifying which information is most important to collect and which questions should be asked. The assessment of your students' performance will be based on the goals that were established at the beginning of the design process.

The detail level of the questions asked, and the questions themselves, will vary depending on the reason for the evaluation, the problems that are perceived, and the resources and time that are available for the evaluation itself. First, it is important that essential questions not be overlooked simply because no one thought of them when the evaluation was being designed, and second, that quality information, once collected, is effectively used to improve the learning of your students.

Resources

Cambridge, B. L. (ed.). *Electronic Portfolios: Emerging Practices in Student, Faculty, and Institutional Learning.* Sterling, Va.: Stylus Publishing, 2001.

> Examines the use of electronic portfolios through interlinks. If you're involved in distance-learning or other nontraditional approaches to teaching, you should take a look.

McGonigal, K. "Getting More 'Teaching' out of 'Testing' and 'Grading.'" *Speaking of Teaching,* 2006, *15*(2). Center for Teaching and Learning, Stanford University. Available at: www.http://ctl.stanford.edu/Newsletter.

The benefits of using assessment as a teaching tool. Describes the required elements and specific techniques. Ideal for addressing the requirements for learning outcomes and assessment.

Tomorrow's Professor (http://ctl.stanford.edu/Tomprof/postings. html).

Below are some of the specific issues that address assessment concerns. Issues are posted two weeks after publication. On the Web site you can also find a complete list of all past publications in the series.

> *#641: Lessons Learned in the Assessment School of Hard Knocks.* C. J. Haessig and A. S. LaPorta

> *#706: Quality and Performance Excellence in Higher Education: Lessons Learned.* C. W. Sorenson, J. A. Furst-Bowe, and D. M. Moen

> *#710: Three Levels of General Education Assessment.* M. J. Allen

> *#716: Learning About Student Learning from Community Colleges.* L. Shulman and P. Hutchings

> *#762: Student Portfolios: An Alternative Way of Encouraging and Evaluating Student Learning.* C. P. White

Wehlburg, C. M. *Meaningful Course Revision: Enhancing Academic Engagement Using Student Learning Data.* San Francisco: Anker/ Jossey-Bass, 2006.

Focuses on course evaluation, outcomes, and the process of continual revision.

Wilson, S. "The Disappointment of Portfolio-Based Teaching," *Inside Higher Ed,* Feb. 15, 2007. Available at http://insidehighered. com/views/2007/2/15/wilson.

An in-depth discussion of one faculty member's experience with using the portfolio approach in the teaching of writing. Don't read this article without reading the extensive comments that follow. Together they provide a comprehensive review of both the benefits and the difficulties with the approach.

PART THREE

Designing, Implementing, and Assessing the Learning Experience

CHAPTER 16

Designing the Learning Experience

The Research on Teaching and Learning

Figure 16.1.

Production, Implementation, and Evaluation for Each Course

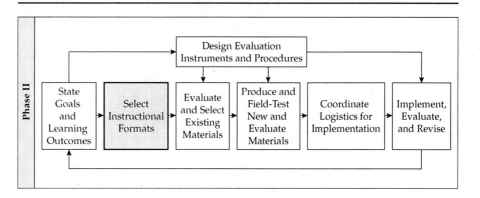

At this point in the design process, you've outlined the overall sequence of your course and identified your general goals and more specific learning outcomes. It is now time to shift your focus from these broader general issues to the more practical concerns of assessment and implementation. For example, how will you facilitate your students' reaching these goals? What will be your role and what will be your students' role? How can the time available be most effectively used? How and when should assessment take place? All are critical questions that each of us must address in every course that we teach. In reality you will often be working on both areas (assessment and implementation of the learning experience) simultaneously. This chapter and those that follow discuss the design of the actual learning experience in your course.

For most of the twentieth century designing the learning experience wasn't a particularly complex process. You knew from the beginning the general structure of your course, lecture, seminar or laboratory, or a combination of the three, how many class hours you had available, and, long before the course was to begin, you had selected your text and requested books to be placed on reserve in the library. You would also have reserved any video tapes or other media you might like to use so that the audio-visual department could schedule equipment delivery to your classroom, if needed. You also could safely assume that your students either lived on campus or in the nearby community and had the same general background as most of their peers.

The process slowly became more complex with the availability of more options, including television, overhead projectors, teaching machines, and programmed instruction. Some faculty in the sciences began to explore the effectiveness of "mastery learning" in their laboratory sections. During the last decade or so an entirely new range of instructional options have become available through advances in technology and experimentation on the part of creative faculty in college and universities throughout the world. As a result, the process of designing the learning experience has become far more challenging than ever before.

In fact the options available to you become more varied with each passing year. We've learned a great deal about teaching and learning in the last twenty years, with far more research available to you as you select your options and design the actual process of learning for your students.

Equally significant is the change that has been taking place in the students we have in our classrooms. Today's students tend to be more diverse, more job oriented, less skilled in reading, speaking, and mathematics, and with far less preparation in how to study than ever before. Although increasingly technologically literate, they also tend to have a shorter attention span, are less willing to read lengthy assignments, and rarely have the ability to transfer learning from one subject to another. In addition there is an increasing possibility that more and more of your students will be working part-time or that your teaching will be in a nontraditional or distance-learning setting.

In a recent issue of *Peer Review,* Crone and Mackay made the following observation about today's students:

Students appear to spend hours surfing Web sites, hanging out in groups, and updating their Facebook sites. They compete for multiple leadership positions from which they often fail to gain all they could because few focus fully on their responsibilities. They forfeit deeper engagement in academic research to earn minimum wage at a retail store in a nearby mall. . . . It is clear that the manner in which students are motivated to engage in higher education has been changing and will continue to change rapidly. The priority students affix to their education is too often usurped by increasingly demanding and time-intensive life priorities such as work, family, or emotional/psychological needs. Many members of this generation of students continue to live in an age of convenience and consumption. A college education has become commoditized, understood as yet another acquisition to be made rather than a process in which you engage. . . . In today's environment of convenience and consumption, how can students be persuaded to move beyond "commodity" thinking and fully engage both in and out of the classroom in activities that enhance their learning? How can they be inspired to become immersed in learning? . . . Rather than expend the time necessary to encounter new ideas, reflect, and make connections with their existing worldview, many of our students carefully budget the minimum amount of time necessary to allow them to achieve the grades they desire while fitting in as many other activities as they possibly can [2007].

In short, although you have far more research on teaching, learning, and student development to help you make design decisions, you also have far more options from which to choose in your effort to effectively teach a far less homogeneous group of students. To do this you will need a solid understanding of what we can learn from the research, a working knowledge of the options open to you, their strengths and limitations, and of what we know about working with adult learners and students from more diverse backgrounds. In addition, you will have to be sensitive to the significant differences in how men and women learn and behave in the classroom. This chapter, and the others in this section, are structured specifically to assist you in designing your course and in selecting and perhaps developing the support materials and assessment tools as needed.

In selecting the instructional approaches that are most appropriate for your course, three interrelated factors must be considered:

- The specific learning outcomes you want to reach (discussed in Chapter 13).
- The research on teaching and learning.
- The instructional options available to you. These could include structural options (lecture, small-group activities, out-of-class experiences), procedural, and technology options (media, computers, and so on), which will be discussed in some detail in the next chapter.

In many instances the design of our courses has been determined more by tradition, ease of implementation, or our own comfort level than by an in-depth look at these three factors.

As you design the learning experience for your course, do not let your personal preferences eliminate effective instructional options. You may have to try new techniques or get outside help from the academic-support center on your campus or from other faculty or staff, not necessarily an unpleasant experience.

The Changing Role of Faculty in the Learning Process

In Chapter 1 we mentioned briefly the shift that has been under way in how we describe the role that faculty have in the learning process—the move from being teaching-centered to being learning-centered. Robert Barr and John Tagg have described this shift as a move from the instructional delivery system, where faculty are conceived primarily as disciplinary experts who impart knowledge by lecturing, to the "learning paradigm," which conceives of faculty as primarily the designers of learning environments where they study and apply best methods for producing learning and student success (1995, p. 24).

Think Research: Think Scholarship

Although we haven't stressed the point, the steps you have been taking up to now and the steps that follow have been laying the groundwork for you to produce scholarly work that could have an impact far beyond your own course and classroom. You've identified a problem, established a specific set of instructional goals, and devised a plan for reaching them. You've collected information about your students, and, in the next stages of your design, you'll review the research, select your instructional strategies, design support materials, implement your plan, and then collect assessment data on whether or not you succeeded. You'll have information on what worked, what didn't work—and why. Best of all, because conducting this research will be an integral part of your teaching assignment, you will be improving your teaching and doing scholarship at the same time. In addition, there will be other advantages. The design and implementation of your course can often be viewed as a series of independent but interrelated research projects, and when you are finished, you will have in place all the elements needed to produce a series of reports or articles. And, most important, what you have done will be of interest to other faculty facing the same problems that you do, and to researchers involved in the study of teaching and learning.

Wilbert McKeachie, in his classic book on college teaching, *Teaching Tips,* made the following observation about this type of study, which has become known as "Classroom Research":

> Much of the progress made in understanding the practical aspects of teaching and learning has come from individual faculty members who have carried out studies in their own and colleagues' classes to get empirical evidence with respect to some issue, such as the effectiveness of some teaching innovation or the student characteristics affecting responses to some aspect of teaching or testing. Planning such a study is one of the best ways of clarifying your thinking, and in my experience, teachers who get involved in such studies become better teachers, not so much from the results per se as from the insights gained in doing and interpreting the research [1994, p. 339].

One of the books we recommend is *Classroom Assessment Techniques* by Thomas Angelo and K. Patricia Cross (1993), which focuses specifically on the type of data you will need to collect during and after you implement your course. Two additional publications you should check out are Caroline Kreber's *Exploring Research-Based Teaching* (2006) and *Classroom Research: Implementing the Scholarship of Teaching* by K. Patricia Cross and Mimi Harris Steadman (1996). As you will be doing a scholarly activity anyway, plan to get the most out of your efforts.

The Research on Teaching and Learning

Fortunately, the great amount of information on learning gives us an excellent starting point as we think through the design of our courses. Unfortunately, many of us have not paid much attention to this body of literature, as evidenced by our heavy reliance on the lecture, which is *the most common means of instruction used on college campuses and one of the least effective and most limited instructional methods available to us.*

The most comprehensive review on the research of how people learn is a report from the National Research Council published by the National Academy Press, *How People Learn: Brain, Mind, Experience, and School* (Bransford, Brown, and Cocking 1999). Many of the conclusions that the authors reach will have a direct bearing on the work you will do as you move ahead in the design process and on the decisions that you will have to make. Among them:

- It is not simply general abilities such as memory or intelligence, nor the use of general strategies that differentiate experts from novices. Instead, experts have acquired extensive knowledge that affects what they notice and how they organize, represent, and interpret information in their environment. This in time affects their abilities to remember, reason, and solve problems.

- Skills and knowledge must be extended from the narrow contexts in which they are initially learned. . . . It is essential for the learner to develop a sense of when what has been learned can be used, the condition of application.
- Learning must be guided by generalized principles in order to be widely applicable. Knowledge learned at the level of rote memory rarely transfers.
- Different kinds of learning require different approaches to teaching.
- Feedback is fundamental to learning . . . but scarce. What are needed are formative assessments,[1] which provide students with opportunities to revise and improve the quality of their thinking and understanding.
- If the goal is to enhance understanding and the applicability of knowledge, it is not sufficient to provide assessments that focus primarily on memory for facts and formulas.
- Because many new technologies are interactive, it is now easier to create environments in which students can learn by doing, receive feedback, and continually refine their understanding and build new knowledge [Bransford, Brown, and Cockling, 1999].

One additional benefit of this report is that it's online (http://books.nap.edu/html/howpeoplel/notice.html) and easy to use. Some of the recommendations focus on K–12, but most apply directly to higher education.

Another excellent resource is Lion Gardiner's *Redesigning Higher Education* (1996), one of the books you should already have in your library. In it you will find an excellent review of the literature and a comprehensive reference section. The information is practical and will be relevant to you as you design the learning experience for your students.

Research Findings on the Lecture

- The lecture is the principal method of instruction in higher education (used about 80 percent of the time).
- Lectures tend to focus primarily on low-level factual materials, with about 90 percent of all questions based on recall.

---

[1]Formative assessment is that data collected for the primary purpose of improving learning.

- A significant number of questions asked during a lecture (about 30 percent) result in no participation by students.

- The students who benefit most from the lecture are those with stronger academic profiles and those from families of higher socioeconomic status.

- When large lecture courses are combined with minimal out-of-class contact with other students and the faculty member, the gap between the quality of the academic experience for residential and commuting students widens significantly. [Primarily from Gardiner, 1996]

Research Findings on Instructional Methods and Learning

Although the lecture is an effective way to transmit low-level factual material, discussion is far more effective for the retention of information, the transfer of knowledge to other applications, problem solving, and changes in attitude.

- Active involvement by students is more effective than passive listening and note taking.

- Learning can take place through several sensory channels; the more channels engaged in learning, the better.

- Compared with competitive or individual learning, cooperation (cooperative learning) leads to greater reasoning ability and higher self-esteem.

- Teaching is more effective when the instructional methods used take into account the diverse ways in which students learn.

- The impact of college is determined largely by the student's effort and involvement in both academic and non-academic activities.

- Students succeed best in developing higher-order thinking skills when such skills are reinforced throughout the education program.

- Changes in students' ability to think critically are significantly and positively correlated with levels of praise from faculty, interaction among students and faculty, and high-level cognitive responses from other students in class.

- Unlearning what is already known is more difficult than learning new information. Identifying misconceptions and correcting them through active discussion and involvement with other students is essential.

- To be remembered, new information must be meaningfully connected to prior knowledge, and it must be remembered in order to be learned.
- New information organized in personally meaningful ways is likely to be retained, learned, and used.
- There is a direct correlation between hours spent studying and all academic outcomes.
- Prior knowledge and experience generally make more difference than intellectual ability in learning success.
- High expectations encourage high achievement.
- Motivation to learn is alterable; it can be affected by the task, the learning environment, the teacher, and the learner.
- Over 50 percent of students report studying five or fewer hours per week.
- Professors rate their own teaching very highly (over 90 percent rate themselves above average or superior).
- There is a positive correlation between the frequency of out-of-class contact between students and faculty and student retention of material and social intellectual development.
- Students tend to routinely use study methods that are known not to work (such as rereading textbooks) and must be taught how to learn effectively.
- Research does not support a positive correlation between the quality of faculty research and the quality of teaching. [Primarily from Gardiner, 1996, and Angelo, 1993]

In the next chapter you will find a number of excellent resources that offer practical suggestions on the use of a wide range of instructional approaches. Many of these include excellent sections on the research related to the approach(es) they are discussing.

Another excellent and brief reference is *The Seven Principles for Good Practice in Undergraduate Education* by Chickering, Gamson, and Barsi (1989). This booklet provides an excellent self-assessment checklist that you can use to compare what you are doing in your courses with what a group of national leaders in education believe is ideal. The inventory is also an excellent way to review instructional strategies you might use in your classes.

The field of psychology has long been an additional source of research on effective teaching. In 1960 Goodwin Watson provided a thirteen-point review of the literature that is as relevant today as it was then. Coming from a psychological perspective, this review provides you with the following additional useful suggestions:

Seven Principles for Good Practice in Undergraduate Education: Representative Items

1. Good practice encourages student-faculty contact.

   I know my students by name by the end of the first two weeks of the term.

   I take students to professional meetings or other events in my field.

2. Good practice encourages cooperation among students.

   I encourage my students to prepare together for classes or exams.

   I create "learning communities," study groups, or project teams within my courses.

3. Good practice encourages active learning.

   I encourage students to challenge my ideas, the ideas of other students, or those presented in readings or other course materials.

   I give my students concrete, real-life situations to analyze.

4. Good practice gives prompt feedback.

   I return examinations and papers within a week.

   I give my students the opportunity to schedule conferences with me to discuss their progress.

5. Good practice emphasizes time on task.

   I clearly communicate to my students the minimum amount of time they should spend preparing for class.

   If students miss my classes, I require them to make up lost work.

6. Good practice communicates high expectations.

   I make clear my expectations orally and in writing at the beginning of each course.

   I encourage students to write a lot.

7. Good practice respects diverse talents and ways of learning.

   I select reading and design activities related to the background of my students.

   I try to find out about my students' learning styles, interests, or backgrounds at the beginning of each course.

Source: Chickering, Gamson, and Barsi, 1989

---

1. Behaviors which are rewarded (reinforced) are more likely to recur.
2. Sheer repetition without indications of improvement or any kind of reinforcement is a poor way to attempt to learn.
3. Threat and punishment have variable and uncertain effects upon learning; they may set up avoidance tendencies which prevent further learning.
4. Reward (reinforcement), to be most effective in learning, must follow almost immediately after the desired behavior and be clearly connected with that behavior in the mind of the learner.

5. The type of reward (reinforcement) which has the greatest transfer value to other life situations is the kind one gives oneself, that is, the sense of satisfaction in achieving purposes.

6. Opportunity for fresh, novel, stimulating experience is a kind of reward which is quite effective in conditioning and learning.

7. Forgetting proceeds rapidly at first—then more and more slowly; recall shortly after learning reduces the amount forgotten.

8. The most effective effort is put forth when tasks are attempted that fall in the "range of challenge"—not too easy and not too hard—where success seems quite possible but not certain.

9. Students are more apt to throw themselves wholeheartedly into any project if they themselves have participated in the selection and planning of the enterprise.

10. Reaction to excessive direction by the teacher may be: (a) apathetic conformity, (b) defiance, (c) scapegoating, or (d) escape from the whole affair

11. Over-strict discipline is associated with more conformity, anxiety, shyness, and acquiescence in students; greater permissiveness is associated with more initiative and creativity in students.

12. What is learned is most likely to be available for use if it is learned in a situation much like that in which it is to be used and immediately preceding the time when it is needed.

13. If there is a discrepancy between the real objectives and the tests used to measure achievement, the latter becomes the main influence upon choice of subject matter and method [Watson, 1960].

Summary

As you address this primary issue of what you and your students will be doing inside and outside your classroom, review the research and think about how you might adapt these ideas in designing your course and planning for what you will be doing on a day-to-day basis; this will prove to be very good use of your time as you work to improve the quality of your students' learning experience. The clearer your vision of where you want to go, the more you understand the research about teaching and learning, and the more you know about the advantages and disadvantages and constraints of the instructional options available to you, the better your decisions will be.

Resources

There are many excellent sources on the research on teaching and learning to which you should have access as you design the learning experience for your students. The following will get you started:

Bransford, J. D., Brown, A. L., and Cocking, R. R. (eds.). *How People Learn: Brain, Mind, Experience, and School.* Washington, D.C.: National Academy Press, 1999.

Gardiner, L. F. "Redesigning Higher Education: Producing Dramatic Gains in Student Learning." *ASHE Higher Education Report,* 23(7). San Francisco: Jossey-Bass, 1996.

McKeachie, W. J., and Svinicki, M. *McKeachie's Teaching Tips: Strategies, Research, and Theory for College and University Teaching.* (12th ed.) Boston: Houghton Mifflin, 2006.

Pascarella, E., and Terenzini P. *How College Affects Students: A Third Decade of Research.* Vol. 2. San Francisco: Jossey-Bass, 2005.

Cooper, J. L. "A Baker's Dozen Ideas to Foster Engagement." *Exchanges: The Online Journal of Teaching and Learning.* California State University, Dec. 12, 2006. Also available at the *Tomorrow's Professor* Web site at http://ctl.standford.edu/tomprof/postings.html (TSP msg #796).

CHAPTER 17

Designing the Learning Experience

Your Instructional Options

Figure 17.1

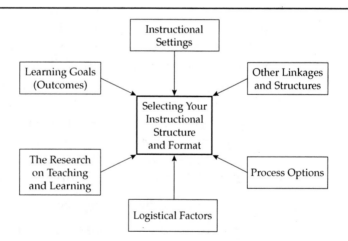

Focusing once more on the goals you have for your course and basing your decisions on what we know about learning, your next challenge is to lay out in detail the actual design of your course. In the process you will focus on two main areas, the sequence of instruction and the approaches you will use in your teaching. In this phase you will match the process of learning with your instructional goals in the most effective way possible.

199

Before you can determine the best structure, sequence, and instructional design for your course, you will need to answer important questions, consider a number of factors, and explore many options. The goals you have for your students, their entering abilities, backgrounds, the setting in which you are teaching, the instructional options available to you, the resources and time you and your students have available will all be key elements in the decision-making process. In the long run it will be up to you, based on your own experience and on the research and resources available, to make the best decision for your students.

Building the Assessment Process into Your Design _____

You will need to consider when and how you will assess your students. In some instances assessment will occur at regular intervals during the semester and at the end of the course. In some course designs, student assessment is an integral element within each instructional segment; in others, it may be the primary focus of the course itself.

For example, in developing a capstone course for a program in marine biology, your goals for the student might include demonstrating the ability to function as part of a team, to be able to apply problem-solving principles and critical thinking skills in addressing a "real-world" problem, and then to demonstrate oral and written communications skills in communicating the results of their efforts. The challenge you would face in this type of course is designing an instructional sequence for your students that would allow you, at the end of the experience, to judge the ability of each student to meet these goals. In this instance you would need to ask a number of key questions that would directly impact the overall design and content of your course. For example:

- If students are to work in teams, how are teams formed?
- What opportunities exist for specific projects?
- What type of assessment procedures will you need?
- If students are part of a team, how can you best determine the quality of the work and contributions of each student on that team?
- What additional instruction and information will students require?
- Should projects be assigned to teams or should you give them the opportunity to choose from a number of options?
- Is there a specific problem-solving sequence that you wish teams to follow? Has it already been taught? If not, when and how should this be accomplished?

A Note of Caution

One of your greatest challenges will be to select that combination of instructional options that is most appropriate for you, your students, and your subject matter and instructional goals. As we describe a number of these options and identify questions that you should ask along the way, there is one additional issue that you should keep in mind. One of the most troubling tendencies is for this decision at times to be impacted by forces that have little to do with what you are attempting to accomplish. In too many instances we find that the decision on how to teach was determined—more than by any other factor—by pressure from advocates of a particular approach, the glamour of technology, or by the effectiveness of advertising by manufacturers. In some instances it is the least expensive, most easily implemented approach that can prove to be the most effective. For this reason, you want to specify your goals, outcomes, and priorities and identify the problems you are addressing before you make any decision as to how you will teach and which technologies you will use.

The Impact of Technology

There is little question that today, as a faculty member, you have far more instructional options available to you than ever before. Nowhere is this more apparent than in the area of technology, when at the same time as your options are expanding, your students are becoming more sophisticated technologically.

In *How People Learn: Brain, Mind, Experience, and School,* the authors made the following observations:

A number of the features of new technologies are consistent with the principles of a new science of learning.

Key conclusions:

- Because many new technologies are interactive, it is now easier to create environments in which students can learn by doing, receive feedback, and continually refine their understanding and build new knowledge.
- Technologies can help people visualize difficult-to-understand concepts, such as differentiating heat from temperature. Students are able to work with visualization and modeling software similar to the tools used in non-school environments to increase their conceptual understanding and the likelihood of transfer from school to non-school settings.
- New technologies provide access to a vast array of information, including digital libraries, real-world data for analysis, and connections to other people who provide information, feedback, and inspiration, all of which can enhance the learning of teachers and administrators as well as students.

- There are many ways that technology can be used to help create such environments, both for teachers and for the students whom they teach. However, many issues arise in considering how to educate teachers to use new technologies effectively. What do they need to know about learning processes? About the technology? What kinds of training are most effective for helping teachers use high-quality instructional programs? What is the best way to use technology to facilitate teacher learning? Good educational software and teacher-support tools, developed with full understanding of principles of learning, have not yet become the norm [Bransford, Brown, and Cocking, 1999, pp. 11–12].

The final sentence here is important. Although more and more instructional materials are coming on the market, many are not well designed. Make sure you check them out before you use them with your students. Technology impacts teaching and learning in two other ways that you should take into consideration as you design the instructional structure of your class: multitasking and changes in class attendance. Both are significant in the impact they can have on student learning.

- *Multitasking.* Today's student lives in a world of doing several things at the same time. It is not uncommon to find students in a lecture hall reading their e-mails, sending and receiving messages, and surfing the web as they are listening to what is going on in the classroom. When homework is being done you can add to the mix listening to music, talking on the phone, and watching television.
- *Diminishing Class Attendance.* On most campuses decreasing class attendance has become a major problem with fewer and fewer students attending class on a regular basis.

Both of these problems directly impact the quality of teaching and learning, which leads to the obvious question, what can you, as a teacher, do about this situation?

Some faculty have found that ensuring that what goes on in the classroom does not duplicate what students can get from the text or from other class materials can make a difference in class attendance. Interestingly, some of the brightest students have the poorest attendance records, as they have learned to spend their energies on those activities that produce the greatest benefit. If they can get what they need from the textbook or other sources, why bother going to class? Multitasking during class can also be reduced by making sure that activities during class require active participation on the part of your students. For more on the issues of class attendance, see "Elephant Not in the Room," by Elia Powers (2007). You will find more information on uses of technology in the chapters that follow.

Beyond Outcomes: Student Engagement _____

In his review of the literature and the findings from *The National Survey of Student Engagement* that he directs, George Kuh observed that the key to academic success is student engagement in the process of learning "by being engaged—sometimes not represented in outcome measures—students develop habits that promise to stand them in good stead for a lifetime of continuous learning" (2007). From his research, Kuh recommends six specific actions:

- Teach first-year students as early as possible how to use college resources effectively.
- Make the classroom the focus of community. (Note: for commuting students this is the only time these students have the opportunity of having face-to-face contact with faculty and other students.)
- Develop networks and early-warning symptoms to support students when they need help.
- Connect every student in a meaningful way with some activity with a positive role model.
- If a program or practice works, make it widely available.
- Remove obstacles to student engagement and success [2007].

As you design your course, keep in mind that although these recommendations are sometimes more difficult to implement, they are equally important for adult, commuting, part-time, and distance-education students as they are for traditional students, and you, as faculty, play the central role in ensuring that these conditions exist in every course you teach. This is particularly important if the course is one of the first that your students take. Administrators can play an important role in supporting your initiatives, but you, as the main interface with your students, must be the primary facilitator of the learning process. For specific suggestions on what you can do in each of these six areas, see Kuh's essay "How to Help Students Achieve" (2007).

Factors to Consider _____

In this chapter we discuss the various factors that you will need to consider as you design your course. Not all factors will be equally important for your situation, and in some instances certain options may not be available or relevant. The key is making sure that you explore all options that are available.

Distance Learning

If your course is designed for students studying off campus, a number of on-campus resources and options will not be available to them. This is important to keep in mind. It also may be that some of the discussion that follows will not be applicable to those planning to teach in distance formats. More applicable approaches will be discussed in some detail in Chapter 19, but we recommend that you still go through the process described in sections that follow. You will have to address many of the same issues as faculty teaching a course on campus and will be able to apply many of the same instructional options. However, there are major differences. You will have to provide your off-campus students with a far more structured support system than for your on-campus students, and you certainly will have to be far more creative in your use of technology. As you design your instructional sequence also keep in mind that, in the traditional classroom, you have the ability to respond immediately to student concerns and questions. Immediate response and adjustment in the content of instruction is not possible in asynchronous distance education.

Logistical Factors

In every class that you teach there will be a number of logistical factors that will have a direct bearing on the design of your course and the instructional options that are available to you. Key among them are:

- The number of students in your class, their ages, and their majors or intended majors.
- The competencies, attitudes, experiences, and knowledge students bring to the course.
- The amount of time your students can devote to course-related work outside of formal instruction periods.
- Whether the instruction takes place on or off campus, and where the students live. Students living near your campus have options not available to students who need to travel long distances. This problem is particularly acute in many graduate programs with numbers of working adults enrolled.
- The instructional time you have available, including time between sessions (there are significant differences in the time available for students to study outside of class between courses taught on campuses using the semester system than there are for those taught during trimesters or summer sessions).

- The number of faculty and graduate students assigned to the course and other human resources that may be available.

Some logistical options to consider as you move ahead

- *Making time available for teamwork.* One of the logistical challenges you may face is how to build in team projects when a number of your students in an on-campus class are working or commuting. Building on the approach long used in the sciences, consider scheduling a three-credit course to meet for two-hour sessions or two one-hour and one two-hour sessions. The extra hour then becomes available for students to work in teams and allows you to schedule two-hour sessions for examinations, special presentations, and so on.

- *Survey your students on the first day of class.* In earlier chapters we discussed the importance of collecting information about your students as early as possible. This information will allow you to find out if your students have the prerequisites you hope for (a short math quiz can easily be included) as well as help you relate the content of your course to the specific priorities of your students. In addition, you will often find students who, based on previous work experiences or class work, can serve as mentors to other students.

- *Use resource people.* Don't overlook the benefits of using outside guests in your class. Keep in mind, however, that every guest must be carefully chosen and have a clear picture of what their specific role is to be. You can find an amazing pool of available talent both on and off campus. Don't overlook the potential of using other faculty, alumni, business and government leaders, and the often overlooked resource of retired people living in your community. As Diamond and Allshouse point out in "Utilizing America's Most Useful Resource" (2006), this group can serve as guest lecturers, members of panels, special advisors to students working on team projects, and as tutors or mentors to students who can use additional assistance or who are interested in addressing advanced topics that may interest them. In addition, retired people can bring to your classroom life experiences that may have nothing to do with their specific professional field of expertise. These individuals can also be of assistance in courses taught in nontraditional settings. Don't be afraid to ask. Most of these folks enjoy being of assistance and are usually available at no cost to you or to your institution.

Instructional Setting

Learning can take place in a number of locations, large lecture halls or auditoriums, traditional classrooms, seminar or conference rooms, laboratories, studios, your office, in off-campus locations, in the student's home or office, or in any combination of these. Although lecture halls, classrooms, laboratories, and studios have been around almost since the beginning of higher education, new technologies are making possible options that add an entirely new dimension to teaching. If your project is to redesign an existing course, you may find that, for the upcoming semester, a decision has already been made regarding where the instruction will be taking place. If you believe that another setting would be preferred, check to see if other options are still available. If not, do the best with what you have and plan to phase in major changes over several semesters. Just don't be discouraged.

Some faculty try to avoid teaching large groups, but this is not always possible. You may find it necessary to include lecture sections in your design for many reasons: a cost-saving approach by your institution, the large number of students registering for your course, the need to administer group tests, or the inability of your department to staff multiple sections. Fortunately, technology is changing the actual configurations of large lecture halls and new approaches to teaching now make it possible for you to significantly change the total feel of the large room experience. We will explore this in more depth in later chapters.

Process Options

In addition to the range of locations in which teaching and learning may take place, there are a number of instructional design options available to you as you structure the learning experience.

• *Mastery learning.* First introduced by Fred Keller (1968) this approach, then called *personalized instruction,* guides the student, step by step, to clearly defined goals. The emphasis in this method is on the design and structure of the sequence of the course with grading of each major step in the process based on clearly articulated and measurable outcomes. Mastery learning, combined with the branching logic first developed in the early days of programmed instruction, are the basics behind many of the computer-based learning modules we use today.

• *Self-pacing.* This approach allows students to move through an independent study unit or an entire course at their own speed based on their ability to pass a test designed for this purpose. Testing is an integral component of mastery learning and is most useful when you expect your students to learn at different rates. Self-pacing requires both excellent instructional materials designed specifically for independent study and often the availability of one-on-one counseling and tutoring. Although useful in many instructional situations, this is often the most effective approach to use when your classes include students with different entry levels.

- *Exemption and remediation.* Part of the formal structure of the course itself, this approach exempts some students from segments of a course or assigns additional work to others to correct a deficiency in entering competencies. It requires both a high-quality testing program and a well-designed remedial sequence. A formal session can be made available for those who require additional work in an area, but a computer-based instructional unit or even a programmed text can be selected to accomplish this in a cost-effective manner without any formal instruction on your part.

- *Content options.* Ideal for use in a course where you have students enrolled from different majors or who have different interests, this approach allows students to choose from assignments that are all designed to meet the same learning objective. These assignments could range from writing about a topic in the student's major area of interest to applying a problem-solving approach that you have introduced to an issue the student chooses.

- *Flexible credit.* When you assign some students additional work or wish to allow others the option of doing additional work in an area that interests them, the use of flexible credit can make a great deal of sense. Continuous registration allows students to enroll in extra credit options during the course after they've reached a certain level of proficiency. In some instances the remedial work, although required, is not awarded additional credit. Some institutions have a system that also allows you to grade each credit independently and for each credit to be listed in this way on the student's transcript, an important advantage for the student. It also makes grading much easier when you do not have to combine work from a number of areas into a single grade.

- *Active learning.* One of the most significant changes that has occurred in teaching over the last two decades has been the increased emphasis on student-faculty and student-student interaction. The traditional lecture format, where the instructor talks and the students (we hope) take notes, has been replaced by a number of approaches designed to increase student involvement and improve learning. In McKeachie's *Teaching Tips* (2006), L. Dee Fink's *Creating Significant Learning Experiences* (2003), and in *Engaging Large Classes* (2002), edited by Christine Stanley and M. Erin Porter, you will find a number of techniques to actively involve your students. A number of these will be described in the chapters that follow. In addition, new feedback systems can provide you with effective alternative methods for getting feedback from your students in both on-campus and distance-learning courses.

You will find examples of how these options have been used in many of the course and curriculum case studies in this book. To use some of these options (such as flexible credit and self-pacing), you will need to check with the Registrar to see if they are or could be available at your institution, For more information on the benefits and use of these two approaches, see Case Study 5, The Flexible Credit and Continuous Registration System.

Other Linkages and Structures

There are a number of structured approaches that you should consider as you design your course. They sometimes overlap, but each has a specific emphasis. The key in deciding to use them will be the match between the benefits of the technique and the specific goals that you have for your course. In most cases they require linking your course to experiences that take place outside of regularly scheduled class sessions. Off-campus practicums and internships are fairly common in professional schools where practical experience has long been perceived as an essential component of the academic experience, but these approaches have only recently begun to be utilized effectively in undergraduate arts and science programs.

Learning Communities

The focus in this approach is to integrate learning across courses by focusing on a major issue or theme. The faculty involved in the two (or more) linked courses work together to integrate all elements and activities with the focus of exploring the common topic or reading through the lenses of the different disciplines. Learning communities might focus on such diverse topics as the history of women's rights, diversity and culture, or the development of the city. At some institutions, students involved in these activities are housed together or provided lounge space in resident halls for group meetings. In others, learning communities are a campuswide initiative that concludes with a senior-year experience for all students. The research on teaching and learning also suggests that this approach is appropriate for the structure of required core programs for students in a variety of academic problems. For more on learning communities see *Sustaining and Improving Learning Communities* (2004), by Laufgraben, Shapiro, and Associates; *Creating Learning Communities* (1999) by Shapiro and Levine: or *Learning Communities* (2005) by Smith, MacGregor, Matthews, and Gabelnick.

Community Service or Service Learning

Sometimes linked with learning communities, these programs focus on providing students with experiences in the community that are directly related to the focus of the individual course in which they are enrolled. For example, students from history, geography, art, and English could work together to develop a public display depicting the evolution of a particular neighborhood, or students in graphics design, advertising, or public relations could assist a local service agency in developing a brochure and information campaign describing its services to potential clients. The goal here is to assist communities in addressing actual problems while expanding students' professional skills and helping them develop a sense of citizenship. This approach, similar to learning communities, has the additional benefits of building interpersonal skills and demonstrating the effectiveness of teamwork when each individual brings to that team different strengths and perspectives. For more on this approach, see "Engaged Learning and the Core Principles of Liberal Education" in *Peer Review* (Association of American Colleges and Universities, 2007).

Cooperative Education

In this approach, your students alternate time in your class with professionally paid work directly related to their fields of study. This approach is now available in over 500 institutions. For example, the University of Cincinnati recently reported over 3,800 students in forty-four disciplines participating in cooperative education programs in and outside the United States. The financial and professional benefits of this approach to students are significant. The specific arrangements vary a great deal, with some partnerships involving government, for-profit or nonprofit organization and institutions from a number of countries. For an excellent overview of the scope of cooperative arrangements see *New Times, New Strategies: Curricular Joint Ventures.*

Internships

Internships, with or without credit, are also being structured into more and more courses. The key is to ensure that the internship assignment relates directly to your goals and course of study. Political science students could, as part of a course, volunteer in the office of a town supervisor, work in a political campaign, or serve on the staff of a community project. A graduate student in a course on assessment or evaluation could be assigned to help another department develop a survey instrument; to collect data from alumni; to be involved in the design and implementation of a community survey; or to help a school or college assess the effectiveness of an academic program. On a growing number of campuses there are offices established for the specific purpose of helping students find internship opportunities in doctors' and lawyers' offices, at newspapers, in government offices, and in businesses throughout the area. Often these unpaid internships lead to paid employment opportunities while the student is in school, and to full employment after graduation.

Simulations and Games

Games and simulations are extremely effective in providing your students with the opportunity to practice applying what they have been learning to "real-world" experiences. Earlier versions were in a board-game format, but most of the newer simulations are computer based. Simulations and games usually involve role-playing with students asked to play a specific role in a carefully structured exercise. The exact character of a simulation is determined by the purpose of the exercise and the content area of your course. With some simulations you have the ability to track your students through the process, see the questions they ask, the information they use, and the decision-making process they follow. Teamwork is also a major ingredient in most simulations. The best way to locate available simulations for use in your class would be through your disciplinary association, as most are specific to a particular field of study.

A Reminder About Core Competencies _____

Earlier, we discussed the importance of reinforcing in all courses the basic competencies introduced in the required core program of your institution. The Association of American Colleges emphasized the importance of institutionalizing these key lifelong competencies in their "Principles of Excellence" in *College Learning for the New Global Century* (2007). Without continual use and reinforcement of these skills throughout their college experience, our students will graduate unprepared for the years ahead.

Since one or more of the core competencies can be taught or applied in almost every course you teach, you should look for the opportunity to build these experiences into your assignments as you design the specific elements of your course. Using these skills as disciplinary focused is an ideal way to demonstrate their importance and to prepare students to use what they have learned after graduation. One example of this approach is the *writing-intensive courses* now found in many curricula. In these required courses, students are encouraged to write and revise reports and papers in a style appropriate to the specific discipline.

Another approach is to combine courses from two disciplines into a single course where the two content areas reinforce each other. For example, you could have an engineering course with a major speech requirement, or a business course with a significant focus on statistical analysis. In such situations, explore the possibility of cross-listing the courses in the two cooperating departments with the teaching load (usually one more credit than was originally assigned) shared, as appropriate, by both. A three-credit engineering course with a report-writing focus might be changed to four credits, with three credits remaining in the engineering department and one credit assigned to the faculty providing assistance in the writing aspect of the course The advantage of this approach is that teaching credit (that is, financial resources) flows to both units. This provides the resources needed to have faculty from engineering courses and from the writing or English program assigned to review and grade papers from the perspective of their respective disciplines, one looking at the accuracy of the content, the other on the quality of the writing itself.

Your Next Steps

Now you will have enough information to design in detail the specific instructional sequence for your course. Figure 17.2 provides an overview of the course design, implementation, and evaluation sequence. You should be able to identify where and when testing will take place, and if and when different instructional options are appropriate. Once the overall design is determined, it becomes

Figure 17.2.

Production, Implementation, and Evaluation for Each Course

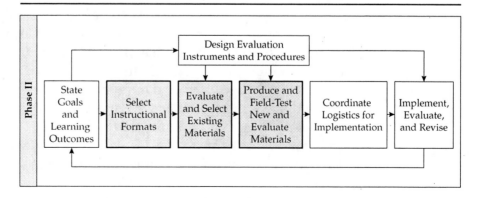

possible, for the first time, to identify possible uses of technology and to select among various instructional materials, student assessment techniques, and instruments. You will also be able to identify areas where you should consider developing your own materials. We strongly suggest that you read the remaining chapters in this section before you go too far along in the design process. The materials included can have a direct impact on the decisions you make.

Funds for Instructional Innovation

At this point in the process, you may feel the need for additional design help in technology or assessment, or for clerical assistance as you start designing your instructional materials and your assessment instruments. You may also have identified published materials or equipment you would like to purchase, a project you might like to visit, or a conference that you believe would prove to be helpful to you as you prepare to complete the work on your course. Although some additional support may be provided through your department, school, or college, and some folks on your campus may be willing to provide limited assistance at no charge, this may be the time to see if some funds may be available to help you complete your work. If you haven't done so already, explore the availability of support from your office of academic affairs. Many institutions have discretionary funds set aside specifically for academic innovation. If you established an external advisory committee for the design of your curriculum or course, you might also explore with them possible sources of assistance. The process you've been following, the description of what you have already accomplished and plan to do, combined with the supporting documentation you've already collected make a most powerful justification for funding support.

A Final Note on Selecting Your Design Options

Finally, as you move ahead to complete the design and overall structure of your course, and select from the various instructional approaches, keep in mind that (1) there always will be trade-offs, and (2) as long as you teach the course, revision will continue. Goals may change, new resources and options may become available, your discipline will evolve, and both you and your students may also change. In addition, you will learn of new instructional techniques, things you tried may not work as well as you might have liked, and you may simply not be able to do everything you had planned. You may find that some units will take far more time than you had anticipated, forcing you to delete some of the material that was to follow. As a result, you will need to make changes in the course design the next time you teach it. The important thing to keep in mind is that teaching is not an exact science and that surprises should always be expected.

Additional Resources

Throughout this chapter we have identified some of the resources that can help you decide on the structure and sequence of your course and how it will be taught. When it comes to teaching and learning, there are a great number of excellent sources of information already available, with new materials and research reports being published regularly. No matter which approach or combination of approaches you decide to use, the more you learn about a specific process, the more successful you'll be in using it.

Although we provide some ideas on where to find more detailed information on the individual teaching techniques, once you have determined the major instructional approaches you would like to explore further, we suggest that you take a few hours and head over to the teaching and learning center on your campus. The materials in their libraries are usually kept up-to-date and in them you will find a wealth of valuable information. The staff of these centers are also extremely helpful if you can't find the specific information you need. It will be time well spent. We hope that such a unit exists at your institution; if not, contact the *Professional and Organizational Network in Higher Education* (e-mail: podnetwork@ podweb.org). The primary focus of this network is the improvement of teaching and learning, and their members are always willing to help.

We suggest you start with three essential sources of information:

- *McKeachie's Teaching Tips*

    For an excellent introduction to what's going on in teaching, learning, and assessment, get your hands on the latest edition of *McKeachie's Teaching Tips: Strategies, Research and Theory for College and University Teachers*, by Wilbert McKeachie and Marila Svinicki. This work is published every few years; make sure you find one of the more recent editions. In it you will find brief but practical chapters on just about every approach to teaching and assessment.

- *Tomorrow's Professor*

  Each issue, approximately four to six pages, may include an entire essay, but more often is all or part of a carefully selected chapter of a recent publication, an article in a newsletter, or a research report. Issues are posted online two weeks after publication. It is an excellent way for you to get a sense of the focus and writing style of books before purchasing. Below are examples of issues that address course-specific concerns. Issues may be retrieved by number through the following link: http://ctl.stanford.edu/Tomprof/postings.html. On the site you can also find a complete list of all past publications in the series.

  #789: Engaged Learning (and the Core Purposes of Education). D. W. Harward

  #784: Integrative Learning: Putting the Pieces Together. M. Huber and M. Green

  #780: Homework Habits: If It Is Broken, Fix It. J. Beister, C. Saviz, and A. Fernandez

  #773: Why Problem-Based Learning? B. J. Duch, J. E. Groh, and D. E. Allen

  #771: Modalities of Teaching and Learning. D. N. Levine

  #757: Calling All Students . . . Come in Students. M. L. Rogers and D. A. Starrett

  #742: Fostering Student Learning and Success Through First-Year Programs. M. S. Hunter

  #738: Getting More Teaching out of "Testing" and "Grading." K. McGonigal

  #657: Student Services for Distance-Education Students. K. I. Roada

  #636: The Challenges of Teaching with Others. J. L. Laufgraben and D. Tomkins

There is one other resource we suggest you check out if you are considering using active learning, mastery learning, computer-based learning, or exploring alternative staffing patterns for your course:

Twigg, C. A. "New Models for Online Learning: Improving Learning and Reducing Costs." Sept./Oct. 2003, *Educause.*

Describes a national project supported by the Pew Charitable Trusts located at Rensselaer Polytechnic Institute. Involving thirty institutions, this project focused on individual courses and used a combination of approaches and instructional techniques to improve learning while reducing costs. The results are impressive. The report is available online from the Center for Academic Transformation Web site at www.center.rpi.edu/.

Although some of the resources listed below discuss more than one instructional approach, many, as their titles indicate, focus on a single technique. To assist you in identifying the publications that will be of greatest interest to you, we have grouped resources, when possible, by instructional approaches. Many of these materials also contain useful recommendations on implementation.

General

Erickson, B. L., Peters, C. B., and Strommer, D. W. *Teaching First-Year College Students.* San Francisco: Jossey-Bass, 2006.

> The latest research-based information on teaching first-year students. Practical, with many useful suggestions on teaching and assessment. Includes examples of active learning and dealing with different styles of learning.

Morrison, G. R., Ross, S. M., and Kemp, J. E. *Designing Effective Instruction.* San Francisco: Jossey-Bass, 2003.

> Provides a model for thinking through the actual design and implementation of your course. Could be extremely helpful as you move along.

Taylor Huber, M., and Breen, M. "Integrative Learning: Putting the Pieces Together." *Carnegie Perspectives #32.* Stanford, Calif. Also available on the *Tomorrow's Professor* Web site, http://ctl.stanford.edu/Tomprof/postings.html.

Active Learning

Amador, J. A., Miles, L., and Peters, C. B. *The Practice of Problem-Based Learning.* San Francisco: Anker/Jossey-Bass, 2007.

> Practical discussion of advantages and challenges of using problem-based learning. Includes sections on implementation and revision.

Bonwell, C. C., and Eison, J. A. "Active Learning: Creating Excitement in the Classroom." *ERIC Digest,* 1991, EDO-HE-91–01.

> This readable literature review, written primarily for faculty and academic leaders, synthesizes current research addressing

essential questions such as: What is active learning and why is it important? What obstacles prevent faculty from making greater use of active learning instructional approaches? How can these obstacles be overcome?

Stanford University Center for Teaching and Learning. "How to Create a Memorable Lecture," *Newsletter,* Center for Teaching and Learning, Stanford University, Winter 2005, *14*(1).

Specific suggestions for use in almost every classroom where lecturing is a part of the instructional pattern.

Stanley, C. A., and Porter, M. E. (eds.). *Engaging Large Classes: Strategies and Techniques for College Faculty.* San Francisco: Anker/ Jossey-Bass, 2002.

Practical advice from faculty at a number of institutions and in a wide range of disciplines.

Collaborating with Other Institutions

Plumb, C., and Reis, R. M. "Creating Change in Engineering Education: A Model for Collaboration Among Institutions." *Change,* May–June 2007.

Reviews the lessons learned from a cooperative project sponsored by the William and Flora Hewlett Foundation which involved schools of engineering at nine different institutions. Discusses such issues of K–12 and higher education cooperation, retention strategies, and collaborative process.

Problem-Based Learning

Duch, B. J., Groh, S. F., and Allen, D. E. (eds.). *The Power of Problem-Based Learning.* Sterling, Va.: Stylus, 2001.

A practical guide on using problem-based learning to increase student participation. Covers selecting problems and managing groups.

Portfolio-Based Teaching

Wilson, S. "The Disappointment of Portfolio-Based Teaching." *Inside Higher Ed,* Feb. 15, 2007. Available at http://insidehighered. com/views/2007/2/15/wilson.

An in-depth discussion of one faculty member's experience with using the portfolio approach in the teaching of writing. Don't read this article without reading the extensive comments that follow. Together they provide a comprehensive review of both the benefits and the difficulties with the approach.

Research as a Teaching Tool

Boyer Commission. *Reinventing Undergraduate Education: A Blueprint for America's Research Universities.* New York: DKA Associates, 2000.

> This report is from the Boyer Commission on Educating Undergraduates in the Research University which began its work under a Carnegie Foundation grant in 1995. After a brief introduction to the challenges facing research universities, the report describes ten projects at different research universities designed to improve the undergraduate experience.

Gurerman, L. "What Good Is Undergraduate Research Anyway?" *The Chronicle of Higher Education,* Aug. 17, 2007.

> The benefits as well as the challenges involved with undergraduate research. Important to read if you're considering this approach.

Kauffman, L., and Stocks, J. (eds.). *Reinvigorating the Undergraduate Experience.* Washington, D.C.: Council on Undergraduate Research, 2003.

> Twenty case studies from a variety of institutions that focus on the integration of research into the undergraduate curriculum. Highlights lessons learned, what can and cannot be done without external support, using difficult approaches, serving different student populations, and stressing the importance of process.

Service Learning: Involving the Community

American Council on Education. *New Times, New Strategies: Curricula Joint Ventures.* Washington, D.C.: American Council on Education, 2003.

> Describes cooperative curriculum projects in a wide range of disciplines and discusses models, strategies, and certification issues. Includes programs between units on the same campus, among different institutions, with community partners, and international associations.

Clarkson, J. (ed.). *In Safe Hands: A Global Concept of Service Learning in Higher Education.* Sterling, Va.: Stylus, 2007.

Describes a voluntary service program in developing countries developed by England's Liverpool Hope University. Down-to-earth, discusses problems faced in developing such a program and other key issues.

Jacoby, B. (ed.). *Building Partnerships for Service-Learning*. San Francisco: Jossey-Bass, 2003.

Focuses on improving teaching, learning, and research by working with community agencies, business, and industry in the design and delivery of instruction using service-learning.

National Service Learning Clearinghouse

www.servicelearning.org

Addresses getting college and university students and faculty actively involved with the community as well as all levels of education.

Simulations

Hertel, J. P., and Miller, B. *Using Simulations to Promote Learning in Higher Education*. Sterling, Va.: Stylus, 2002.

A comprehensive overview of designing and using simulation in your classroom.

Team-Based Learning

Michaelsen, L. K., Knight, A. B., and Fink, L. D. (eds.). *Team-Based Learning: A Transformative Use of Small Groups in College Teaching*. Sterling, Va.: Stylus, 2004.

Discusses the benefits and limitations of small-group and team activities. Practical suggestions on getting teams under way with a range of examples written by faculty from different disciplines.

Testing as a Teaching Tool

McGonigal, K. "Getting More 'Teaching' out of 'Testing' and 'Grading.'" *Speaking of Teaching*, Center for Teaching, Stanford University, 2006, 15(2). Available at www.http://cti.stanford.edu/Newsletter/.

The benefits of using assessment as a teaching tool. Describes the required elements and specific techniques. Ideal for addressing the requirements for learning outcomes and assessment.

CHAPTER 18

Using Technology to Support Learning

Wallace Hannum

One of the more obvious changes on university campuses in recent years is the use of technology. Courses previously taught by lecture and discussion now include online activities such as discussion forums, links to online readings, and group exercises. Some courses are taught entirely online with faculty and students never coming together in the same place or even at the same time. There is also a growing number of courses that combine both online and traditional instruction. The use of technology on campuses has been one of the most significant movements in higher education over the last decade. Several years ago Green (2000) reported that a third of all college courses have a Web page, 60 percent use e-mail, 40 percent include Web resources on the syllabus, and 55 percent of universities offer some online courses. The numbers continue to increase.

Mention technology on campus today and many people immediately think of students and faculty working with computers and the Internet. Of course, computers and the Internet are examples of technology, but they are not the only examples. Technology in education extends far beyond applications of communications hardware to include all the processes used for designing and delivering

Note: Portions of this chapter are based on materials by W. Hannum in "Technology in the Learning Process." In R. M. Diamond (ed.), *Field Guide to Academic Leadership.* San Francisco: Jossey-Bass, 2002.

instruction. Adding technology to the instructional mix without considering changes to the instruction itself might add some benefits, but these will be negligible. Technology is best when considered more broadly, when you totally rethink how to teach a course rather than just taking what you have always done and simply do the same thing, but with technology. For example, shifting teaching practices and materials to some form of a technology delivery system, such as placing lecture notes on a Web site, is the lowest form of technology use in instruction, and this change will add little in terms of improving the quality of your teaching and the learning of your students.

Benefits of Using Technology

There are many reasons to use technology in instruction. These include:

• *Enhanced Learning.* When used appropriately and thoughtfully, technology can enable students to learn more than they might learn sitting in lecture classes.

• *Increased Enjoyment and Engagement.* Although the primary outcome we seek is student learning, it is not altogether a bad thing if students also enjoy our courses. If they find our courses enjoyable, they are more likely to put forth extra effort and more likely to be more engaged in the instructional content. Technology used well has been shown to increase students' positive response to and engagement in courses.

• *Greater Job Relevance.* Because you are preparing students for a world in which technology is ubiquitous, especially in the world of work, you should make use of technology on campus. When universities use technology widely, they better prepare students for their futures. Indeed, skills in using technology have become a basic required competence for work in most occupations.

• *It's Expected.* Technology is so accepted in our society that parents and students alike expect universities to use technology widely in their programs. Employers also expect students to have used technology in school.

• *Improved Quality.* If instruction is carefully designed and delivered with technology, it can be of higher quality than traditional instruction—whether you use PowerPoint presentations in the classroom, assign computer simulations as homework, or offer classes entirely online.

• *Increased Quantity.* Technology can improve the amount of instruction available to students in terms of the breadth and depth of instruction available to students. Technology-based classes are not limited to the textbook, readings, and notes from lecture sessions. Through technology, a wide array of instructional materials can now be available to your students via the Internet.

- *Improved Access.* Students can now have access to your resource materials at any time. In addition, distance learning enabled with technology makes instruction available to many people who would otherwise not have such access. On campus, the use of technology makes instruction more widely available outside of the regular class times. Office hours can also be made available electronically, instead of requiring students to come to campus to talk with faculty.

- In addition to the above benefits, technology can also be a change agent that helps you rethink *how* to teach. When technology plays such a role, there are a number of additional benefits; these include:

- *Instructional Model.* Technology can change the roles of both instructors and students. If implemented in a thoughtful way, following systematic course design principles that include active learning, technology can alter the dominant instructional model from students passively receiving information to having a more active role in their learning process. Students engaged more directly with learning enhance their understanding of the subject matter when under the guidance and coaching of faculty.

- *Modes of Representation.* Technology allows students to gain access to knowledge in more than one mode. Reading and listening to lectures are both highly symbolic activities that are removed from the events and objects they describe. Through technology, students can interact with representations of the material they are studying, seeing and hearing phenomena and controlling interactions, such as in simulations. Multimedia presentations allow students a greater range of stimuli.

- *Deep Processing and Understanding.* When students learn with technology, it can enhance their deep processing of content and provide a richer understanding. These approaches can shift the learning from rote memorization of facts presented in textbooks or lectures to a deeper interaction with the content and a richer understanding of concepts and principles.

Keep in mind that while proponents argue for increased use of technology on campus, others argue against its use, especially against using technology in the form of distance learning to replace traditional classroom instruction. These opponents feel that faculty members interacting with students on campus do much more than simply dispense information, which, they say, is all that happens in distance learning. Considerable evidence challenges this view. Perhaps some of the opponents have seen unimaginative uses of technology where it was used to repackage old notes and not as part of a redesigned course. The key will always be how the use of technology improves the total quality of the learning experience.

Although widespread instructional use of technology may be a recent phenomenon on some campuses, there is a substantial history of technology use in education going back to World War II as well as a rich research base for us to understand its use and limitations. Hundreds of empirical studies of instruction using technology appear in the literature. Although sometimes inconclusive, in general the studies support the position that instruction delivered by technology is at least as good as traditional instruction and often produces greater learning. Students using technology also learn at faster rates than in traditional classrooms and report more favorable attitudes towards the instruction and the subject matter. But there's one caveat: *the research suggests that how technology is used to deliver instruction—a systematic design process—matters much more than what technology is used or even whether technology is used.*

Misuses of Technology

Reducing Costs by Replacing Faculty

It is tempting for some administrators and faculty to embrace technology, then convert existing instruction using some form of technology, such as placing content on a CD or Web site, and assume that this can replace traditional classroom instruction. The potential for technology to replace instructors is nothing new and dates back to the printing press, when it was thought that widely available and inexpensive books would replace teachers. It didn't and neither did other technologies, including the radio, which could deliver the audio presentations, nor television, which could deliver both the audio and visual portions of lectures. When computers were applied to deliver instruction directly to students in the form of computer-assisted instruction, it was thought that this, too, would replace faculty. Today, we have rich interactive multimedia and online courses, but these are not likely to replace faculty any more than books did. The reason why faculty cannot be replaced is a basic one: *quality instructors do more than dispense content; they motivate, they modify instruction to meet the needs of the student, and they design the entire learning experience.*

Changing Delivery but Not Content

Decades of evidence suggest that simply changing how you deliver instructional materials while retaining the same content—such as videotaping lecture classes and uploading them as streaming video on a Web site—adds little instructional value. Instead, faculty must redesign their courses to take full advantage of instructional possibilities offered by technology. Nowhere is this clearer than in distance-learning classes offered over the Internet. Some faculty post their lecture notes and readings on a Web site and consider this to be online instruction that can replace the traditional classroom. Distance learning offers the possibility of using technology to replace traditional classroom instruction, but doing the same thing with few changes is never an improvement and is often far worse.

Appropriate Uses of Technology

Taking Advantage of the Options

Instructional content and pedagogy must be modified to take full advantage of the possibilities that technology offers. It is important to build on what we know about the characteristics of effective teaching and then incorporate these into instruction delivered in part or whole by technology. Properly done, distance learning affords the opportunity to replace the traditional brick-and-mortar classroom—but does not replace the need for the instructor. Some form of instruction via technology can be combined with face-to-face instruction to create blended learning environments that have some of the benefits of both. Technology, when used well, allows faculty, students, and other experts to interact with each other and with content. More on quality distance learning will be found in the next chapter.

Technology to Supplement Instruction

You can use technology to supplement current instruction without having to offer your whole course via technology. For example, rather than drawing a diagram of a process on a blackboard, it is often far easier to use a computer with presentation software to project the diagram on a screen. Instead of making copies of resource materials to distribute to your class, you can put these materials on a Web page with links to an article to be downloaded and read, or to an audio or video file to listen to or view. You can place a copy of your notes on a course Web site and give students access to these, directly freeing them from the burden of extensive note taking. You could even record your lectures and make these available as audio files (podcasts) that students could download and listen to on their iPods or MP3 players. You can also make your course syllabus available in this way. However, experience has shown that the only way to make sure these materials are used is to refer to them constantly during discussion or lecture sessions and to make sure their content is an important part of the testing process. All these uses may offer some benefits; however, they obviously do not take full advantage of technology.

The foregoing are examples of using technology to accomplish something we've always been doing in instruction. As mentioned before, doing the same instructional activities but only changing their display or delivery format is not likely to add significant instructional value. The supplemental use of technology can make for more efficient use of your time and that of your students, but it cannot improve the quality of the overall learning experience.

Improving the Quality of the Learning Experience

Most significantly you can use technology to do things you were simply not able to do without it. For example, you can

- Use a computer simulation to show changes on an archaeological site over a period of centuries
- Use real-time computation of data from a space shuttle to explore physical forces
- Have students interact with complex engineering models to learn how to design electrical power plants
- Use virtual reality for your students to learn about chemical compounds by "walking" through them
- Use patient simulations to allow students to learn about diagnosis and treatment of diseases
- Use video-conferencing to bring authorities from around the world into your course to interact with your students
- Have students produce multimedia projects rather than written term papers
- Connect your students with students at other universities worldwide for collaborative group projects
- Introduce a richer depth and breadth of content in your course through using the Internet rather than being bound to a textbook

Guidelines for Using Technology Effectively _____

Successful learning requires quality instructional design. It does not happen by chance. Numerous people have suggested various principles for effective instruction, and there is considerable overlap. Rather than reviewing all the different recommendations that have been offered for effective college teaching, this section is organized around a set of seven principles for effective instruction in undergraduate teaching that were discussed by Chickering and Ehrmann (1996). These principles have been widely recognized in higher education as representing some of our *best practices* with regards to teaching.

Principle 1: Good Practice Encourages Student-Instructor Interaction

We have long known that good-quality interaction between students and faculty promotes effective learning. Outstanding faculty try to interact frequently and well with their students both inside the classroom and during office hours. Technology can add another dimension to this interaction, as it offers more ways to interact with our students when they are not physically present. An obvious example is e-mail, which faculty use routinely to interact with students. This extends both the quantity and quality of interactions over what is likely to happen during a class. E-mail allows students to ask you a question at night or on a weekend when they are reading and encounter a problem. Often students will hesitate to interrupt class to ask a question but will be more forthcoming via e-mail. This method gives them a little more time to formulate their question; it also gives you a little more time to formulate your response. In your reply you can also insert a direct link to a resource on the Web that will provide further assistance to the student. You can use a discussion forum for your whole class or for subsets to address issues that may begin in the classroom. This gives students more opportunity to hear from each other as well as more time to construct a better reply. Students can also bring other digital resources into the discussion to add richness and depth. Your comments and interactions with your students will motivate and engage them.

Several years ago a colleague at a different university was teaching the same course as I was. Together, we created a blog in which we carried on a running discussion about the content of our classes and about how best to convey this content to our students. While the two of us taught a course with the same name and the same textbook, our approaches could not be more divergent because our backgrounds were almost opposite. After the courses were under way we decided to open up our blog to our students. Although we had not planned to do this, it was a big hit as students gained insight into why we were teaching as we did. Further, many of them jumped into the blog and extended the conversation. This blog became another vehicle for student-instructor interaction. For more on this distance-learning course see Case Study 14.

Not all student-faculty interaction has to happen with e-mail or blogs. One greatly underutilized technology for interacting with students is the telephone. Maybe you don't want to give out your cell number and be called at all hours by your students. I know I don't. However, at times I encourage students to give me a call if they have questions, especially as an examination nears or a paper is due. You can also pick up a phone and call a student as you are reading his or her paper to discuss a point. This is fast, easy, and often less time-consuming—much more so than arranging a meeting at your office in several days to talk about it. Besides, you can convey much more in two minutes on the phone than by writing a note in the margin that the student will later read. You can also use a Voice-over-Internet Protocol (VoIP) such as Skype to make completely free telephone calls regardless of where you are. In addition, you can use collaborative software with students so that you are both looking at the same document, perhaps their paper, at the same time and each can see what the other writes or draws. Even if not communicating directly with your students, you can use features of some word processing programs that allow you to mark up as well as comment on your students' papers and have them respond to this. These approaches can lead to a rich interaction that guides, instructs, and motivates your students. The point of each of these approaches is the same—to extend and enhance interactions between you and your students.

Principle 2: Good Practice Encourages Cooperation Among Students

For many years we have considered individualized instruction as the most desirable form of instruction. As theoretical and empirical evidence has grown in recent years, we have begun to recognize the many ways students benefit from cooperatively working together. In addition, team building and learning how to work in groups are considered basic competencies required for the modern workforce. Research shows that students are likely to acquire more content knowledge when they interact and cooperate with other students. Quite simply, faculty are not the only resource available to help students learn. Other students working cooperatively can support and assist each other as they develop richer knowledge. Using technology, you can create shared workspaces in which students can work collaboratively. Students can communicate with each other by e-mail, instant messaging (IM), chat, telephone, and discussion forums. Students can use conferencing software to communicate and collaborate with each other as well as to share documents on which they are working. These approaches free students of space and time restrictions while allowing them to communicate and collaborate during your course. Students can work cooperatively to create digital products, such as a podcast, video clip, or multimedia. In the process of developing these products they will undoubtedly learn from each other. Technology can act as a lever to engage students, and it also gives them the tools they use for production, a vehicle for gathering information necessary for this project, and the means for their communication.

Principle 3: Good Practice Encourages Active Learning

We have long known that when students are actively engaged in the learning process they will learn more. When thoughtfully integrated into our classes, technology allows us to change our role from presenters of information and the students' role from passive recipients of information. Today's technology has the potential to revolutionize teaching and learning and place the student in an active role as never before. Shifting the focus from the instructor to the student may be education's greatest benefit from technology use. In the traditional classroom it is the instructor who is active while the students sit quietly, perhaps taking notes, for the majority of time. Technology can allow us to place students in a more active role, whether they are working through complex computer-based simulations, searching out information on the Web, collaborating with others, actively producing products related to course content, or solving real problems through technology-based service-learning or problem-based learning. Technology can extend your classroom and bring in the external world through video-conferencing, Webcams, realistic simulations, or virtual worlds, and it can place the student at the center of the instruction.

Principle 4: Good Practice Gives Prompt Feedback

Feedback is essential for learning, and to be effective it needs to be timely and informative to your students. Often the first feedback students receive in a course is when they get their midterm examinations back, and this may be several days after they took the examination. Often the feedback is little more than a grade and seeing what questions were missed. Instructionally this is too little and too late. So that it can be helpful to them, students should receive more feedback, and they should receive it in a prompt manner. This can be difficult to accomplish in a classroom of forty students, much less a classroom of three hundred students; there is little opportunity for students to respond, and little opportunity for you to provide effective feedback to them. Technology can be helpful with this in several ways. You can use e-mail to ask students or groups of students questions, then respond to them promptly via return e-mail. When students have group assignments you can set up a listserv for that group and provide feedback to them in this manner. You can have students interacting in a discussion forum that you scan on a regular basis and in which you can provide feedback. In a similar manner, you can encourage students to participate in discussion forums and respond to other students by providing feedback. In essence, you can arrange for some peer-tutoring in your classes, facilitated by technology. This removes you from being the sole source of feedback to students. It also has the advantage of fostering cooperative learning and active learning on the part of your students. Of course, you will need to monitor the discussions and jump in if a student is giving inaccurate or incomplete information when responding to another student. But by using other students to provide feedback, you extend what you can accomplish, and you create an active learning environment for your students in which they have a more direct role. A number of studies have shown that the student giving the feedback will also be learning from this experience.

It is often very time-consuming to provide more feedback to your students the first time you use this approach in a specific course. A suggestion: one way to reduce this burden is to save the feedback you are giving students in a categorized file. You will find that in time you can almost predict the questions students will ask and you can anticipate their problems. Knowing this, you can formulate replies to these common questions with appropriate suggestions. Then when a student asks for help you don't have to start with a blank screen to construct your reply; simply go to your file for this question or problem, copy what you have previously written, and then tailor it to that specific student. This is the concept of mass customization. While you give your students feedback that is customized to them (to their question, problem, or misunderstanding), you draw from a large file that's already stored and modify it to fit. This is akin to providing a customer a previously made off-the-rack suit that you have taken in at the waist a bit and cuffed the pants to get an exact fit. The result is a suit that fits perfectly, produced in far less time.

Another way to use technology to provide prompt feedback is to select and use software that has feedback embedded in it. There is a wide collection of computer-assisted instruction for most subject matter that offers tutoring to students, including frequent and immediate feedback, including instant feedback each time students interact with the simulation.

Principle 5: Good Practice Emphasizes Time on Task

A consistent finding from research on teaching is that the more a student focuses on the learning task and stays with it, the more he or she will learn. Anything we can do to get our students to devote attention to the learning task is likely to produce learning gains. We can start by being clear about what students should be doing. We can develop and use a student-centered syllabus that communicates all assignments and expectations in a clear, easily understood manner. We can place the syllabus on a course Web site and directly link all the resources they will need from the syllabus. However, this should not replace a copy that they have available in class and in discussion periods. This minimizes any time they would spend in trying to figure out what they should be doing or in assembling the resources they would need to accomplish this. You can be available by e-mail, chat, or IM to provide a more immediate response to a student who might need additional guidance—rather than having him or her wait until the next class or the next time you have office hours.

Another way to maximize students' time on task is through careful course design and field-testing your instructional materials before use. All the instruction should be focused on accomplishing your goals for the course. This keeps students focused and spending time on the essential tasks. Through good course design, you help ensure that the efforts of the learners keep them on task whether they are participating in activities or reading content. When the course activities and reading align with the course goals, you are more likely to have your students spending more time on task. Through the process of formative evaluation you can field-test instructional activities and materials ahead of time to spot potential deficiencies that might trip up students. Anything you do to smooth the path for your students will help. If directions are not clear, students will focus on trying to figure out the directions, rather than thinking about and learning the content. If a reading is poorly written, students' energies will be devoted to figuring out what the author is trying to say and little will be gained.

Principle 6: Good Practice Communicates High Expectations

To an extent, students will achieve what we expect of them. If we set low expectations, we will not see much growth from our students.

They have other demands on their time, such as other courses, work responsibilities, family responsibilities, or social demands. If they see that we do not expect much from them, they will take the rational course of diverting their attention to where they perceive a greater need, rather than spending more time with our course. This is not to say that we should be unreasonable in our expectations, as this tends to suppress motivation; we should set expectations that are high but attainable by most students with effort. This is when learning happens.

We can communicate our expectations clearly in the syllabus, which can also be made available and updated electronically. Information on the Web site can communicate what our students are expected to do and accomplish during the course. Expectations about the quality and quantity of their work can be made explicit through instructional outcomes, examples of student work products, and practice examinations. We can reinforce and annotate these expectations to students in e-mails or announcements so that this information is fresh in their minds.

Principle 7: Good Practice Respects Diverse Talents and Ways of Learning

Students have different ways of approaching learning tasks; one size does not fit all with regards to learning. Trying to teach everything and everybody the same way at the same time will not be successful any more than a restaurant can be successful serving only one dish. Technology can strengthen our abilities to add variety to our instruction. This should not be variety for variety's sake, but rather variety to accommodate our students' needs, capabilities, and interests. We can use rich multimedia environments to stimulate multiple senses through text, graphics, video, audio, and animation and, as a result, be more engaging to different learners whose interests vary. We can use hypermedia that allows students to explore our instructional content using a path of their own choosing, rather than one prescribed path for all. Students who are familiar with some aspect of content can skip this and move to content that is new to them, while others needing more support can elect to spend more time on a specific section and receive additional instruction. We can develop computer-assisted instruction that has a variety of different instructional events, such as examples, explanations, practice exercises, podcasts, video representations of the content, and so on, and let our students determine what will be most helpful in learning the content at any particular moment. In essence, we can use technology to create flexible learning environments that allow students to tailor what and how they study to their diverse ways of learning.

How to Go Wrong (or, What Not to Do) _____

Most mistakes stem from a rush to use technology or a failure to think through why and how we should use technology. We create problems when we

- Start by assuming we will use technology, rather than starting with questions about course purpose and design
- Focus on the technology because it appears glamorous and sophisticated, rather than keeping the focus on learning and instruction
- Rely exclusively on technology advocates and outside vendors to guide us
- Fail to allow sufficient time for development or find support for using technology in meaningful ways in our classes
- Fail to make sure that the development and use of technology is considered as valued faculty work in promotion and tenure reviews
- Fail to consider the cost of maintaining and continuing technology-based projects
- Do not make arrangements for technical assistance for ourselves and our students when using technology

Conclusion _____

A few things are important with respect to using technology for instruction. To be effective—and technology can be very effective in learning—start with a focus on your instructional goals and your students. Think about what should happen to help your students reach these learning goals. Then think about how technology can assist you. Let concerns about learning and pedagogy drive your choices. Apply guidelines for effective instruction, such as those included in this chapter, and use them to see how you might be able to employ technology to better accomplish some of your instructional goals and enhance your students' learning. Talk with students and other faculty about their technology use. Read about how other faculty are applying technology in their courses and see if something they are doing might be modified to fit your course. Gather ideas and try them out. Students will appreciate your attempts to make better use of technology; make sure that you keep them informed of what you are doing, how they are doing, and what you are learning along the way.

Additional Resources _____

Web Sites

Association for the Advancement of Computers in Education (www.aace.org/)

> A nonprofit international association that focuses on improving the quality of teaching and learning at all levels through applications of information technology. This organization publishes several journals and holds several conferences on different topics each year.

Association for Educational Communications and Technology (www.aect.org/default.asp)

> This is a professional association for those interested in the use of technology in education at all levels. They publish journals as well as books related to technology.

Campus Technology (http://campustechnology.com/)

> This Web site contains information about technology use in higher education, including reviews of hardware and software, a newsletter, a collection of related resources, news about what's happening with technology on campuses, and features about specific applications.

Chronicle of Higher Education: Information Technology (http://chronicle.com/infotech/)

> This is the Chronicle's section related to information technology use in higher education. It contains interesting articles about technology on campuses.

Education Atlas (www.educationatlas.com/instructional-technology-higher-education.html)

> A collection of annotated links to technology in higher education.

Educational Technology Organizations (www.educational-software-directory.net/organizations.html)

> An annotated listing of various organizations worldwide that are involved in using technology in education.

Educause (www.educause.edu/)

> A major nonprofit organization that attempts to advance the use of information technology in higher education. They publish two journals that can be of interest to faculty engaged in technology use.

Instructional Technology Connections (http://carbon.cudenver.edu/~mryder/itcon.html)

> A large but organized collection of links to readings about instructional technology—defined broadly to include the process as well as hardware aspects. There are selections on theory, research, teaching, and the news.

International Society for Computers in Education (www.iste.org/)

> A nonprofit organization that seeks to provide leadership to advance the use of technology in education. Although their focus is on K–12 schools and teacher education, this is a good source for information about technology use.

National Center for Academic Transformation (www.center.rpi.edu/)

> This is an independent, nonprofit organization dedicated to the effective use of information technology to improve learning outcomes and reduce the cost of higher education. They provide expertise and support to institutions and organizations regarding technology use in higher education. Their Web site contains many examples of courses that were redesigned to include technology as well as information about how to accomplish this.

Teaching and Learning with Technology Group (www.tltgroup.org/Index.htm)

> A nonprofit organization dedicated to assisting educational institutions in improving teaching and learning through better use of technology. This Web site includes numerous resources and sources of assistance to those using technology.

Books

Bates, A. W., and Poole, G. *Effective Teaching with Technology in Higher Education: Foundations for Success.* San Francisco: Jossey-Bass, 2003.

> Demonstrates how to incorporate technology into higher education based on theoretical and practical foundations. It provides guidance for selecting and using technology to deliver instruction.

Bonk, C. J., and Graham, C. R. (eds.). *The Handbook of Blended Learning.* San Francisco: Pfeiffer, 2006.

> A collection of thirty-eight chapters on different aspects of using technology to combine traditional face-to-face

instruction with computer-mediated instruction. This book includes different models for blended learning from a global perspective.

Bullen, M., and Janes, D. P. (eds.). *Making the Transition to E-Learning: Strategies and Issues.* Hershey, Pa.: Information Science Publishing, 2007.

> An edited book that discusses issues associated with the transition to technology-based instruction. The chapters are organized into three main sections: (1) institutional and conceptual issues, (2) learning and teaching issues, and (3) instructional design and technology issues. Each chapter provides some insight and practical advice from those with experience teaching in higher education.

Clyde, W., and Delohery, A. *Using Technology in Teaching.* New Haven, Conn.: Yale University Press, 2005.

> Offers practical guidance for faculty members who embark on using technology in their classes. The approach is very straightforward; suggestions are accompanied by clear examples.

Conole, G., and Oliver, M. (eds.). *Contemporary Perspectives in E-Learning Research: Themes, Methods and Impact on Practice.* New York: Routledge, 2007.

> This edited book explores key themes of research into e-learning in higher education. Included are chapters reviewing the research on design of learning technologies, application of learning theory to e-learning, designing digital resources, assessment, collaboration, and social issues, among others. This book gives a good picture of the landscape related to e-learning in terms of what research has shown.

McConnell, D. *E-Learning Groups and Communities.* New York: McGraw-Hill, 2006.

> Describes how students learn in e-learning groups and communities. The focus of the book is on learning in virtual communities and the collaborative and cooperative processes essential for learning. The book also examines traditional teaching practices in light of what is possible through new technology.

Mishra, P., Koehler, M. J., and Zhao, Y. (eds.). *Faculty Development by Design: Integrating Technology into Higher Education.* Charlotte, N.C.: Information Age Publishing, 2007.

A collection of chapters describing how technology can be integrated into higher education from the perspectives of faculty members and graduate students in one university who participated in a multiyear project. Chapters document the challenges faced as well as the processes they followed.

Naidu, S. (ed.). *Learning and Teaching with Technology: Principles and Practices.* New York: Kogan Page, 2003.

An edited book that discusses the use of information and communications technologies in education. It describes different uses of technology in teaching including simulations, interactive multimedia, online discussions, problem-based learning, and others, with an international perspective.

Newby, T., Stepich, D., Lehman, J., and Russell, J. *Educational Technology for Teaching and Learning.* (3rd ed.). Upper Saddle River, N.J.: Pearson, 2005.

A survey of technology use for teachers. It includes chapters on planning for technology use, ways to involve students, using computers to support learning, evaluation, issues, and trends in using technology. Although it is aimed primarily at K–12 teachers, it is a useful resource for teaching in higher education.

Seale, J. K. *E-Learning and Disability in Higher Education: Accessibility Research and Practice.* New York: Routledge, 2006.

Focuses on making e-learning accessible to students with disabilities. It includes a description of the tools, methods, and practices for improving accessibility.

CHAPTER 19

Distance Learning

Wallace Hannum

The crucial starting point for those interested in distance learning has already taken place. Before you can even start to focus on the distance-learning experience itself, you need to have clearly stated goals and outcomes, collected data about your students, and have reviewed the literature on teaching and learning. At this point you would have already taken this action. As part of your next step, you'll be reviewing the instructional options discussed in the previous two chapters. Too often faculty start by considering what kind of distance-learning course they want to create and focusing on what technologies to use to create their course.

The overwhelming message from decades of research on technology use in education, including distance learning, is that there is no magic in the hardware. If you are to have quality in your distance-learning course, you must build this quality into the course through strong instructional design and appropriate pedagogy. Time and time again we have learned that as fancy as technology and distance learning can be, simply porting existing content over the Internet for delivery as an online course will not give a quality course. Nor will your students learn much from the experience. However, if you pay attention to the process of course design, you can create and offer a course via distance learning that will actively engage your students and will produce results as good as or better than found in a traditional on-campus course.

The Growth in Distance Education

In recent years we have seen a dramatic rise in distance-learning courses, especially courses taught online. The vast majority of colleges and universities now offer both courses and complete degree programs through distance learning. Over 96 percent of large postsecondary institutions offer online courses and two-thirds offer complete degree programs online. If you are considering, or are currently teaching, an online course, you are part of a rapidly increasing phenomenon. In the fall of 2005, 3.2 million students were taking at least one online course. This number was up considerably from the 2.3 million students who took an online course the year before. Distance learning is now a well-established part of postsecondary education. Some speculate that this trend portends the demise of traditional brick-and-mortar institutions, but these folks are in the minority. You can expect a future where higher education takes place on traditional campuses, entirely through distance education, and in many instances by a combination of both delivery systems.

There are a number of forces supporting the significant expansion of distance learning:

Advances in technology. Advances in computing and communications technologies have made distance learning more feasible. The Internet and the ubiquity of networked computers have made it possible for students to access courses at any time from almost any place.

Student comfort with technology. In addition, distance learning is a good match for today's students, who have grown up as users of technology. Although extensive technology use may feel foreign to some faculty, it feels comfortable and familiar to their students. They interact with friends through e-mail and instant messaging; they create and share videos on YouTube; they use Google to find information; they develop and share their own Web pages; they form online communities that serve as their "neighborhoods"; they live in a multitasking world and are doing many things simultaneously through technology; they are in constant contact with others and with information sources regardless of where they are; they have cell phones, iPods, PDAs, DVD players, MP3 players, and ultra-portable computers in their pockets. Using these technologies for learning is as natural to your students as using a spiral-bound notebook was for most of us.

Student demand. Students, especially adult students, appreciate the flexibility that distance learning offers them. As the demographic of undergraduates continues to include greater numbers of students older than the traditional eighteen- to twenty-four-year-old students, the demand for flexibility has increased. More students have work or family obligations that make it far harder to meet the schedules of a traditional institution. Being able to determine their own schedule is a benefit for these students who find it very difficult, if not totally impossible, to be on campus certain days at specific times. Distance learning excels at allowing students to time-switch and complete courses on a schedule that fits with the rest of their obligations.

The institutional setting. Distance learning fits the modern workplace, which has become a technology-rich environment. A growing proportion of adults use e-mail constantly for communications at work, and they do their work from home or on the road, not just from their office. They complete tasks for work at all hours of the day and night. Many of the resources they require for work are accessed in digital format, and many of their work products are created and distributed using technology. In addition, the members of their work team are as likely as not to be in different locations and working on different schedules as they interact at a distance enabled by technology; they are comfortable with this format.

Competition. As Internet access has made geography largely irrelevant, a student living almost anywhere can consider taking a distance-learning course from an institution located anywhere on the planet—not just near where he or she is living. As a result, the local university is now competing with institutions worldwide when offering courses to people in its own backyard. As students demand more distance-learning courses, pressure has mounted for every institution to offer distance-learning courses or risk losing local students—who, before the expansion of distance learning, had only one realistic choice.

In all probability the expansion in distance learning will continue, although it is questionable if the current rate of expansion can be maintained. However, distance learning fits many of today's realities and is likely to continue to be a major form of education. To us as faculty members, both those favoring distance learning and those who oppose it, *the key issue will always be the instructional quality of the distance-learning experience.* This is a main focus of this chapter. As a faculty member, your instructional quality must be your primary concern and something over which you, more than anyone else, have the greatest influence.

Benefits of Distance Learning

Numerous books and articles have identified the benefits of distance learning. Most include the flexibility of time, place, location, and pace as major benefits. Students can complete an online course when they have the time to do so because they determine their own schedule. In distance-learning courses, students also determine where studying takes place, unlike in traditional courses where students are required to come to campus to a prescribed building, room, or laboratory. The pace at which a student advances is another dimension of flexibility. Although rare in most on-campus courses, distance-learning students typically can progress through the course at their individual rates, independent of others taking the same class, and thus ensure their mastery of the course content. Some institutions even allow multiple entry and exit points for courses throughout the academic year rather than holding registration only at the beginning of each semester and requiring course completion at the end of the semester. Interestingly, faculty at a number of institutions are exploring ways to adapt some of the advantages of distance learning to their traditional on-campus courses and programs.

There are other benefits to distance learning that also have a direct bearing on learning outcomes. These include:

- Improved instructional quality
- Increased productivity of learning
- Greater access to learning
- Improved student attitudes toward learning and the subject matter
- Encouragement of greater student independence and self-regulation of learning
- More active involvement of students in the learning process
- Greater opportunity for students to share and co-construct knowledge with others
- More immediate feedback to students, as tests and papers are graded more quickly
- Enhanced communication between faculty and students, especially part-time students
- Greater use of multimedia as opposed to exclusive reliance on text
- Developing a higher level of knowledge rather than simple acquisition of content
- A shift from instructor-centered learning to student-centered learning

The Challenges

We are not suggesting that distance learning has ushered in nirvana as far as teaching and learning go. Distance learning does bring with it some important limitations. We want to be very clear that simply placing content into a course management system and declaring you have developed a distance-learning course is irresponsible. This is not a defensible practice because it is not the technology itself that causes learning—it is the design of the learning process that makes the difference. Creating and teaching an effective distance-learning course is neither quick nor easy. Teaching a high quality distance-learning course may also require that you reach a new level of competency in a number of areas.

Certainly you have to be facile with technology extending considerably beyond word processing and e-mail. To achieve the benefits that distance learning offers, you will find yourself interacting with individual students much more than in most traditional lecture courses. In fact, you will note that your role will evolve from that of information dissemination to that of guiding and monitoring students. You will be monitoring students' progress, providing individual feedback and encouragement, and making sure your students are moving along at an appropriate pace. A distance-learning course taught in this manner is going to take more of your time than is normally anticipated in on-campus teaching. Many see this as a limitation of distance learning because it requires more faculty time. However, we see the increased faculty-student interaction as a benefit in terms of producing enhanced learning outcomes. You should also anticipate that developing and teaching an online course will take more of your time than you might at first anticipate; this is especially true the first few times you teach in this setting.

Access to Resources and Services

There are three other challenges that you will have to deal with as you design your courses:

• When a student is taking an online class, he or she is not physically on campus and thus does not have access to the facilities and services that are available on campus. Most notably, students may not have easy access to the campus library or student services such as registering and advising. You will need to make up for these limitations by making available all the resources on the Internet including the digital collections in many libraries.

• The lack of face-to-face contact. In the traditional classroom, you have the key advantage of being in the classroom with your students, and so you can immediately respond to questions, add new materials when you see your students are confused, adjust your pace when it is necessary, modify your sequence, or make other adjustments. You can also stop and ask questions to make sure that major points are understood. As an effective teacher, you will always be looking for clues of discomfort, inattention, and boredom. This is not possible in distance education. In this format you have to anticipate problems, build in review, and develop creative ways to address issues of clarity and confusion when they do occur.

• The lack of student-student interaction. Although much can be gained through distance-learning opportunities, the unexpected, informal "water cooler" conversation will rarely happen unless it is built into your course. Certainly you can design your distance-learning courses to include informal learning opportunities, even unexpected ones in which students have the opportunity for quick informal discussions with other students. Unfortunately these experiences are missing in many online courses that have students paying attention to completing assignments independently and little else. Students often report feeling lost and isolated in these courses. Indeed, the drop-out rate is higher in distance-learning courses, likely as a result of this isolation and frustration. But this problem is neither inevitable nor necessary. Once again, this is a result of poor planning and poor course design. The Internet makes it easy for students to interact with many other people and form strong online communities. However, this does not happen unless you plan for it and build these opportunities. If you want your students to work together and to learn from each other, you must structure your course to make sure this occurs.

Categories of Distance Learning

Distance learning is hardly a single entity or concept. There is considerable variety of distance-learning courses. One way to begin to understand the variety and richness within distance learning is to examine some major categories of distance learning. One way to categorize distance learning courses is by technologies, similar to the following taxonomy of distance learning:

- Print-based courses (correspondence courses, independent study)
- Pre-recorded audio courses (audio tapes, podcasts)
- Broadcast audio courses (radio)
- Pre-recorded video courses (videotape, DVD)
- Broadcast video courses (television)
- Conferencing courses (video-conferencing, computer-mediated communications)
- Online courses

Recently there has been a tendency to equate distance learning solely with online learning, but as you can see in the above taxonomy, this ignores many other forms of distance learning. Certainly the growth in this area has been in online learning; however, there are many distance-learning courses that do not use the Internet.

If you are going to offer a distance-learning course, one of the decisions you have to make is what type of distance learning you will use. Since most distance learning being developed today is online learning, we will focus on this approach in this section. Keep in mind that another approach or combination of approaches may make more sense for your particular course and students.

At the risk of being redundant, we want to stress that at the point you are deciding what type of online course you will offer, you should have already completed many of the steps in the systematic design model. Online learning and its technologies will not mask any mistakes you make by failing to follow a systematic design approach. If anything, online learning will enhance flaws and make them more apparent. Remember that technology alone does not enhance instruction—never has and never will. Pedagogy is what matters—always has and always will.

It may be desirable for you to learn more about the technologies used to deliver distance learning as well as learn how to use some of the software packages necessary for creating digital content. But never confuse this with knowledge of pedagogy. Many people can develop digital content, but fewer can develop a decent online learning course—because they do not understand teaching and learning. Start with good pedagogy, then add technology when developing a distance-learning course, and you are much more likely to create an effective course.

Blended Learning

More recently many faculty members have begun to use some distance learning in conjunction with their traditional face-to-face classes to take advantage of the features of both. This is typically called *blended learning* and brings, or blends, some of the flexibility of distance learning into a regular class. While different faculty may go about blended learning in a different manner, most have their classes meet in a regular, face-to-face format for some of the semester at their regularly scheduled class time, and then have them participate in distance learning in lieu of other class meetings, thus blending some of both approaches into one class. This approach is a less dramatic change than going to a total distance learning format in which the class never meets face-to-face. However, it does allow faculty to bring some of the advantages of distance learning to their students while preserving aspects of the traditional classroom.

Some Recommendations

Focus on Your Student

We suggest that as you begin to develop an online learning course you take the point of view of your students. That is, start by thinking what your students should do that will cause them to grasp the course content rather than by thinking about what you will do to present the content. This is the reverse of what most faculty members do, but it has the distinct advantage of helping us develop more learner-centered courses that, in turn, will contribute to greater learning outcomes. As you start planning for your distance-learning course, you have already identified goals, collected information about your students, and explored various instructional options. You have all the elements required to design a quality course. Now you must carefully plan the activities for your students on a week-by-week basis. We don't recommend that any faculty member should "wing it" in a traditional face-to-face course, but doing so is a road to certain failure in a distance-learning setting.

Synchronous Versus Asynchronous

Online learning courses can be subdivided as being either synchronous or asynchronous. *Synchronous* courses happen in real time as the instructor and students are engaged at the same time although they are in different locations interacting via the Internet. This is similar to a telephone call in which the people talking are in different locations but interacting at the same point in time, that is, synchronously. In *asynchronous* courses the interactions among instructors and students happen at different points in time. This is similar to e-mail in which one person writes his communication at one point in time, and it is read by another person or persons at different points of time, that is, asynchronously.

An initial decision you want to make is whether to offer your distance-learning course as a synchronous course or as an asynchronous course. Both synchronous and asynchronous distance-learning courses can be effective, but there are some typical differences shown in the research. In general, students report a preference for synchronous courses. Perhaps this is because these courses meet at a fixed time on a predictable schedule and thus more closely mimic traditional courses that they are used to taking.

However, *data demonstrate that the learning outcomes are slightly better in asynchronous courses.* We don't intend this as a call to abandon synchronous distance-learning courses; we want you to understand that you may have to build in more support for learning if you plan to teach a synchronous course. You should also note that synchronous courses do not have the advantage of anytime learning, since students have to be online at the same point in time although they can be in different locations. This is another consideration in making the decision about having a synchronous or asynchronous course. However, if you elect to teach an asynchronous course, you should know that some of your students are likely to manage their time poorly and fall behind. This contributes in part to the high drop-out rate when this approach is used.

Establish Deadlines Involved

Certainly we favor letting the students have some control over the pacing of their progress through a distance-learning course, but many students have not yet developed the self-regulation necessary to do this successfully. We suggest that you set some deadlines throughout the semester and monitor students' progress against these deadlines. For example, you may establish a recommended pace through the course and get in touch with students who fall two weeks behind to make sure that everything is all right or if they are having problems and what those problems are. The key here is that they "feel" your presence in the online course. Students quickly get a sense of whether a faculty member is paying attention to them. If they sense you are often absent, they will be also. You must create and maintain a *virtual presence* in your online course for it to be effective. We are not suggesting that you have to be heavy-handed or dominate the discussion in the course. Far from it—we recognize that student-centered courses produce superior learning results. However, you should not relinquish your role as the faculty member and let the students work independently without any input from you. The students can remain the center of your course, but you should monitor their work almost daily and provide frequent feedback, especially when you detect they are going astray or are not making necessary progress.

Course Management Systems

Although you may start by creating a Web site from scratch for your online learning course, we recommend you use some of the course management systems software, such as BlackBoard,

WebCT, or Moodle, because this makes it so much easier and quicker to develop an online course. These or similar systems allow you to structure your course into a series of units, or modules, and assign activities within each. They allow you to include digital materials for your students to read or view online. You can embed links to any resources available on the Internet as part of your course to make a vast array of materials available to your students. You can also include a rich variety of mediated materials that you locate or that you produce including video clips, PowerPoint files, and podcasts. These content management systems include communications tools to support discussion forums, chat, and e-mail as part of your course. Students can submit assignments, you can review them and provide feedback all within the content management system. You can register students for your course, track their progress, administer examinations, and keep their grades all by using the course management software. It will require some time for you to learn how to use this software, but this is not substantial especially in light of the software's benefits.

The Crucial Role of the Course Syllabus

We suggest you create your course design by starting with your course learning outcomes and identifying the resources your students will need to help them meet these goals. You can include these resources on a calendar for the semester (much as you would in a typical syllabus), showing each week's or each class session's goals and outcomes, the resources available to the students, the activities students are expected to undertake, any products students are to create, and how they will be assessed. This gives your students a detailed road map for your course that will help them use their study time most efficiently. A student-centered syllabus is helpful in any course, but it is vital to the success of an online course. Without it students are likely to get lost and off track. With such a syllabus they know what they are to do, why they are doing it, how to go about it, and even how they will be evaluated. This will improve the quality of their online experience, eliminate or reduce many problems, and it will make it easier for you to help your students be successful.

Your Role in Online Courses

You have two important roles as a teacher in an online course. The first is as *course designer*. Building on the research on teaching and learning and using the best instructional options available, you must design a high-quality learning experience. This extends far beyond rounding up some readings and putting links to these online. The course design should include a detailed plan for what students should do on a week-by-week basis, much like the detailed playbook that a coach has for his or her players, or the sheet music with notations that a conductor has for all his musicians. You have the responsibility for creating this detailed plan for how your students will learn and for communicating the information to your students.

It is extremely important that your goals, learning outcomes, and the specific responsibilities are clearly spelled out in your syllabus. Students need to know where they are going, how they will get there, how they will be assessed, and how to locate the resources that they will need.

Your second key role is as a *monitor of learning*. Of course you can't predict everything perfectly ahead of time—neither can a coach or conductor—but you have to start with a detailed plan just the same. Similar to a coach or conductor, you have to pay attention when the course is under way by monitoring the performance of your students and making any changes that appear necessary to help the students achieve your learning goals. Online learning does not equate with independent learning. Although your students will not be in the classroom with you three days a week, you need to be engaged with and monitoring them just as closely, perhaps even more so. If you notice that students are not getting some point or not grasping some concept, then you must provide additional resources, such as new examples with explanations, or enter into discussions with students to understand and clarify their confusion.

A successful online learning experience will require that you attend to both of your roles of course designer and course monitor. This is not really new—all good instruction requires careful design of the learning experience and then careful monitoring of your students during the course of study. The roles are especially crucial in distance-learning courses where opportunities for rapid responses to problems are limited.

Is Distance Learning Right for You?

Is teaching a distance-learning course right for you? Although more and more faculty are beginning to teach distance-learning courses, we don't suggest that all faculty members be coerced into teaching distance-learning courses. Let us first quickly dispel the idea that distance learning is something of interest only to younger or more technologically literate faculty and thus not appropriate for more "seasoned" faculty. Some of the finest distance-learning teaching we have seen came from faculty members well above the typical retirement age who have had no prior experience teaching with technology. What they brought to their first distance-learning experience was deep knowledge of their subject matter, some sound ideas about pedagogy, and a keen interest in teaching well. Likewise, we have seen many younger faculty members struggle to be effective with distance learning because of some rather flawed concepts regarding appropriate pedagogy. Consider the following:

- If your primary approach to teaching is lecturing
- If you see distance learning as a great way to distribute your lectures
- If you don't see the potential use of technology to expand the library of resources available to your students
- If you see your primary function as a faculty member is to give assignments to students and then to test them on what they recall

. . . don't get involved with distance education! Both you and your students will suffer.

Distance education is not effective without engagement and without exposing your students to different ideas from different people. It is a way of ushering in a richer concept of teaching that extends far beyond the older transmission of information models. If you are ready to look at teaching this way, then, and only then, will distance learning make sense for you.

Conclusion

Distance learning can bring a new dimension into your teaching. It is flexible along many dimensions, including where learning takes place, when learning occurs, and at what pace. Your students also could be working towards different learning objectives that are matched to their own purpose and goals. Different students could be using different learning resources and they could assume different roles in the course at different times, taking full advantage of the knowledge and experience they bring to the class. There can be flexibility in the assignments and in the products that students create, both for learning and for assessment. If your concept of teaching allows such flexibility, distance learning will be a good choice for you. If you see teaching as an active process in which you are engaged with your students, if you see teaching as something you jointly create with learners, then distance learning will make sense for you. You will find that teaching a distance-learning course will be a rich and exciting learning experience for you and for your students.

Resources

There are a host of excellent Web sites and readings available on distance learning. When combined with the resources in previous chapters these will provide you with the information you need to design and implement a high-quality distance-learning course.

Web Sites

American Center for the Study of Distance Education (www.ed.psu.edu/ACSDE/)

> The center, located at Penn State, is devoted to distance education and learning. It has resources on distance learning as well as archives of a distance-learning discussion group.

American Distance Education Consortium (www.adec.edu/)

> This is a group of state universities and land grant colleges devoted to supporting distance learning. This site contains links to distance-learning programs and resources, funding opportunities, conferences and workshops, trends, and learning resources.

Distance Education Clearinghouse (www.uwex.edu/disted/index.cfm)

> A large collection of information about distance learning that includes basic information about distance-learning conferences, distance-learning organizations and associations, distance-learning journals, news, research, policies, and information on technologies. This is a good starting point.

Distance-Educator.com (www.distance-educator.com/index.html)

> A portal from Western Governors University devoted to distance learning that contains information, news, and tools for distance learning.

Educause (www.educause.edu/)

> A major nonprofit organization that attempts to advance the use of information technology in higher education. They publish two journals that can be of interest to faculty engaged in technology use, including those using distance learning.

Instructional Technology Council (www.itcnetwork.org/reports.htm)

Includes a substantial collection of links to literature on distance learning. This listing is categorized for easy use and includes topics from academic advising and copyright to assessment and computer software.

Journal of Asynchronous Learning Networks (www.sloan-c.org/publications/jaln/index.asp)

A publication of the Sloan Consortium that bills itself as the premier journal of online learning. It contains refereed articles on topics related to online learning in higher education.

MERLOT: Multimedia Educational Resource for Learning and Teaching Online (www.merlot.org/merlot/index.htm)

A repository of peer-reviewed online teaching and learning materials for higher education.

Self-Evaluation Quiz Related to Online Learning (www.online learning.net/InstructorCommunity/selfevaluation.html?s=226. r080g675u.0888026h00)

This self-scoring online quiz of twenty-five items purports to help faculty determine whether teaching online courses is right for them. Regardless of the specific results, it gives you some things to consider.

Teaching, Learning & Technology Group (www.tltgroup.org/Index.htm)

A nonprofit corporation that works with educational institutions to help them make better use of technology for teaching and learning. This site contains links to many good practical resources.

The Open and Distance Learning Association of Australia (http://odlaa.une.edu.au/)

The professional association of teachers, researchers, and administrators involved in distance learning. This site contains many publications and resources as well as information items.

United States Distance Learning Association (www.usdla.org/)

A national group that provides advocacy, information, and networking for those interested in distance learning. This site includes links to journals, reports, conferences, and a rich variety of other resources about distance learning.

World Lecture Hall (http://web.austin.utexas.edu/wlh/)

A large collection of online courses of varying quality, classified by subject matter. It is a good resource that will allow you to peek in on courses that other faculty have developed.

Books

Barab, S. A., Kling, R., and Gray, J. H. (eds.). *Designing for Virtual Communities in the Service of Learning.* Cambridge: Cambridge University Press, 2004.

> An edited collection of chapters that focus on theoretical, learning, and methodological issues associated with virtual learning communities. Chapters address such issues as designing, supporting, and researching online learning communities.

Berge, Z. L., and Clark, T. (eds.). *Virtual Schools: Planning for Success.* New York: Teachers College Press, 2005.

> A collection of chapters on the context of virtual schools and case studies of virtual schools. The settings are usually K–12, but the roles of universities are included. This can give you a good foundation in what your students may have experienced in distance learning in high school.

Bruning, R., Horn, C. A., and PytlikZillig, L. M. (eds.) *Web-Based Learning: What Do We Know? Where Do We Go?* Greenwich, Conn.: Information Age Publishing, 2003.

> A compilation of articles from a symposium of researchers, practitioners, teachers, technologists, and developers that came together to explore the use of electronic technologies in education. It contains chapters on the research on web-based learning, multimedia, at-risk students, course management systems, intellectual property, and recommendations for practice.

Burge, E. J., and Haughey, M. (eds.). *Using Learning Technologies: International Perspectives on Practice.* London: Routledge, 2001.

> This collection gives an international perspective on using technology for distance learning. One set of chapters focuses on policy issues. Another focuses on issues associated with the practice of distance learning, with examples from various countries. The final set of chapters focuses on issues of quality in courses, especially evaluation of courses.

Collis, B., and Moonen, J. *Flexible Learning in a Digital World: Experiences and Expectations.* London: Kogan Page, 2001.

This book explores four dimensions to flexible learning: the institution, implementation, pedagogy, and technology. Contained within this book is a discussion of eighteen lessons learned about flexible learning that are practical and widely applicable.

Dabbagh, N., and Bannan-Ritland, B. *Online Learning: Concepts, Strategies, and Application.* Upper Saddle River, N.J.: Pearson, 2005.

This book introduces online learning, describing the roles of both instructors and students in online courses. Discusses constructivist-based pedagogical models, instructional strategies, evaluation, and authoring online courses. It also includes a description of course management systems.

Discenza, R., Howard, C., and Schenk, K. (eds.). *The Design and Management of Effective Distance Learning Programs.* Hershey, Pa.: Information Science Publishing, 2002.

An edited collection of chapters on different aspects of distance learning, providing an overview to administrators and faculty interested in distance learning. Individual chapters address the status and future of distance learning, faculty perceptions, social needs in distance learning, quality assurance, and factors that contribute to success in distance-learning programs.

Dooley, K. E., Linder, J. R., and Dooley, L. M. *Advanced Methods in Distance Education: Applications and Practices for Educators, Administrators, and Learners.* Hershey, Pa.: Information Science Publishing, 2005.

This book examines several aspects of distance learning including teaching and learning at a distance, adult learning theory, instructional design, technology and administrative issues. The intent of this book is to focus on learner-centered instructional design and principles of adult learning rather than the technologies of distance learning.

Driscoll, M. *Web-Based Training: Designing E-Learning Experiences.* San Francisco: Jossey-Bass, 2002.

This text provides practical advice for distance learning that is grounded in solid theory and research. It discusses the advantages and limitations of delivering instruction over the Web, best practices, principles of adult education and instructional design, selecting appropriate distance-learning strategies and methods, designing synchronous and asynchronous instruction, and implementation.

Duffy, T. M., and Kirkley, J. R. (eds.). *Learner-Centered Theory and Practice in Distance Education: Cases from Higher Education.* Mahwah, N.J.: Lawrence Erlbaum Associates, 2004.

> This is a collection of case studies about distance learning organized into five sections: community building, problem-centered learning, innovations in technology use, scaling up, and alternate views. Eight different distance-learning programs are described in detail, addressing issues of theory, pedagogy, design, assessment, collaboration, and faculty development. Each program is described by someone involved in that program. A formal reaction follows from someone who is a specialist in the relevant aspect of distance learning. Then an edited transcript of an open discussion among participants at a symposium follows.

Figueiredo, A. D., and Afonso, A. P. *Managing Learning in Virtual Settings: The Role of Context.* Hershey, Pa.: Information Science Publishing, 2006.

> This is a collection of chapters about different issues associated with online learning internationally. Several chapters explore the context of online learning. Specific chapters discuss team building, learning agency, quality assurance, isolation, narrative, activity theory, and implementation from a variety of perspectives.

Fiore, S. M., and Salas, E. (eds.). *Towards a Science of Distributed Learning.* Washington, D.C.: American Psychological Association, 2007.

> This is an edited book that focuses on what we know about learning at a distance—distributed learning as they call it. There are chapters on theoretical models of distributed learning, team learning, and cognitive processes in distributed learning. This is a compilation of a considerable amount of research.

Keegan, D. *Foundations of Distance Education.* (2nd ed.) London: Routledge, 1990.

> Although dated, this book provides an overview of distance education, including several chapters discussing the concept of distance and theories of distance education. It attempts to provide a synthesis for distance education through a theoretical framework and typology of distance education. Finally, this book seeks to evaluate distance education.

Khan, B. (ed.). *Flexible Learning in an Information Society.* Hershey, Pa.: Information Science Publishing, 2007.

> This is an edited book containing chapters on a variety of topics associated with flexible learning. There are chapters on community learning, problem-based learning, motivation, storytelling, virtual exhibits, peer coaching, authentic learning, assessment, evaluation, multimedia, mobile learning, management, ethical issues, and obstacles encountered—all within the context of flexible learning.

Lambropoulos, N., and Zaphiris, P. *User-Centered Design of Online Learning Communities.* Hershey, Pa.: Information Science Publishing, 2007.

> This book provides a comprehensive look at online learning communities. The individual chapters contain reviews of the literature as well as suggestions for practice when working with online learning communities.

Lockwood, F., and Gooley, A. (eds.). *Innovations in Open and Distance Learning: Successful Development of Online and Web-Based Learning.* London: Kogan Page, 2001.

> An edited collection of chapters on innovations in distance learning including a discussion of lessons learned. A variety of topics are included, such as use of flexible tools for distance learning, lifelong learning, student recruitment and retention, online assessment, video production, and teacher beliefs, among others.

Meyer, K. *Quality in Distance Education: Focus on On-Line Learning.* Hoboken, N.J.: Wiley, 2002.

> A monograph that focuses on research on online learning. It reports research findings and discusses research issues as they apply to online learning.

Monolescu, D., Schifter, C. C., and Greenwood, L. (eds.). *The Distance Education Evolution: Issues and Case Studies.* Hershey, Pa.: Information Science Publishing 2004.

> An edited book that focuses on issues in distance education in higher education and includes several case studies about teaching distance education courses. Although the context of this book is the experience within one university, lessons are widely applicable.

Moore, M. G., and Kearsley, G. *Distance Education: A Systems View.* (2nd ed.) Belmont, Calif.: Thomson Wadsworth, 2005.

A good introduction and overview of the field of distance education. It provides the historical context, describes the scope of distance education, discusses technologies used for distance education, reviews the course development process, discusses the role of the instructor and of the students, describes issues related to the management of distance education, discusses research on distance education, describes distance education in several countries around the globe, and discusses why distance education involves change.

Palloff, R. M., and Pratt, K. *The Virtual Student.* San Francisco: Jossey-Bass, 2003.

Offers practical suggestions for facilitating online learning with an emphasis on the student. It discusses issues and concerns with working with students in online courses and provides strategies for teaching online in a learner-centered manner.

Simonson, M., Smaldino, S. E., Albright, M., and Zvacek, S. *Teaching and Learning at a Distance: Foundations of Distance Education.* (3rd ed.) Upper Saddle River, N.J.: Prentice Hall, 2005.

A basic textbook that includes chapters on the history of distance learning, research, technologies used for distance learning, instructional design, considering the students, teaching in distance learning, managing and evaluating distance learning.

CHAPTER 20

Meeting the Needs of Adult Learners

G. Roger Sell

The orientation of this chapter is that *educators contribute to, but cannot directly cause, adult learning*, as summarized by Christopher Knapper:

> . . . we must recognize that all learning is self-directed—in the sense that no one can learn on behalf of another. Learning is an inevitable and natural human activity that takes place in a wide variety of contexts and through many different agencies in addition to formal educational institutions and professional educators. At the same time, educators do make a difference, especially through their role in motivating students, providing guidance on learning strategies, offering feedback on students' performance, and generally serving as "validators" of students' own learning efforts and accomplishments [2004, p. 1].

In this chapter, we focus specifically on learners who are adults—persons older than traditional college-age students (18–24) and those who have major responsibilities (such as work, family, and community) other than, or in addition to, participating in postsecondary education. Our concern here is primarily the needs of adult learners and how adults learn—both of which are essential to the planning and design of courses and curricula intended for an adult population as well as courses in which you have a combination of both traditional and adult students.

A National Perspective for Adult Learning _____

In the introduction to *Returning to Learning*, the following argument is made:

> In the United States, postsecondary education has long driven individual mobility and collective economic prosperity. Nonetheless, the nation's labor force includes 54 million adults who lack a college degree; of those, nearly 34 million have no college experience at all. In the 21st century, these numbers cannot sustain us. Increasing global economic competition and the rapid pace of technological change are revolutionizing the skills and educational qualifications necessary to individual job success and national economic well-being [Pusser, and others, 2007, p. 1].

This argument for connecting continuing education to the quality of life is strengthened by adding that lifelong learning contributes to individual and community well-being through the development of knowledge and skills, not only for jobs and careers, but also for health, personal finances, recreational opportunities, safe communities, and other facets of adult life.

As part of the Emerging Pathways Project supported by the Lumina Foundation, a national survey of adult learners and two-year and four-year postsecondary institutions was conducted in 2004–05. Four key implications or "lessons" from these survey findings are summarized below (from Pusser, and others, 2007, p. 4):

• *There is no typical adult learner.* Institutional leaders and policymakers should view "the adult learner" as a diverse set of individuals with distinctive demographics, social locations, aspirations, and levels of preparation.

• *The broad range of adult learning programs does not receive the attention deserved.* A vast world of site-based and online, short-term, non-credit classes serve millions of learners. Because it is often excluded from state resource-allocation models, this "hidden college" is little understood by policymakers. Yet, because of the demands of the emerging knowledge economy, this arena is critical to the nation's future.

• *The well-worn path of traditional courses and programs often does not work, or does not work well, for many adults.* Many adult students choose nontraditional paths to postsecondary education because they work, are responsible for dependents, and can sometimes obtain tuition assistance from an employer if they enroll in a part-time program. The pathways open to adults tend to offer fewer resources per student than do traditional resident and commuter campuses. In addition, the range of the adult curricular interests, and offerings available to them, is distinctly different. Adult learners generally seek convenient access and a high degree of certainty in choosing a program. As a result, they may select private or for-profit institutions that offer organized programs specifically designed to serve them. Yet these institutions cannot necessarily meet the needs of a wide range of adult learners or the public goals for adult higher education. A variety of extenuating factors, including student characteristics; access to information; and the nature of local, state, and national subsidies shape the probability of success for adult learners.

• *To find the right path, adult learners need a guide.* Complex choices face the adult learner in deciding which courses or programs will meet individual interests and needs. Many adults can benefit from sound guidance in making enrollment decisions about particular courses and programs, how academic programs and career opportunities mesh, financial aid available, and child care services available, to name a few of the areas that influence adult student success. Mapping the adult student's path to postsecondary success is crucial.

In the next section you will find a closer look at adult needs and implications of these needs for learning programs.

Priorities of Adult Learners: Implications of Self-Determination Theory

If we begin with the assumption that there is no typical adult learner, then a key issue is whether there are common needs in the adult population served by one or more educational programs. Diversity of adult learners does not preclude the identification of common needs, especially when needs are viewed as fundamental requirements for the well-being of individuals.

One of the most useful models of "needs" for educational purposes is associated with Self-Determination Theory or SDT (Deci and Ryan, 1985, 2000). Within the SDT framework, three basic psychological needs are treated as innate and universal for all human beings: the need for competence, the need for autonomy, and the need for relatedness. Briefly summarized (see Levesque, Sell, and Zimmerman, 2006, for more details):

• *Competence* is the ability to interact effectively with one's environment. Competence is associated with the sense of self-efficacy. It is the belief that one is able to effectively accomplish tasks or perform certain behaviors.

• *Autonomy* refers to the individual's choice of the reasons behind one's behaviors and actions. Autonomy involves volition (choice) and the desire to organize and behave in a way that is consistent with one's sense of self. Researchers and scholars have often confused the need for autonomy with the concept of independence. Autonomy signifies choices, and the consequences of choices, not independence. An individual could choose to be interdependent (that is, being a member of a team), or in contrast could choose to act independently.

• *Relatedness* means attachments to and connections with other people. Relatedness signifies a sense of belonging or affiliation with others. It involves secure relationships that also contribute to the satisfaction of needs for autonomy and competence.

SDT basic psychological needs are not hierarchical but rather are continuous, to be satisfied on a daily basis. The human condition of well-being results from fulfilling all three needs for competence, autonomy, and relatedness—which are primary sources of intrinsic motivation. Both of these differences have significant implications for educational programs for adults. For example:

1. Earning academic credit or achieving a degree or certificate may be important for some adults, but these are usually not the main reasons for adult enrollment in an educational program. *Becoming more competent, for professional or personal reasons, is a fundamental need that adults seek to satisfy.* Striving to achieve competence is an intrinsic motivation for enrolling and persisting in an educational program. Therefore, effective educational programs for adults (a) build on competencies that learners already possess and (b) focus objectives on knowledge and skills to be acquired or further developed. While subject matter, teaching-learning methods, and assessment tools are components of an educational program, they are secondary to what adults desire to know and be able to do.

2. Regarding autonomy, *adult learners desire flexibility in choices of what, when, how, and where to engage in educational programs.* Considering the diversity of backgrounds, ongoing commitments, and interests in the adult population, providing multiple ways in which adults can engage in educational programs is essential. Not every educational program can be fully individualized for each adult learner. At the same time, there are choices that can be designed into a single program or across program offerings. For example, a mixture of face-to-face, online, and blended learning opportunities can enhance adult access while being responsive to a range of learning styles supported by different instructional formats. The following chart (adapted from Rossett, Douglis, and Frazee, 2003, p. 1) provides examples of different formal and informal approaches that can be used in blended programs for adult learners in a variety of contexts or settings:

Context	Formal Approaches	Informal Approaches
Face-to-Face	Instructor-led classroom Workshop Coaching/mentoring On-the-job (OJT) training	Collegial relationship Work team Role model
Virtual-Electronic Collaboration	Live e-learning class E-mentoring	E-mail Listserv Online bulletin board Online community
Self-Directed	Web learning module Online resource link Simulation Scenario Video and audio CD/DVD Workbook	Help system Print job aid Knowledge database Documentation Performance/decision support tool

Source: Rossett, Douglis, and Frazee, 2003.

3. *Learning is a social activity as well as an individual process or outcome.* Making connections with others—for example, teachers, peers, employers, or family members—is another ingredient for effective educational programs for adults. In just about every study of exemplary teachers, one of the characteristics that learners identify is "the teacher demonstrates that he or she cares about students." Personal contact with teachers, both within and outside classrooms, often makes a difference in how learners feel about their experiences and themselves. The sense of belonging or affiliation extends to connections with other adult participants, whether the means of connection is established through collaborative learning groups, e-mail or other electronic communications, or friendships that develop within a group of participants. Family and employer support of adults who enroll in an educational program is another aspect of meeting the need for relatedness.

Much more could be said about the needs of adult learners. However, in the context of this chapter, we have intended to introduce you to a foundation for one of the most important aspects of any educational program—adult needs as related to the motivation of adult learners. The study of motivation seeks answers to the question, "Why do people do what they do?" The engagement of adults in any purposeful activity, such as learning, is not possible without motivation. Building on this introduction, we now turn to an overview of research findings on how people learn, and then some implications of these findings for adult educational programs.

How Adults Learn: Implications of the Research_____

The past ten years or so have marked a very productive time for synthesizing literally hundreds of experimental and non-experimental studies of how people learn. A number of the more important reports on research findings are found in the References section. Using sources such as these, empirically based generalizations can be summarized for what we know about how adults learn, and then implications can be drawn from these findings for adult educational programs. In the remainder of this section, five major generalizations are identified and followed by several implications for programs serving adult learners. It is important to keep in mind that these generalizations are equally applicable to students at all levels. The key is to use these principles in the context of the adult students' needs and expectations.

1. *What and how much adults learn depends, in part, on their prior knowledge, skills, experiences, expectations, and beliefs.*

In addition to age differences, adult learners generally have a different mix of characteristics from traditional college-age students. More specifically, with regard to entering knowledge and beliefs, "Students come to the classroom with preconceptions about how the world works. If their initial understanding is not engaged, they may fail to grasp new concepts and information . . . or they may learn them for purposes of a test but revert to their preconceptions outside the classroom" (Donovan, Bransford, and Pellegrino, 1999, p. 2.1).

Either prior to, or at the beginning of, an educational program for adults, you can obtain and use information to describe participants' expectations and their desired outcomes from participation in an educational program.

Where feasible, it is useful to do an assessment of the participants' entering competencies (knowledge and skills), experiences, and beliefs relevant to learning goals and objectives, and then you can use this information to personalize and fine-tune the design and implementation of the educational program.

Information is more readily accommodated, organized, and recalled if it is meaningful to the adult's life and connected to his or her prior knowledge and experiences.

Unlearning what has been previously learned is often necessary to advance the development of new knowledge and skills. One way to approach misconceptions or unfounded beliefs is to create dissonance (for example, discrepancy between a pretest score and the adult's belief about his or her knowledge related to a course). Pretests also can serve as diagnostic assessments to locate and improve weaknesses through guided learning activities.

2. *Different forms of extrinsic motivation can have positive or negative effects on intrinsic motivation and adult learning.*

Intrinsic motivation refers to purposive behavior (including learning) wherein the goal (intention) is the action itself. Some examples of intrinsically motivated actions are pursuing curiosity, seeking meaning, developing competence, making choices autonomously, and serving others without the promise of external rewards or the threat of punishment. For intrinsically motivated behaviors, satisfaction is inherent in being fully engaged in the activity; the activity is both the means and end for involvement. *Extrinsic motivation* refers to purposive behavior (including learning) wherein the activity is instrumental for reaching a goal (reward) that goes beyond the activity itself. Some examples of extrinsically motivated actions are studying to get a good grade, completing a project in order to get a salary increase, participating on a committee to gain status or recognition, and obtaining an advanced degree to get a better job or earn more money. For extrinsically motivated behavior, satisfaction can result from the instrumental outcomes of an activity but not necessarily from engaging in the activity per se.

Different forms of motivation can have different effects on adult learners. While intrinsic motivation is the ideal for self-determined behavior, many of the behaviors people perform, particularly in a formal educational program, are extrinsically motivated. Deci and Ryan (2000) described the effects of four different kinds of extrinsic motivation in relation to amotivation (the absence of motivation) and intrinsic motivation (involvement in activities that are satisfying in and of themselves, including activities directed at satisfying the three basic psychological needs).

Wherever and whenever possible, you should emphasize two forms of positive extrinsic motivation—*identification* (the process by which adults begin to internalize the value of their behaviors and to accept them as their own) and *integration* (the process by which adults identify with the behaviors performed, fully endorse them, and integrate those behaviors with other aspects of the self).

In contrast, you should use sparingly, if at all, two forms of negative extrinsic motivation—*external regulation* (the process by which adult behavior is controlled by specific external contingencies such as rewards and punishments) and *introjection* (the process by which adult behavior is controlled by creating guilt or shame).

In addition, "Learning is more effective and efficient when learners have explicit, reasonable, positive goals, and when their goals fit well with the teacher's goals" (Angelo, 1993, p. 4).

3. *Active learning requires the engagement of adults in sustained and meaningful learning experiences resulting in knowledge and skills that are transferable to their own lives.*

Learning is not a spectator sport, but activity by itself is not meaningful for developing new knowledge and skills.

It is not so much what you do in your classroom, but rather what your adult students do, that makes the difference in the quality of their learning experiences and outcomes. Adults "construct" their own learning and not external agents such as teachers, texts, or online programs.

Teaching as telling is not an effective strategy if the intent is to actively engage adults in understanding complex problems and solving non-routine problems.

Meaningful learning experiences involve subject matter that is worth knowing. Moreover, "To develop competence in an area of inquiry, your students must: (a) have a deep foundation of factual knowledge, (b) understand facts and ideas in the context of a conceptual framework, and (c) organize knowledge in ways that facilitate retrieval and application" (Donovan, Bransford, and Pellegrino, 1999, pp. 2–3).

More content does not equal more or better learning. With expanding knowledge in every field, there always will be more content to teach and learn. Content or subject matter is important, but related directly to the amount, breadth, and depth to what is to be acquired, retained, and used by adults.

Adult learner engagement that involves any complex set of knowledge and skills also requires focused attention, an awareness of what is important to learn, practice with diagnostic feedback about strengths and areas for improvement, and the devotion of sufficient amounts of time and sustained effort.

Questioning, and the quality of questions, is one of the most important parts of learning any new knowledge or skill.

A major purpose for any educational program is the transfer of learning, that is, applying what is learned in one role or task to a new role or task, or from a role or task learned in one setting to another setting. Whether in subject matter or environment, or both, some degree of similarity between the learning context and the application context is necessary to enable the effective use of knowledge and skills that are learned. Service learning, internships, and on-the-job training are examples of educational experiences that have been found useful in the transfer of learning.

4. *Effective adult learning programs communicate clear, consistent, and reasonably high expectations for the success of all participants.*

No one rises to low expectations; most adult students will strive to attain high expectations if they are within reasonable reach (but beyond their immediate grasp).

Although prior knowledge, skills, and achievements are indicators of content mastery, they are not the only predictors of who will learn or do well. Amount and quality of effort, along with appropriate kinds of support, also are powerful predictors of learning outcomes. All adult students can be successful learners.

Clarity of expectations for adult learners is enhanced through *transparency* and *alignment*. Adults learn best, and educators are most effective, when the alignment is transparent among course goals and objectives, content, learning activities, and formative and summative assessments of learning performance (such as tests and grades, but also written and verbal feedback).

The course syllabus, or some other plan for learning, must meet the requirements for transparency and alignment by clearly conveying the instructional design of your course and should be used regularly and reinforced through ongoing communication with your students.

Test scores or grades by themselves are not sufficient feedback to help guide your adult students in their learning activities. "Learners need feedback on their learning, early and often, to learn well; to become independent, they need to learn how to give themselves feedback" (Angelo, 1993, p. 5). Clear, timely, and substantive feedback that adults understand and can use helps them to assess their accomplishments and to diagnose where and how they can improve their performance.

"The ways in which learners are assessed and evaluated powerfully affect the ways they study and learn" (Angelo, 1993, p. 6).

Student feedback is a primary source of the information you need. Participant feedback contributes to both teacher professional development and the scholarship of teaching and learning. Angelo and Cross (1993) and Cross and Steadman (1996) are excellent sources of data collection tools and project designs for gathering learner-generated feedback used for the study and improvement of adult learning programs.

5. *Adult learning success is enhanced by emphasizing appropriately challenging objectives and activities while providing adequate support that is responsive to individual needs, interests, and expectations.*

In addition to stimulating discussions and demonstrations, your adult students often can be inspired through a variety of "hands-on" activities (for example, case studies, computer simulations, writing, visualizing, and researching) that are clearly linked to the learning objectives.

In addition to, or as a substitute for, "objective" tests (e.g., multiple-choice items that are machine scored), carefully selected research papers, case studies, and projects can be effective for assessing learning performance and providing formative feedback.

The continuing development of knowledge and skills, both personal and professional, is aided by your adult students' reflections on their use of particular learning strategies and skills as well as their self-regulation of learning goals, activities, assessments, and resources. You may find that reflection and self-regulation present significant challenges for adult learners, so they may require additional support in these areas.

Positive interaction with you and other participants, both within and outside formal educational settings, is one of the most important aspects of support for your adult students. In addition, some adults may require assistance in particular content areas of professional or personal development, such as math or writing or science. Mentoring, tutoring, and self-help aids can be effective forms of support for adult participants in educational programs.

To summarize, based on a synthesis of findings from empirical research, effective educational programs for adult learners:

- Build on your adult students' prior knowledge, skills, experiences, expectations, and beliefs while correcting faulty preconceptions, strengthening gaps in prior learning, and developing more complex, connected, and deeper knowledge.

- Take steps to ensure that the learning goals, tasks, and outcomes are relevant, useful, appropriately challenging, intrinsically rewarding, and related to your adult students' efforts and expectations.

- Actively involve your adult students in deep (rather than superficial) learning through experiences that involve sufficient time, effort, and practice in ways that enhance the acquisition, retention, and transfer of knowledge and skills that are developed.

- Establish expectations for learning activities and outcomes that are clear, consistent, and reasonably high for all of your adult students.

- Challenge your students to do their best while providing adequate support to help them self-regulate their learning through reflection by setting goals, monitoring progress, and improving their learning strategies and skills.

What Should I Do If I Have a Mix of Adult and Traditional Students in My Course or Program?

The summary of research findings in this section, and related implications for educational programs, applies to adults of all ages. However, adults generally require more flexibility because they are likely to be part-time students, full-time workers, or care providers, and those with other major time commitments. Where possible, you can build in options for adult students to satisfy course or program requirements, for example with regard to attendance, where and how learning activities occur, and appropriately different ways in which achievement can be assessed and graded. Also, adult learners who have not been involved in educational programs for some time may lack confidence or particular skills such as using newer technologies. You may need to provide some additional assistance to help adult students in these areas. A strong asset of adult learners is that they bring a wealth of experience to postsecondary education, and both educators and traditional students can benefit from their presence. Survey the adult students in your course or program early and use this information to design and implement your course. You will discover other areas in which to adapt your course to the needs and interests of adult learners. We have suggested but a few of the possibilities you might consider when having a mixture of adults and traditional students in your course or program.

Institutional Strategies for Meeting the Educational Needs of Adult Learners

This closing section of the chapter identifies some kinds of institutional support that can help meet the needs of adult learners. Based on findings from their national survey, Pusser and others recommend the following actions that institutions can take to increase adult student success:

- Develop instruments for tracking the number of credit-bearing and non-credit-bearing courses and for tracking student enrollments and student characteristics in those courses.
- Track resource allocation to credit-bearing and non-credit-bearing courses.
- Provide students with detailed information on the impact of credit-bearing and non-credit-bearing courses on short-term and long-term postsecondary attainment and lifetime earnings.
- Work with industry and community partners to develop credit-bearing, pre-baccalaureate programs that offer labor market training and credit toward future postsecondary degree attainment, particularly in emerging areas of knowledge and expertise.
- Integrate non-credit and English-as-a-Second Language (ESL) education with larger strategies for student success and mobility, with transitions to credit-earning courses and sustainable employment markets [2007, p. 14].

Four other key areas of institutional support that contribute to adult learning are:

- Professional development opportunities for full-time faculty, part-time (adjunct) faculty, and graduate teaching assistants

(TAs) to enhance their knowledge and skills for serving adult students.

- An institution-wide agency for working with faculty and academic units in course and curriculum development, including but not limited to face-to-face, online, and blended courses for adult students.

- Institutional and organizational unit policies for hiring, placing, supervising, tenuring, promoting, and paying faculty in ways that reinforce the importance of effective teaching for adult learners.

- Collaboration among academic affairs and student affairs personnel in support of all facets of the adult student's introduction to, financial aid for, participation in, and post-graduation relationships with programs sponsored by the institution.

As a concluding note, we offer this thought: There is no greater calling than to serve others through our profession as educators. These are difficult and trying times as we struggle to better understand, and improve where possible, ourselves and our relationship with others and the world. At the same time, the satisfaction we receive from seeing our students develop and progress toward realizing their aspirations is an incomparable reward for being a teacher.

Additional Resources

Angelo, T. A., and Cross, K. P. *Classroom Assessment Techniques.* (2nd ed.) San Francisco: Jossey-Bass, 1993.

> An excellent source of fifty different instruments and procedures for obtaining and using feedback from students in your course. Following a brief description of selected "classroom assessment techniques" or CATs, you will find a thumbnail sketch of its purpose, related teaching goals, suggestions for use, one or two examples, step-by-step implementation procedures, pros and cons for using the assessment tool, and related references and resources.

Barkley, E. F., Cross, P. K., and Major, C. H. *Collaborative Learning Techniques.* San Francisco: Jossey-Bass, 2005.

> Another useful handbook that offers descriptions and notes on using thirty collaborative learning techniques (CoLTs). Commentary also is provided for applying each CoLT in an

online learning context. Following a brief review of relevant research, the three parts of the handbook address in order the why, how, and what questions of collaborative learning. These materials are particularly relevant to the social dimensions of learning and interactions of students with peers.

Cross, K. P., and Steadman, M. H. *Classroom Research: Implementing the Scholarship of Teaching.* San Francisco: Jossey-Bass, 1996.

A resource that both complements and extends *Classroom Assessment Techniques* (Angelo and Cross, 1993). It is complementary in the common purpose of providing materials that support classroom research which is learner-centered, teacher-directed, collaborative, context-specific, scholarly, practical, relevant, and ongoing. It goes beyond CATs by discussing and illustrating key issues for the design of studies that contribute to the scholarship of teaching and learning. Using case studies coordinated with related research reviews, the authors engage readers by raising both fundamental and stimulating questions that address the why and how of doing classroom research.

McKeachie, W. J., and Svinicki, M. *Teaching Tips: Strategies, Research, and Theory for College and University Teachers.* (12th ed.) Boston: Houghton Mifflin, 2006.

The classic, yet thoroughly updated, text for teachers of traditional students as well as adults. First used as a guide for teaching assistants at the University of Michigan in the early 1950s, the longevity of this resource is a signal of its usefulness for so many teachers, both new and experienced. Connections of the twelfth edition to earlier versions of *Teaching Tips* are most noticeable in the first two parts— "Getting Started" (for example, an introduction to the culture of teaching, course planning, and the first class meeting) and "Basic Skills for Facilitating Student Learning" (reading, discussing, lecturing, assessing learning, and assigning grades)—and the last part—"Lifelong Learning for the Teacher." The middle parts of the book cover various challenges and opportunities for adapting to differences among students, skills and strategies for dealing with other aspects of teaching, and educational goals that go beyond memorization of facts and concepts. Professor McKeachie writes in the preface (p. xviii): "*Teaching Tips* has stressed learner-centered teaching since the very first edition, in which I emphasized the importance of active learning. . . . What counts in education is not so much what the teacher does as what goes on in the students' minds. . . . 'Learner-centered' may appear to diminish the importance of the teacher. Not so! Your unique qualities as a person, your integrity, your commitment to your students' development—these are even more important than they were when the teacher's role was simply that of a talking textbook. . . . *There is no one best way of teaching.* . . . I do not offer a set of rules to follow. Rather I suggest strategies to consider and modify as needed by the ever-changing dynamics of your classes." In using this resource, you will discover or rediscover, as many of us before you have, that Bill McKeachie is indeed an exceptional mentor!

Walvoord, B. E., and Anderson, W. J. *Effective Grading: A Tool for Learning and Assessment.* San Francisco: Jossey-Bass, 1998.

An informed discussion of different approaches to grading and how grading affects student learning. Procedures and examples are provided for managing the grading process, making assignments worth grading, criteria and standards for grading, calculating course grades, communicating with students about their grades, making grading more time efficient, and using the grading process to improve teaching. A part of this sourcebook also covers "how grading serves broader assessment purposes."

CHAPTER 21

Addressing Diversity

G. Roger Sell

In the second edition of *Designing and Assessing Courses and Curriculum*, Diamond (1998) framed a set of issues that remain highly relevant ten years later in addressing educational concerns for diversity:

> Most higher education institutions include on their list of major goals some reference to developing in their students a respect for diversity, an understanding of different cultures, and the ability to work constructively with others who have different backgrounds, goals, and priorities. The growing movement in this direction is as significant as it [is] substantial. . . .

> Unlike most of the other basic goals for all students, cultural diversity cannot be addressed within one course or curriculum. Reaching this goal presents faculty and institutions with a unique challenge. . . .

> Developing in our students the ability and willingness to work effectively in a multicultural environment is a complex task for a number of reasons. First, to do it successfully we must actively involve the entire campus community and reach far beyond the classroom. We cannot successfully teach our students to deal with diversity if they find intolerance and bigotry in their residence halls or in offices around campus. Second, few issues create more tension in our classrooms because in this instance students are asked to question beliefs that have been developed since childhood. Third, until we deal with prejudice directly, a significant portion of students will find the environment of our classrooms is simply not conducive to learning. . . . Fourth, most of us are not particularly comfortable addressing these issues in our courses, in our classrooms, or in conversations with our students. Nor have we been prepared to do so [pp. 203–204].

This chapter takes a fresh look at diversity, focusing particularly on connections between diversity and what and how we teach and learn. One university is used as a case example to illustrate ways in which institution-wide concerns for diversity can be addressed.

Dimensions of Diversity and Its Values in Postsecondary Education

Diversity is not limited to a particular individual or group characteristic such as race, ethnicity, age, sex, class, or religion. The concept of diversity is inclusive of these characteristics, and much more, that is directly relevant to the what, how, and why of teaching and learning in postsecondary education. For example, Missouri State University described diversity as follows in its strategic plan, "Imagining and Making Missouri's Future":

> Diversity is comprised of the multiplicity of people, cultures, and ideas that contribute to the richness and variety of life. It broadly encompasses a mixture of similarities and differences along a multitude of dimensions including, but not limited to, values, cultures, concepts, learning styles, and perceptions that individuals possess. According to the Higher Learning Commission of the North Central Association of Colleges and Schools, diversity "is represented in many forms, such as differences in ideas, viewpoints, perspectives, values, religious beliefs, backgrounds, race, gender, age, sexual orientation, human capacity, and ethnicity of those who attend and work in the organization." [2006].

In a related initiative, the President's Commission for Diversity at Missouri State endorsed the American Council on Education's *Statement on Academic Rights and Responsibilities* (1998) as a set of values that inspired an institutional commitment to diversity:

1. *Diversity enriches the educational experience.* We learn from those whose experiences, beliefs, and perspectives that are different from our own, and these lessons can be taught best in a richly diverse intellectual and social environment.
2. *Diversity prompts personal growth—and a healthy society.* Diversity challenges stereotyped preconceptions; it encourages critical thinking; and it helps students learn to communicate effectively with people of varied backgrounds.
3. *Diversity strengthens communities and the workplace.* Education within a diverse setting prepares students to become good citizens in an increasingly complex, pluralistic society; it fosters mutual respect and teamwork; and it builds communities whose members are judged by the quality of their character and their contributions.

4. *Diversity enhances America's economic competitiveness.* Sustaining the nation's prosperity in the twenty-first century will require us to make effective use of the talents and abilities of all our citizens in work settings that bring together individuals from diverse backgrounds and cultures.

As a result of these values, Missouri State University is committed to creating physically and psychologically safe environments where students, faculty, and staff will be valued for both their similarities and differences. Differences should be viewed as valued resources for academic, cultural and personal development. A challenging atmosphere which fosters the exploration of issues from multiple perspectives will enhance intellectual exploration as well as personal, professional and institutional growth [2005–06].

Resource Q is the outline of a faculty seminar on "Diversity in the Classroom: Inclusive Teaching and Learning in a Multicultural Environment" that illustrates one approach for addressing diversity issues with faculty at the classroom level. Each institution decides how it will address diversity issues. However, we all can benefit from sharing experiences, approaches, and what works and does not work at different institutions. The following examples are some of the other ways that Missouri State University is addressing various aspects of diversity.

1. The 2005–06 report of the President's Commission for Diversity at Missouri State University. Available at www.missouristate.edu/diversitycommission/10110.htm.

2. A Declaration of University Community Principles. Available at www.missouristate.edu/declaration/.

3. A Committee on Freedom of Expression Policies and Procedures. Available at www.missouristate.edu/president/committees/expression/finalreport.htm.

4. Equity and Diversity Online Training. Available at www.missouristate.edu/human/training/equity.htm.

5. Suggested Wording for Course Syllabi/Policy Statements. Available at www.missouristate.edu/assets/provost/Course PolicyStatements2007–2008.doc.

Statements similar to those above can be found at a multitude of colleges and universities—public and private, large and small, rural and urban, two-year and four-year, undergraduate and graduate. While some might argue that diversity is divisive and that quality of education suffers when diversity is promoted, the large majority of postsecondary institutions and faculty freely endorse the value of diversity and seek responsive and responsible ways to act in accordance.

Major Recent Events and Their Implications for Diversity in Postsecondary Education _____

Colleges and universities, however, are not isolated from major events that shape public views and have a widespread impact. Which recent developments, since the publication of the second edition of this guide, have had or are having a significant impact on diversity policies and practices of postsecondary institutions? Although the choice of any small number of events having a particularly significant impact on diversity in postsecondary education is arguable, five broad-ranging developments are discussed briefly and some implications are suggested for consideration.

September 11, 2001, and Its Aftermath

Resulting in enormous fatalities and casualties, the attacks on the World Trade Center and the Pentagon, along with the crash of Flight 93 in Pennsylvania, have continued to affect the emotions and outlook of people in the United States and other countries. Although affecting all Americans in one way or another, the most immediate impact has been on the individuals involved and the losses felt by their family members and close acquaintances. Consequential actions related to 9/11 include, but are not limited to, involvement in (and the associated loss of life and casualties in) the Afghanistan and Iraq wars, broad-based awareness of and reactions to political and religious extremism, and aggressive security measures to counteract future acts of terrorism and to protect individuals and national security. With few exceptions, actions such as these tend to fuel negative attitudes toward diversity among persuasive outspoken critics and single-purpose organized groups in the United States who associate "appreciation of differences" with liberal thought, radicalism, and threats to the "American way of life." More specifically, some implications for colleges and universities include:

• Which content to include in courses, curricula, and special programs to help students understand, and be better prepared for, acts of terrorism and reasoned responses.

• How to respond to verbal and physical attacks, as well as more subtle forms of discrimination, against students, faculty, and guest speakers who are from particular countries, of particular religions, speak particular languages, or appear to be associated (directly or indirectly) with terrorism or extreme groups.

• Which policies and procedures to establish to protect the security of people, information systems, and facilities on campus.

• How to deal with the disruption to, and added concern for, the enrollment of international students and the international travel of, and exchange programs for, students and faculty.

Some of the more positive implications associated with 9/11, or stemming from actions associated with 9/11, are:

- Time and concern given during classes and special programs on campus to students, and their family members or friends, involved in an act of terrorism or international conflict.

- Attention to the seriousness of messages that state or imply terrorist acts, or the intent to do harm to others, involving students, staff, faculty, or administrators.

- Beginning efforts to create a kind of GI Bill for military personnel who have served in Afghanistan or Iraq, including special provisions for veterans with disabilities.

In many ways, 9/11 changed the psyche of the American people and beyond. Each teacher should consider how 9/11 and its aftermath affects what is taught, how, and for which reasons.

University of Michigan Affirmative Action Cases

With regard to recent court cases involving the University of Michigan, Ann Springer (2005), Associate Counsel of the American Association of University Professors, filed an update on diversity and affirmative action (excerpted below):

> The University of Michigan's two affirmative action cases (undergraduate and law school) became the cases on which the issue of affirmative action in admissions was once again addressed by the Supreme Court. The Court heard oral argument on both cases on April 1, 2003, and a decision was issued on June 23, 2003.
>
> In the fall of 1997, two class action lawsuits were filed by the Center for Individual Rights on behalf of white students denied admission to the University of Michigan's undergraduate and law school programs. (*Gratz v. Bollinger, et al.* and *Grutter v. Bollinger et al.*) The suits allege that the University utilizes different standardized test score/grade-point average standards for white and minority students, but the University counters that race is only one among a number of factors taken into account in its admissions processes. (It has since adopted new admissions guidelines that assign points to applicants for academic and non-academic factors, including race.

The University asserts that the new system maintains its commitment to affirmative action and was under development before the lawsuit. The Center for Individual Rights (CIR) has faulted the new system for also making race too large a factor in admissions.) The state's efforts have been quite successful in increasing minority representation within its programs over the past decade or so.

On June 23, 2003 the U.S. Supreme Court finally issued its much awaited decisions in these two cases. The Court issued its *Grutter* decision first—a 5–4 decision written by Justice Sandra Day O'Connor. In it the Court endorsed Justice Powell's decision in Regents of the University of California v. Bakke, finding diversity in higher education to be a compelling state interest and upholding the law school admissions program. The Court noted the individuality of the review in the law school, and held that race can be considered as a "plus" factor in admissions if it is considered in the context of a "highly individualized, holistic review of each applicant's file, giving serious consideration to all the ways an applicant might contribute to a diverse educational environment."

In contrast, however, in the 6–3 *Gratz* decision, Justice O'Connor joined the opinion's author, Justice William Rehnquist, and four other justices in striking down Michigan's undergraduate admissions program. Importantly, the *Gratz* decision upheld the concept of affirmative action and diversity as a compelling interest. But it also struck down Michigan's undergraduate admissions process, finding its award of 20 points out of 150 to underrepresented minority applicants solely because of race to be insufficiently "narrowly tailored to achieve the interest in educational diversity that respondents' claim justifies their program" [Springer, 2005].

Although these legal cases that reached the Supreme Court are focused on issues of race and admission to an undergraduate or graduate program, they have much broader diversity implications for colleges and universities:

• Who is admitted to an institution defines, in part, the range of differences in the student population, characteristics of students enrolled in courses you teach, and the kinds of experiences that students have both within and outside classrooms.

• If race is important in the mix of student characteristics, then colleges and universities have much at stake in decisions about whom is admitted and under which criteria or conditions.

• Both proponents and critics of the educational role of social justice are actively involved in debates about not only race and admission but also other aspects of diversity and admission related to courses and curricula (for example, academic preparation, academic standards, student support services, and outcomes assessment).

Claims of Liberal Bias Among Faculty

Professors are all Democrats, except for those who are communists. Professors all hate [President George W.] Bush. Professors favor like-minded students and love converting those who love God, country, and the president . . .

—Jaschik, 2007

So begins a recent article in *Inside Higher Education*, citing claims made in blogs and columns authored by "right-leaning" authors. Results of research studies are used by David Horowitz (www. FrontPagemag.com) and others to provide empirical evidence of professors' liberal biases and have been used as arguments to support the students' Academic Bill of Rights (http://www.students foracademicfreedom.org/abor.html).

Lee (2006) examined eight studies published between 2003 and 2006 that, as a group, "presented evidence purporting to show that higher education in the United States displays a systematic liberal bent. This, in the opinion of the critics, marginalizes conservative voices on the faculty and results in political views being presented in the classroom. . . . These critics also suggest that students with conservative views are at a minimum uncomfortable in this environment and at worst may be punished with lower grades" (p. 1). Using five widely used criteria for evaluating research quality, Lee found that none of the eight studies met all of the criteria, three met two of the criteria, and three met none of the criteria.

Nonetheless, whether supported by valid research findings or not, perceptions strongly influence behavior. In the United States, parents and the public at large have long contended that political orientations should be kept out of education. Concerns are heightened when this anti-political orientation toward education is combined with the publicity of events that indicate the liberal bent of faculty, especially with regard to academic expectations for students. Some implications for postsecondary institutions are:

- Protection for students to express their concerns about teacher behaviors that inhibit or restrict student freedom of expression.

- Support for faculty to use their professional judgment in the design and implementation of courses while respecting student rights and creating an environment that is conducive to learning for all students.

- Institutional responsibilities to support the constitutional freedoms of all members of the college or university community and to provide an ongoing educational program that develops sensitivities, knowledge, and skills for implementing important principles for educational communities.

Student Success Initiatives

Approximately 25 percent of all full-time, first-time students counted in the fall enrollment for U.S. four-year public institutions do not re-enroll at the same institution the following fall term. Overall, 50 percent of these first-time students do not graduate within six years from their matriculating institution. These numbers are considerably lower for students who begin their postsecondary enrollment at a two-year college as well as for African-American, Native-American, and Hispanic students. Moreover, those who graduate from four-year colleges and universities often do not possess the knowledge and skills expected by employers or needed for active civic engagement. These are some of the findings relevant to the Commission on the Future of Higher Education (U.S. Department of Education, 2006), who in turn recommended strong actions for reversing these trends, including more effective student support programs and assessments of student outcomes.

Implications similar to those drawn from research on how people learn are applicable to teacher-student relationships that increase student success, such as:

- Communicate clear, consistent, and reasonably high expectations for all students
- Emphasize appropriately challenging coursework that stretches students beyond where they are
- Take into consideration students' backgrounds and pre-college experiences
- Actively engage students in meaningful learning experiences
- Provide support that is responsive to individual needs, interests, and expectations
- Recognize the importance of students' experiences outside the classroom

Diversity and Community Study

Robert D. Putnam, Harvard political scientist, unveiled an alarming report in summer 2007 that increasing ethnic diversity, which is occurring in most advanced countries, tends to reduce trust, solidarity, altruism, and cooperation. He found, from his study of U.S. communities, that residents of ethnically diverse neighborhoods tend to "hunker down," interact less, and have fewer friends.

If there is any "good news" in these findings from a highly credible researcher, it is that the effects of increasing diversity are probably seen in the short run. Putnam is confident that, in the long run, diversity has important cultural, economic, and developmental benefits. The key seems to be to "hang in there" until the longer-term benefits start to kick in (2007).

If we assume that these findings are generalizable to states, and at least to larger communities in the United States, then there are some strong implications for educational institutions, such as:

- Revisiting the values that support the promotion of diversity and involving all members of the educational community in open dialogue regarding their endorsement.

- Nurturing diversity content in courses throughout the curriculum, and actively engaging faculty and students in discussions related to significant public and private issues dealing with trust, altruism, competition, and cooperation.

- Distinguishing the difference between short-term and long-term impacts of diversity, and engaging in systematic efforts to examine the effects of diversity on students and faculty, the institution and its programs, and surrounding communities.

Some of the other major recent events that could have been discussed with clear implications for diversity and postsecondary education include legal and illegal immigration, rights of gay and lesbian couples, prayer in public places, and equity issues dealing with faculty employment, evaluation, and reward systems.

The Diverse Classroom

Chism (2002) discusses four key areas for inclusive teaching: (1) make all students feel welcome in the classroom and the course, (2) treat students as individuals, (3) create an environment in which all students feel they can participate fully, and (4) treat students fairly. Although these topics focus on what teachers can do, they also include interactions of students with teachers and students with students. Therefore, as a set, these behaviors support the values of teaching and learning with diversity. Because this excellent resource is no longer in print, behaviors addressed by Chism are covered here in some detail.

Making All Students Feel Welcome

- Use care and sensitivity in selecting terms that refer to social groups (for example, "gay and lesbian students" rather than "homosexual students," "Asian" rather than "Oriental," "women" rather than "gals") and people with disabilities (for example, "sight impaired" rather than "blind" and "physically disabled" rather than "handicapped").

- Use terminology and define terms so that concepts are readily understood by all students.

- Help students orient themselves to the college experience as the course progresses.

- Acknowledge the presence of each student (by calling students by name, greeting students before class meetings, allowing for personal comments, and so on).

- Make explicit at the beginning of a course that diversity is valued by welcoming different perspectives and accommodating different needs.

- In larger classes, move around to different locations in the room, invite and schedule students to meet with you outside of class, and rotate among groups of students who meet during class time.

- Plan, prepare students for, guide (as needed), and monitor active student participation in collaborative or cooperative learning, team learning, peer teaching, study groups, or other small groups formed for your course.

- Form groups of two or three occasionally to discuss a relevant issue or topic related to the course goals and objectives.

- Include content, authors, and examples that represent a range of multicultural perspectives for understanding the subject matter of the course and for serving as role models of scholars, practitioners, and artists in various fields and disciplines.

- Include references to scholars or issues connected with socially diverse groups.

- Create an atmosphere conducive to open inquiry and new or different perspectives that challenge existing views and present new possibilities for understanding.

- Avoid behaviors that patronize students who have a disability or are members of a particular racial or ethnic group.

- With expert consultation, provide reasonable accommodations for students with diagnosed disabilities.

- Listen to a range of student voices and concerns in discussing issues, planning class activities, and selecting means for assessing student performance.

Treating Students as Individuals

- Avoid praise or censure of any student with regard to their social identity.
- Avoid tokenism.
- Maintain reasonably high standards for all students enrolled in the course.
- Be aware of stereotypes that cloud individual characteristics.
- Invite students to express their own opinions and interpretations rather than the views of a particular social group or group of persons with disabilities.
- Serve as a mentor with students from diverse social and disability groups.

Creating an Environment in Which All Students Feel They Can Participate Fully

- Recognize that individual students probably have learning styles different from your own style and that of at least some other students in the course.
- Avoid the interpretation of differences from the traditional norm as deficits.
- Be aware of whom is called upon to answer questions or do other things in the course, and whether there is a pattern of bias in your behavior.
- Ask an observer to record participation levels in one or more of your classes to get a sense of the patterns and to avoid pitfalls of unequal or biased behaviors for participation.
- Encourage students to speak with you about their needs.
- Insert comments in the course syllabus about alternative formats or options that students have with regard to learning in the course and how assessment of performance will occur.
- Attend to student needs for course relevance to their life experiences.
- Be flexible when the personal responsibilities of students (such as child-care or workplace issues) call for different learning arrangements.
- Use varied instructional approaches (lecture, discussion, small-group work, experiential activities, and so on) as well as varied modalities (for example, redundancy in print and

visual resources) that allow students to use their preferred learning style while being appropriately challenged to expand their learning repertoires.

- Use a range of means for evaluating student work, including both qualitative and quantitative assessments that span objective items (such as multiple-choice tests), essay items, performance items, and other ways to assess performance.

Treating Students Fairly

- Recognize that equal (fair) treatment is not necessarily the same treatment for all students but rather treatment that is appropriate and effective for the circumstances of particular learners.

- Communicate expectations that are relevant and appropriate to each student.

- Hold a discussion at the beginning of a course on expectations and standards, coupled with a clear syllabus of course objectives, activities, due dates for papers, scheduled tests, and so on.

- Be aware that, when class participation is part of the grade, some students may be socialized to value listening more than speaking and, therefore, not the number but the quality of contributions may be the most important.

- Design and implement the course with inclusion in mind.

To summarize, Chism offered these concluding thoughts:

As faculty, we play a crucial role in the success of students from socially diverse groups. To help these students get the most from their education and to help the institution benefit from the talents and perspectives the students bring, we can:

1. Help to make the students feel welcome by displaying genuine interest, personalizing our interactions with them, and honoring and including their perspectives and experiences.
2. Treat students as individuals, rather than as representatives of social groups.
3. Ensure that students from diverse social groups have ample opportunity to participate fully through providing options for different learning styles and modes of expression.
4. Strive for fair treatment by communicating appropriate expectations and making instructional decisions with inclusion in mind [2002, pp. 146–147].

A Closing Note

In this chapter, we have attempted to identify and discuss some of the dimensions of diversity, why it is crucial in education and society, and the values associated with its nurture. We also highlighted some recent events that have enlivened discussion of diversity in higher education and their implications for education. More specifically, diversity-related issues were linked to teacher-student relationships and teacher behaviors in postsecondary settings.

How to live constructively and responsibly with diversity is in many respects the most important issue of our time. We in postsecondary education have a special responsibility to increase sensitivity, develop knowledge, and cultivate wisdom related to diversity so that our individual and collective efforts strive toward creating a future that provides opportunities for all to realize their potential.

Additional Resources

The breadth and depth of diversity resources are constantly changing. The following Web sites provide useful resources to stay abreast of new developments. All of these Web sites appear to be regularly updated and maintained.

Association of American Colleges and Universities (AAC&U) Diversity Web (www.diversityweb.org/)

> This site provides "a compendium of campus practices and resources for campus practitioners seeking to place diversity at the center of the academy's educational and societal mission." It includes Diversity Innovations, Diversity Research and Trends, access to issues of Diversity Digest and On Campus with Women (OCWW), and Diversity Postings of conferences, papers, and position openings.

Chronicle of Higher Education (http://chronicle.com/)

> A weekly newspaper that covers items relevant to all sectors of higher education. A total of 527 items were identified in July 2007 from the single search term "diversity."

Jossey-Bass Publishers (www.josseybass.com)

> One of several major publishers of educational books and monographs on various aspects of diversity. In July 2007, a total of 285 items were identified using the single search term "diversity."

National Education Association (NEA) (www.nea.org/webre sources/diversitylinks.html)

> This Web site includes materials relevant to a range of diversity concerns for elementary and secondary education as well as postsecondary education. Some of the topics include a civil rights project, culturally responsive teaching, access to a diversity calendar, multicultural education and ethnic groups, and other equity and diversity resources.

CHAPTER 22

Developing a Learning-Centered Syllabus

The clearer the picture your students have of what you expect them to be able to do by the end of your course, and the greater their understanding of what their role will be and of the criteria that will be used to determine success or failure, the more effective the course will be. A learning-centered syllabus is based on the question, "What information will help my students succeed in my course?" Using such a syllabus can improve learning and, at the same time, avoid many of the frustrations caused by poor communication. In addition, providing your students with more information about the goals of your course, and the rationale behind any new instructional approaches that you might be using, can significantly reduce the resistance to change and frustrations so common with most students. Grunert-O'Brien, Millis, and Cohen have observed: "Your syllabus represents a significant point of interaction, often the first, between you and your students. If thoughtfully prepared, your syllabus will demonstrate the interplay of your understanding of students' needs and interests, your beliefs and assumptions about the nature of learning and education, and your values and interests concerning course content and structure. If carefully designed, your syllabus will provide your students with essential information and resources that can help them to become effective learners by actually shaping their own learning" (2008, p. x).

Throughout this book, you have focused on the design of courses and curricula that will help your students develop the competencies they need to be successful in college and after graduation. The models that we have used shift the focus away from what you will teach to what your students will learn, so that you as a faculty member will serve less as a disseminator of knowledge than as a facilitator of learning. This shift calls for changes in how you think about the courses you teach, how you design students' learning experiences, how you use class time and your students' time outside of class, what you expect from your students, and what they can expect from you.

Technology, changing demographics, failure to engage students, and new ways of thinking about the nature of knowledge in the Information Age have prompted many instructional changes on college and university campuses. In addition, new opportunities available through the Internet and e-mail, increased use of active learning, as well as internships and extended-classroom activities, have significantly altered how we teach by requiring enhanced interaction among all members of the learning community. The traditional syllabus, designed for a teacher- or content-centered classroom, is ineffective for helping students understand their expanding role in the learning enterprise. To understand the expectations we have of them and our plans for the learning experience, students need more comprehensive information than the traditional syllabus provides. The learning-centered syllabus places students at the center of the question, "What do students need to know in order to derive maximum benefit from this educational experience?"

In their review, *How College Affects Students: A Third Decade of Research* (2005), Pascarella and Terenzini reported that the two most important dimensions of teacher behavior in predicting student learning were clarity of presentation and course structure and organization. Other reports have consistently focused on the importance of a clear and detailed syllabus as the best indicator of a well-organized course.

Many faculty have already gone far beyond the one- or two-page syllabus with which most of us are familiar. John Lough (1996), in a study of faculty members who have been recognized as Carnegie Professors of the Year, found important similarities in syllabi designed by these exemplary teachers. Most obvious was their "detailed precision." Each contained clearly stated course objectives, a day-by-day schedule identifying specific reading assignments and due dates, and clear statements regarding make-up dates, attendance, and grading standards. They also provided students with the times faculty members would be available in their offices, by e-mail, and by phone at home. Lough observes: "One gets the very clear impression the . . . award winners have extraordinary expectations for their own behavior in and out of the classroom. Perhaps it is not so surprising, therefore, that these professors might impose some of these same standards on the students with whom they share so much" (Lough, 1996, p. 223).

Obviously, it is through their actions—what they do in the classroom and how it is manifested in what they say in their syllabi—that these faculty communicate these standards to their students.

We faculty often invest a great deal of time in improving the content and structure of our courses, the quality of the materials we use, and the equity of our examinations. Despite these efforts, many of us spend countless hours with individual students reviewing content, attempting to clarify assignments, and generally helping them (and perhaps ourselves) to understand requirements, assignments, and standards. Faculty are also reporting a significant increase in the litigious attitude on the part of students (and their parents). In most instances these problems are caused by unclear grading criteria or poorly communicated or understood expectations of what students' responsibilities are to be.

Although many of the instructional problems we face are to be expected, others are unnecessary. If our students do not understand their assignments, if they study the wrong content for a test, or are confused about how grades will be determined, they will not learn effectively. Such problems can be avoided. In a review of the problems faced by students, a course-approval committee at the University of Maryland (Rubin, 1985, p. 56) identified a series of important questions that were repeatedly not answered in the syllabi provided by the faculty to their students:

- Why would a student want to take this course?
- What are the course objectives? Where do they lead, intellectually and practically?
- What are the prerequisites? What does the faculty member assume that the students already know? Will the missing necessary skills be taught during the course?
- Why do the parts of the course come in the order they do?
- Will the course be primarily lecture, discussions, or group work?
- What does the professor expect from the students?
- What is the purpose of the assignments?
- What will the tests test? memory? understanding? ability to synthesize, to present evidence logically, to apply knowledge in a new context?
- Why have the books been chosen? What is their relative importance in the course and in the discipline?

An effectively used and carefully designed comprehensive syllabus can improve the students' learning by helping to answer these and other questions. It can improve communication, significantly reducing problems for you and your students.

Just as courses differ, no two syllabi should be alike. The final decision about the form and content of a learning-centered syllabus must be based on the structure of the course (lecture, laboratory, distance learning, field experience, discussion, and so on), the number of students, the learning goals and expectations for students, and how much direction you wish your students to have. For some, the syllabus becomes a comprehensive manual.

Why Use a Learning-Centered Syllabus?

A learning-centered syllabus serves a wide variety of functions, all designed to make your role easier and your students' roles and responsibilities clearer. Your syllabus can do the following:

• *Define student responsibilities for successful completion of the course.* One of the biggest problems students have is managing time effectively. If your students have a clear idea of what they are expected to accomplish and a time frame for completion, they are more likely to finish assignments on time and be appropriately prepared for exams. As students assume greater responsibility for their own learning, they need to know what is expected of them.

• *Reduce significantly the resistance to change.* Student resistance to anything unfamiliar has been identified as one of the biggest obstacles to improving teaching (Rehm, 2006). By anticipating this immediate reaction and by discussing the rationale behind the structure and design of the course, you can significantly reduce your students' resistance to these changes.

• *Improve students' note taking and studying.* Students frequently spend class time copying detailed formulas and diagrams or attempting to distinguish important from unimportant information. As a result, they often miss the major points of the presentation or discussion. By including outlines of information to be covered, essential diagrams and tables, and copies of overhead transparencies, the manual helps students organize and focus their note taking and studying.

• *Reduce test anxiety and improve test-taking skills.* Providing your students with sample questions in a manual has a positive impact on learning and reduces text anxiety. The more students know about the instructional priorities, the more effective and efficient they can be in their studying.

- *Review important policies and procedures.* Since procedures and standards vary from course to course, students are often confused as to the policies that each faculty member will be following. Your syllabus is the ideal place to inform students of the key policies and procedures for your specific course and what they can expect from you as their teacher. What, for example, are your policies toward academic dishonesty, late papers, and attendance? If you are encouraging students to contact you by e-mail, how soon can they expect you to respond? Unfortunately, unless told otherwise, students often anticipate that you will answer e-mails almost immediately which, for most of us, is impractical if not impossible. If you are allowing students to call you at home make sure that you set time limits; students are prone to study far later than the working time of most of us. For more on these types of problems see Mary McKinney's excellent article "Setting Boundaries."

- *Acquaint your students with the logistics of the course.* Courses vary significantly in the schedule of classes, the instructors for each class, and the type of sessions (guest lecturers, simulations, group projects, and so on). A learning-centered syllabus details this information so that students know what to expect at each class meeting.

- *Provide readings that are difficult to obtain.* If a course is developed before comprehensive literature on the topic is available, the manual can include copies of articles you want your students to read. (If a syllabus is used in this way, be certain that the necessary copyright clearances are obtained.)

- *Include handouts that might otherwise have been distributed individually.* We frequently distribute handouts as they become appropriate to the topics covered. If these handouts are included in the syllabus, students find it easier to keep all the course information together and accessible. Materials of this type often include important tables, charts, graphs, and diagrams that are not found in the required texts.

- *Improve your students' efficiency.* By including detailed descriptions of major assignments, you can help your students prepare for their work and improve their time management.

Faculty who have developed comprehensive syllabi have found the approach helpful for their students. Typical comments follow:

"[The expanded syllabus] provides a succinct presentation of relevant course materials, which helps the student to define what is important for this particular course."

"It helped a great deal. Faculty colleagues from other institutions have been able to adapt and adopt the course with limited guidance from me. In addition, I have very few requests for clarification of course requirements, time lines, grading criteria or standards, or weekly assignments. Perhaps some faculty look forward to such repeated discussions—I prefer to teach."

"A terrific idea. The students can refer to [the syllabus] throughout the semester, and they considered it to be one of the most positive aspects of the course."

"The greatest advantage for me is that it enables me to get a variety of materials in students' hands efficiently and effectively."

"[The expanded syllabus] provided necessary coherence for the class. Without it, the course would have appeared not only 'experimental' but unorganized or even incoherent."

"The syllabus provided important information and a semblance of rationality. It gave all of us a common plan and reference."

Equally important, the very process of putting a learning-centered syllabus together can lead you to a more carefully designed course because it allows you to review, in a logical manner, the major decisions you have made up to this point.

Content and Style

The content of a syllabus varies from course to course, as does its general format. However, the following items are usually included. (The specific order in which these items are covered is not absolute.)

- Title and number of the course, section number, class time, and location.
- Faculty and staff (TAs) involved in the course—how to contact them (office hours, phone, email, Web site)
- General course description written in an engaging manner, perhaps including examples of practical application or the framing questions or theories underlying the course
- Rationale (how this course fits into the general program and for whom it was designed)
- How you will communicate with students regarding notices, grades, and so on (e-mail, in-class, course Web site)
- Overview of content
  - Course outline
  - General course and individual unit learning outcomes
  - Your expectations for student behavior and performance

- Important policies and procedures
  - Academic dishonesty
  - Late papers and missed exams
  - E-mail messages and phone calls
  - Other
- Evaluation or grading procedures
  - Credits and grades (how determined)
  - Requirements and assignments
  - Criteria
- Materials
  - Texts or other materials—where and how to get them and how to use them
  - Bibliographies, resources, and so on
  - Calendar—places and times for units, projects, meetings, deadlines, and so on
  - Application of technology—e-mail, course management software, course Web site, online research capabilities, and so on
  - Facilities—learning laboratory, library, museum, and so on; where they are and how to use them
  - Checklist of all deadlines
  - Self-tests (with answers optional)—designed to give the students an opportunity to see whether they can meet the stated objectives
  - Copyright or credit notices
  - Readings (optional) or other materials (such as forms to be turned in) that are necessary and not available elsewhere. Also included in this section may be copies of complex diagrams or other visuals that will be used by the faculty member during lectures, chronologies, and materials on using the library or computing center.

Some Specific Suggestions

Because your syllabus will be used by students, it should be written to students, using "you" whenever possible. It should be clear and precise, especially for courses with complex structures. Flow diagrams, if used well and designed with care, can outline the scope of the course and provide logistical information. If complex drawings are to be used in large lecture sections, reduced copies should be included. Also effective is leaving space for taking notes if the syllabus is to be referred to during the lecture. *The Course Syllabus* by Grunert-O'Brien, Millis, and Cohen (2008) is an excellent guide to writing a learning-centered syllabus; it includes representative pages from a number of syllabi in various disciplines.

A Matter of Style and Tone

In his article discussing problems with many course syllabi, Manlo Singham (2007) raises concerns about the style and tone of many of these documents where their approach, often "authoritarian," may actually be detrimental to effective teaching. Your syllabus is students' first introduction to you and to the course. It should be engaging, explanatory, and inviting in addition to including all the pertinent particulars. It is vitally important that students clearly understand the goals and purpose of the course, their responsibility, how they will be assessed, the grading criteria that you will use, and important procedures, and it will be up to you to establish the overall supportive tone for your course. This article is available from *Tomorrow's Professor.*

Obtaining Permission to Reproduce Copyrighted Material

At times you may want to include materials from other sources in your syllabus. In most instances you are permitted to quote words, tables, figures, and other material as long as the quotation is accurate and appropriately credited. In recent years the Copyright Law and the definition of "fair use" have undergone a number of major revisions and, with the onset of new computer and electronic transfers, applications have become much more complex.

If you are planning to use copyrighted material, there are two major steps you should take:

1. Make sure that all copyrighted materials are properly cited in your syllabi.

2. Read Resource R, where you'll find a summary of the copyright law dealing with the use of copyrighted material in other publications.

Important: Pay particular attention to the Fair Use section of Resource R, since most syllabi would fall under this section of the law. The primary exception would be if the syllabi were to become part of a course that would be published and distributed beyond your institution.

Fortunately, the recent changes in the copyright law have paid increased attention to educational use which gives you, as a teacher, more flexibility than ever before. However, before you include major sections from published materials by other authors in your syllabus or other course materials, you should check the most recent revision of the copyright laws. Unfortunately, the law itself is long and complex and open to many interpretations. As checking with a legal expect on your campus may be difficult, if you want more detailed information, see Chapter 7, Academic and Educational Permission, in Richard Stim's *Getting Permission and How to License and Clear Copyrighted Material On-line and Off* (Stim, 2004), which includes a major section on publications of this type and other materials relevant to faculty.

Putting Your Syllabus Online

Although an increasing number of faculty are placing their syllabi online for easy retrieval and to cut costs, others are finding that this approach can actually reduce the effectiveness of the document. They report that because the syllabus is an outstanding reference, it should be used in class on a regular basis. When it is online, many students do not print copies and, as a result, do not have it available for use in class. Of course you can require students to print the syllabus or sections of it for use in class. An advantage to the online syllabus is that it is easily modified or updated as the course progresses. Especially for new courses, this makes good sense.

Royalties and Copyright

As noted previously, writing a high-quality learning-centered syllabus takes time and effort—time that you could devote to research, to other writing, or to other financially rewarding activities. Collecting royalties on the sale of a syllabus recognizes the value of the effort and, in one small way, helps to balance the reward system for teaching, research, and publication. The key is how much new material is in the final product. If it contains extensive original work (intellectual property), you may want to discuss with your chair or dean the possibility of collecting royalties. Some faculty are comfortable doing so; others are not. In addition, collecting royalties may negate your ability to use other materials without paying some royalties to the copyright holder.

Because a syllabus may contain important new material, some consideration should be given to copyrighting it. On some campuses a formal royalty and copyright policy is in place. If sales are anticipated outside the institution or if significant new material is contained in the manual, you can hold the copyright or it can be held by the institution if you were awarded funds for the project.

If the syllabus does not contain much new material and is for use only in a specific course, you can simply include a notice of copyright and the year of publication on the title page. No other formal action on your part is required.

Summary

This chapter has described the kind of material you might include in your syllabus in order to support student learning and success in your course. However, no matter how good a syllabus is, its content must be enacted in your classroom. The best syllabi are effective only if they manifest a lively, active, and engaged practice in your classroom.

Resource

Denman, M. "How to Create a Memorable Lecture." *Speaking of Teaching*, Winter 2005, *14*(1). Center for Teaching and Learning, Stanford University, Stanford, Calif.

PART FOUR

Your Next Steps

CHAPTER 23

Using Your Data: Curriculum and Course Revision

Figure 23.1.

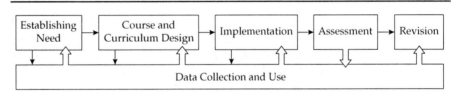

Throughout this book we have stressed the importance of collecting, analyzing, and using good information. Data played a major role in helping you decide if you should begin your curriculum or course design effort. Knowledge of your students, the needs of your discipline, the priorities of your institution, and the competencies needed to succeed in today's world were necessary elements in developing the goals for your project. A review of the literature on teaching and learning, as well as a number of other factors, helped you design the actual learning experience for your students.

Your next step will be to use the information you have collected from students, other faculty, and from alumni or employers to determine what worked, what didn't work, and why. You will use this data to identify the changes you should make in procedures, in content, and in sequence to improve the quality and effectiveness of your course or curriculum. Keep in mind that all the way through the design process you used the data you collected to make some immediate changes in the design—but for the most part, these adjustments did not require major structural changes or a great deal of time to implement.

At this point in the process you'll focus on a number of questions that are far more substantial. Among them:

- Were all of your instructional goals reached?

- For those goals that were not achieved for a significant number of students, what were the problems?

- Was the program successful for certain students and not for others? If so, what were the differences between the two groups?

- Which specific elements of your program were less successful than you had hoped? If there were specific problems with the units, what were they?

- Was the overall curriculum or course cost-effective? Did it efficiently utilize resources, and student and faculty time?

- If important changes are required, what specific problems are most important and should be given priority in the revision process? Where do you start?

In many instances the information you have collected will not only identify major problem areas but will also often provide enough information to determine how to eliminate or reduce the problem. Content can be restructured and resequenced to address unanticipated prerequisite problems, to reduce the time required for completing a unit by reducing the amount of work required, and in some instances, less important material can be reduced or even eliminated. In addition, instructional materials might be improved in both clarity and effectiveness. Only after you have carefully reviewed your data can you determine which specific actions you should take.

Course and curriculum revision is not a one-time occurrence. Students change, new faculty with different perspectives become involved, the priorities of institutions and disciplines change, and new instructional and assessment methods are introduced. Although it will be far less complex than your initial design effort, anticipate that continual revision will and should always be a component of your teaching.

Learning from Others

A great source of information is faculty involved in innovative instructional programs at other institutions. You can anticipate that many will have faced or are now facing some of the same problems as you are.

For this reason you should always explore reports from other institutions focusing on the type of information that was collected, the problems that were being faced, and how they were addressed. An interesting *Inside Higher Ed* report on a number of redesign efforts is "Introductory Course Makeover" by Elia Powers (2007), which describes initiatives at several institutions as part of a project of the *Center for Academic Transformation* supported by the Pew Charitable Trusts.

Another excellent essay on the use of assessment to improve the quality of teaching and learning is "Assessment from the Ground Up" by Donna Englemann (2007). The author describes the use of data as an integral part of a campuswide study of teaching and its impact on both students and faculty. One of the ongoing challenges you'll face when you read reports of innovative programs is finding out what didn't work and why. This information, while often lacking in traditional press releases and reports, will be among the most useful you can collect. For this reason we recommend that whenever possible, you call, e-mail, or visit with colleagues who have designed courses that you find most interesting. Sometimes an hour of conversation with the faculty involved will be well worth the cost of the trip.

Case Studies in Course and Curriculum Revision

A number of the case studies in the back of this book are examples of how programs changed based on the information obtained during the implementation process. While most revisions within a curriculum will take place at the individual course level, there are exceptions. There have been instances where the sequence of courses needed to be modified, where entirely new content areas had to be added, or where changes in the discipline, changes in accreditation requirement, or new research in the field led to major revisions in the curriculum. However, most redesign efforts will focus on individual courses within the curriculum and not on the curriculum as a whole. The following two case studies are representative of the types of revisions that often occur after the initial offering of a new course.

The Evolution of an Introductory Psychology Course: A Case Study

A number of years ago, the psychology department at Syracuse University, building on an earlier project, introduced a new first-year course that was designed to provide all students with the same basic program. Previously, individual sections had been taught by different faculty, each using textbooks supporting his or her own approach to psychology. As a result, the faculty teaching the courses that followed could make few if any assumptions about what the students already knew, causing major problems for the department.

Recognizing the potential problems associated with having faculty and nearly a dozen graduate students offering a single course to approximately eight hundred students per semester, the department asked the teaching support center to formally evaluate the department's first attempt to develop a single introductory course and to make recommendations based on their findings. An evaluation protocol was cooperatively developed and administered, and student performances on tests and examinations were analyzed.

To collect these data, several steps were taken. Staff attended lectures, a random number of recitation sections, and meetings of faculty involved with the course. Interviews were conducted with the recitation leaders (graduate students), the large-group lecturers, other faculty, the department chair, and the course coordinator. The students were also surveyed in the middle and at the end of the course.

Although the course generally ran smoothly for a first-time offering, several specific problems were identified:

- The course, while crucial to the department, was perceived by many as not addressing all the content that many faculty considered essential.

- The lecturers (four different faculty members) were not equally well prepared and their presentations were uneven in quality and often lacked continuity.

- The room in which the lectures were held was poorly suited to the use of the visuals (vital to the course) and had an inadequate sound system.

- The readings assigned by the four lecturers were uneven in both length and difficulty.

- There was too much emphasis on "word lists" and definitions and too little emphasis on important concepts.

- The role of the course coordinator was not clear to faculty or to students.

- Quizzes and examinations were based primarily on textbook materials and did not include questions related to the lecture topics or the recitation discussions; consequently, the students perceived the lectures and recitations as unimportant.

- There was some disagreement about the role of the recitation leaders as well.

To address these concerns, a number of actions were taken:

- The location of the lectures was changed.

- To provide greater continuity, the department tried to reduce the number of new lecturers from semester to semester and to improve the quality of materials used. Greater effort was also made to ensure that the content of the lectures meshed with the specific goals of the course.

- A comprehensive student manual was produced. This manual, in addition to describing the general operation of the course and the role of each of its components, spelled out grading procedures and instructional outcomes and provided representative questions and vocabulary lists. The manual also provided content guidelines to faculty responsible for the large lectures. (In a later version, selected readings were also added.)

- Quizzes and examinations were restructured to be more comprehensive, to stress the major goals of the course, and to include elements covered in both lectures and recitations. Scored items were analyzed, and poorer items were replaced or rewritten.

The results were positive. Ratings of the lectures improved significantly; students found grading to be fairer and exams to be better indicators of knowledge. In addition, and perhaps most significant to some, enrollment increased from eight hundred to thirteen hundred students. In addition, the student manuals were rated extremely useful and clear. In the following semester, the student survey indicated an improvement of the lectures but increased concerns about the recitation sessions. Improvements in the recitation sessions were made during the following year, and a major revision of the entire course followed to meet the significant increase in student enrollment. A comment from the course coordinator best describes the success of this project:

> During the current fall semester, attendance at the lectures runs about 90 to 95 percent (up from about 50 percent in its first year). In addition, there is close cooperation, and weekly meetings are held among the TAs [teaching assistants] and lecturers. Although a fair amount of experience with this format would inevitably tend to improvement, the contributions by the teaching support center, I feel, in terms of diagnoses of problems and specific recommendations, were invaluable in the speed with which the course has improved and reached this status. I also found the data extremely valuable as I trained new teaching assistants entering the program.

Revising an Existing Course: Music for the Non-Major

Figures 23.2 and 23.3 are the field test and revised outlines of the first four-week module of a music course for non-majors at the State University of New York College at Fredonia. (Although this project was completed some time ago, the process that was used in its development and modification was identical to the model described in this book.)

The introductory module was designed to provide each student with an orientation to and framework for the entire course along with the prerequisites that were necessary for the units that follow. Because the student population was extremely diverse—some students had as many as eight years of formal music training while others had none—three tracks were used, with assignments based on the performance of the students on the pretest. Level 1 students had the most comprehensive music background; Level 2 students had some musical experience or coursework; and students assigned to Level 3 had little, if any, background in music.

The changes that were made as a result of the field test and reasons for them are as follows (notice how these changes affected the operational sequence):

- The course overview and the pretest were separated to improve the orientation session.

    Rationale: with its emphasis on independent study and options, the course was such a major departure from traditional courses that many students found the transition difficult. As a result, additional time had to be spent reviewing how to use the student manual as well as explaining to students how they could use the statements of instructional outcomes to improve learning and increase the effectiveness of their study time.

- The sequencing of seminars within the module had to be substantially changed.

    Rationale: for a seminar to be effective, a certain amount of background information is essential. The original sequence did not provide students with enough study time to complete the necessary units before they were discussed in the seminars. The seminars, therefore, were rescheduled later in the module.

- New instructional units were required.

    Rationale: on the posttest, students did not perform at the anticipated level in their ability either to read scores or to discriminate aurally. Two additional independent-study

Figure 23.2.

Fall Field-Test Version of Introductory Module for Music in the Western World

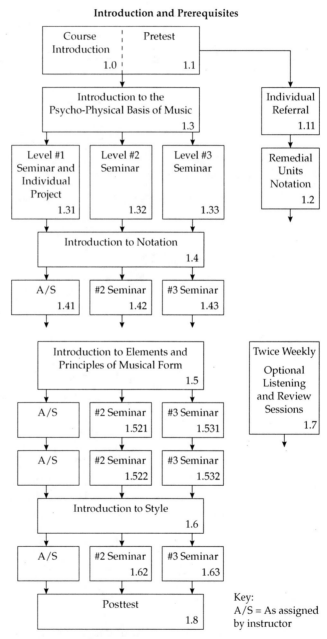

Source: Thomas Regelski and Robert M. Diamond.

Figure 23.3.
Spring Revision of Introductory Module for Music in the Western World

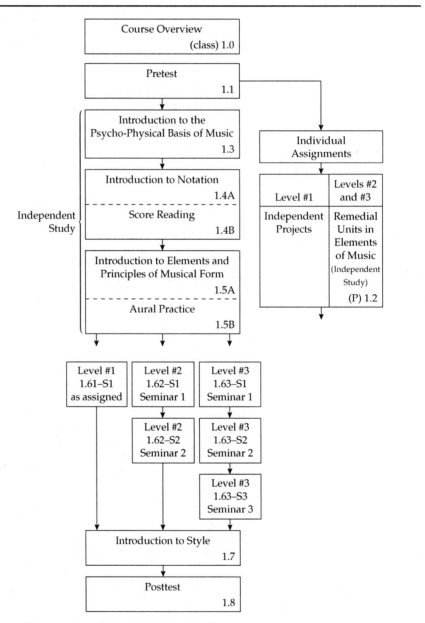

Source: Thomas Regelski and Robert M. Diamond.

units were added, and, as a result, students' deficiencies were corrected.

- One unit had to be completely redesigned.

  Rationale: the original multiscreen presentation style proved to be instructionally ineffective and was disliked (an understatement) by the students. This approach also proved cumbersome and inefficient as it forced all students to move at the same pace. It was replaced by a far more effective instructional sequence used in conjunction with written materials.

- The number of seminars was reduced.

  Rationale: as sometimes happens, the fall and spring semesters did not have the same amount of time available for instruction, forcing a modification in design. By placing the seminars later in the sequence and scheduling more seminars for the Level 3 students and fewer for the well-prepared group, the number of seminars was reduced from fourteen (including three optional ones) to six. This decrease did not appear to have a negative effect on either attitudes or achievement. In addition, to permit maximum flexibility, this three-hour course was scheduled for an hour a day (five hours each week) so that every student could attend any session scheduled during that period. However, the maximum number of live meetings a student would attend during the four-week module was six.

- The twice-weekly optional listening and review sessions were replaced by oral practice and the use of recordings made available through a number of approaches.

  Rationale: because of a heavy assignment load, many students did not attend the regularly scheduled, optional, faculty-led review sessions.

In addition, minor modifications were made in the pretest, in some of the introductory sequences, and in the remedial units that were used. Several remedial assignments were also eliminated, and a more realistic time frame was established. The effectiveness of the new remedial module made it possible to eliminate grouping the students by entering levels of proficiency once this unit was completed.

A Final Word on Course and Curriculum Revision_____

Revision of courses and curricula is a constant that will impact your role as an educator throughout your career. The continual use of good information is one of the major factors in helping you keep your sanity through the entire process. It will provide you with the information you need to make decisions along the way and prevent you from making mistakes that could have a negative effect on your students. The availability of good data can also make the entire change process much less risky and will, in addition, save you a great deal of time and effort. The key is using the information once you have it.

Note: One additional approach you might like to consider is using the *Teaching Goals Inventory* by Angelo and Cross (1993) to review how well the emphasis of your course meshed with the priorities you had established for it (see Resource S). While not designed for this purpose, this instrument can be extremely useful for relating course goals to content.

CHAPTER 24

Learning from Experience

The challenges we face today as teachers and administrators at colleges and universities are more complex than ever before. Our students are more diverse and often come to us inadequately prepared (academically, emotionally, and socially); there are more and more demands on our time; resources are often diminishing; and the critics of higher education are convinced that we place our highest priorities on everything but the education of our students. In addition, if our students are to be prepared for the years ahead, they will require a wide range of additional competencies beyond what has been traditionally taught in our classrooms—competencies that John Abbott, director of the 21st Century Learning Initiative (www. johnsonfdn.org/summer96/search.html) described in an interview with Ted Marchese as "the ability to conceptualize and solve problems that entail abstraction (the manipulation of thoughts and patterns), system thinking, experimentation, and collaboration" (Marchese, 1996, p. 4).

It is certainly not an easy time to be a faculty member or an administrator at any American college or university. On one hand we are asked to become more accountable to the public, more accessible to students from a broader spectrum of society, more proactive to responding to international competition, and, on the other hand, we are asked to reduce our costs per student, improve the quality of our academic programs, and address the needs of a student population that is more diverse, less prepared, and often less motivated than ever before.

A number of additional factors make this challenge even more difficult:

- A faculty reward system on many campuses that places far more emphasis on research and publication than on teaching

- A national ranking system that focuses more on fame, wealth, and exclusivity than it does on how well an institution educates its students (Carey, 2006)

- Boards of Trustees and alumni who often are more interested in and willing to support athletics than they are in devoting their energies to improving the quality of academic programs

- A growing reliance on part-time or untenured faculty who are given little encouragement or time to take an active role in advising students, in course and curriculum design, in instructional improvement, and in serving in the broad spectrum of institutional roles normally assigned to faculty

- A continuing shift in budgeting away from academic programs to security, to addressing legal issues, to meeting unfunded governmental mandates, and to addressing the many demands generated by an expanding technological infrastructure

Equally problematic are the inefficiencies caused by the serious disconnect often found between courses, curricula, and the basic core competencies most faculty believe are required of every college graduate. A 2002 report from the Association of American Colleges and Universities made the following observation: "The fragmentation of the curriculum into a collection of independently 'owned' courses is itself an impediment to student accomplishment because the different courses students take, even on the same campus, are not expected to engage or build on one another. . . In the absence of shared learning goals and clear expectations, a college degree more frequently certifies completion of connected fragments than a coherent plan for student accomplishment" (2002, p. 7).

Is it any wonder that faculty and administrators concerned with the quality of teaching and learning on their campus feel frustrated, overworked, and often under-appreciated?

To reach the goals of a high-quality education will require major changes in what we do as faculty, in how we design the instructional experience of our students, in our students' role in the learning process, and in where this learning takes place. We can anticipate that more and more teaching and learning will occur outside of the traditional classroom, and that the teaching that does take place on campus will be significantly different from what is common today. We will find ourselves focusing more on assessment, and using technology more frequently with students, and the diversity of our communities will increase. Change in how we teach and in the materials we use will become a constant. The stereotype of senior faculty reading from yellowed and somewhat brittle notes almost as old as many of the students in the class will become part of American folklore.

A Respected, Honored Activity

For years, those faculty who spent their energies on teaching-related activities were viewed by some as incapable of doing research, as individuals who cared little about promotion, merit pay, or recognition, and thus were often seen as second-class citizens. On many campuses the message was clear: if you spend your energies on teaching, you do so at your own risk.

Fortunately—for our students, for our institutions, and for many of us—the situation is changing. As the direct result of changes in accreditation requirements and increased demands from state and national governments and business and industry leaders, teaching and the type of course and curriculum activities described in this book are not only becoming respectable but are being encouraged. Each year more internal monies are being set aside to fund course and curriculum activities, and the promotion and tenure systems are being modified to include these endeavors under the rubric of scholarly work. These changes do not imply that research is no longer important. Rather, faculty reward systems are expanding their definitions of scholarship to recognize a far wider range of activities as they become more sensitive to the differences among disciplines and among individuals. The strongest academic units and the most effective institutions recognize that their vitality comes not from every faculty member's having the same strengths, but from the efforts of individuals with different interests and abilities.

It is one thing to have an activity supported, but it is another to do it well. A successful effort in course and curriculum design requires a comprehensive approach. The elements of your course or curriculum must be carefully orchestrated to interrelate and connect. The most talented teacher on your campus will not be successful if what he or she teaches is out of date or if essential goals or elements are missing.

A Quality Educational Experience: Impossible Without a Quality Curriculum

Throughout this book, we have stressed the crucial interrelationship between curriculum and a comprehensive educational experience for your students. This relationship between the curriculum and the courses within it is quite often the weakest link in the total educational experience of students. Tightening up this relationship is not easy. It requires everyone involved—faculty, administrators, and staff—to work together and to be willing to put the needs of the students and the institution above their own personal interests.

In Exhibit 24.1, which you will find at the end of this chapter, Lion F. Gardiner, from his work with the National Academy of Academic Leadership, provides an excellent overview of this key relationship.

Learning from Experience: The Basic Principles of Change

Heeding the important lessons learned over the years will enable you to reduce the problems you have to face and improve the quality of the educational experience of your students. The following principles apply to all aspects of academic innovation; from designing a lesson or a course to totally restructuring an entire academic curriculum.

• *Have a plan and follow it.* This book has proposed one specific model for course and curriculum design. There are others. Select one approach and follow it. Do not skip steps or change models. Every step is important.

• *Do not do it alone.* Having someone from outside your department facilitate the design process not only will result in a better product but will also improve the efficiency of the process itself by reducing the time required. Involving such a facilitator—a staff member from your faculty-support or instructional-support center or a faculty member from another discipline—who can ask questions, test assumptions, and explore options with you, will make your life much easier by eliminating the problems that often occur when you play the dual roles of content expert and facilitator. The design process is far more efficient when you are supported by an objective individual whose primary function is not as a content expert but as a facilitator and devil's advocate, double-checking assumptions and ensuring that all options are explored.

• *Establish a sense of urgency.* In his excellent book on leading change, John Kotter (1996) identified establishing a sense of urgency as a major step in any successful change initiative. Make sure that everyone directly involved with your project and your key administrators understand why your project is important. Failure and complacency go hand in hand.

• *Create ownership and keep key individuals informed.* Before you begin a project, make sure you have the necessary support. In a course project your chair, dean, and other key faculty should be kept informed. In a curriculum project every department that will be involved must participate. Don't hesitate to ask for advice or suggestions. The more people involved, the greater your support. Key administrators and faculty often are extremely helpful. Share information and seek advice as you move through your project. Too many great ideas are never implemented because key decision makers were not kept informed along the way.

• *Strive for the ideal.* Do not focus on what exists; focus on what ideally could be. Not only does this approach reduce "turf" wars, particularly in curriculum projects, but it will lead to exciting new approaches and structures that would, under other conditions, rarely even be discussed.

• *Collect information before you begin.* Whether you are designing a course or a curriculum, collect information for three purposes: to establish need, to test your assumptions about your students, and to provide base data so you can document the significant changes that occur. All too often we wait until we are almost finished before we think about writing a report about our accomplishments. As a result, the information you'll need is no longer available. If you are going to work on a course, collect data before you begin on attrition, student attitudes, learning styles, and so forth. In a curriculum project look for enrollment data, information on the profile of applicants, job-placement data, number of transfers out, and so forth. All decisions must be data driven.

• *Be sensitive to human problems.* At times, design projects can significantly affect others, including other faculty members, secretaries, custodians, technicians, or administrators. Remember that change can be an emotional process, and be sensitive to the feelings of others. If you know where problems might occur down the line, bring everyone who may be impacted into the conversation as early as possible. And if you are going to need more or different kinds of space or a different credit structure, talk to your registrar. Few administrators can open more doors for you or give you more problems in certain areas. Registrars are always complaining, usually for good reason, that faculty members do not advise them early enough of what they have in mind. Do not forget your students either. Be sensitive to the problems of students who are in a course or program that is being offered for the first time or that is being revised. Schedules may not work well, the workload may be excessive, and there may be a gap in your instructional materials. Keep the students informed. Let them know that their assistance, responses to your questions, and patience are extremely important, and be prepared to adjust and modify the course on the basis of their responses.

• *Expect some student and faculty resistance.* Most people do not like change. Students are often not prepared to study as hard as you expect, and, particularly in their first year, rarely use their time effectively. While the use and constant reinforcement of the materials in a well-designed syllabus will significantly reduce many of the problems, don't expect them to totally disappear. Faculty are also often resistant to change, particularly if it impacts what they do in their own classrooms. Once again, getting them involved early makes a difference.

• *Do not reinvent the wheel.* Whenever possible, use available course and curriculum designs, evaluation instruments, and instructional materials. Using existing software and publications is a lot cheaper and certainly faster than trying to develop these items yourself. However, do not try to use material or tests designed for a different purpose or for a different population of students. Keep abreast of what is new, what is being tried, and if it makes sense, use it, borrow it, and always give credit. Learn from the experience of others. Do not waste resources by doing what has already been done or in trying approaches that have failed again and again. Throughout this book, relevant printed materials and Web sites have been listed; they should prove helpful.

• *Pay attention to support systems and logistics.* As noted earlier, the registrar's office, perhaps more than any other, can encourage or discourage academic innovation by being supportive or obstructive. The library can also play a key role. We faculty have a tendency not to worry about logistics, but you need to keep on top of the details if your project is to succeed. Make out schedules and room assignments far in advance. Make sure that book orders have been processed, that multiple sets of materials are ready, and, if needed, that you have available the necessary computer access or laboratory supplies. Keep students informed of any changes, and be sure that your departmental secretary and any other staff members who need to respond to questions from students seeking help have accurate, up-to-date information. Leave nothing to chance.

• *Keep technology in perspective.* Do not select the technology solution before identifying the problem and exploring the alternatives. One of the strengths of the approach we use is that all instructional options are explored before decisions are made. When technology is used, make sure it is the most effective solution. If e-mail and computer-based instructional modules are to be used, make sure the hardware that students have available will support the software you have chosen. Careful selection is essential. When properly used, technology can be a major asset in improving instructional quality and effectiveness. All too often we find faculty and staff starting with the solutions and then attempting to modify the project accordingly, a process that usually leads to poor results.

• *Build in assessment.* An effective data-collection program can significantly improve the quality of your course or curriculum. Data provide a base for good decision making throughout a project. Determine what information is needed, and develop an evaluation system that provides this information. The data can also be used for your tenure and promotion dossier as evidence of your teaching effectiveness and efforts in this area.

• *Ensure that the data collection approaches you use are designed to give you the information you need.* Some packaged, commercial products may not do what they are reported to do and data can be misleading. For example, if your student cohort includes many part-time or working students, be sure that you collect attrition data for more than six years. Recent studies (Attewell and Lavin, 2007) indicate that this population tends to drop out and then return, making the traditional six-year benchmark highly misleading.

• *Sometimes, when more than one faculty member is involved, agree to disagree and move on.* Problems of this type do occur, but they are rare. They are most common when goals for curricula are set, because that is when fundamental differences can occur on a specific issue. For example, a task force at the University of Northern Iowa, in an effort to describe the "qualities of an educated person," posed the following questions: Is there one ideal of an educated person, or are there many ideal types? If there are multiple types, to what extent is it feasible to identify common, desired qualities of an educated person? As the task force obviously anticipated, in answering such questions, faculty will have some basic areas of disagreement, but there will be far more areas of agreement. These common goals should become the focus of the conversations that follow. You cannot allow disagreement on one topic to stall the implementation of an entire project.

• *Expect the unexpected.* There are power failures, people get sick, boxes get lost, students may not listen to what they are told or read materials they are given. A snowstorm can play havoc with a schedule, and a computer system always manages to be down on the most crucial day of the year. We have had guest speakers miss their planes and a faculty member scheduled to handle a major course orientation end up having a baby on that day, two months early. At times like these, one can only do his or her best, be creative, and maintain a sense of humor.

• *Keep your chair and dean informed.* When students are frustrated or uncomfortable with change, you can be sure the first person they will turn to is your chair. Make sure he or she knows what you are trying to do and the rationale for the change; supplying a copy of a new syllabus is always a good idea. Also, let your chair know, as you go along, about what is working and what is not. The last thing that any administrator wants is surprises.

• *Expect the effort to be an educational experience for you, as well as for your students.* The students will learn, but so will you. Faculty tell us that after they go through the design process, they never see their classes as a single class but as a group of individuals, each with their own backgrounds, needs, interests, and abilities.

The whole is indeed greater than the sum of its parts. Loacker and Mentkowski made the following observation about Alverno College's experience in restructuring its entire curriculum: "With administrative direction that fosters faculty responsibility and focuses on accountability to the student, the Alverno faculty has developed a coherent system of education that incorporates assessment as an integral part. That system has been put into place within a strong, supportive culture. The coherence of the system rests on articulating and inter-relating educational mission, values, assumptions, principles, theory, and practice. It relies on the reconceptualization of the use of time, academic structures, and other resources to bring about increasingly effective learning for students" (1993).

Exhibit 24.1.

Designing a College Curriculum

Lion F. Gardiner

The curriculum is the heart of a student's college experience. The curriculum is a college's or university's primary means of helping students develop in directions valued by its faculty. Curricula should be reviewed and, if necessary, revised on a regular basis, better to serve the changing needs of both students and society. Today, we are being urged to assess especially carefully the quality of our curricula.

Faculties are responding to this challenge by turning their attention to what are in many cases long-neglected curricular matters. They are doing so as a practical means of both attracting and retaining more students and ensuring their success and producing high-quality outcomes for everyone.

SOME CHARACTERISTICS OF EFFECTIVE CURRICULA

A number of important characteristics of effective curricula emerge from the professional literature in higher education. These characteristics are relevant to both college-wide and more specialized disciplinary curricula and to curricula at both the undergraduate and graduate levels.

An effective curriculum has:

A coherent philosophy. A curriculum should be based on a carefully thought-out philosophy of education and should be clearly connected to an *institution's* stated mission.

Clear purpose and goals. A *curricular* mission statement and written curricular goals (*intended* student learning outcomes or results) articulate curricular purpose and aims—what graduates should know and be able to do and those attitudes and values a faculty believes are appropriate to well-educated men and women. These goals and their more specific objectives are described in considerable detail and in behavioral language that will permit designing the curriculum and assessing its degree of achievement (its *actual* outcomes).

A theoretically sound process. Student learning activities are chosen that are capable of developing the desired outcomes, as indicated by empirical research on learning and college student development. A curriculum has its desired effect primarily through its courses. Therefore, the choice of course experiences and the specific quality and efficacy of these experiences in producing the stated intended outcomes for all students is fundamental to the quality of any curriculum. Current empirically based education theory is essential to effective instruction and thus the improvement of curricular quality. For example, there is little evidence that using traditional lectures will develop in students the higher-order cognitive abilities such as critical thinking and principled ethical reasoning a faculty may value. Nevertheless, lecturing is still the predominant method of instruction in many institutions today.

A rational sequence. Educational activities are ordered in a developmental sequence that carefully considers prerequisite knowledge to form a coherent curriculum based on the stated intended outcomes of both the curriculum and its constituent courses.

Continuous assessment and improvement of quality. Reliable and valid assessment is preplanned to monitor on a continuing basis the effectiveness of the curriculum in fostering learning and student development—the actual achievement of the defined institutional and curricular outcome goals. In many or most institutions there exist two potentially quite different curricula: one, the array and sequence of courses offered by the institution and intended by the faculty to be taken and a second, composed of the specific courses actually taken and the sequence followed by a student. The intent, content, educational experience, and thus outcomes of the two may be—and, as judged from research, can be—quite different from each other. Careful monitoring of actual student course-taking behavior through transcript analysis can reveal the degree to which students are experiencing the faculty's intended educational process to achieve their intended outcomes.

High-quality academic advising. An effective curriculum—one that produces the results it claims in all of a college's diverse students— depends for its success upon a high-quality program of academic

(Continued)

Exhibit 24.1. *(continued)*

advising. Modern academic advising is developmental, starting with each student's values and goals, and helps all students design curricular, co-curricular, and other experiences that can help them achieve their own goals and the institution's intended learning outcomes.

Defining Curricular Outcomes

Clearly defined intended curricular outcomes enable a faculty to understand, communicate about, and control—manage—learning through the curriculum more effectively. Today, clearly stated, written outcomes are essential to good curriculum design, implementation, and assessment.

Specifically, curricular outcome goals and objectives:

- Provide the solid foundation of clearly specified *intended* outcomes.

- Provide specific direction for the continuous monitoring—assessment and evaluation—of the *actual* outcomes the curriculum produces.

- Reduce the potential for untoward teaching to the test—corruption of the curriculum by instruction directed toward chosen assessment indicators. Instead, both the instruction and the indicators are aligned with the outcomes previously defined by the faculty.

- Obviate the dumbing down of curricula in response to increased student diversity and under-preparedness by providing firm, clearly identified, high outcome standards and by requiring the educational process to change in response to altered student needs.

- Guard against grade inflation and the consequent reduction in student, and perhaps faculty, quality of effort and the devaluation of degrees.

- Help an institution resist academic drift, where a college or program with one mission or curricular purpose gradually and unconsciously drifts away toward some other purpose or purposes.

- Enable a faculty to deal more straightforwardly and rationally with conflict over curricular content, such as disputes related to departmental turf.

- Help everyone involved—faculty members, students, administrators, trustees, parents, legislators—understand the institution or program and the results it claims to produce.

- Increase the perception of institutional openness, candor, and integrity among all of the institution's customers and stakeholders.

Source: Gardiner, 2007. Reprinted with permission.

Summary

Obviously, lists like this are never complete. Many of the suggestions, once one thinks about them, are obvious. Unfortunately, we often find that we faculty and administrators have created many of our own problems by rushing, by not worrying about details, by not listening, or by not being as sensitive to the feelings of others as we should be. However, as difficult as the process of course and curriculum design can be, it is also challenging, exciting, and most rewarding.

"The academy needs a new, more encompassing vision of excellence—a vision that takes account of opposing views of higher education's purpose and underscores the importance, interdependence, and useful tensions among the goals of academic excellence *and* those of service and operational excellence. It should identify the academy as a place that not only *advances* knowledge but also one that *applies, tests,* and *uses* that knowledge—one that practices what we teach and that genuinely aspires to excellence in all that we do" (Ruben, 2003).

Few things we do in our careers will have more significant impact on the lives of more students or will make us feel as good. Enjoy the experience.

RESOURCES

Achieving Educational Objectives: Teaching and Learning

Western Association of Schools and Colleges

Criteria for Review

2.1   The institution's educational programs are appropriate in content, standards, and nomenclature for the degree level awarded, regardless of mode of delivery, and are staffed by sufficient numbers of faculty qualified for the type and level of curriculum offered.

2.2   All degrees—undergraduate and graduate—awarded by the institution are clearly defined in terms of entry-level requirements and in terms of levels of student achievement necessary for graduation that represent more than simply an accumulation of courses or credits.

• Baccalaureate programs engage students in an integrated course of study of sufficient breadth and depth to prepare them for work, citizenship, and a fulfilling life. These programs also ensure the development of core learning abilities and competencies including, but not limited to, college-level written and oral communication; college-level quantitative skills; information literacy; and the habit of critical analysis of data and argument. In addition, baccalaureate programs actively foster an understanding of diversity; civic responsibility; the ability to work with others; and the capability to engage in lifelong learning. Baccalaureate programs also ensure breadth for all students in the areas of cultural and aesthetic, social and political, as well as scientific and technical knowledge expected of educated persons in this society. Finally, students are required to engage in an in-depth, focused, and sustained program of study as part of their baccalaureate programs.

• Graduate programs are consistent with the purpose and character of their institutions; are in keeping with the expectations of their respective disciplines and professions; and are described through nomenclature that is appropriate to the several levels of graduate and professional degrees offered. Graduate curricula are visibly structured to include active involvement with the literature of the field and ongoing student engagement in research or appropriate high-level professional practice and training experiences. Additionally, admission criteria to graduate programs normally include a baccalaureate degree in an appropriate undergraduate program.

2.3   The institution's student learning outcomes and expectations for learning and student attainment are clearly stated at the course, program, and, as appropriate, institutional level. These outcomes and expectations are reflected in academic programs and policies; curriculum; advisement; library and information resources; and the wider learning environment.

2.4.   The institution's expectations for learning and student attainment are developed and widely shared among its members (including faculty, students, staff, and where appropriate, external stakeholders). The institution's faculty takes collective responsibility for establishing, reviewing, fostering, and demonstrating the attainment of these expectations.

2.5   The institution's academic programs actively involve students in learning, challenge them to achieve high expectations, and provide them with appropriate and ongoing feedback about their performance and how it can be improved.

2.6   The institution demonstrates that its graduates consistently achieve its stated levels of attainment and ensures that its expectations for student learning are embedded in the standards faculty use to evaluate student work.

2.7.   All programs offered by the institution are subject to systematic program review The program review process includes analyses of the achievement of the program's learning objectives and outcomes, program retention and completion, and, where appropriate, results of licensing examination and placement and evidence from external constituencies such as employers and professional organizations.

Student Learning, Assessment, and Accreditation

The Higher Learning Commission of the North Central Association

Among the public's many expectations of higher education, the most basic is that students will learn, and in particular that they will learn what they need to know to attain personal success and fulfill their public responsibilities in a global and diverse society. Student learning is central to all higher education organizations; therefore, these organizations define educational quality—one of their core purposes—by how well they achieve their declared mission relative to student learning. A focus on achieved student learning is critical not only to a higher education organization's ability to promote and improve curricular and cocurricular learning experiences and to provide evidence of the quality of educational experiences and programs but also to fulfill the most basic expectations and needs of higher education.

In October 1989 the Commission first posited that assessment of student learning is an essential component of every organization's effort to evaluate overall organizational effectiveness. In February 2003 The Higher Learning Commission adopted a newly revised position statement on assessment of student learning (see Section 3.4–2 of the *Handbook of Accreditation, Third Edition*) to reaffirm and strengthen this position. Through the Criteria for Accreditation and multiple Core Components, the Commission makes clear the centrality of student learning to effective higher education organizations and extends and deepens its commitment to and expectations for assessment. Indeed, the Commission asserts that assessment is more than a response to demands for accountability, more than a means for curricular improvement. Effective assessment is best understood as a strategy for understanding, confirming, and improving student learning.

Fundamental Questions for Conversations on Student Learning

Six fundamental questions serve as prompts for conversations about student learning and the role of assessment in affirming and improving that learning:

1. How are your stated student learning outcomes appropriate to your mission, programs, degrees, and students?

2. What evidence do you have that students achieve your stated learning outcomes?

3. In what ways do you analyze and use evidence of student learning?

4. How do you ensure shared responsibility for student learning and for assessment of student learning?

5. How do you evaluate and improve the effectiveness of your efforts to assess and improve student learning?

6. In what ways do you inform the public and other stakeholders about what and how well your students are learning?

In using these questions, an organization should ground its conversations in its distinct mission, context, commitments, goals, and intended outcomes for student learning. In addition to informing ongoing improvement in student learning, these conversations will assist organizations and peer reviewers in discerning evidence for the Criteria and Core Components.

The fundamental questions and the conversations they prompt are intended to support a strategy of inquiry into student learning. Further, the questions are intended to support this strategy of inquiry, built on principles of good practice, as a participative and iterative process that

- Provides information regarding student learning

- Engages stakeholders in analyzing and using information on student learning to confirm and improve teaching and learning

- Produces evidence that confirms achievement of intended student learning outcomes, and
- Guides broader educational and organizational improvement

In other words, organizations assess student learning in meaningful, useful, and workable ways to evaluate how they are achieving their commitments and to act on the results in ways that advance student learning and improve educational quality. Effective assessment of student learning is a matter of commitment, not a matter of compliance.

Evaluating the Student Learning Organization's Efforts to Assess and Improve

The centrality of student learning and the fundamental nature of assessment as a strategy for understanding and improving that learning are embedded directly into the Criteria and Core Components. Thus, peer reviewers seeking evidence for the Criteria and Core Components will discern evidence of the commitment to student learning and the meaningful use of assessment to confirm and improve student learning. Neither the Criteria nor Core Components prescribe specific methods for assessing and improving student learning. It is inevitable and desirable that diverse organizations exhibit a wide variety of approaches and embed assessment of student learning in a variety of institutional forms and processes. Thus, the Commission and its peer reviewers will not approach the review with expectations for specific ways in which assessment efforts are structured and implemented but rather with a focus on student learning and the use of assessment to confirm and improve that learning within the context and mission of the organization.

To remain focused on student learning and assessment as a strategy for confirming and improving that learning, peer reviewers may use the fundamental questions as prompts to engage faculty, staff, students, and administrators in conversations about the organization's (a) commitment to improving student learning and educational quality; (b) sustained effort to collect, analyze, and use data and information on student learning; (c) evidence that students have achieved the learning intended; (d) shared responsibility for student learning and assessment of student learning; and (e) successes and challenges in improving student learning and educational quality through assessment. These conversations will assist peer reviewers in understanding the organization's commitment to student learning and approaches to assessment of that learning within the organization's context and mission. Further, the conversation will assist in discerning areas for consultation and in identifying and validating evidence related to the Criteria and Core Components. Peer reviewers will base their accreditation-related judgments and recommendations on this evidence as it relates to the Criteria and Core Components.

Finally, the Commission realizes that assessment of student learning is an ongoing, dynamic process that requires substantial time; that it is often marked by fits and starts; and that it takes long-term commitment and leadership. It is reasonable for organizations to use different approaches and timetables in implementing their assessment of student learning efforts. Nevertheless, the Commission expects that each organization can demonstrate a sustained effort to implement assessment processes that are workable, reasonable, meaningful, and useful in confirming and improving student learning and in assuring and advancing broader educational and organizational quality.

The Proposal Templates

Ohio Board of Regents

The Proposal Template was developed to address all the criteria in Rule 3333–1–08 (Standards for Issuing Certificates of Authorization under Chapter 1713 of the Ohio Revised Code), and to standardize the proposal writing process.

The template also attempts to eliminate the confusion and most complexities related to the writing of a proposal to Regents.

Staff will guide each institution through the development of the writing of a proposal requesting authorization in Ohio.

Proposal writing workshops are also held periodically throughout each year. Check the Regents' Web sites for schedules.

The Proposal Template was developed in sequential sections.

Only a large and very comprehensive university with many sites might be required to address every section of the template.

Each institution will only write to those sections that are relevant to their proposal. (Staff will also provide guidance in making those determinations.)

If an institution is requesting authorization for multiple programs, the institution will begin by only developing one proposal first with the guidance of Regents staff. Many sections of the first proposal can be copied into the remaining proposals after the sections of the first proposal have been completed.

All sections are identified below:

- Section 1: Directions, Executive Summary, Institutional Profile, Accreditation, Institutional Mission/Purpose

- Section 2: Institutional Governance Structures and Academic Control
- Section 3: Institutional Academic Divisions
- Section 4: Institutional Administrative Services and Grievance Policies
- Section 5: Institutional Distance Ed and Off-Site Initiatives
- Section 6a: Institutional Undergraduate Curriculum Policies
- Section 6b: Institutional Graduate Curriculum Policies
- Section 7: Proposed Program Development/Maintenance Policies
- Section 8: Proposed Curriculum Components
- Section 9: Proposed Course Descriptions and Syllabi
- Section 9a: Proposed Clinical Sites
- Section 10: Proposed Curriculum Sequencing
- Section 11: Proposed Program Assessment and Evaluation
- Section 12: Institutional Library Resources
- Section 13: Proposed Program Grading Policies and Measuring Student Success
- Section 14: Proposed Program Application Process
- Section 15a: Institution Undergraduate Faculty Policies
- Section 15b: Institution Graduate Faculty Policies
- Section 16: Proposed Program Faculty
- Section 16a: Proposed Program Faculty Additional Sites
- Section 16b: Proposed Program Clinical Faculty
- Section 16c: Proposed Program Doctoral Faculty
- Section 17: Proposed Faculty Orientation and Mentoring Policies
- Section 17a: Proposed Faculty Orientation and Mentoring Policies Additional Sites
- Section 17b: Proposed Clinical Faculty Orientation and Mentoring Policies
- Section 18: Proposed Faculty Professional Development and Scholarship Policies
- Section 19: Institutional Support Services
- Section 20: Proposed Program Budget and Financial Plan
- Section 21: Diversity, Institutional Research, and Submission of Proposal Materials
- Section 22: Consultants' Review of Proposal

Before beginning the development of a proposal, please consult with Regents staff first to review the sections above that will be relevant to your request. Thank you!

Section 13 (Selected Portions) _____

Institution/Proposed Program—Grading Policies and Measuring Student Success

(Overview of institution/department/program goals and objectives for measuring student success.)

Goals/Purposes:

Objectives:

Outcome Focus:

(Grading/Evaluation Policies. Insert requested information below.)

Describe Institutional Grading/Evaluation System (if described previously, direct reader to section and page number where that information may be found):

Appendix Item(s):

Describe Minimum Grade/Evaluation Requirement for Continued Matriculation in Undergraduate Programs:

Appendix Item(s):

(Describe grade/evaluation appeals process)

(List and describe program-specific assessment and evaluation processes for proposed program as related to student performance/outcomes by providing requested information below. If same as institution, then state that. If information was provided previously, direct reader to section and page number where that information can be found. Submit documentation/instruments as Appendix items.)

Student/Learner Assessment and Evaluation Processes for Measuring Student/Learner Success for Matriculated Students/Learners:

1. Name Process for Measuring Student/Learner Success:
   - Outcome Focus:
   - Description of Process (include tables/charts for added clarity):

- How Will Data Inform the Program?:
- How Will Results Be Operationalized?:
- Forms/Instruments Used:
- Appendix Items:

(Continue with this format if more need to be identified, or delete unused items.)

(List and describe institution/department/program initiatives for tracking student success/outcomes after completion of program. Submit documentation as Appendix items. If institution has no initiative for such tracking, then state that.)

1. Name of Process:
   - Outcome Focus:
   - Description of Process (include tables/charts for added clarity):
   - How Will Data Inform the Program?:
   - How Will Results Be Operationalized?:
   - Forms/Instruments Used:
   - Appendix Items:

(Continue with this format if more need to be identified, or delete unused items.)

(Statement related to alignment of grading/student success measures (i.e. goals) and institution mission/purpose. Provide documentation as Appendix items, if applicable. Leave a double space between the last line of this response and the Consultant Comments line below.)

Criteria for Accrediting Engineering Programs

Effective for Evaluations During the 2007–2008 Accreditation Cycle

Accreditation Board for Engineering and Technology (ABET)

These criteria are intended to ensure quality and to foster the systematic pursuit of improvement in the quality of engineering education that satisfies the needs of constituencies in a dynamic and competitive environment. It is the responsibility of the institution seeking accreditation of an engineering program to demonstrate clearly that the program meets the following criteria.

1. General Criteria for Baccalaureate Level Programs

Criterion 1: Students

The quality and performance of the students and graduates are important considerations in the evaluation of an engineering program. The institution must evaluate student performance, advise students regarding curricular and career matters, and monitor student's progress to foster their success in achieving program outcomes, thereby enabling them as graduates to attain program objectives.

The institution must have and enforce policies for the acceptance of transfer students and for the validation of courses taken for credit elsewhere. The institution must also have and enforce procedures to ensure that all students meet all program requirements.

Criterion 2: Program Educational Objectives

Although institutions may use different terminology, for purposes of Criterion Two, program educational objectives are broad statements that describe the career and professional accomplishments that the program is preparing graduates to achieve.

Each engineering program for which an institution seeks accreditation or re-accreditation must have in place

a) Detailed published educational objectives that are consistent with the mission of the institution and these criteria

b) A process based on the needs of the program's various constituencies in which the objectives are determined and periodically evaluated

c) An educational program, including a curriculum that prepares students to attain program outcomes and that fosters accomplishments of graduates that are consistent with these objectives

d) A process of ongoing evaluation of the extent to which these objectives are attained, the result of which shall be used to develop and improve the program outcomes so that graduates are better prepared to attain the objectives

Criterion 3: Program Outcomes and Assessment

Although institutions may use different terminology, for purposes of Criterion Three, program outcomes are statements that describe what students are expected to know and be able to do by the time of graduation. These relate to the skills, knowledge, and behaviors that students acquire in their matriculation through the program.

Each program must formulate program outcomes that foster attainment of the program objectives articulated in satisfaction of Criterion Two of these criteria. There must be processes to produce these outcomes and an assessment process, with documented results, that demonstrates that these program outcomes are being measured and indicates the degree to which the outcomes are achieved. There must be evidence that the results of this assessment process are applied to the further development of the program.

Engineering programs must demonstrate that their students attain

a) An ability to apply knowledge of mathematics, science, and engineering

b) An ability to design and conduct experiments, as well as to analyze and interpret data

c) An ability to design a system, component, or process to meet desired needs within realistic constraints such as economic, environmental, social, political, ethical, health and safety, manufacturability, and sustainability

d) An ability to function on multidisciplinary teams

e) An ability to identify, formulate, and solve engineering problems

f) An understanding of professional and ethical responsibility

g) An ability to communicate effectively

h) The broad education necessary to understand the impact of engineering solutions in a global, economic, environmental, and societal context

i) A recognition of the need for and an ability to engage in lifelong learning

j) A knowledge of contemporary issues

k) An ability to use the techniques, skills, and modern engineering tools necessary for engineering practice

In addition, an engineering program must demonstrate that its students attain any additional outcomes articulated by the program to foster achievement of its education objectives.

Criterion 4: Professional Component

The professional component requirements specify subject areas appropriate to engineering but do not prescribe specific courses. The faculty must ensure that the program curriculum devotes adequate attention and time to each component, consistent with the outcomes and objectives of the program and institution. The professional component must include:

a) One year of a combination of college-level mathematics and basic sciences (some with experimental experience) appropriate to the discipline

b) One and one-half years of engineering topics, consisting of engineering sciences and engineering design appropriate to the student's field of study. The engineering sciences have their roots in mathematics and basic sciences but carry knowledge further toward creative application. These studies provide a bridge between mathematics and basic sciences on the one hand and engineering practice on the other. Engineering design is the process of devising a system, component, or process to meet desired needs. It is a decision-making process (often iterative) in which the basic sciences, mathematics, and the engineering sciences are applied to convert resources optimally to meet these needs.

c) A general education component that complements the technical content of the curriculum and is consistent with the program and institution objectives

Students must be prepared for engineering practice through the curriculum, culminating in a major design experience based on the knowledge and skills acquired in earlier course work and incorporating appropriate engineering standards and multiple realistic constraints.

Providing Institutional Support

*The Academy for Assessment of Student Learning
of the Higher Learning Commission of the North
Central Association*

The Academy for Assessment of Student Learning offers the Higher Learning Commission (HLC) member institutions a four-year sequence of events and interactions that are focused on student learning, targeted at accelerating and advancing efforts to assess and improve student learning, and designed to build institution-wide commitment to assessment of student learning. When planned comprehensively and carefully by the institution, participation in the Academy (1) can produce evidence for Criteria and Core Components in upcoming accreditation evaluations; (2) can serve in place of mandated progress reports, monitoring reports and focused visits on assessment of student learning (PEAQ); and (3) can serve in place of one or more action projects (AQIP).

Year 1: Apply, Propose Action Portfolio Student Learning Projects, Attend Academy Roundtable. An institution joining the Academy proposes one or two potential Student Learning Projects related to assessing and improving student learning and sends a team to the multi-day Academy Roundtable. At the Roundtable, institutions

Source: The Higher Learning Commission. For additional information, contact: Jonathan Keiser, jKeiser@hlcommission.org; 312-263-0456 x 128.

critique and improve their own and other institutions' Student Learning Projects in consultation with Academy mentors and HLC staff.

Years 2 and 3: Complete Annual Progress Analyses, Participate in Optional Learning and Assessment Exchange and Showcase, Conduct Optional Events and Interventions. Institutions implement their Student Learning Projects and receive mentoring, critique, and validation through Annual Progress Analyses and participation in the Academy's Electronic Network, which serves as a gathering place for resources and meetings throughout the four-year Academy experience. Institutions may customize the Academy with optional Events and Intervention Strategies (on-campus consultation, on-campus conversation day facilitation, visit to good practice site, open space facilitation, and so on). Institutions may choose to participate in the annual Student Learning and Assessment Exchange and Showcase.

Year 4: Complete Results Report, Participate in Results Forum, Prepare Sustainability Plan, Complete Academy. Each institution writes a brief Results Report and sends a team to the two-day Academy Results Forum to showcase accomplishments, to compare and share good practices, and to define post-Academy strategies to sustain their efforts. Each institution receives a Results Response from its reviewers. In addition, HLC intends to compile a compendium of case studies for publication that showcases accomplishments and inventory good practices.

Exhibit E.1.

Academy Features and Benefits for Institutions

Academy Features	Academy Benefits
Action-focused, four-year sequence of events, interactions, and analyses focused on student learning results	Achieved results on key action Student Learning Projects that impact student learning
Team- and institutional-based forums for networking, feedback, experimentation, and evaluation of good practices strategies	Increased institutional commitment to and ability for assessing and improving learning
Analysis, critique, and feedback on key Student Learning Projects	Compilation and dissemination of good practices and innovative strategies in assessing and improving student learning
Forums for documenting and disseminating good practice in assessing and improving student learning	Support for ongoing institutional effort, experimentation, and good practice development in assessment of student learning

Web-based library of action projects, progress analyses, and outcomes	Collaborative relationship with the Commission in building institutional commitment and ability to assess and improve student learning
Web-based peer review and feedback structures to support follow-through on Student Learning Projects	Development of institutional culture for assessing and improving student learning
Forums for comparing measures, strategies, and outcomes and showcasing learning and results	Opportunity to compare stated student learning outcomes, assessment strategies, and project results
Multiple, innovative interventions, activities, and events that customize the Academy to individual institutions	Proactive replacement for Commission-mandated follow-up on assessment
Documentation of results and accomplishments as evidence for accreditation evaluations	Documented evidence for accreditation evaluations and follow-up

Outcomes of the Academy

- Establish institutional commitment to understanding, confirming, and improving student learning
- Achieve intended results as defined by an institution's Student Learning Projects
- Develop institutional culture around assessing and improving student learning
- Improve institutional capacity to engage multiple stakeholders in efforts to assess, confirm, and improve student learning
- Develop institutional leaders and mentors
- Test and document effective practices in assessing, confirming, and improving student learning
- Interact with diverse institutions striving to assess, confirm, and improve student learning and teaching, building a collaborative network for ongoing comparison of efforts and results
- Assessment of student learning evidence for accreditation evaluation and follow-up.

An Exercise in Diagramming a Course

The description below of an introductory science course includes a number of the structural options that we will describe in case studies later in this book. Take a piece of paper and a pencil (with a good eraser—you will need it!) and diagram this course. Remember that there is no single answer; as long as your diagram shows all the important relationships and flow, it will be fine.

Course Description

- In this course the instructor faced several design problems. While some students were missing prerequisites in mathematics, others, having had advanced courses in high school, were able on the first day of class to pass the first of the six unit tests. To address these differences, the course that evolved was structured in a specific way. It began with an orientation session, which included a placement test. Depending on their test results, some of the students were assigned remedial work in mathematics, which had to be completed by the beginning of Unit Two; others were advised to drop the course and take additional math courses before re-enrolling; others were placed in Unit One; and the students with the best knowledge of mathematics were exempted from Unit One.

- Units One and Two were sequential; Units Three through Five could be taken in any order.

• During Unit Five students also had the option of selecting a special project for one additional credit. This project had to be turned in at the final exam, which followed the final unit. To meet the needs of the students, the final unit consisted of three sessions on science careers; the first session covered careers in business and industry; the second, careers in research; and the third, careers in the health professions. Students were required to select one of these sessions.

When you are finished, look at Figure F. 1 to see one possible way to diagram this course. Keep in mind, there is no single correct answer. The key is clarity of both content and sequence.

Figure F.1.
One Possible Flow Diagram: Exploratory Science 118

One Possible Flow Diagram: Exploratory Scene 118

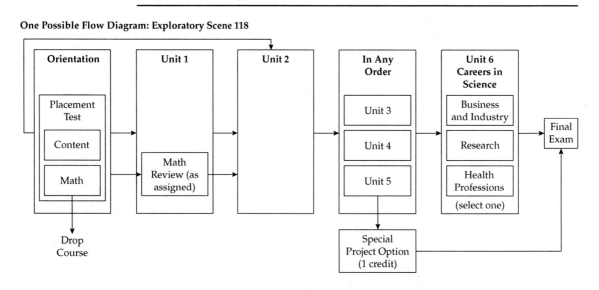

Questions for Evaluating a College Course

Richard R. Sudweeks and Robert M. Diamond

No two evaluation designs will be the same. In each instance the evaluation must be structured to serve the information needs of those involved in the decision-making process. However, some general questions tend to recur in the evaluation of courses and other programs of instruction. The following list has been designed to assist faculty and administrators who are or will be charged with the task of evaluating a course. Although no list can ever be considered complete, this one has been developed from efforts on several campuses that have designed and implemented new courses and programs and have evaluated existing courses and curricula. The list is intended to be a guide in the design stage of an evaluation. It should serve as a checklist for making sure that all relevant questions have been considered.

All the questions in this list may not be appropriate in a single project because of limitations in time, staff, and money. Those involved must select the specific questions that should be addressed and prioritize them. This list is intended to be comprehensive so that those involved can omit questions intentionally rather than by accident. The evaluation methodology selected should match the questions that are being asked.

Participants in the evaluation process should consider each of the following questions and check those that are appropriate for the specific course they are evaluating.

I. RATIONALE

  A. What population of students is the course intended to serve?

  B. What student needs is the course intended to meet?

  C. What institutional, community, or societal needs is the course intended to meet?

  D. What other defensible reasons exist for offering this course?

  E. What other courses fulfill these same needs?

  F. To what extent does this course overlap with or duplicate these courses?

II. DEVELOPMENT AND CURRENT STATUS

  A. When and under what circumstances was the course developed?

  B. How frequently and how regularly has the course been offered?

  C. How much has enrollment increased or decreased from year to year, or has it remained stable?

  D. What problems have been associated with the course and how have they been resolved?

  E. To what extent is the course intended to be replicable from instructor to instructor or from term to term?

  F. To what degree do the plans or design for the course exist in a written or documented form? In what documents (course-approval forms, course outlines or syllabi, memos, and so on) do these plans exist?

  G. How does the current version of the course differ from earlier versions? Why?

III. CREDIT AND CURRICULAR IMPLICATIONS

  A. What credit is awarded for successful completion of the course? On what basis is this credit allocation justifiable?

  B. How does this course fulfill graduate and degree requirements?

  C. At what level (lower division, upper division, or graduate) is the course classified? On what basis is this classification justified?

  D. How does the course fit into the overall curriculum of the department and college?

  E. In which departments is the course cross-listed? Why? How does it fit into the curricula of these departments or colleges?

F. What prerequisite skills or experiences are needed in order to succeed in this course?

G. What problems are experienced by students who do not have these prerequisites?

IV. OBJECTIVES

A. What are the formal stated objectives of the course?

B. How feasible and realistic are these objectives given the abilities of the target population and the available time and resources?

C. How are the stated objectives related to the competencies students will need in everyday life outside of school?

D. How are the objectives related to the competencies students will need in their subsequent academic careers?

E. If the course is designed to prepare students for a specific professional or vocational field, how are the objectives related to the competencies they are likely to need in their future careers?

F. What values are affirmed by the choice of these objectives as goals for this course?

G. What other purposes or goals do the faculty, administrators, and other interested audiences have for the course?

H. What goals and expectations do students have for the course?

I. To what extent are these additional goals and expectations compatible with the stated course objectives?

V. CONTENT

A. What (1) information, (2) process, and (3) attitudes and values constitute the subject matter or content of the course?

B. How are the various content elements related to the objectives?

1. Which objectives receive the most coverage or emphasis? Why?

2. Which objectives receive only minor coverage? Why?

C. How is the content sequenced or arranged? Why is this sequence appropriate or inappropriate?

D. How are the various content elements integrated into a coherent pattern or structure? To what extent does fragmentation or lack of coherence appear to be a problem?

E. What values and assumptions are implicit in the content selected and emphasized?

VI. INSTRUCTIONAL STRATEGIES

A. What kinds of learning activities are used?

1. What activities are the students expected to engage in during class sessions?

2. What assignments or projects are students expected to complete outside of class?

3. In what ways are these activities appropriate or inappropriate in light of the course objectives?

4. How could these activities be made more effective?

B. What instructional materials are used?

1. How and for what purpose are the materials used?

2. How accurate and up to date are the materials?

3. In what ways do the materials need to be improved?

4. How could the materials be used more effectively?

C. What instructional roles or functions are performed by the teacher(s)?

1. How could these roles be performed more effectively?

2. What important instructional roles are not provided or are performed inadequately? Why?

D. What premises and assumptions about learning and the nature of the learner underlie the selection of instructional strategies? How and to what extent are these assumptions warranted?

VII. PROCEDURES AND CRITERIA FOR EVALUATING STUDENTS' ACHIEVEMENTS

A. What instruments and procedures are employed to collect evidence of the students' progress and achievement?

B. What criteria are used to assess the adequacy of the students' work or achievement? On what basis were these criteria selected?

C. How well do the assessment procedures correspond to the course content and objectives? Which objectives or content areas are not assessed? Why?

D. Are the assessment procedures fair and objective?

E. What evidence is there that the assessment instruments and procedures yield valid and reliable results?

F. How are the assessment results used? Are the results shared with the students within a reasonable amount of time?

G. How consistently are the assessment criteria applied from instructor to instructor and from term to term?

H. Is the amount of assessment excessive, about right, or insufficient?

VIII. ORGANIZATION

A. How is the course organized in terms of lectures, labs, studios, discussion sections, field trips, and other types of scheduled class sessions?

B. How frequently and for how long are the various types of class meetings scheduled? Is the total allocation of time sufficient or insufficient? Why?

C. If there is more than one instructor, what are the duties and responsibilities of each? What problems result from this division of responsibilities?

D. What outside-of-class instruction, tutoring, or counseling is provided? By whom? On what basis?

E. How well is the student workload distributed throughout the course?

F. Are the necessary facilities, equipment, and materials readily available and in good working condition when needed?

IX. OUTCOMES

A. What proportion of the enrollees completed the course with credit during the regular term? How does the completion rate vary from instructor to instructor or from term to term?

B. What proportion of the enrollees withdrew from or stopped attending the course? Why?

1. To what degree does their withdrawal appear to be related to factors associated with the course?

2. How does the attrition rate vary from instructor to instructor or from term to term?

C. At the end of the course, what evidence is there that students have achieved the stated objectives?

1. Which objectives does the course help students meet the most and the least?

2. For what kinds of students is the course most and least successful?

D. What effects does the course have on students' interest in the subject matter and their desire to continue studying and learning about this subject?

E. What other effects does the course have on the students?

　　1. How are their values, attitudes, priorities, interests, or aspirations changed?

　　2. Are their study habits or other behavioral patterns modified?

　　3. How pervasive or significant do these effects appear to be?

Curriculum-Related Issues Raised by *The Engineer of 2020: Visions of Engineering in the New Century*

In either your core program or areas of concentration, are there specific learning outcomes (skills, attitudes, and knowledge) that students should have that are not now being addressed?

- Who is your major competition regionally, nationally, and internationally? How can you best compete?

- Are there existing programs, courses, or instructional units that should be reduced or eliminated?

- What assumptions are you making about entering or transfer students? Are you accurate?

- How do you build into your academic programs an ongoing process of renewal and improvement?

- What is the role of your school or college in the education of non-engineering students, the general public, and political leaders? Should you be involved in the liberal arts core? If so, how?

- With the rapid development of new technologies combined with the ongoing challenges facing society (protecting the environment, an aging population, a crumbling infrastructure, and so on), do you need to modify your existing programs or design new ones? What are the trade-offs?

- To address these issues, what specific knowledge and skills do you need in your faculty that you do not now have? Do you bring in new people or retrain those already on staff, or a combination of the two?

- How do you integrate other essential disciplines into your curriculum (such as business and management, the sciences, social sciences and humanities, law, and communications)?

- What is your role in the continuing education of professionals in the field?

- Looking at the future needs in the engineering profession, the strengths of your program and the resources that you have available, are there certain areas of the newer specializations that you should emphasize? If so, which ones?

- As you design new programs or revise existing ones, are there certain individuals outside of the institution or in other schools or colleges that you should involve? What specific skills, knowledge, and resources could even add to the process?

- What should be the goals of your core program for all engineering students? How much time should be devoted to it and must the core program be limited to the lower division? How can these core competencies be reinforced throughout your curriculum? How can you determine that your products have the knowledge and competencies that you feel are essential for success?

Multicultural Competencies for Counselors

American Counseling Association

The student should be able to describe a situation in a culture so that a member of that culture will agree with the student's perception of it. Such an awareness would require an individual to have:

Required Competencies:

- Ability to recognize direct and indirect communication styles
- Sensibility to nonverbal cues
- Awareness of cultural and linguistic differences
- Interest in the culture
- Sensitivity to the myths and stereotypes of the culture
- Concern for the welfare of persons from another culture
- Ability to articulate elements of his or her own culture
- Appreciation of the importance of multicultural teaching
- Awareness of the relationships between cultural groups
- Accurate criteria for objectively judging "goodness" and "badness" in the other culture

---

Source: Reprinted from P. Pedersen, *A Handbook for Developing Multicultural Awareness*, American Counseling Association, 1988, pp. 9–11. Reprinted with permission. No further reproduction authorized without written permission of the American Counseling Association.

Guidelines for Measuring Assessment:

- Does the student have specific knowledge about the culturally defined group members' diverse historical experiences, adjustment styles, roles of education, socioeconomic backgrounds, preferred values, typical attitudes, honored behaviors, inherited customs, slang, learning styles, and ways of thinking?

- Does the student have information about the resources for teaching and learning available to persons in the other culture?

- Does the student know about his or her own culture in relation to the other culture?

- Does the student have professional expertise in an area valued by persons in the other culture?

- Does the student have information about teaching or learning resources about the other culture and know where those resources are available?

Guidelines to Measure Skill Development:

- Does the student have a teaching or learning style that will be appropriate in the other culture?

- Does the student have the ability to establish empathetic rapport with persons from the other culture?

- Is the student able to receive and accurately analyze feedback from persons of the other culture?

- Does the student have the creative ability to develop new methods for work in the other culture that will go beyond what the student has already learned?

Guidelines to Measure Awareness:

- Is the student aware of differences in cultural institutions and systems?

- Is the student aware of the stress resulting from functioning in a multicultural situation?

- Does the student know how rights or responsibilities are defined differently in different cultures?

- Is the student aware of differences in verbal and nonverbal communication styles?

- Is the student aware of significant differences and similarities of practices across different cultures?

Ethics

The Commission on Public Relations Education

In today's practice of public relations, ethical conduct is quintessential. Modern public relations is defined by ethical principles, and no public relations practice should exist in contemporary society without a full commitment to ethical practice. Ethics for the public relations profession can be defined as a set of a priori principles, beliefs, and values that should be followed by all who engage in public relations practice.

Ethical conduct transcends geographical and geopolitical boundaries, and a common standard for ethical conduct should apply across different countries and regions. Thus, international ethical standards should be closely examined and followed. Of course, cultural variables must be considered when public relations professionals practice abroad. However, practitioners should be cautious about determining that questionable practices are "culturally bound." Rather, public relations professionals should carefully examine whether these practices are indeed commonly adopted within a culture and are considered to be ethical by the majority of local professionals. Also, a practice is not necessarily ethical just because it is widely adopted in one or more countries, as research on international media transparency has pointed out (http://www.commpred.org/report/pdf/ethics.pdf).

Recent business and communication scandals have emphasized the importance of honest, fair, and transparent public relations, which is a must in today's business environment. One of the greatest challenges for public relations professionals is to demonstrate and prove that new ways of thinking and new practices are indeed founded

Source: The Report of the Commission on Public Relations Education. 2006. Reprinted with permission. (www.commpred/org)

on ethical principles. New-generation professionals should follow honest practices to build a fundamental trust between publics and organizations. This transparency requires ethical decision making and an increasingly influential role at the table where decisions are made.

The successful public relations practitioner is highly intelligent, literate, and well read, an educated global citizen with an extensive knowledge of both the history of civilization and of global current events. The practitioner possesses excellent professional communication skills and has both exceptional depth and breadth in public relations theory.

Equally as important as this professional competence is public relations practitioners' ethical conduct in both their professional and personal lives. Reflexively, the traits of successful practitioners help to assure that these professionals are capable of making informed and well-reasoned ethical decisions. Practitioners also must appreciate the societal, organizational, and personal necessities for abiding by the highest ethical conduct. And, although public relations professional education perhaps cannot make students ethical, either professionally or personally, such education can define and teach professional ethics. It can provide a body of knowledge about the process of ethical decision making that can help students not only to recognize ethical dilemmas but to use appropriate critical thinking skills to help resolve these dilemmas in a way that results in an ethical outcome.

2006 Recommendations

1. All learning objectives in public relations education must be placed within the framework and context of public relations ethics. Professional ethics must not only be integrated into all coursework in public relations but must also be given priority as a discrete component of the public relations curriculum. Public relations ethics are critically important because public relations practitioners share with other professional occupations not only the ability to significantly help (or hurt) their clients but also the ability to greatly influence stakeholders and society at large.

2. Public relations practitioners have an unquestionable moral obligation to act professionally, that is, in a socially responsible manner, within their own societies as well as within an emerging global community. To do so, the community of public relations professionals, both practitioners and educators, must publicly define their relationship to society as earning a position of trust.

Their behavior must be consonant with the expectations of society, although they have the freedom and responsibility to determine what they ethically may and may not do as a professional community within their society's moral parameters. These professional ethics must consider both the wider moral values of society as well as the aims of public relations practice.

Of course, this professional role with its accompanying need for professional ethics necessarily elevates public relations practitioners above the organizational role of obedient technicians who blindly do the will of managers. Complex organizations depend on a range of professionals who have unique knowledge and skills and who exert great influence over the behavior of these organizations through their professional ideologies, theories, values and worldviews.

3. The ethical values of such public relations professionals influence the behavior of their organizations, and thus their professional values become organizational values. Those in the public relations professional community must develop, continually refine and publicly acknowledge their professional ideology, values and belief systems to fulfill their professional responsibilities. These values can and must be taught to students who hopefully will accept and assimilate these common values that result in a morally defensible body of professional ethics.

Mathematics, Prerequisites, and Student Success in Introductory Courses

Adapted from a Final Report by William J. Hardin

Introduction

In the fall of 1986, Syracuse University in cooperation with the economics department undertook a pilot project to see if addressing mathematics prerequisite deficiencies could reduce the course failure rate. The project demonstrated that for some students, a brief review could in fact, improve their success rate in an introductory course (Evensky, 1991). This project explored the possibility of using this approach in other introductory courses.

This study was a pilot effort to determine which mathematics skills were assumed in selected freshmen courses and to determine to what extent weaknesses in these prerequisite mathematical skills adversely affect the academic performance of students. It was our hypothesis that if such a relationship exists, special attention could remove certain mathematical barriers for "at-risk students," resulting in academic success and reduced failure rate. If this approach was successful, the university could improve its overall retention rate of students while maintaining academic standards.

The courses selected for this study were Anthropology 101, Astronomy 201, Chemistry 103, Chemistry 106, Geography 105, Physics 101, Political Science 121, and Psychology 205.

The study consisted of three phases: (1) math prerequisite identification, (2) course specific prerequisite test generation, and (3) test administration and data analysis.

Phase 1: Mathematics Prerequisite Identification

Instructional materials from introductory undergraduate courses were collected and evaluated to determine which mathematical skills or concepts are assumed. A basic skills mathematics inventory was used as a frame of reference for reviewing course tests and associated materials as well as for discussions with the faculty member. After conversations with the appropriate dean and department chairs, faculty responsible for several courses were asked, and agreed, to participate in the project.

It was our basic assumption that:

- There are certain basic mathematics skills assumed for all courses.

- An understanding of mathematical processes and products would improve understanding of course material.

- When advanced mathematics skills are used in texts, it is assumed that the students have the prerequisites. For example, to solve algebraic equations a text assumes the students understand basic operations, fractions, the concept of variable, and (perhaps) the concept of a constant.

- Although our list of basic skills was developed over time and is extensive, there is a possibility that for some first-year courses additional mathematics skills may be required. For example, in GEO 105 students were expected to know the meanings of certain vocabulary terms such as per capita, and sic fold decline.

To provide a check on the process, the faculty member and the project coordinator reviewed the materials independently and generated two independent lists. Then they met to discuss and resolve discrepancies between these two lists. The lists were then combined to result in one list.

It should be noted that while some prerequisite skills were assumed in every course, others were course specific. For example, fractions and percents were assumed in all courses. Only Chemistry 106 assumed linear interpolation, the ability to solve inequalities and work problems using decimals (see Table K.1).

Table K.1. Prerequisite Mathematics Skills Identified by Course

Course	ANT 101	CHE 103	CHE 106	PHY 101	POL 121	PSY 121	AST 201	GEO 105
Basic Skills								
Arithmetic								
a) Basic arithmetic operation	×	×	×	×	×	×	×	×
i) Order of operations		×	×	×	×	×		
ii) Prop. of addition			×	×				
iii) Prop. of multiplication		×	×	×	×		×	
b) Place value			×					
c) Exponents		×	×	×			×	
d) Fractions	×	×	×	×	×	×	×	×
e) Percents	×	×	×	×	×	×	×	×
f) Decimals	×	×	×	×	×	×	×	×
g) Significant digits			×					
h) Powers	×		×	×			×	
i) Roots			×	×				
Measurement systems								
a) Unit conversions	×	×	×	×		×	×	×
b) Scientific notation		×	×	×			×	
c) Orders of magnitude				×			×	
Calculator skills								
a) 4-Function calculators		×	×				×	
b) Scientific calculators								
c) Statistics calculators								
d) Graphic calculators								
Other general skills								
Probability								
a) Naïve definition of probability	×	×	×	×	×	×	×	
b) Probability distributions	×	×	×	×	×	×		
c) Normal distribution			×			×		
d) Uniform distribution			×			×		

Statistics								
a) Descriptive statistics	×	×	×	×	×	×	×	
i) Measures of center of distribution (mean, mode, median)	×	×	×	×	×	×	×	
ii) Measures of the spread of a distribution (sample variance)	×	×	×	×	×	×	×	
b) Infernal statistics								
i) Z-test								
ii) T-test								
iii) Confidence interval estimation								
Estimation and approximation								
a) Estimation	×	×	×	×	×		×	
b) Approximation	×		×				×	
Working with graphs								
a) Rectangular coordinates	×	×	×	×	×	×	×	×
b) Polar coordinates		×	×	×			×	
c) Graph points	×		×				×	
d) Graph lines							×	
e) Graph algebraic expressions								
f) Bar graphs	×	×	×	×	×			
g) Pie charts	×	×	×	×	×			
h) Line graphs	×	×	×	×	×		×	×
Working with tables								
a) Reading data from tables	×	×	×	×	×	×		×
b) Making tables	×	×	×	×	×	×		×
c) Linear interpolation	×		×					
d) Linear extrapolation	×		×	×				
Logic and set theory								
a) Baby set theory						×		
i) Unions and intersections						×		
ii) DeMorgan's laws								
iii) Venn diagrams					×			

(continued)

Table K.1. (*Continued*)

Course	ANT 101	CHE 103	CHE 106	PHY 101	POL 121	PSY 121	AST 201	GEO 105
b) Logic conjunction, disjunction								
c) Notion of proof								
Map skills								
Translate symbols	x	x	x	x			x	x
Categorization	x	x					x	
Genetic addition	x							
Algebra								
Real numbers:								
a) Basic definitions	x		x			x	x	
b) The number line			x	x				
c) Concept of variable			x	x			x	
d) Concept of constant			x	x			x	
e) Equality and inequality	x	x	x	x	x	x		
f) Operations on real numbers				x				
g) Numbers in other bases (base 2, octal, hexadecimal) and conversions							x	
h) Scientific notation		x		x			x	
Linear equations and inequalities								
a) Solve linear equations in one variable			x	x			x	
b) Solve linear inequalities in one variable			x	x				
c) Absolute value inequalities			x					
d) Compound inequalities					x		x	
e) Absolute value inequalities								
Exponents and polynomials								
a) Integer exponents		x	x	x				
b) Properties of exponents		x	x	x			x	
c) Multiplication of polynomials								

Topic							
d) Greatest common factors; factoring by grouping							
e) Factoring trinomials							
f) General methods of factoring							
g) Solving equations by factoring							
Rational expressions							
a) Basics of rational expressions	×	×	×	×	×	×	×
b) Ratios and proportions	×	×	×	×	×	×	×
c) Multiplication and division of rational expressions		×					
d) Complex fractions							
e) Dividing polynomials		×	×				
f) Synthetic division							
g) Solve equations with rational expressions							
h) Solve inequalities with rational expressions							
Rational exponents and radicals							
a) Rational exponents		×					
b) Radicals							
c) Simplifying radicals							
d) Adding and subtracting radical expressions							
e) Multiplying and dividing radical expressions							
f) Equations with radical		×					
g) Complex numbers							
Quadratic equations and inequalities							
a) Solve quadratic expressions by completing the square		×					
b) The quadratic formula							
c) Non-linear inequalities							
The line	×						
a) The slope of a line	×					×	

(continued)

Table K.1. (*Continued*)

Course	ANT 101	CHE 103	CHE 106	PHY 101	POL 121	PSY 121	AST 201	GEO 105
b) The equation of a line								
i) Slope intercept form								
ii) Point slope form								
iii) Standard form								
c) Linear equations								
d) Linear inequalities								
Systems of linear equations								
a) Linear systems of equations in two variables								
b) Linear systems in three variables								
c) Matrices and determinants								
d) Solutions to linear systems of equations by matrix methods								
Conic sections								
a) The parabola							x	
b) The circle and ellipse				x			x	
c) The hyperbola							x	
d) Nonlinear systems of equations							x	
e) Second degree inequalities								
Functions								
a) Definition of function		x						
b) Functional notation			x	x				
c) 1–1 functions and inverses of functions								
d) Domain and range								
Exponential and logarithmic functions								
a) Exponential functions								
b) Logarithms								
c) Properties of logarithms								
d) Calculating with logarithms								
e) Logarithms and exponential equations								
f) The natural logarithm								

Trigonometry

Sequences and series

a) Sequences

b) Series

c) Arithmetic sequences

d) Geometric sequences

e) The binomial theorem

Vectors

a) Definition

b) Vector operations

c) Graphing

Geometry

Lines

Angles

Area

Perimeter

Concept of congruence

Concept of similarity

Geometric figures in the plane

a) Triangles

b) Quadrilaterals

c) More general polygons

d) Circles

Solid geometry

a) Cubes

b) Spheres

c) Pyramids

Applications (word problems)

Problems involving decimals

Problems involving percents

Problems involving interest

Problems involving geometry

Problems involving mixture

Problems involving motion

Problems involving loans

Examples of Outcome Statements

Lion F. Gardiner

Note: The professional literature of higher education uses a variety of terms when discussing the outcomes or results of learning. The three examples below use *goal* to refer to a relatively broad intended outcome and *objective* to describe a more specific or narrow outcome—a component or aspect of a goal—at any organizational level of a college or university.

These first two broad exemplar goals and their narrower, more specific objectives describe what many people believe are the preeminent learning outcomes that any college or university should strive to produce: the capacity and will to engage in skilled critical thinking and principled ethical reasoning and the translation of the latter into consistently ethical behavior.

Goal 1: Critical Thinking

Graduates will consistently and skillfully use critical thinking to comprehend the world and reason about situations, issues, and problems they confront.

Source: Revised from Gardiner, L. F. *Working with Goals and Objectives in Colleges and Universities,* 1988, p. 20. Reprinted with permission.

Objectives

Graduates will

1.1 Identify the elements of reasoning—its purpose(s), the question(s) to be answered or problem(s) solved, the requisite information or evidence required, inferences made and assumptions they are based on, concepts and principles being used, implications or consequences of the reasoning, and points of view or frames of reference being used—when thinking about personal, professional, and civic situations, issues, and problems

1.2 Skillfully use the universal intellectual standards of clarity, accuracy, relevance, precision, logicality, breadth, depth, completeness, significance, and fairness to assess and evaluate the quality of reasoning used when considering each of the elements of reasoning in Objective One

1.3 Reliably and consistently engage in rational thinking by recognizing and avoiding their own and others' egocentric and sociocentric biases

1.4 Exhibit the intellectual traits or dispositions of intellectual humility, intellectual autonomy, intellectual integrity, intellectual perseverance, intellectual courage, confidence in reason, intellectual empathy, and fair-mindedness

Goal 2: Ethics

Graduates will reason and act in a consistently ethical fashion with respect to other people, animals, and the natural environment.

Objectives

Graduates will

2.1 Distinguish among examples of complex reasoning based on ethical principle, religious dogma, legal prescription, and social conditioning, including traditional customs and political propaganda

2.2 Identify the elements of reasoning (purpose of the reasoning, question to be answered, information needed, concepts and principles required, assumptions being made, points of view that should be considered, inferences made and conclusions drawn, and implications for self and others of these and other possible conclusions), and use these elements to analyze reasoning about complex ethical dilemmas

2.3 Analyze reasoning about complex moral dilemmas in terms of their clarity, accuracy, precision, depth, breadth, logic, and significance

2.4 Use the analyses in Objectives Two and Three to discern moral content and determine a principled ethical course of action

2.5 Exhibit respectful behavior toward other people, animals, and the natural environment that is consistently characterized by the traits of humanity, empathy, fair-mindedness, integrity, ethical perseverance, and ethical courage

A Discipline-Specific Example: Ecology

Goal. Use concepts and principles of ecology, together with plausible evidence, to describe the interactions of organisms with their environments and with each other.

Objective 1. Demonstrate that organisms are both interdependent and dependent on their environments using specific examples from various major taxa as well as from marine, freshwater, and terrestrial environments

Objective 2. Show how ecosystems consist of populations of organisms, together with abiotic inputs, nutrient cycles, energy cycles, and limiting factors

Objective 3. Explain how species and populations interact in a dynamic fashion in communities

Objective 4. Propose one or more hypotheses that plausibly suggest how different species can occupy the same ecological niche, and support the hypothesis(es) with convincing evidence

Objective 5. Show how the various world biomes reflect global physical and biotic diversity

Objective 6. Use the concept of ecological succession to explain temporal changes in communities and ecosystems

Objective 7. Demonstrate the range of human impacts on the natural environment, together with their specific causes

Based on outcomes developed in the Department of Biological Sciences, Rutgers University, Campus at Newark. Note: This goal might be appropriate for a biology major curriculum or for an introductory course in ecology. Different biological science faculties might include other content and use different wording, numbers of outcomes, and specific formatting with this goal. The overall format of the relationship of the goal and its objectives, however, would probably be similar.

One Approach to Categorizing Your Learning Outcomes

Taxonomies of Educational Objectives

Cognitive Objectives

1. Knowledge—Recognizing or recalling facts, terminology, principles, theories, and so on

2. Comprehension—Simple understanding; ability to describe in one's own words, to paraphrase, to give examples, or to translate from one form to another (words to numbers)

3. Application—Using material in a new way; applying concepts, laws, or theories in practical situations to solve problems

4. Analysis—Understanding the organizational structure of material as well as content—breaking it down into component parts, drawing comparisons between elements, distinguishing cause and effect relationships

5. Synthesis—Combining the parts into a *new* whole; creatively arranging or rearranging to get patterns and structures new to the learner

Source: For cognitive objectives: adapted from Bloom and others, 1956; for affective objectives: adapted from Krathwohl, Bloom, and Masia, 1964.

6. Evaluation—Comparing material to known standards; judging or decision making based on appropriate criteria—either internal criteria (such as organization) or external criteria (for example, relevance to purpose)

Affective Objectives

1. Receiving—Being aware or willing to attend to something; learner is passive but attentive, listening with respect

2. Responding—Complying to given expectations; learner participates actively by reacting as well as showing awareness

3. Valuing—Accepting importance of the attitude; learner displays behavior consistent with a belief or attitude though not forced to comply

4. Organization—Committing oneself to a set of values; bringing together different values and resolving conflicts between them; building an internally consistent value system

5. Characterization—Behaving according to a characteristic "life style" or value system; maintaining a consistent philosophy regardless of surrounding conditions

Decision-Making and Problem-Solving Skills of a Critical Thinker

Category description: The skills used in decision making and problem solving are those involved in the generation and selection of alternatives and in judging among them. Many of these skills are especially useful in quantitative reasoning problems.

Skill	Description	Examples of Use
a. Listing alternatives and considering the pros and cons of each	Every problem and decision involves selecting among alternatives. This is a systematic way to consider the advantages and disadvantages of various alternatives.	Several ways of increasing sales are described. CT (critical thinker) combines the advantages and disadvantages of each and adds his own alternatives and combination of alternatives.
b. Restating the problem to consider different sorts of alternatives	Most real life problems are "fuzzy"; that is, there are many possible goals and ways to achieve them.	Several ways of increasing sales are described. CT redefines the problem as too little profit and considers other ways to increase profits.

Source: Greenwood, A. (ed.). *The National Assessment of College Student Learning: Identification of the Skills to be Taught, Learned, and Assessed.* NCES #94–286. 1994. National Center for Education Statistics, U.S. Department of Education, Washington, D.C.

Skill	Description	Examples of Use
c. Recognizing the bias in hindsight analysis	Hindsight analysis is the reevaluation of a decision after it has been made and its consequences known, with the belief that the consequences should have been known with greater certainty when the decision was made.	After a parolee goes on a killing spree, the townspeople want to fire the parole board. CT knows that the decision to release the parolee may have been reasonable given the information available at the time it was made.
d. Seeking information to reduce uncertainty	Decisions based on more information are likely to be better than those made with greater uncertainty.	A company is deciding whether to increase its advertising budget. CT gathers relevant information on the effect of increased advertising before making the decision.
e. Recognizing decision based on entrapment	Entrapment is a situation in which much money, time, or effort has been invested and the decision to continue with a course of action is based on this investment.	The Pentagon argues that the government needs to continue spending money on a new weapon because it has already invested large sums of money on its development.
f. Producing graphs, diagrams, hierarchical trees, matrices, and models as solution aids	Graphic representation of problems can be useful in solving them.	A problem is described verbally. The task for the CT is to depict the information in a graphic display in order to solve it.
g. Understanding how worldviews can constrain the problem-solving process	There are limitations on the way individuals approach problems placed upon them by social class or other group membership.	A company president is confronted with a takeover. The possibility of cooperating with the competitor does not occur to the president because of his worldview.
h. Using numerous strategies in solving problems, including means-ends analysis, working backwards, simplification, analogies, brainstorming, contradiction, and trial and error.	This is a collection of common strategies that every problem solver should know and use. They all require the planning and monitoring of solution strategy.	Several stages of action need to be completed by a due date. CT works backward from the due date to decide how much time should be spent on each stage.

Curriculum Review: The Questions to Ask

Robert M. Diamond and Lion F. Gardiner

A quality educational program must

- Be consistent with its institution's mission
- Have clearly defined outcomes that it intends to produce
- Use the best combination of learning experiences to help each learner achieve these results
- Include an assessment process that shows whether the results are being achieved
- Use the findings of assessment to improve program effectiveness

An approach to continuous program improvement that asks the right questions can provide academic administrators, faculty members, and others with the information they need to develop an appropriate, effective, and efficient academic program. The focus here is on undergraduate programs, but identical principles apply to curricula at the graduate level as well.

Listed below are a number of key questions to ask when reviewing curricula. Most of them are germane whether a curriculum is in general education or a specialized field. Although designed for reviewing curricula that already exist, many of these questions also can be helpful when beginning to design a new curriculum.

Asking these questions can help ensure the maximal learning possible with available resources and minimal waste.

Source: The National Academy for Academic Leadership. Copyright 2003. Reprinted with permission.

Be Clear About Purpose and Desired Results: Mission Statements, Goals, and Objectives

1. Is the curriculum consistent with and does it naturally flow from the institution's or unit's mission statement?

2. What assumptions have been made about entering students' developmental levels, knowledge, skills, and affective characteristics—all important inputs for the curriculum and each course. Have entering students been carefully assessed to ensure these assumptions are correct?

3. Does the curriculum have a formal set of intended learning outcomes that articulate the knowledge, skills, attitudes, and values it proposes to introduce or reinforce and that every student should have achieved upon graduation?

4. Are these intended outcomes written in specific language that is understandable in the same way to students, faculty members, and all other users?

5. Are the intended outcomes stated in terms of effective goals and objectives that permit assessment of students' success in achieving them?

6. When identifying and developing these intended outcomes, was there appropriate input from all concerned stakeholders, depending on the type of curriculum, such as faculty members, professionals in various fields, employers, and alumni?

7. Have agreed-upon intended learning outcomes been identified for each of the major areas within the curriculum— for the humanities, natural and social sciences, and fine arts within general education, or for a major field curriculum within the disciplines?

8. Does each course have a set of clearly stated intended outcomes derived from the intended outcomes of the curriculum?

9. Do these outcome goals and objectives prominently include higher-order cognitive and other complex behaviors as appropriate?

10. Will achieving each course's intended outcomes materially contribute to learners' achieving the outcomes of the curriculum in a deliberate and predetermined way?

11. When the intended outcomes of all the curriculum's courses are considered together, will every student have ample opportunity to achieve each of the specific intended outcomes of the curriculum itself?

12. For a major field in which certification or accreditation exists, are all of the outcome goals and objectives required for certification built into the curriculum's intended outcomes; or if requirements are stated in terms of courses, are all of these courses part of the curriculum?

13. Is the curriculum carefully sequenced so that the learning outcomes of prerequisite courses provide all required inputs for successive courses?

Monitor Program Quality: Know and Improve Actual Results

1. Is there an assessment plan that can ensure that graduates of the program have the knowledge, skills, attitudes, and values described as intended outcomes of the curriculum?

2. Is the curricular program being assessed as a whole and not merely by assessment of the intended outcomes of each of its individual courses?

3. Are diverse methods of assessment being used as appropriate for each type of learning engaged in and outcome desired?

4. Is there a close alignment between the intended outcomes of each course and the ways in which students are assessed in the course? Are a variety of assessment techniques being used?

5. Are intended outcomes being measured directly in both curriculum and courses—as opposed to surveying students' opinions about their learning—to reveal clearly what graduates know and can do, including their important affective qualities?

6. Are the findings of assessment made public and effectively communicated, as appropriate, to all interested stakeholders in a timely manner and in language they can understand?

7. Specifically, how have faculty members used information generated by assessment to improve the amount of learning produced?

8. Do faculty members collect data from students about their perceptions of and their level of satisfaction with the courses they have taken? Specifically, how is this information being used to improve courses?

The Education Process: Producing Learning

1. Are the educational processes employed to help students learn in each course or activity fully consistent with research on learning and student development and thus appropriate

for reaching both the course's or activity's specified outcomes and those of the curriculum?

2. Has the curriculum been designed so that each student has the sustained opportunity to apply to important issues, situations, and problems the knowledge, skills, attitudes, and values that have been identified as intended outcomes?

3. What percentage of class time do students spend passively listening to traditional lectures?

4. Are students consistently and actively involved in learning, not only in their courses but also through such methods as participating in internships, practica, and work-study and study-abroad programs?

5. Do students understand the purpose, structure, and processes of the curriculum, their responsibilities for learning, and how their progress will be assessed? Is each student helped to understand these things at the beginning of the curriculum and throughout every course?

6. Is the formal academic curriculum specifically linked to noncourse-based opportunities for learning on campus such as orientation, developmental academic advising, the cocurriculum, residence life, and employment?

Other Important Considerations

1. Are students able to enroll in both required and elective courses as needed? Are they completing the curriculum in a timely manner? If not, specifically why not?

2. Is the program attracting an adequate number of students to support accomplishment of the institution's or unit's mission and to make it cost-efficient? If not, specifically why not?

3. Are students completing the program and each of its courses at a high rate? If not, specifically why not?

4. Do the dropout or failure rates in the curriculum as a whole and in each of its courses indicate a problem and, if so, has the problem been identified and is it being appropriately addressed?

5. Do graduates find appropriate employment in their major fields after graduation? If not, specifically why not?

Writing Goals Inventory

Elizabeth A. Jones

	Extreme Importance			Medium Importance			No Importance		
	1	2	3	4	5	6	7	8	9

(Please place an "X" in one box per item.)

Awareness and Knowledge of Audience—Goals

College graduates should be able to:

	1	2	3	4	5	6	7	8	9
a. Address audiences whose backgrounds in the topic vary widely	☐	☐	☐	☐	☐	☐	☐	☐	☐
b. Address audiences whose cultural and communication norms may differ from those of the writer	☐	☐	☐	☐	☐	☐	☐	☐	☐
c. Define their anticipated multiple audiences	☐	☐	☐	☐	☐	☐	☐	☐	☐
d. Clearly understand their audiences' values, attitudes, goals, and needs	☐	☐	☐	☐	☐	☐	☐	☐	☐
e. Consider how an audience will use the document	☐	☐	☐	☐	☐	☐	☐	☐	☐

(continued)

Source: Jones, 1994, pp. 1–3. Used with permission of Elizabeth A. Jones, Ph.D., National Center on Post-Secondary Teaching, Learning, and Assessment.

	Extreme Importance			Medium Importance			No Importance		
	1	2	3	4	5	6	7	8	9

(Please place an "X" in one box per item.)

f. Choose words that their audience can understand ☐ ☐ ☐ ☐ ☐ ☐ ☐ ☐ ☐

g. Understand the relationship between the audience and themselves ☐ ☐ ☐ ☐ ☐ ☐ ☐ ☐ ☐

h. Understand the relationship between the audience and the subject material ☐ ☐ ☐ ☐ ☐ ☐ ☐ ☐ ☐

Purpose for Writing—Goals

College graduates should be able to:

a. Be aware of the multiple purposes and goals they are acting on when they write ☐ ☐ ☐ ☐ ☐ ☐ ☐ ☐ ☐

b. State their purpose(s) to their audiences ☐ ☐ ☐ ☐ ☐ ☐ ☐ ☐ ☐

c. Use vocabulary appropriate to their subject and purpose(s) ☐ ☐ ☐ ☐ ☐ ☐ ☐ ☐ ☐

d. Arrange words within sentences to fit the intended purpose(s) and audience ☐ ☐ ☐ ☐ ☐ ☐ ☐ ☐ ☐

e. Use appropriate tone of voice ☐ ☐ ☐ ☐ ☐ ☐ ☐ ☐ ☐

f. Make appropriate use of creative techniques of humor and eloquence when approaching a writing task ☐ ☐ ☐ ☐ ☐ ☐ ☐ ☐ ☐

g. Draw on their individual creativity and imagination to engage their audience (for example, using narrative, description, metaphor, and/or similar means of expression) ☐ ☐ ☐ ☐ ☐ ☐ ☐ ☐ ☐

Pre-Writing Activities—Goals

College graduates should be able to

a. Analyze their own experience to provide ideas for writing ☐ ☐ ☐ ☐ ☐ ☐ ☐ ☐ ☐

b. Create ideas for their writing ☐ ☐ ☐ ☐ ☐ ☐ ☐ ☐ ☐

c. Retrieve material from their memories to write ☐ ☐ ☐ ☐ ☐ ☐ ☐ ☐ ☐

d. Plan the writing process, using effective writing strategies and techniques ☐ ☐ ☐ ☐ ☐ ☐ ☐ ☐ ☐

e. Clarify their policy and position before writing ☐ ☐ ☐ ☐ ☐ ☐ ☐ ☐ ☐

f. Discuss their piece of writing with someone to clarify what they wish to say ☐ ☐ ☐ ☐ ☐ ☐ ☐ ☐ ☐

g. Research their subject ☐ ☐ ☐ ☐ ☐ ☐ ☐ ☐ ☐

h. Locate and present adequate supporting material ☐ ☐ ☐ ☐ ☐ ☐ ☐ ☐ ☐

i. Focus and then narrow their plan by recognizing the rhetorical problem(s) they wish to solve ☐ ☐ ☐ ☐ ☐ ☐ ☐ ☐ ☐

j. Identify problems to be solved that their topic suggests ☐ ☐ ☐ ☐ ☐ ☐ ☐ ☐ ☐

Organizing—Goals

College graduates should be able to

a. Develop patterns of organization for their ideas ☐ ☐ ☐ ☐ ☐ ☐ ☐ ☐ ☐

b. Use knowledge of their subject matter to shape a text ☐ ☐ ☐ ☐ ☐ ☐ ☐ ☐ ☐

c. Use knowledge of potential audience expectations and values to shape a text ☐ ☐ ☐ ☐ ☐ ☐ ☐ ☐ ☐

d. Organize the material for more than one audience ☐ ☐ ☐ ☐ ☐ ☐ ☐ ☐ ☐

e. Create and use an organizational plan (such as outlines, lists, and so on) ☐ ☐ ☐ ☐ ☐ ☐ ☐ ☐ ☐

f. Select, organize, and present details to support a main idea ☐ ☐ ☐ ☐ ☐ ☐ ☐ ☐ ☐

Diversity in the Classroom: Inclusive Teaching and Learning in a Multicultural Environment

A Faculty Seminar—Spring 2006
Missouri State University
Academic Development Center

Effective learning and teaching practices integrate diversity into the experiences of students *and* faculty. This seminar focuses on dimensions of diversity with implications for designing courses and interacting with students in a multicultural environment. Discussion will emphasize making connections with students that promote active engagement while increasing sensitivity to individual and group differences. In particular, and integral to the Missouri State mission in public affairs, participants will explore democratic practices that encourage full participation in learning and teaching processes. Our intention is to provide an opportunity for participants to reflect on their own values of diversity, exchange views with colleagues, and

Source: Kirkpatrick, D. L. *Evaluating Training Programs: The Four Levels.* San Francisco: Berrett-Koehler, 1996.

come away with a heightened inclination to think about diversity issues.

Outline of Seminar

Introductions

Perceptions of Diversity (Question 1)

Diversity can be viewed from many different perspectives, each with benefits for individuals and institutions. What is your perception of the most important aspects of diversity and their benefits for individuals and institutions?

Experiences That Have Shaped Perceptions of Diversity (Question 2)

Can you describe and share one or two experiences that have strongly contributed to shaping your view of diversity and its benefits or shortcomings?

Missouri State Nondiscrimination Policy (Question 3)

"Biases" and "prejudices" are acquired through cultural experiences, including the teaching of others. How are biases and prejudices similar to, or different from, the kind of discrimination referred to in the Missouri State University nondiscrimination policy (www.missouristate.edu/equity/Nondiscrimination_Statement.htm)?

Student and Teacher Behaviors That Demonstrate Valuing Diversity (Question 4)

Which student and teacher behaviors—reflecting particular knowledge, skills, or sensitivities—would demonstrate that you and your students value diversity?

Ways to Improve Inclusive Teaching (Question 5)

Chism (2002) suggests that some ways to implement inclusive teaching in a multicultural environment are to (1) make all students feel welcome in the classroom and the course; (2) treat students as individuals; (3) create an environment in which all students feel they can participate fully; and (4) treat students fairly. Regarding diversity, if you could do one or two things to improve your (inclusive) teaching and your students' learning experiences, what would you choose to do?

The materials distributed and used in the workshop are described in some detail in Chapter Twenty-One.

The most widely used approach to evaluating the impact of workshops and seminars is Kirkpatrick's four-level approach to assessment. Approximately six months after the seminar was completed, a follow-up questionnaire was distributed to all participants. The instrument focused on four areas:

- Level 1: Response—What was the participants' overall reaction to the seminar?

- Level 2: Learning—What did they learn?

- Level 3: Performance—Did the faculty use the knowledge and skills they developed? How did their behaviors change?

- Level 4: Results—What impact did these changes have on the teaching, research, or service activities of the participants?

It will be the Level Four responses that will determine the actual success of the program and its long-term impact.

Copyright: Handling Permissions and Releases

Background on Copyright Law and Fair Use

As an author, you have two concerns with copyright law: as the content proprietor of your own work and as the user of copyrighted works by other authors.

Your manuscript is protected by copyright from the time of its creation. The protection will extend for 70 years following your death. Copyright allows the copyright owner the exclusive right to reproduce, distribute, and adapt work and make derivative works from it.

The second concern relates to material owned by others which you wish to use in your manuscript. Such material is protected whether or not it has been published. The only times you do not have to seek permission for using material created by others is if (1) it is in the public domain, (2) you already have permission by an implied license, or (3) your use of the material constitutes "fair use" under the law.

Copyright protects the *expression* in the work, not the facts, information, or ideas. However, since copyright protects the format, organization, sequence, and style of the presentations as part of the expression, paraphrasing is only appropriate for limited portions of the original and should credit the source. *Close paraphrasing is akin to direct quotation.* Also, a translation of a public domain work

The following are selected portions of "Part Four" Handling Permissions and Releases, *Guidelines for Authors,* John Wiley and Sons, Inc., November, 2005. Reprinted with permission.

is protected, as is a copy or photograph of a building or a public domain painting or sculpture.

Public Domain _____

The following chart is a shorthand tool for determining whether material has fallen into the public domain by reason of time:

Date of Publication or Registration	Status
United States	
Before 1923	Public domain
1923–1963	95 years from publication or registration *unless* only U.S. authors and not renewed, in which case, public domain
1964–1977	95 years from publication or registration
1978 and later, including still unpublished	Life of the author plus 70 years or to December 31, 2047, whichever is greater
	OR, in the case of works for hire, earlier of 95 years from publication or 120 years from creation
Canada	
All years	Life of the author plus 50 years
Other countries	
All years	Life of the author plus 70 years

In addition, under the law, works of the U.S. government are in the public domain. This includes, for example, the text of federal court opinions, Congressional reports, and Agency reports. It does not include material created under federal grants, nor does it include material from state or local governments.

Finally, although some material is dedicated to the public domain by its creators, it may be difficult to recognize because material can have the full protection of the copyright law even if it does not use a copyright notice or make any statement about copyright. More often, and frequently on the Internet, an author specifically grants the public the right to quote material is properly attributed. If you are taking material off the World Wide Web, be sure to look for any place on the Web site that provides a policy on copyright, quotation, and reuse. If that policy permits you to quote with proper attribution, you should provide us with a copy of that notice as your permission. If no such notice is posted, you will need to confirm permission in writing with the author or creator of the material.

Fair Use

One of the trickiest issues authors encounter is determining whether a particular use constitutes a "fair use" for purposes such as criticism, comment, news reporting, teaching, scholarship, or research under the law. This is a fact-based determination on a case-by-case basis, with no specific numbers of words or percentages supplied by the courts. The following four factors should be considered:

- *The purpose and character of the use of material from a copyrighted work,* including whether such use is of a commercial nature or is for nonprofit educational uses.

- *The nature of the copied work.* The more creative or expressive the work (such as poetry over general fiction, and fiction over nonfiction), the less material you can use from it.

- *The amount and substantiality of the material used in relation to the entirety of the original copyrighted work.* Copyright law does not dictate absolute rules regarding length. The longer the length of *the original copyrighted work,* the more that can be quoted; the length of your manuscript is not a determining factor. Also of significance is whether the material used is the most moving or interesting part or in some way the "heart" of the original copyrighted work, which cuts against fair use even if the number of words is small.

- *The effect of the use upon the potential market for or value of the copyrighted work.* This may be the most important of the four factors and is always considered. The existence, as in the case of song lyrics, of an established market to grant quotation rights weighs very heavily against fair use.

Remember, contractually, final responsibility for the use of material belonging to another rests with you. If there is any reasonable doubt whether a use falls within "fair use," the most prudent thing to do is to request permission to use the material. Even when material does fall within fair use, you are obligated to ensure that:

- The quoted material is clearly presented as a quotation.

- The quotation is not taken out of context, and the true meaning is not distorted.

- The quotation is accurate.
- Full credit is given.

What Requires Copyright Permission

The following list presents some common examples of the different types of material for which permission generally *is* required. These examples are not to be considered determinative or to be a statement of what does or does not constitute "fair use" in every case.

1. Tables, figures, exhibits (including charts and graphs), and other representations taken in their entirety or adapted substantially from another work, since the form of presentation of the data constitutes the copyrighted expression. Note that if you present the data in a different way, permission is not needed, but the source should be credited. For example: "Source: Data from Jones, 1992, pp. 25, 67."

2. Itemized lists or checklists from another work (for example: "The 14 Principles of Management" or "Teaching Guru's 7 Steps"), whether used verbatim or picked up from headings throughout a section of the text.

3. Photographs (the photographer owns copyright to the picture but may not own all rights), illustrations, cartoons, maps, advertisements, and other artwork.

4. Epigraphs, because of their expressive value, which disfavors a finding of fair use. Permission is required unless the material is 1) short; 2) from a long work that is narrative rather than poetry, lyrics, or the like; and 3) has a direct content relationship to the content that follows.

5. Quotations in excess of approximately three hundred words that are taken from a book-length nonfiction work, with more leeway from a lengthy work and less for a short one such as a journal article.

6. Quotes of as few as approximately one hundred words from a book-length work of narrative fiction, with less leeway the more artful or literary the expression.

7. Quotations of as few as approximately fifty words from newspaper or magazine articles and even fewer words from short newspaper editorials or opinion pieces and even less than that from plays, scripts, movies, and television productions.

8. Poetry, unless the quotation is a few words from a lengthy piece; song lyrics; music from any composition (whether run into

the text or set off). Be careful when using arrangements of music and lyrics, which are usually copyrighted.

9. Quotations from informal writings such as speeches, interviews, position papers, corporate in-house documents, annual reports, mission statements, questionnaires, training or teaching materials; from conferences, seminars, or meetings; from instructional presentations, classroom discussion, or student work and dissertations. Sometimes the nature of the material and the way in which it is distributed indicate that the author intends to allow quotation, but this should not generally be assumed, especially if the work is short, literary, or unpublished.

10. Quotations from government agencies other than those of the U.S. government. This includes quotations from publications of many state, city, and local governing boards, such as school districts, but as in Nine above, sometimes the nature of the dissemination will convey the right to use it. Some states have declared that material produced by their agencies is fair use, but no good list of which states have done so exists, so you must check in each individual situation.

11. Letters, diaries, and other correspondence, including e-mail (the recipient owns the physical letter, but copyright is retained by the author; in the case of correspondence written for work the owner is the employer).

12. Computer representations, such as the depiction of results of research on computerized databases and the on-screen output of software, reproduction of Web pages and the capture of Internet or other online screen shots. *Note: If a Web site authorizes copying of its material, that does not automatically extend to permission for third-party material (such as photographs) that may be included in that site.*

13. Third-party software to be distributed as an electronic component should have a separate agreement.

14. Your own previously published works for which rights have been granted to the publisher, from whom you should, therefore, get permission.

Be aware that you cannot assume that permission has been granted for any third-party material (such as artwork or quotations) embedded in the text you receive permission to use. It is your responsibility to seek permission for those items. It is important to remember, in general, that you must always provide a citation for and, if necessary, seek permission from the *original* source of any third-party material.

RESOURCE S

Teaching Goals Inventory: Self-Scorable Version

Purpose: The Teaching Goals Inventory (TGI) is a self-assessment of instructional goals. Its purpose is threefold: (1) to help college teachers become more aware of what they want to accomplish in individual courses; (2) to help faculty locate Classroom Assessment Techniques they can adapt and use to assess how well they are achieving their teaching and learning goals; and (3) to provide a starting point for discussions of teaching and learning goals among colleagues.

Directions: Please select ONE course you are currently teaching. Respond to each item on the inventory in relation to that particular course. (Your responses might be quite different if you were asked about your overall teaching and learning goals, for example, or the appropriate instructional goals for your discipline.)

Please print the title of the specific course you are focusing on:

_____

Please rate the importance of each of the fifty-two goals listed below to the specific course you have selected. Assess each goal's importance to what you deliberately aim to have your students accomplish, rather than the goal's general worthiness or overall

Reproduced from Thomas A. Angelo and K. Patricia Cross, *Classroom Assessment Techniques: A Handbook for College Teachers.* (2nd ed.) *Teaching Goals Inventory,* pp. 393–397. San Francisco: Jossey-Bass, 1993.

importance to your institution's mission. There are no "right" or "wrong" answers; only personally more or less accurate ones.

For each goal, circle only one response on the 1–5 rating scale. You may want to read quickly through all fifty-two goals before rating their relative importance.

In relation to the course you are focusing on indicate whether each goal you rate is:

(5) Essential:	A goal you always or nearly always try to achieve
(4) Very important:	A goal you often try to achieve
(3) Important:	A goal you sometimes try to achieve
(2) Unimportant:	A goal you rarely try to achieve
(1) Not applicable:	A goal you never try to achieve

Rate the importance of each goal to what you aim to have students accomplish in your course.

	Essential	Very Important	Important	Unimportant	Not Applicable
1. Develop ability to apply principles and generalizations already learned to new problems and situations	5	4	3	2	1
2. Develop analytic skills	5	4	3	2	1
3. Develop problems-solving skills	5	4	3	2	1
4. Develop ability to draw reasonable inferences from observations	5	4	3	2	1
5. Develop ability to synthesize and integrate information and ideas	5	4	3	2	1
6. Develop ability to think holistically: to see the whole as well as the parts	5	4	3	2	1
7. Develop ability to think creatively	5	4	3	2	1
8. Develop ability to distinguish between fact and opinion	5	4	3	2	1
9. Improve skill at paying attention	5	4	3	2	1
10. Develop ability to concentrate	5	4	3	2	1
11. Improve memory skills	5	4	3	2	1
12. Improve listening skills	5	4	3	2	1
13. Improve speaking skills	5	4	3	2	1
14. Improve reading skills	5	4	3	2	1
15. Improve writing skills	5	4	3	2	1
16. Develop appropriate study skills strategies and habits	5	4	3	2	1

17. Improve mathematical skills	5	4	3	2	1
18. Learn terms and facts of this subject	5	4	3	2	1
19. Learn concepts and theories in this subject	5	4	3	2	1
20. Develop skill in using materials tools or technology central to this subject	5	4	3	2	1
21. Learn to understand perspectives and values of this subject	5	4	3	2	1
22. Prepare for transfer or graduate study	5	4	3	2	1
23. Learn techniques and methods used to gain new knowledge in this subject	5	4	3	2	1
24. Learn to evaluate methods and materials in this subject	5	4	3	2	1
25. Learn to appreciate important contributions to this subject	5	4	3	2	1
26. Develop an appreciation of the liberal arts and sciences	5	4	3	2	1
27. Develop an openness to new ideas	5	4	3	2	1
28. Develop an informed concern about contemporary social issues	5	4	3	2	1
29. Develop a commitment to exercise the rights and responsibilities of citizenship	5	4	3	2	1
30. Develop a lifelong love of learning	5	4	3	2	1
31. Develop aesthetic appreciations	5	4	3	2	1
32. Develop an informed historical perspective	5	4	3	2	1
33. Develop an informed understanding of the role of science and technology	5	4	3	2	1
34. Develop an informed appreciation of other cultures	5	4	3	2	1
35. Develop capacity to make informed ethical choices	5	4	3	2	1
36. Develop ability to work productively with others	5	4	3	2	1
37. Develop management skills	5	4	3	2	1
38. Develop leadership skills	5	4	3	2	1
39. Develop a commitment to accurate work	5	4	3	2	1
40. Improve ability to follow directions, instructions, and plans	5	4	3	2	1
41. Improve ability to organize and use time effectively	5	4	3	2	1
42. Develop a commitment to personal achievement	5	4	3	2	1
43. Develop ability to perform skillfully	5	4	3	2	1
44. Cultivate a sense of responsibility for one's own behavior	5	4	3	2	1
45. Improve self-esteem or self-confidence	5	4	3	2	1
46. Develop a commitment to one's own values	5	4	3	2	1
47. Develop respect for others	5	4	3	2	1
48. Cultivate emotional health and well-being	5	4	3	2	1
49. Cultivate physical health and well-being	5	4	3	2	1
50. Cultivate an active commitment to honesty	5	4	3	2	1
51. Develop capacity to think for one's self					
52. Develop capacity to make wise decisions					

In general, how do you see your primary role as a teacher? (Although more than one statement may apply please circle one.)

1. Teaching students facts and principles of their subject matter
2. Providing a role model for students
3. Helping students develop higher-order thinking skills
4. Preparing students for jobs/careers
5. Fostering student development and personal growth
6. Helping students develop basic learning skills

1. In all, how many of the fifty-two goals did you rate as "essential"?_____

2. How many "essential" goals did you have in each of the six clusters listed below?

	Cluster Number and Name	Goals Included in Cluster	Total Number of "Essential" Goals in Each Cluster	Clusters Ranked— from 1st to 6th— by Number of "Essential" Goals
I	Higher-Order Thinking Skills	1–8	_____	_____
II	Basic Academic Success Skills	9–17	_____	_____
III	Discipline-Specific Knowledge and Skills	18–25	_____	_____
IV	Liberal Arts and Academic Values	26–35	_____	_____
V	Work and Career Preparation	36–43	_____	_____
VI	Personal Development	44–52	_____	_____

3. Compute your cluster scores (average item ratings by cluster) using the following worksheet.

	A	B	C	D	E
	Cluster Number and Name	Goals Included	Sum of Ratings Given to Goals in That Cluster	Divide C by This Number	Your Cluster Scores
I	Higher-Order Thinking Skills	1–8	_____	8	_____
II	Basic Academic Success Skills	9–17	_____	9	_____

III	Discipline-Specific Knowledge and Skills	18–25	_____	8	_____
IV	Liberal Arts and Academic Values	26–35	_____	10	_____
V	Work and Career Preparation	36–43	_____	8	_____
VI	Personal Development	44–52	_____	9	_____

CASE STUDIES

Developing an Institutional Assessment Culture

Truman State University

Bronwyn Adam

Truman State University's assessment plan has "evolved into a mature program over the past thirty years" (Pieper, 2005, p. 1). At Truman State University (formerly Northeast Missouri State) an assessment culture was cultivated over the nineteen-year tenure of the institution's president, Charles J. McClain. When McClain arrived at Northeast Missouri State University in 1970, he brought with him a commitment to institutional quality and accountability that was a decade ahead of mainstream higher education. Along with a new dean of instruction, Darrell W. Kreuger, he worked though the 1970s to focus the institution's attention on measuring— so as to improve—student learning. Working along with faculty, these two leaders developed an assessment core as the center of the university initiative to improve student learning.

Three Phases of Assessment

1. Value Added

Suzanne Pieper, Assessment Specialist at Truman State, describes the first of three distinct phases in the development of the assessment culture as the *value-added phase*. From 1973 to 1983, President McClain worked to establish "degrees with integrity" at Truman State (Pieper, 2005). This effort included the use of standardized measures such as the Sequential Test of Educational Progress and the ACT College Outcomes Measurement Project. Graduating seniors were required to complete a senior exam in their majors. Truman State also began using surveys to better understand student perceptions and experiences.

2. Performance Measures

Attempts to assess value added at the institution attracted the attention of external constituencies. In 1985 the Missouri General Assembly designated the university as "the public liberal arts and sciences university for the state." This second phase of assessment—which Pieper identifies as 1984–1997—was a "time of expansion of University-wide and discipline assessment to include *performance measures*" (2005, p. 1). Specific initiatives included the development and implementation of a liberal arts and sciences' portfolio assessment, a sophomore-level writing assessment, and capstone courses and assessments in the majors. By the end of the 1990s, the institution had developed a robust assessment model focused on performance measures that could substantiate value added for its students—especially at graduation.

3. Reflection and Refinement

In 1995 the General Assembly renamed the institution Truman State University. This new identity accompanied the third phase of assessment—1998–present—a time Pieper characterizes as a "period of *reflection and refinement* of Truman's assessment plan" (2005, p. 1). The 2001 University Master Plan Review led to a new Assessment Action Plan in 2002. Campus constituents—students, faculty, and staff—were asked to contribute feedback and comments regarding the existing Assessment Plan, and the new Action Plan "was crafted to address a number of concerns, from the need to more clearly map current assessments to University core outcomes, to the call for more effective discipline-level assessment, to the need to assess students' level of motivation" (Pieper, p. 1). According to Pieper, "three initiatives were particularly important to the continuing vitality of assessment: (1) the implementation of a new writing assessment, (2) participation in a state-wide value-added student learning project, and (3) the launch of a new discipline assessment website" (p. 2).

Leadership, Involvement, and Change _____

Truman State is an excellent example of planned institutional change and illustrates some of the features of successful change initiatives. This case also reminds us that "successful assessment is much more than techniques, processes, or even outcomes; it is a cultural issue that affects how a community of scholars defines its work and its responsibilities to its students" (Magruder, McManis, and Young, 1997, p. 17).

Administrative Leadership

The transformation of Northeast Missouri State was undeniably a presidential initiative; however, McClain was careful to build community ownership in the change process by involving faculty and challenging them to answer difficult questions about how well the university was accomplishing its mission and goals. He worked to create a consciousness of the need for change by demonstrating to faculty that they had no way of assessing how well they were preparing students for life after college.

Since Truman State's roots were as a teachers' college, placement records and feedback from school districts who worked in partnership with the college provided an information base from which to begin thinking about student performance assessment. The first attempt to collect additional data on which to base improvement initiatives came in 1972 when graduating seniors were invited to take nationally standardized mastery examinations in their majors. For a number of years these exams were taken voluntarily. The results were reviewed with faculty, allowing them to consider the outcomes and their implications as they were asked to make recommendations about which examinations were most appropriate for assessing knowledge in the field. Additional means of assessing outcomes were used including student satisfaction surveys and value-added tests so as to provide feedback from multiple sources and perspectives.

McClain's nineteen-year tenure as Truman's president was certainly an important variable in this case. Consistent leadership as the assessment culture evolved undoubtedly contributed to the transformation of this institution.

A Community Effort

Another important variable in this case was the purposeful manner in which McClain involved faculty in developing and implementing the assessment plan. Making this initiative a community effort involving multiple measures of students' knowledge and perceptions and supporting this effort over a period of years fostered an ambient climate for institutional change.

Faculty are often wary of assessment initiatives; however, McClain's careful, consistent efforts worked to reassure faculty that the data collected about student learning would not be used in punitive ways. This assurance made it possible for assessment to become part of the ongoing improvement processes under way at Northeast Missouri State University. Performance data were shared, and occasions were provided for faculty to analyze the data publicly. Moreover, the president and dean modeled for the campus community the ways in which assessment data would be used for ongoing improvement. Their public and private communications with faculty consistently communicated that decisions about existing and future programs and initiatives needed to be informed by assessment data. Faculty also came to take for granted that the focus on student learning goals would be paramount at the institution.

Staged Implementation

Having established a climate accepting of assessment as the means to a mutually desirable end of "improvement," an assessment *system* developed at Truman. By 1980 all students were required to take pre- and posttests of general education, to pass a locally designed writing assessment, to complete three student surveys, and to take a nationally normed examination in the major. It is important to note that there were no negative consequences for individual students to taking the various examinations. In fact, there was a benefit for individual students insofar as mentoring and advising were available to refer them to campus services based on assessment results.

Group scores were considered as information and feedback about how well the institution was achieving its goals and objectives. By 1990 more qualitative measures were added to the evaluation design, incorporating such methods as capstone experiences in the major and student portfolios. In 1992 an annual initiative was launched to interview students concerning their undergraduate experience.

The institution continues to explore methods for gathering good data on which to make improvements. While recognizing the centrality of such data collection to this case, Truman's success demonstrates the importance of institutional climate in change initiatives, particularly those in the assessment domain. A campus culture that accepts assessment as part of the business of teaching and learning and supports self-evaluation makes ongoing improvement possible. Magruder, McManis, and Young (1997) identified four essential factors in developing this culture: (1) administrative clarity and commitment; (2) timing and motivation for the assessment initiative; (3) integration of assessment into the management and operation of the institution; and (4) reliance on faculty to develop and implement the assessment.

Making Good Things Visible

Sustaining any change initiative is difficult if participants in the process do not see tangible outcomes and experience the impact of those outcomes in positive ways. "Part of the successful strategy used by McClain and Krueger was to assure that good things happened because of assessment" (Magruder, McManis, Young, 1997). Faculty received generous, positive reinforcement for their work in improvement efforts. Moreover, as the University's reputation changed, it attracted better-prepared students, and students responded to the institution's interest in their success and became more engaged in academic life. Finally, the University's strong benchmark data attracted support for a number of focused initiatives to improve the academic environment and ultimately led to the State's designation of Truman as a selective, statewide, liberal arts university. Assessment has paid off for Truman State University.

Important Lessons

An important factor for faculty was that over time they came to trust that assessment would pay off for them personally as faculty—or at least that it would not hurt them in any way. Faculty and staff evaluations were never linked to the assessment plan. The institution was careful to provide opportunities for dialogue and input and to introduce change systematically.

Making changes visible to outside constituencies was also accomplished purposefully. Truman was in the advantageous position of being ahead of the accountability movement, allowing the institution time and freedom to explore options and find measures that worked within the institutional culture. The public policy environment in Missouri was supportive of Truman's efforts and recognized and rewarded the institution for its self-study. The rewards the University received for its efforts were a strong payback to members of the campus community.

Sustaining the System

Higher education enjoys little stability in terms of major stakeholders. Students rotate out of the system continuously, and faculty and administrators turn over, although certainly with less frequency or regularity. Keeping the culture in-tune with the assessment system requires ongoing socialization. Keeping the system fresh and current requires consideration of new ways of measuring, displaying, and using data. New people need to become involved in order to bring fresh perspectives to bear, and "veterans" need to be reinvigorated. Maintaining the energy that comes with innovation is a challenge. Because Truman's success has been so highly dependent upon the assessment *culture* as opposed to the assessment *program,* this aspect of the Truman case cannot be underestimated. Magruder, McManis and Young note that "new leaders have to be socialized to understand the use of data. The temptation for leaders to delegate the assessment processes to others can quickly make assessment just one more report" (p. 26).

Everyone's Input: Everyone's Responsibility

Modifications in the assessment plan are the result of ongoing evaluation of the plan and the success of particular measures to provide useful information about student learning and development. It is important to keep in mind that recent changes to the plan were prompted by the 2002 Assessment Action Plan through which faculty, students, and staff provided feedback about assessment activities and their utility and vitality. One important change in the assessment culture at Truman State has been to incorporate more students in assessment processes. The Student Interview Project has solicited feedback from Truman State juniors each spring since 1992–93. This project incorporates a written survey and a personal interview and provides a venue for faculty-student interview teams to talk with students about their experiences at Truman. Focus questions are modified each year, and study results are made available to the campus community. Students are involved in a variety of other ways as contributors or co-creators of assessment methods or data, and self-assessment has been encouraged as an important part of the assessment process.

A 2005 Truman State Self-Study Report identified a variety of direct and indirect measures as components of the Assessment Program. In addition to students, who are assessed by multiple measures in all but the sophomore years, faculty, staff, alumni, and employers of alumni contribute to assessment efforts each year. Eight surveys are used along with four nationally normed exams, three performance assessments, and the Interview Project. Truman State's commitment to assessment is highly visible—and everyone contributes.

At a time when many in academe continue to haggle over questions of student outcomes' assessment, Truman State University has over twenty-five years' experience measuring student learning. In

1991, Peter Ewell, a national assessment expert, described Truman State's success as "astonishing" in terms of the extent to which the institution had embraced and engaged assessment. Ewell's remarks highlight a key reason for Truman's success—focused, conscious efforts to involve a campus community in assessing student learning. In 2002, Trudy Banta cited Truman as an example of an institution that had engaged questions of student learning as part of the "scholarship of assessment" made possible by years of careful collection and analysis of data—what Banta calls a "culture of evidence" (2002, p. 122). The culture of assessment at the university has made great strides in helping the institution understand how teaching and learning take place in its institutional context. This case also reflects the importance of times of reflection and inquiry as opportunities to take stock of progress to-date and to adjust to changing needs and contexts. This case has much to teach us about the importance of community and culture in institutional change.

For more information, visit the Truman State University Assessment Web site at http://assessment.truman.edu/.

Resources

Banta, Trudy J., and Associates. *Building a Scholarship of Assessment*. San Francisco: Jossey-Bass, 2002.

Ewell, P. Oral Report to Board of Governors, Truman State University, Nov. 1991.

Magruder, J., McManis, M., and Young, C. "The Right Idea at the Right Time: Development of a Transformational Assessment Culture." In P. J. Gray and T. W. Banta (eds.), *The Campus-Level Impact of Assessment: Progress, Problems, and Possibilities*. New Directions for Higher Education, No. 100. San Francisco: Jossey-Bass, 1997.

Pieper, S. *Higher Learning Commission of Self-Study*. Truman State University, 2005.

Developing a Statement of Learning Outcomes
Alverno College

Alverno College, a small Catholic liberal arts college in Milwaukee with a student body of twenty-six hundred, has long been a national leader in its coordinated effort to describe the instructional goals of the institution in the development of an academic program to meet these goals and in the design of a program to measure student learning in terms of the progress of each student as well as of each program and of the institution as a whole.

As a first step in the curriculum design process, the college identified and then described in detail eight basic abilities:

- *Communication:* Make connections that create meaning between you and your audience. Learn to speak and write effectively, using graphics, electronic media, computers, and quantified data.

- *Analysis:* Think clearly and critically. Fuse experience, reason, and training into considered judgment.

- *Problem solving:* Define problems and integrate a range of abilities and resources to reach decisions, make recommendations, or implement action plans.

- *Valuing:* Recognize different value systems while holding strongly to your own ethic. Recognize the moral dimensions of your decisions and accept responsibility for the consequences of your actions.

- *Social Interaction:* Demonstrate ability to get things done in committees, task forces, team projects, and other group efforts. Elicit the views of others and help reach conclusions.
- *Developing a Global Perspective:* Act with an understanding of and respect for the economic, social, and biological interdependence of global life.
- *Effective Citizenship:* Be involved and responsible in the community. Act with an informed awareness of contemporary issues and their historical contexts. Develop leadership abilities.
- *Aesthetic Engagement:* Appreciate the various forms of art and the context from which they emerge. Make and defend judgments about the quality of artistic expressions.

For each ability the faculty then developed specific levels of performance. For example, the Effective Citizenship ability had these four levels:

Level 1. Assess own knowledge and skills in thinking about and acting on local issues.

Level 2. Analyze community issues and develop strategies for informed response.

Level 3. Evaluate personal and organizational characteristics, skills, and strategies that facilitate accomplishment of mutual goals.

Level 4. Apply developing citizenship skills in a community setting.

The faculty then went one step further and described in detail each of these four levels. The following example is from Level 2 of the Analysis ability.

Level 2 focuses on the student's ability to draw reasonable inferences from her observations and requires her to distinguish between fact and inference, evidence and assumption.

For example, a student in a science investigative learning laboratory might learn to hypothesize about possible results of an experiment that she designs herself. A student in a psychology course on life-span development might learn to infer theories of human development by interacting with people at differing stages of life—by taking a young child to lunch, for example, or interviewing a grandparent. After carefully examining her observations and inferring the subject's stage of development, the student would review the theories of human development that she had learned in class to see how her experiences reinforced her understanding and how her inferences corresponded to the theories.

In teaching and assessing the individual student, the faculty determined that the abilities must be integrated into disciplinary or interdisciplinary content and be expressed as student learning outcomes. For every course, faculty at Alverno develop a syllabus outlining the ability levels available in the course, the means by which they will be taught in the given disciplinary context, and the methods used for validating attainment. This detailed documentation is the basis on which the educational experience at Alverno rests.

One of the major strengths at Alverno is the approach to assessment—specifically, the use of video and written portfolios to record the development of each student as a communicator and a learner.

The specifics of the Alverno approach are unique to that college, as the faculty insist they should be to any institution involved. However, the systematic approach that was used to develop an integrated curriculum, the documentation required, and the assessment protocol used have applications far beyond the institution. For additional information write to Kathleen O'Brien, Senior Vice President for Academic Affairs, Alverno College, 3400 South 43rd Street, P.O. Box 343922, Milwaukee, WI 53234-3922.

Developing Learning Outcomes

Southeast Missouri State University

Southeast Missouri State University in Cape Girardeau was established in 1873. It has a current enrollment of over eight thousand students and offers undergraduate liberal arts, teacher preparatory, and professional programs. It also offers graduate study beyond the master's level but does not offer doctorates. The university was one of the first institutions to bring coherence to its basic academic program by developing a comprehensive set of academic goals to serve as the underpinnings of its core curriculum. In 1981, nine overarching objectives were developed for the University Studies, or core, program. This program was described as follows:

> The University Studies program at Southeast Missouri State University is designed to provide all students with the knowledge, concepts and competencies necessary for them to assume productive leadership roles in a pluralistic society. The purposes of the University Studies program are to ensure the acquisition of knowledge common to educated people; the ability to process, synthesize and evaluate such knowledge for use in making intelligent decisions; and the ability to use such knowledge in everyday life for a more rewarding, fulfilling existence and to disseminate such knowledge to others in one's society and world.

> The entire undergraduate program at the University encourages students to develop an intellectual orientation—to build reasoning powers capable of integrating personal experience with collective human experience. In particular, students educated by a coherent University Studies program learn ultimately how to discover and

comprehend, how to create and communicate, how to appreciate and use knowledge for themselves and for others. Reason fostered by education thus prepares them for their future academic, professional, personal, and societal lives.

The core program had as its goal "equipping students to make sound choices by critically thinking through a problem and assessing its implication in the world at large. By integrating the various disciplines and thus identifying the interconnections of thoughts and ideas, students will increase their understanding of their physical, social, political, psychological and cultural intellectual environment." As you read the nine goals of Southeast Missouri State University presented here, notice that although they overlap considerably with the Alverno statements, they are different in both character and description.

Objective 1: Demonstrate the ability to locate and gather information

The explosion of knowledge in the twentieth century and the variety of formats in which information is being presented have resulted in the need for more sophisticated tools and capabilities to access that information. At the same time, the need for information has accelerated. Information is necessary for making intelligent decisions and judgments and for the enrichment of personal life. The ability to locate or retrieve this information efficiently is an important component in the preparation for living a fulfilling life and for assuming a responsible and creative role in society.

Objective 2: Demonstrate capabilities for critical thinking, reasoning, and analyzing

Since information exists in a wide variety of formats, students often encounter it as disjointed and disparate facts. Thus, it is necessary for students to learn to evaluate, analyze, and synthesize information in order to make intelligent use of it. Students need to learn that there are numerous ways of discovering and processing information and applying it to a given situation. The University Studies program should equip students with the ability and the desire to think critically and to reach well-reasoned conclusions about specific issues. Only as students become skillful in evaluating, analyzing, and synthesizing information will they be able to engage in the level of intellectual activities required for critical thinking.

Objective 3: Demonstrate effective communication skills

The mastery of verbal and mathematical symbols is an essential component of the University Studies program. The ability to understand and manipulate such symbols is a fundamental requirement in any society that encourages and thrives on the free interchange of ideas and information. In this context mere functional literacy can never be an adequate goal; students must attain a level of proficiency that will enable them to become informed, effective citizens in their society and world.

Objective 4: Demonstrate an understanding of human experiences and the ability to relate them to the present One important characteristic of human beings is their ability to understand and transmit the accumulated knowledge of the past from one generation to another. This ability enables each generation to build on the experiences of the past and to understand and function effectively in the present. The degrees to which individuals and societies assimilate the accrued knowledge of previous generations is indicative of the degree to which they will be able to use their creative and intellectual abilities to enrich their lives and the culture of which they are a part.

Objective 5: Demonstrate an understanding of various cultures and their interrelationships Understanding how other people live and think gives one a broader base of experience upon which to draw in the quest to become educated. In the University Studies program, students explore the different interrelationships among cultures that must be understood in order to appreciate the differences and similarities in customs throughout the world.

Objective 6: Demonstrate the ability to integrate the breadth and diversity of knowledge and experience The educated person is not one who possesses merely isolated facts and basic concepts but one who can correlate and synthesize disparate knowledge into a coherent, meaningful whole. Even though modern society encourages a high degree of specialization in some areas, students should be encouraged and empowered to perceive connections and relevancies within the multiplicity of data experience.

Objective 7: Demonstrate the ability to make informed, intelligent value decisions Valuing is the ability to make informed decisions after considering ethical, moral, aesthetic, and practical implications. Valuing is a dynamic process that involves assessing the consequences of one's actions, assuming responsibility for them, and understanding and respecting the value perspectives of others. As a result, valuing is a natural dimension of human behavior and an integral component of the University Studies program.

Objective 8: Demonstrate the ability to make informed, sensitive aesthetic responses A concern for beauty is a universal characteristic of human cultures. Although the term aesthetic is usually associated with such fine arts as literature, theater, art, music, dance, and architecture, in actuality the term need not be so narrowly defined. All areas of human endeavor—science, history, business, and sport, for example, as well as the arts—contain elements of beauty. Toward the end of exercising an informed sensibility, students should be exposed to various definitions of beauty, equipped with the appropriate methods of investigation and evaluation, and encouraged to make independent judgments.

Objective 9: Demonstrate the ability to function responsibly in one's natural, social, and political environment The existence of mankind depends on countless interrelationships among persons and things. Students must learn to interact responsibly with their natural environment and with other citizens of their society and world. The University Studies program should help students to realize that individual freedoms may necessarily be limited and that natural, social, and political harmony begins with the individual. Further, the University Studies program should foster a desire for a political and social system based on a concern for human rights and just public policy determined through reasoned deliberation. Such an ideal presupposes an educated, enlightened citizenry that accepts its responsibility to understand and participate in the governance process.

Imagining Missouri's Future

Missouri State University

In order for Missouri State University students to be educated and successful in the fullest sense, the process of incubating new ideas must also be accompanied by informed discussion, debate, and understanding of the uses, values, and purposes of new discoveries and creative products. What implications will such advances have for how individuals live and work? How will they affect our local communities and our global partners? What risks might they pose, and what dangers could they reduce? How should new discoveries be regulated, by whom, and for what duration of time?

Missouri State must assure that its education of students prepares them to confront these and many other vexing questions. To do so, the University must provide educational experiences that

- Simulate informed dialogue and scholarly engagement about public policy
- Afford students the best that can be offered in terms of global education
- Support special research efforts that will address the most substantial problems our local communities are likely to confront in the future

Source: Missouri State University, 2006. Copyright 2006 Board of Governors, Missouri State University. Available at www.missouristate.edu/longrangeplan/imagining.htm.

Ultimately, to imagine a well-conceived future, the University should insist on rigorous expectations for its students, and it must be clear about what it means to be well-educated for the twenty-first century. There are five traits of educated students:

They cultivate their aesthetic tastes. Educated students push their creative limits and stretch their aesthetic appreciation. The University years are a great time for students to sharpen their eyes for art, tune their ears to music, and turn their minds to all kinds of dramatic and creative expression.

They become critical thinkers. They can discern what is a sturdy basis for knowledge and beliefs versus what is mere bias or preference. Universities should recruit people away from illusions and toward truth. One of the main goals of a first-rate university is to teach students how to think and reason well, and that is what we will ask students to embrace as a personal goal.

They are serious readers who become broadly literate. Reading is the vehicle by which students travel and learn their own interiors. It introduces them to the life of the mind, and it opens windows on their own lives. Habitual reading remains one of life's single most empowering and liberating activities.

They dedicate themselves to becoming curious and contributing citizens. Students need to find a personal intellectual interest that captures their hearts and drives them to approach each day eager to learn a little more. Students need to grow an obsession for some area of knowledge where they insist on being an expert and through which they make a difference for others. The specific expertise also should be complemented by an understanding of the global issues that effective citizens need to develop throughout their lives. Further, students need to develop the skills necessary for successful collaboration and teamwork.

They balance an in-depth mastery of at least one academic discipline with a broad appreciation of the liberal arts. By the time they graduate, students should be extremely capable in the academic field of their choosing. But that specialty should be built on a broad educational foundation to help provide context and understanding.

Academic Philosophy

The focus of Missouri State's mission continues to be the development of educated persons who have an understanding of themselves and the diverse social and natural world in which they live, who are creative people of vision, and who are capable of making informed and meaningful decisions. These educated persons should possess the five traits previously identified. In order to achieve these aims, it is essential that the faculty, staff, and administration of Missouri State University serve as role models and leaders.

The mission of the university, with its rededicated emphasis upon student learning as its primary purpose, and with a statewide mission in public affairs, acknowledges that teaching, scholarship, and service are to be regarded as integrated, complementary activities. The University's new performance-based compensation system will reward faculty who excel in these three areas, as well as provide a stronger basis for the granting of promotion, tenure, and salary increases.

Academic departments, schools, and colleges support both the individual and collective efforts of faculty in fulfilling their obligations to the University and the public they serve. These units have several important responsibilities:

- To critically examine the curriculum (both major programs of study and individual courses) using a variety of available measures. Programs and courses that are not appropriate for the University mission should be eliminated, while those that are should be strengthened, subject to resource constraints.

- To review their offerings in light of providing effective efficient learning experiences for students. Unnecessary duplication of courses and sections, frequent offering of low enrollment courses, and inefficient use of facilities and resources must be avoided.

- To expand the use of instructional technologies, both within and outside the classroom, or order to improve efficiency, enhance student learning, expand accessibility, and support collaborative offerings among institutions.

- To achieve the goal of increased partnerships, Missouri State campuses, departments, schools, and colleges will pursue and promote cooperative and collaborative programs and learning experiences. Some examples that are currently in place or will be pursued include:

  Partnerships with Springfield Public Schools to provide a seamless experience in K–16 and to enhance student learning through improved teaching skills and accessibility to courses. Faculty exchanges with the R–12 school district, the University's participation in the eMints program, and the Missouri Virtual School will continue.

  Joint offerings with other institutions, at both the graduate and undergraduate level. On the horizon is a cooperative undergraduate engineering program with the University of Missouri-Rolla in civil and electrical engineering. That will be added to the undergraduate partnerships in education with Crowder Community College, Ozarks Technical Community College (OTC), and Missouri State University-West Plains; undergraduate partnerships between Missouri State and Crowder College in Agriculture and Industrial Management; a cooperative doctorate in educational leadership with the University of Missouri-Columbia; and a cooperative Master of Arts in Teaching degree program with Missouri Southern State University; and a cooperative Master of Arts in Library of Science with the University of Missouri-Columbia.

Accelerated graduate degree programs with Springfield-area colleges and universities in areas where Missouri State can address unmet needs.

Cooperative efforts, both at the graduate level and undergraduate level, with a number of international institutions, particularly in Asia.

Possible creation of a College of Public Health which, along with the Ozarks Public Health Institute, will promote collaborative program development both within the University and outside the University.

Joint ventures with business and industry to provide improved opportunities for Missouri State students and faculty. The most notable venture to date is the JVIC, which includes the Center for Applied Sciences and Engineering (CASE) and the Center for Biomedical and Life Sciences (CBLS). JVIC/CASE/CBLS not only benefit the University, community, and a host of businesses but also will increase Missouri State's research activity in the sciences.

- In an effort to support lifelong learning and to be of service to the community, it will be necessary to provide and promote nontraditional learning experiences. The Center for Continuing and Professional Education and Ozarks Public Television will use their expanded facilities to offer additional noncredit opportunities for people in the metropolitan community served by the University.

Public Affairs

On June 16, 1995, Missouri Governor Mel Carnahan signed into law Senate Bill 340 which gave Missouri State University a statewide mission in public affairs. This mission defines a primary way in which a Missouri State education is different from that of other universities and one way by which we educate our students to imagine the future.

The United States, a pluralist gathering of races and cultures, banded together not by blood or religion, by territory or tradition, but by a political idea, is a nation formed by its dedication to civic principles. These principles embedded in our fundamental national documents make it clear that American citizens are expected to fulfill civic responsibilities by competent participation in public affairs. The obligations of civic participation are not unique to Americans but are incumbent on all those who are fortunate enough to live in democratic republics.

A leading American political thinker and statesman, Thomas Jefferson, contended that the status of "citizen" called for every member of the community to become involved in the business of society. To imagine the future, the University has a special responsibility to educate students about social goals, public purposes and values, and the ethics of citizenship as well as to encourage students to have a personal sense of responsibility for the global society.

Good citizenship takes place at several different levels. Students are members of multiple communities—the University, the neighborhood, the city, and the state, as well as the nation. Students also are citizens in a larger philosophical sense. Students belong to a moral community composed of all human beings. The members of the Missouri State campus community affirm their citizenship in the larger world community by ensuring that differences of nationality, ethnicity, or social-economic class do not become barriers between us. Helping students become responsible citizens at these different levels takes time and deliberate efforts on the part of all educators.

Public affairs in higher education is not restricted to politics, humanities, or the social sciences. It is present in all areas of life that require knowledge, participation, civic skills, and the willingness to work for the common good. Public affairs involves educating persons to become responsible citizens and leaders. The University should define the skills of responsible citizenship and ensure that its unique education develops these skills.

In order to educate for public life and for the future, the University must foster a community where all individuals are called upon to respond to public affairs issues and to develop a sense of public spiritedness, tolerance, and understanding of multicultural concerns. Students are exposed to a common core of knowledge through the General Education Program in order to promote the general welfare of community, state, nation, and globe. This common core imparts historical and comparative perspectives on public affairs—for example, problems of order, justice, liberty, equality, stability, and avoidance of civil and international strife. Capstone courses allow the student to investigate in depth a particular social problem or issue of his or her choice.

Education in public affairs should be a recognizable and measurable goal. Public affairs, although not a curriculum, must be present and expressed through all academic disciplines. Students are taught how to communicate effectively in the public sphere through the arts, through logic, and through the written and spoken word. They are exposed to ethical and global issues; political, environmental, and technological concerns; and issues of human diversity. Teachers are prepared for public and private schools, underscoring the importance of educated persons for a flourishing civic society. Scientific and social research are used to promote a healthy citizenry, which is vital to stable and productive societies. Students are educated to participate in our democratic society as fully involved and informed citizens; and science and the environment are studied to promote environmentally responsible growth. Being exposed to these issues in public affairs will help develop the student's capacity to analyze and resolve contemporary problems in the metropolitan area, in the nation, and in the international community.

Public affairs education takes place not only in the public space of the classroom but also outside the University. Internships, field experiences, practica, cooperative projects, government service, volunteer programs, and residential life programs that help develop leaders all contribute to inculcating in students a sense of individual and community responsibility.

Community outreach through public affairs research centers, adult continuing education, distance learning courses, public broadcasting, and telecommunication linkages with other universities will use faculty expertise to address state and community problems. Missouri State's commitment to its statewide mission also is reflected in campus lectures on public issues in which the community is invited to participate. The challenge presented by a focus on public affairs, however, is not just about what kind of curriculum, community service, or public forums should be in place. It is about discovering solutions to the problems that all citizens face as members of a democratic society in a world shared by many.

International Programs

We live in a world of increasingly political, economic, social, cultural, linguistic, environmental, and geo-strategic interdependence and complexity that requires educated persons to have a global frame of reference. Therefore, Missouri State University must provide its students, faculty, and administrators, as well as the community it serves, with cross-cultural experiences that develop mutual understanding and respect of cultural differences.

To develop these abilities and sensibilities is part of a college education that prepares students for their future obligation to become active global participants and citizens. For this reason, Missouri State University is committed to provide all stakeholders with increased opportunities for educational and experiential exchanges and study tours, and contacts with foreign students and scholars on campus.

To fulfill its obligations to be an effective force for global understanding, the University will pursue several strategies, including:

- Promoting global citizenship by emphasizing international issues and perspectives in its course offerings.

- Enhancing international opportunities for students, faculty, administrators, and community members by participation in study abroad programs (semester, summer), study tours (short-term), experiential programs, and global issue events on campus and in the community.

- Establishing joint academic programs with international programs leading to diplomas, degrees, or certificates, and dual degree options.

- Increasing Missouri State's visibility abroad in order to attract more international students, teachers, and scholars to this institution. This will require aggressive, consistent, and coherent recruitment strategies, including personal contacts between Missouri State faculty, administrators, and international colleagues and advertising through multiple media.

- Enhancing curriculum and programmatic offerings with a global focus, especially by strengthening courses and programs in foreign languages, comparative studies, international affairs, globalization, and aspects of interdependence.

- Strengthening research collaboration with foreign scholars in such areas as business, agriculture, industrial development, technology, physical and biological sciences, social sciences, arts, and humanities.

- Hosting seminars, workshops, exhibitions, and other programs at various locations and with a variety of client groups, with home, host, and guest personnel serving as resources.

- Focusing our efforts at globalization on regions of the world that offer the best opportunities, including Latin America,

Europe and the former Soviet Union, Asia, the Middle East, and Africa, and on select countries in each of these regions.

- Focusing on relationships with key universities or research institutions in these various regions.

- Increasing the number of foreign students attending Missouri State or enrolling in a University outreach program abroad to at least 800, or 4 to 5 percent of the student population.

- Doubling the number of foreign students attending the English Language Institute (ELI) to at least 100 students annually.

- Doubling the number of Missouri State students going abroad during exchange and study-abroad programs to at least 300 students annually.

- Doubling the number of students participating in study tours, experiential learning experiences, and other short-term programs to at least 120 students.

- Increasing the opportunities for Missouri State faculty to go abroad or interact formally with foreign faculty through such avenues as international conferences, collaborative research, and public forums.

- Offering an interdisciplinary Global Studies Major, beginning in 2007, which includes a significant foreign language component.

- Establishing and fully implementing the Office of International Programs under the leadership of a Director of International Affairs, who will be responsible for administering and overseeing internationalization efforts and programs at Missouri State. This office will report to the Provost via the Associate Provost and Dean of the Graduate College.

The Community and Social Issues Institute

A major way in which the University can help imagine the future is to form centers that assemble faculty and student talent and focus that talent on those issues that loom as the biggest threats to a progressive future. The Community and Social Issues Institute (CSII) has been developed with this purpose prominently in mind.

The mission of the Community and Social Issues Institute is to provide high-quality research and data that accurately and honestly portray social conditions and problems in the community. The Institute will work with existing agencies to develop strategies that address and remediate significant social problems. The Institute's research can range from studies that generate primary data to projects that focus on evaluating program effectiveness.

One example of a social problem that could be attacked by the Institute is risk-related behavior, particularly by youth. Young people are drawn to risky behavior (examples include alcohol and drug use, sexual behaviors, tobacco use) because of psychological temperament, physiological predispositions, peer pressure, and feelings of invincibility. These behaviors are usually established during early childhood, strengthened in adolescence, and persist into adulthood. In addition to causing serious dysfunctions and health problems, these behaviors also contribute to the educational and social problems that confront the nation, including failure to complete high school, unemployment, and crime. For example, children living around or near methamphetamine production and use face double jeopardy: they are often victims of different types of abuse; and, they tend to take on risky behavior patterns that follow them throughout their youth and persist into their adult lives.

The Institute will focus its research efforts on:

- Collaborating and complementing efforts of the many agencies that are serving the citizens of southwest Missouri (for example, the Community Partnership of the Ozarks, Inc. is sponsoring the Methamphetamine Awareness Project).

- Working with nonprofit and government agencies to conduct a gap analysis of types of data that are required to monitor the community's social health over time.

- Developing and maintaining indicators that enable the community to monitor social issues.

- Sponsoring and promoting faculty research focusing on specific community problems and issues.

- Becoming self-supporting and sustaining through internal investment and by seeking external funds through grants and contracts for services.

- Partnering in the overall network of agencies that are providing essential social services to the community. Its role will be to complement existing agencies while avoiding duplication of services already being rendered.

- As a first step to build the CSII, the University will recruit a senior-level scholar to serve as the Director.

The Flexible Credit and Continuous Registration System

Meeting the Needs for New Instructional Formats

Robert M. Diamond and Peter B. DeBlois

New demands for more flexibility in the delivery, structure and effectiveness of courses has significantly increased the need for new administrative support systems that provide the structural capabilities that are required. Integral to the development of these systems is the active involvement of the registrar in the design process. First developed over twenty-five years ago, the flexible credit and continuous registration systems described in this case study although capable of meeting these needs, are still not widely used.

A Case Study

In 1971, in an effort to refocus the university on the quality of instruction, Syracuse University established the Center for Instructional Development within the office of Academic Affairs.

Source: This article was first published in *Inside Higher Ed,* Jan. 20, 1997. Reprinted with permission.

This office, with staff experienced in instructional design, faculty development, evaluation, and media production, was charged with working with faculty and academic leaders in the design and structure of new courses and curricula more attuned to the needs of the disciplines, the students, and the community. There were no charges for these services. As work began in a number of high priority programs in academic units throughout the university at both the undergraduate and graduate levels, a number of common questions began to surface for which we had no clear answer:

• What were the assumptions being made by faculty about the students entering their courses and degree programs, and how accurate were the assumptions?

• What knowledge and skills did students actually bring to particular classes or programs? If students entered an introductory course with a wide range of knowledge and competencies, why should they all start at the same place?

• If students had advanced skills or knowledge, could they be exempted from certain units within a course or curriculum?

• Must all students move through a course or program at the same pace? If some students required more time to complete a unit, how could we handle grades at the end of the semester when the work was not yet complete? How could we address financial aid and academic progress requirements for full-time enrollment when a student might be enrolled full-time but had only earned six credits by the end of the semester? How could we handle enrollment fees when certain students were taking more time and using more resources than others to develop the required level of competence before advancing within a course or program?

• How could we allow students who were interested to take additional credits in a course to do so? Could this decision be made during the semester? How could fees be established for such additional work?

• How could we take advantage of technology and independent study to make better use of faculty and student time?

• If we had students with different majors enrolled in a course, could we have small concurrent group sessions that applied the same principle or concept to their respective fields of study? If we used faculty from other departments or faculty from other areas of specialization in the same department to teach these groups, how could we handle teaching loads for such short assignments?

• If different topics in a course were offered by different faculty, must we average the grades of each unit to get a final course grade?

The Need for Flexibility in Time and Structure _____

As these questions surfaced and data on students began to be collected, it soon became apparent that the existing time-frame and credit and fee structures significantly limited our ability to use new patterns of instruction designed to address these issues.

It should be noted that with the recent growth of independent study, new applications of technology, service learning, and distance education, these limitations have become even more pronounced as faculty have attempted to address the increased diversity among students, an increasing number of part-time students, and the lack of prerequisite skills characteristic of an increasing number of students. At the same time, more students are entering postsecondary study with credits earned from advanced placement coursework in basic skill areas and from previous learning via work experience. More than ever, the enhanced academic placement and transcripting options that current systems allow and that the registrar manages are essential elements in planning for curricular innovation. Unfortunately, the traditional credit and semester structures with which most of us are familiar no longer meet today's instructional needs. Without major changes in instructional delivery and support systems, it will be impossible for institutions and faculty to address the concerns of national leaders, state and federal legislators, senior campus executives, employers, accreditation agencies, faculty, the community at large, and students themselves.

What is needed are smarter ways of aligning instructional strategies, academic policies, and the new generation of information systems that have the technical capacity to support transformational change. Fortunately, the work that began in Syracuse in the mid 1970s provides us with a structure that other institutions can build upon. In a joint effort between the Office of the Registrar and the Center for Instructional Development, with grant support from the Fund for the Improvement of Postsecondary Education (FIPSE), a major effort was begun to address the administrative and structural problems. A way had to be found to allow for more options in the design and delivery of instruction. What evolved from this effort was one of the first flexible credit and continuous registration systems in the country. As an added benefit, the structures developed also facilitated the use of new and cost-effective instructional patterns and assessment procedures.

These approaches, as effective as they were in the mid-1970s, are still not available, or if technically available, were not in use at most institutions in 2006. To be sure, some institutions, especially those with a strong commitment to distance or distributed learning and "nontraditional" learners, are adapting instructional strategies and support systems in advanced ways that go beyond even what Syracuse did in the seventies. The University of Phoenix, other commercial distance learning providers, and community colleges constitute a new generation of pioneers that have, in large measure, attracted nontraditional students by being more responsive more quickly to flexible learner models—with information systems to match. Four-year and research institutions are only beginning to catch up.

The key has always been the willingness of the faculty, the registrar, and key support offices to work together in designing and implementing the use of flexible administrative systems, structured to meet the specific needs of the institution. Experience has shown that the registrar, academic leaders, or the faculty can either be effective facilitators and supporters of change or major barriers to innovation in academic affairs. The keys are institutional leadership and the ownership of all groups in the final product.

What Such a System Allows

Flexible Credit

With flexible credit, a course or a curriculum may be offered for variable credit (one to three credits, two to four, three to six, thirty to forty-five, and so on) based on the needs or the interests of the individual student and the instructional goals of the faculty. For example, in an introductory course, students who do not have the required prerequisites may be required, based on diagnostic testing, to take additional credit or noncredit units while others, with more extensive knowledge or a higher skill level, may have the option of taking additional work for additional credit.

Within a given course, students may take separate units of instruction, each of which may generate its own grade and credit. A student may earn two A's and a B in a three-credit course, with the transcript showing the specific name of each unit under the overall course title. This would be particularly advantageous for students doing more advanced, in-depth work.

Units in a course may have different weights with credit assigned based on the work and time required (some units, for example, may be assigned two or three credits with others worth only one).

Courses may be combined in clusters for a set number of credits depending on the structure and needs of the academic program.

The system facilitates faculty load and time flexibility. Faculty not only can be given variable load assignments based on their course responsibilities, but this load can be distributed unevenly throughout a course. For example a team of faculty could offer a series of one-credit units at different times throughout a course, or two faculty, based on their areas of specialization, could divide a course into major blocks with each having their teaching load focused on only one part of the semester.

Although grades are reported at the end of the semester, or when work in a specific unit is finished, final grades are not necessarily recorded until the entire sequence is completed, with nonpunitive Incompletes posted for a specified competence-development period.

Overall, such a system allows student performance to be more accurately reflected on the official academic record or transcript and, perhaps, allows a faster or slower, more rational timeframe to degree completion. The latter possibility resonates with calls for more global alignment of U.S. higher education (with all due caveats about quality and independence) with the emergence of the three-year "Bologna degree" that is being regularized in the European Union, Australia, and India.

Continuous Registration

Designed to remove the many constraints of the semester system, continuous registration allows work within a course or program to continue beyond the semester framework. With current online, Web-based registration services at most institutions, this process is considerably less burdensome to students and staff than it used to be.

- It allows students to enroll in individual course units as the semester progresses.

- It allows students to register for additional credits during the academic year, and for faculty to assign additional work if the need becomes apparent.

- Course units may be established and offered continuously throughout the semester; there is no single starting date for beginning options.

Administrative Issues

As the structures were developed a number of administrative issues surfaced. For the most part, these needed to be addressed by the registrar's office. The university transcript had to be modified to accept within a single course, a number of options or additional work for additional credit. Each unit needed to have its own description and assigned grade. New procedures for students and faculty using these options (a paper-based Continuous Registration Form that would now be electronic) had to be developed, tested, and revised. An information booklet for faculty on using these systems also had to be developed and field tested.

One of the more complex challenges was the need to add new grade designations to the university transcript. Three new letter designations were required: one to designate a variable-credit modular course ("VC"), one for the base course which would not have a grade required as the grade would be assigned to the individual modules or units of the course ("NR"), and one to use at the end of the semester if the student were going to resume the same module in the following term. Complicating the process was the need for all changes to be approved by the University Senate where there was no agreement among members as to which committee needed to sponsor the final recommendation, because several thought that changes of this type fell under their jurisdiction. After a decision was made to have the proposal made jointly by all interested groups, there was little agreement on which letter or letters to use to designate an in-progress grade for those modules that were to carry over to the next semester and where the work of the student was not yet complete. After extensive discussion, the committees finally agreed on "V" which is used to signify that the student is making normal progress in a particular module of a variable length course and that work is not yet complete.

Two other issues surfaced. First, we were concerned that although a student could be carrying a full load, he or she might not, under certain circumstances, be earning enough credits to maintain eligibility for certain scholarships or federal assistance programs. In checking with state and federal officials, the university registrar was able to obtain approval to determine full-time status on the basis of "credits enrolled" rather than on "credits earned." This was most important decision for entry-level courses where remediation is essential if the students were to succeed. The second key factor was the policy already on the books for undergraduate students to be allowed to earn twelve to nineteen credits for the same basic tuition. This helped in two ways: First, students interested in doing so in a variable credit course, could earn up to nineteen credits a semester without an additional tuition charge. Second, students requiring more time and additional resources could be earning fewer credits while paying more for each credit earned, because they were consuming additional instructional resources. In institutions where a large number of students are requiring more time to earn course credit, moving away from the traditional cost-per-credit-hour enrolled system may make a great deal of sense.

Learning Outcomes, Accountability, and Retention _____

A key element in a quality course and curriculum design process is the requirement that diagnostic tests be used to determine the entry level of undergraduate and graduate students enrolled in a course or curriculum, to determine where remediation or additional course work may be required or where exemption is possible. In both instances the evaluation process requires that the faculty define their assumptions and the goals of each course or program in outcome terms. Decisions are to be based on accurate data and well-defined outcomes.

Using outcome statements and quality student data for important placement decisions has a number of significant advantages:

1. The data that is collected and the impact of its use are important elements in the information on student learning outcomes that is being demanded by disciplinary and regional accreditation agencies.

2. The use of remediation and exemption can have a direct and positive impact on students' attitudes about degree programs and the institution.

3. As a number of studies at Syracuse found, this approach can result in major improvements in student learning and retention, critical goals of all institutions and a major focus of the Spellings Commission report.

In short, flexible credit, continuous registration, and new grading systems, overseen and shaped by the registrar on behalf of the faculty, provide instructional design options that are more attuned to today's instructional problems and to the various course and curriculum design opportunities that now exist through the use of technology and the research on teaching and learning. Their use provides a wide range of benefits to students and to faculty, while supporting new forms of departmental and institutional accountability for learning outcomes. In addition their implementation requires the active support of the academic leadership and the involvement of the registrar, key support staff, and faculty.

Three key lessons can be learned from the Syracuse experience. First, without the registrar as a key player from the start, no easy synergy can be developed between instructional innovation, academic policy, records procedures, and system adaptation. Second, new technology innovations such as e-portfolios and course and learning management systems are often implemented under accelerated pressure, jeopardizing compliance with external privacy regulations that the registrar could have anticipated. Third, unless an individual or a design organization, such as the registrar or a teaching and learning support unit, becomes a visible proponent of opportunity to adapt technology and policy, new visions will chafe against tradition and sputter at best. The registrar knows the institutional change culture, doesn't forget political and technical history, and remembers what has worked and why. Institutions ignore this player at the cost of inefficient or retarded progress.

Addressing Math Deficiencies and Collecting Student Data

Introductory Economics

Entry-level deficiencies in mathematics may be due to students' avoidance of the subject rather than the neglect of math skills (multiplication, division, fractions, decimals, percents, word problems, and graphing) in the final three or four years of pre-college education. Whatever the reason, however, these deficiencies need to be remediated before students can take many courses.

Economics, for example, like many of the social sciences, relies heavily on mathematics for the presentation and interpretation of data. It was therefore not surprising to find that the lack of mathematics preparation would have to be addressed in a project that included the redesign of two existing introductory courses, micro-economics and macro-economics, and the design of a new course specifically for non-economics majors.

As a first step, a review was made of the text that would be used and of past examinations to identify the specific mathematics competencies required of the students. Identified competencies were basic operations with fractions, decimals, and percents, and the use of tables and graphs to represent the relationships between economic variables.

Before major design work began, a basic mathematics test was constructed to assess these prerequisite competencies; it was administered on the second day of class to a group of students enrolled in the basic micro-economics course that was then being offered. This testing not only provided data on the mathematics skills of the students enrolled in the course but also permitted items on the test itself to be evaluated. Data collected showed that nearly 70 percent of the students had inadequate mathematics skills in at least one area. As a result, a diagnostic and remedial sequence was built into the three introductory courses for all first-time economics students.

Beginning Sequence for Introductory Economics Courses _____

Figure CS6.1.
Beginning Sequence for Introductory Economics Course

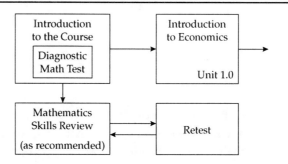

A decision was made to use a diagnostic test followed by remedial tutorial units assigned on the basis of test results. Although students are actively encouraged to complete the sequence, the tutorial units are not required. Students are, however, provided with their test results and an analysis of the relationship of test results to performance in the course. An exhaustive search of available programmed and computer materials failed to locate appropriate materials for use in economics. For this reason, a new computer-based instructional sequence was designed.

In addressing problems of this type, it is possible to build the remediation into the regular instructional sequence and exempt those students who have the competency from the class session. This option was not taken in this instance because faculty agreed that using in-class time for this purpose would be wasteful; the problem could be effectively eliminated for most students by two to three hours of study outside of class.

It has now become possible to advise some students, on the basis of extensive data, either to complete these units or, in severe cases, to take additional mathematics courses prior to enrolling in the economics course.

The Course Syllabus

In courses of this size, the student manual can play an important role in informing the students about the course and how it operates. This is extremely important when the format may be new to them. For example, the following is the introduction to the self-test and tutorial included in the latest edition of the course syllabus (2007).

Graph Skills for Introductory Economics

INTRODUCTION

Good graphing skills are essential to the study of economics. This Graph Skills Self-Assessment provides you with a pretest to assess your skill level in this area and offers you the opportunity to review these skills. Data analysis of students' performances in past semesters suggests those who are weak in these skills often have difficulty with the material because the "language" used in class (the graphs) confuses them. (As one student put it: "It's Greek to me.") It is very important that you determine as early as possible if you have a problem with these skills because if you do, there is something you can do to help yourself. You can tune-up your skills.

You should complete this pretest early in the semester so you can determine if you need review in these skills. If you wish to review any of these skills, there is a button at the bottom of the pretest that will take you to the tutorial. Before going to the pretest, read through the instructions below.

INSTRUCTIONS

There are two versions of the pretest available. If you have a web browser that will allow you to use JavaScript you should take the *self-scoring* version of the test. (If you are accessing this pretest from a University computer cluster, you should use the self-scoring version.) If you do not have a browser that will recognize JavaScript, you will need to take the *paper-and-pencil* version. You can also find a copy of this pretest on reserve in the library. The entire sequence, test and tutorial is available at http://sage.syr.edu/AboutSage.Aspx. For more information on this and other material developed for the course, contact Jerry Evensky at jevensky@maxwell.syr.edu.

Collecting Student Data to Improve Teaching

Data collected during a course can often be used to improve teaching effectiveness. This technique is particularly helpful in multisection courses in which teaching assistants or junior faculty teach the sections, laboratories, or discussion groups, usually coordinated or supervised by senior faculty members.

In the micro-economics and macro-economics courses at Syracuse University a single faculty member supervised more than a dozen teaching assistants responsible for approximately twenty discussion sections. To assist the supervising faculty member in this role and to provide information that could help these beginning teachers improve their teaching, questions focusing specifically on their performance in the classroom were added to the student end-of-course questionnaire (see Exhibit CS6.1).

Other sections of the questionnaire dealt with such areas as course objectives, the student manual, the remedial mathematics sequences, course materials, the evaluation procedures, and instruments that were used. It also included a number of open-ended questions focusing on strengths and weaknesses of the course as students perceived them.

To make the questions about the discussion leaders particularly useful, the information collected was presented to the course coordinator and the discussion leaders in three different ways (see Exhibit CS6.2).

Exhibit CS6.1.

Selected Portion of Questionnaire Regarding Small-Group Discussion Leaders

A one (1) represents *Not at All (N)*, a three (3) represents *Somewhat (S)*, and a five (5) represents *Very Much (V)*.

Please indicate the degree to which you perceive your instructor as:

	N		S		V
1. Prepared	1	2	3	4	5
2. Organized	1	2	3	4	5
3. Understandable in terms of level of presentation	1	2	3	4	5
4. Understandable in terms of language	1	2	3	4	5
5. Being open to questions	1	2	3	4	5
6. Treating students with respect	1	2	3	4	5
7. In control of the class	1	2	3	4	5
8. Enthusiastic	1	2	3	4	5
9. Answering questions effectively	1	2	3	4	5
10. Caring about the subject	1	2	3	4	5
11. Making students interested in the subject	1	2	3	4	5
12. Providing high-quality instruction	1	2	3	4	5
13. Motivating you to perform well in this course	1	2	3	4	5

Exhibit CS6.2.
Selected Portion of Report to Individual Discussion Leaders

Class/section/prof: EDN20204
Overall Mean Score = 4.4
Rank over all classes = 3 of 19

Score

Item/Question	This Class	All Classes	STD	N
Instructional pace about right	3.7	3.6	0.9	31
Required workload about right	4.0	3.6	0.8	31
Degree exam questions were fair	3.4	3.4	1.2	31
Degree exam grading was fair	3.5	3.6	1.0	31
Degree exams covered what was taught	3.9	3.7	1.1	31
Degree exam time to finish was right	2.5*	3.7	1.3	31
Feedback was timely	3.5	3.7	1.0	31

*Problem area

- For each question the course coordinator received an analysis of data for every discussion section. Because most teaching assistants were responsible for two sections, specific problem areas were easy to identify, and counseling could begin.

- All discussion leaders were provided with a summary mean ranking of all sections.

- Each discussion leader also received his or her own summary for all items on the questionnaire and could then compare that data with the data for all discussion leaders.

As a result of reporting information in this way, the coordinator was able to meet with individual discussion leaders to review the specific problems identified and suggest how they could be resolved.

Expanding the Course Time Frame to Compensate for a Lack of Prerequisites

General Chemistry

Another interesting and successful project in which time, rather than content, was the significant variable was the redesign of the introductory general chemistry course at the University of Rhode Island.

The problem was not unusual: a high failure rate (30 percent) and a related frustration level on the part of both the faculty and many students. From an analysis of student profiles, faculty learned that the majority of those who failed or dropped the course could be identified even before the course began by analyzing their entering SAT scores, high school class rank, and standardized test scores in mathematics.

The instructor, Jacklyn Vitlimberger, proposed an experiment that was implemented with the approval of her chair during the 1985–86 academic year. A number of high-risk students were enrolled in a new two-semester general chemistry course that had the identical content, assignments, instructional objectives, and instructor as the existing one-semester program. The additional time was used to provide the students with an increased opportunity to practice the problem-solving skills that were identified as necessary for success in general chemistry. The examinations in both courses were also identical; the midterm in the traditional program became the first-semester final in the experimental two-semester program, and both sections took the same final examination. The performance of students in the two-semester program was then compared with that of students in the one-semester program who had the same range of SAT scores, class rank, and math-test scores.

The results were positive:

- 70 percent of the high-risk students in the two-semester program passed the course and the final examination.

- Each of the students in the experimental section who completed the two-semester sequence scored above the median score of the students in the traditional sections on the final examination.

- The overall failure rate in the course was significantly reduced (from 30 percent to approximately 10 percent).

- Students who completed the two-semester sequence also performed satisfactorily in subsequent science and math courses.

As a result of this project, the experimental two-semester course was regularized, and entering students who are identified as being in the high-risk category are encouraged to enroll in this option.

In the experimental course, students received no credit for the first semester and three credits for the second. This approach placed a hardship on students. Because they had to earn twelve credits to maintain full-time academic standing for purposes of financial support, work-study, and so on, they were forced to enroll in five courses the first semester rather than four, an academic load too heavy for high-risk students. These issues were resolved by granting three credits for each semester of the revised course but with the stipulation that only the second-semester credits count toward a degree. Grades for the first semester are, however, included in the student's grade point average. Awarding credit in this manner allows an institution to meet the needs of academically disadvantaged students without lowering the academic standards of the course, the department, or the institution.

Expanding the Course Time Frame to Compensate for a Lack of Prerequisites

Introductory Calculus

The basic sequence in calculus as traditionally taught at Syracuse University consisted of four sequential three-credit courses taken during the freshman and sophomore years. The sequence was required of all engineering, mathematics, economics, and science majors. Over the years, faculty teaching the course had become increasingly concerned with a high failure rate. In addition, studies had shown a direct and high correlation between achievement on the mathematics placement test taken by all entering freshmen and success in the traditional course. In other words, those students who entered with a solid mathematics background tended to pass; others did not. To address these issues, a self-paced program based on the mastery concept of learning was developed and introduced. This program used the continuous-registration and flexible-credit systems implemented earlier for use in other courses.

Students enrolled in the initial field-testing version of the course slightly over four months after design work began. The design and implementation phase was short because the content and the sequential materials presented were traditional (not open to significant review) and the course was built around an available commercial text. Student guides, manuals, and some instructional materials, however, were developed specifically for the new program.

The goal of self-paced calculus was to permit students to master the materials covered in an introductory college calculus course at a pace most comfortable to them. The subject matter was divided into one-week units (or blocks of material). The students used a standard calculus textbook and a set of detailed study guides to learn the material in each unit. Regularly scheduled tutorial periods were also available. Problem-solving sessions were provided on an optional basis, and two programmed booklets were written to teach content not covered adequately or effectively in the available materials. A section of a page from the student manual describing the courses is shown in Figure CS8.1.

For each unit a series of equivalent tests was prepared. When the students believe they had mastered the material in a unit, they could request a test. A student who passed at a pre-specified level of mastery could begin to prepare for the next unit test. Students who did not pass were given tutorial help or remedial assignments and then took another version of the test for that same unit. Again, a pass was required before proceeding to the next unit. Unit tests

Figure CS8.1.
Self-Paced Calculus (MAT 295, 296, 397, 398) Course Sequence

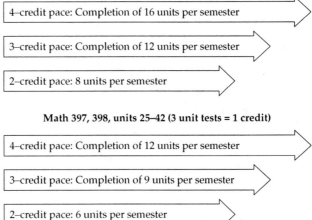

- Tests for all units will be available during the tutorial periods and may be taken when you become prepared for them.
- Failed unit tests may be retaken until passed, with no penalty.
- Satisfactory completion of each unit test is required before proceeding to the next.
- There is no limit to the number of credits that you may earn in any semester.

Math 295, 296, units 1–24 (4 unit tests = 1 credit)

4–credit pace: Completion of 16 units per semester

3–credit pace: Completion of 12 units per semester

2–credit pace: 8 units per semester

Math 397, 398, units 25–42 (3 unit tests = 1 credit)

4–credit pace: Completion of 12 units per semester

3–credit pace: Completion of 9 units per semester

2–credit pace: 6 units per semester

were taken as often as needed with no grade penalty for not passing. Tests for all units were available from the beginning of the course so that any student who had prior preparation in calculus could receive credit by passing the appropriate unit tests.

In the early weeks of the course, to earn one academic credit students needed to pass four units successfully; eight units passed earned two credits; and so on. As students advanced to the more difficult concepts, they needed to pass three unit tests in order to earn one credit. The speed at which the students progressed through the course and the number of credits individuals earned depended on how rapidly they could master the material. A separate letter grade was earned and recorded for each credit hour.

A follow-up study of 248 students, 60 in the self-paced program and 188 in the conventional course, showed that the primary goals were reached. First, for those in the self-paced course the direct correlation between entry-level test results and performance in the course was significantly reduced as entry-level problems were dealt with and corrected. In the conventional course, placement-exam results had a direct relationship to semester examination scores (see Figure CS8.2). Second, there was a major improvement in overall student performance.

As in any self-paced course, it was necessary to build into the program a minimum pace—a rate of movement below which students

Figure CS8.2.

Correlation Between Mathematics Preparation and Performance in Introductory Calculus

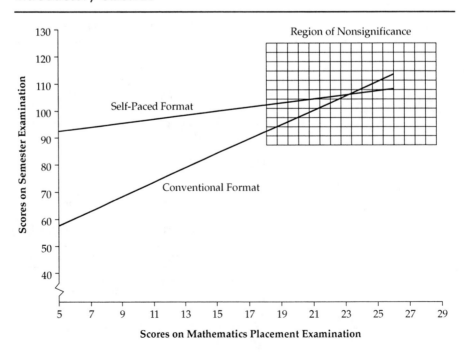

could not fall—although there was no maximum pace. Students were required to complete eight units in their first semester—a two-credit-per-semester pace.

One caution about materials should be noted. Because the initial course relied on a published text, it was necessary to rewrite all the associated materials with each revision of the text. This soon became a problem because the publisher has tended to publish new editions every two or three years. To reduce the need for extensive rewriting of associated materials, the university at first stockpiled extra copies of the text for use after the new editions are published. More recently print materials of this type were moved to a computer-based module which significantly improved the ease of use and of editing and the ability to develop far more effective instructional self-study units.

Dealing with Prerequisites at the Graduate Level

A Course in Cost-Effectiveness

A graduate course in cost-effectiveness in instruction and training, offered by a school of education, forced the faculty member teaching it to answer three important questions:

- How could the course meet the needs of an extremely diverse student population—majors in higher education, management, and instruction technology, many from different countries?

- How could the course deal with entering students who do not have all the prerequisites?

- How could the course meet the needs of entering students with very different backgrounds, different expectations, and very different situations in which they would be expected to achieve cost-effectiveness in instruction and training.

Those who lacked prerequisites and who had an inadequate background for the course were assigned additional readings and other assignments, and the course design was modified to relate course content to individual professional goals. As part of the enrollment procedure that was developed, students are asked to complete a brief questionnaire that provides the instructor with information about why they are enrolling, related courses and

Figure CS9.1.
Course Description for Second Part of Cost-Effectiveness in
Instruction and Training

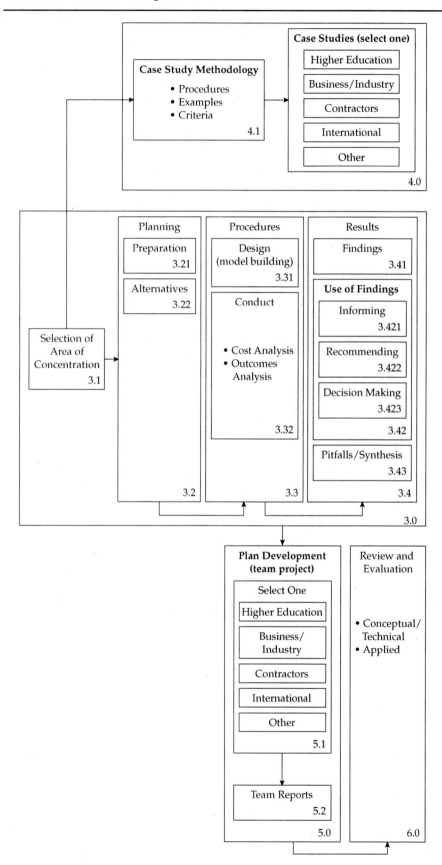

Source: Philip Doughty.

work experiences they have had, and their professional goals. This information is then used by the instructor to prepare assignments and identify student teams for projects later in the course (see Figure CS9.1). This design is unusual in that students are allowed to focus on their own areas of interest as they apply the general model that is being taught. This flexibility occurs in two areas: Unit 4.0, in which the students apply the model to case studies, and Unit 5.0, team projects.

This is an excellent example of how the basic content of a course can be left unchanged while the course itself is restructured to meet the specific needs of the students who are enrolled.

Using Data from Students

Introductory Course in Religion

In this project a survey instrument was prepared and distributed to a sample of students enrolled in an introductory religion course the semester before classes were scheduled to begin (see Exhibit CS10.1). The instrument was intended to identify levels of interest in various topics that could be included in the course. The instrument was developed jointly by evaluation specialists and faculty from the Department of Religion.

When responses had been collected and tabulated, the students' interests were viewed in the context of the faculty's expectations. The data generated by this instrument were quite different from faculty's expectations and resulted in significant changes in the intended course design. In addition, the faculty could anticipate fairly accurately the number of students who would later choose different options within the course.

The value of this instrument to the project is best described by the faculty member who served as the course coordinator for the department:

> The test instrument employed in the development of experimental Religion 105 was designed to indicate what patterns, if any, of student interest, disinterest, expectation, recognition, or dislike would be likely to characterize a typical population involved in this course. The results of the application of this instrument at first appeared so ambiguous as to be useless. Under continuing consideration, however, they proved most helpful.

Exhibit CS10.1.

Survey of Student Interest in Various Topics in Religion

The following list contains topics that could be included in this course. Rate each topic according to your level of interest in it. Use the following scale.

A = Very high interest

B = Moderate interest

C = A little interest

D = No interest at all

1. Women's lib and mythologies of creation
2. Ecology and creation stories
3. Psychotherapy and mystical experience
4. The problem of a good God and the existence of evil in the world
5. Science and religion
6. Abortion and the church
7. Pacifism and the holy wars of Judaism, Christianity, and Islam
8. Sex and an absolutist ethic
9. Number symbolism in the problem of the Trinity
10. Technology as a new religion
11. Apocalypticism and progress
12. Modern mythologies of the creative hero
13. The death of God in ancient religions
14. The religious history of the future
15. Should churches be taxed?
16. The artist as the religious hero of our time
17. God as relative rather than absolute
18. Is Zen possible in the West?
19. Yoga and drugs
20. Traditional religions and the occult
21. The religion of the American Indian and paleface Christianity
22. The end of religion
23. Polytheism in our time
24. Modern pantheons
25. Dreams and religion
26. The poetry of the Bible
27. Ballad and rock music as scripture
28. Job and psychology
29. "Jesus freaks"—then and now
30. Witchcraft
31. Capitalism in church and synagogue
32. Communes and religion
33. The birth and death of religious institutions
34. Are there other topics in religion of interest to you that are not listed here? Please list them on the back of your answer sheet.

Although initial analysis showed no clear pattern of interest for any particular subject matter, or issue, or method in the study of religion, it did reveal a wide variety of levels of recognition as well as diverse preferences for formats of presentation. What we came to see was that the concern for diversity, for flexibility, for variety of instructional formats was specifically the pattern that was common to the sample population. The test instrument clearly suggested modular construction and a flexible selection procedure. It also became apparent that a common base of meaning and of definitions had to be developed before the course could be effectively taught.

The data collected during this project indicated a wide diversity in backgrounds and areas of interest. The structure developed was based on this information and other priorities of the department. Several key goals for the course evolved:

- A common framework for the course had to be set, and appropriate vocabulary had to be introduced.
- The course had to include major interest areas of the students.
- Because the course was the initial contact the students had with the department, it had to serve as a recruiting vehicle for majors and for enrollments in other religion courses.

The unique course design that was developed proved most effective in meeting these objectives (Exhibit CS10.2). Seminars and programmed materials were used to introduce the term religion and religion as a field of study. From this point, students were required to take one four-week option from each of three major areas: Forms of Religious Expression, Forms of Religious Issues, and Methodologies. Additional options could be taken for extra credit. An advantage of this design (referred to by some as the "Chinese-menu" approach) was that it allowed first-year students to have direct contact in small-group sessions with senior faculty teaching in their areas of specialization. Options with higher enrollments were repeated as needed.

An interesting sidelight is that when the new course was first taught, some students in the class felt strongly that religion as a formal subject did not belong in a university. For this reason the optional unit Objections to the Study of Religion was built into the program. As the political climate of the country changed, the number of students enrolling in this option declined significantly, and the option was dropped.

Exhibit CS10.2.
Ratings for Levels of Interest in Possible Religion Course Topics

HIGH INTEREST

Percentage of students who judged their interest in the topic to be "moderate" or "very high"

Psychotherapy and mystical experience	63%
Abortion and the church	58%
Sex and an absolutist ethic	60%
Is Zen possible in the West?	57%
Yoga and drugs	53%
Traditional religions and the occult	56%
The end of religion	65%
Dreams and religion	60%
Witchcraft	70%

LOW INTEREST

Percentage of students who judged their interest in the topic to be "little" or "no interest at all":

Number symbolism in the problem of the Trinity	62%
Apocalypticism and progress	71%
Should churches be taxed?	62%
Modern pantheons	82%
The poetry of the Bible	61%
Capitalism in church and synagogue	57%

Figure CS10.1.
Structure of Introductory Course in Religion

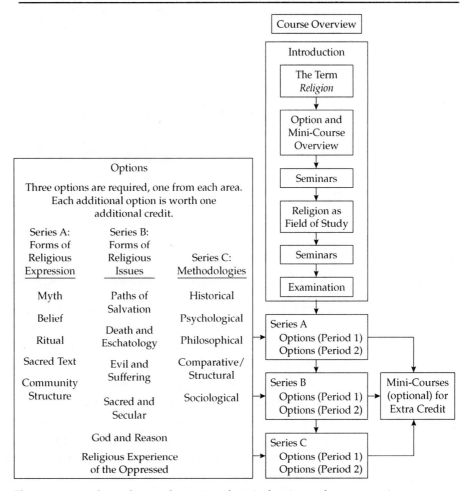

This course provides students with a variety of required options and an opportunity to earn extra credit by taking additional options or mini-courses. Classes are scheduled for two hours, twice weekly, with a different series of options offered each hour, permitting a student to complete two option credits in any four-hour period.

Source: Ronald Cavanagh, Robert Diamond.

CASE STUDY 11

Designing an Ideal Curriculum

Music/Music Industry

Figure CS11.1 presents the lower-division structure of a new curriculum, Music/Music Industry. Notice in particular the features that create sequential movement: (l) attention has been paid to general entrance requirements and then to the program itself; (2) in the first two years only one additional course is required—Music Industry; (3) those students who enter with competency in two instruments have the option of taking a special three-course sequence in the School of Management. Discussions with professionals in the field, an extensive review of the literature, and numerous surveys were used to provide the data on which both the curriculum and course designs were based.

The faculty thought that adding the overview course on the music industry was essential not only for introducing the students to the field but also for providing them with an understanding of the profession before they were required, at the end of their sophomore year, to select a major field of specialization and to apply for formal admission into the program.

Figure CS11.1.

Structure of Bachelor's Degree Program in Music/Music Industry

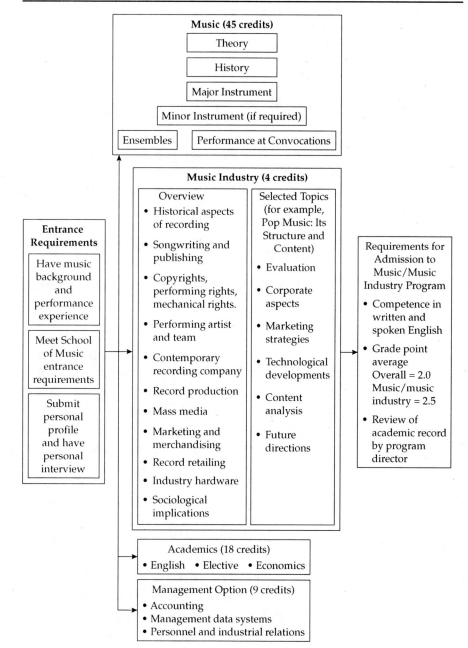

Source: Ronald Lee, Paul Eickmann.

Designing an Ideal Curriculum: Surveying Alumni

Master's Program in Management

Figures CS12.1 and CS12.2 are the beginning parts of two drafts of the curriculum for a proposed master's degree in business administration program (MBA) in management. Designing this complex curriculum, which involved several departments, took many months. Notice that although some elements in the sixth draft appear to have undergone little change by the fourteenth version, the overall structure has changed and has become far more specific. Major emphasis was on two issues: what topics should be required of all students and in what order. In addition, the fact that many MBA students enter with work experience had to be addressed.

This project did not begin until all departments in the school agreed to actively participate—a process that took nearly one year. By the time the project was completed eighteen months later, the design included a general description of the total curriculum with a list of student performance outcomes for each course or unit within it.

The design that evolved had several significant structural elements. Notice how sensitive this structure was to the entry level of the students. Although some students enroll directly from an undergraduate program, which may or may not be in the field, others are older students entering after several years of work experience. Individual counseling and formal evaluation permit assigning prerequisite courses as they are needed. The Managerial Team Dynamics

Figure CS12.1.
Part of Draft 6: Proposed Master's Degree in Business Administration Program in Management

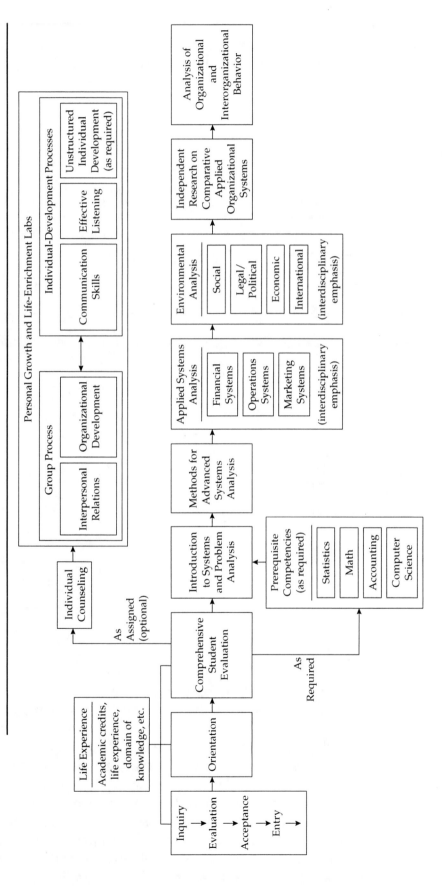

Figure CS12.2.

Part of Draft 14: Proposed Master's Degree in Business
Administration Program in Management

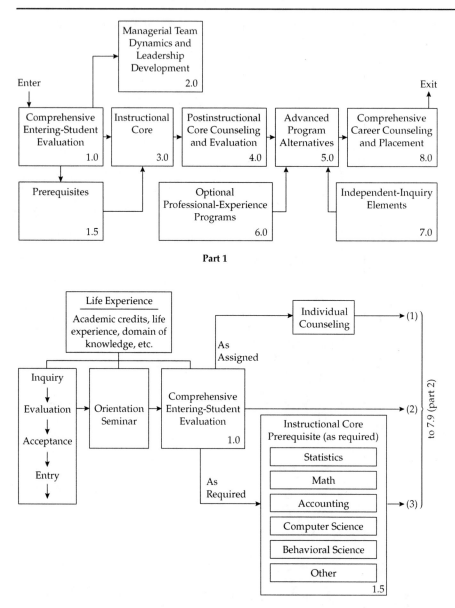

Part 1

and Leadership Development sequence (Figure CS12.3) was added
specifically to develop the "survival skills" (speaking, interpersonal,
and writing skills, and so on) that were mentioned repeatedly by
employers and recruiters as being essential for success in the field.
In the Instructional Core (3.0), although some units (or courses) are
required of all students, others are assigned according to the student's specific major on the basis of decisions made in each academic
area. Also note that career counseling and placement are not left to
chance but are proposed as an integral part of the total curriculum.
(Notice also how the use of the phrases "as required" in Unit 1.5 and
"as assigned" in Unit 3.4 simplify the diagramming process.)

Figure CS12.3.
Part of Draft 14: Proposed Master's Degree in Business
Administration Program in Management (continued)

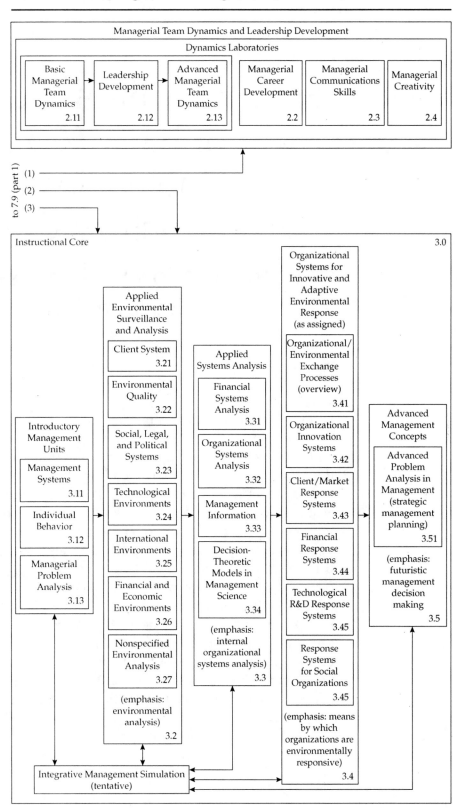

Ensuring the Acquisition of Basic Core Competencies in an Introductory Course

Introduction to Business and Management

Before the fall semester of 1992 the School of Management at Syracuse University did not offer a freshman management course. Students began their formal discipline-related coursework in their sophomore year, after spending the first year meeting core requirements in the College of Arts and Sciences. The School of Management found that the delay in direct instructional contact with students led to a lack of community and caused a great deal of student frustration. The faculty had also come to believe that if their students were available to them during the first year, they could begin to teach a number of skills that students needed for success in their programs and later as professionals.

As a result, the faculty decided to develop an introductory first-semester course to be required of all first-year students in the School of Management. A team of faculty representing each of the departments in the School of Management was established. The teaching support center was asked to facilitate the design, implementation, and assessment process.

The team established three overarching objectives for this new course: to build a community of the students, faculty, and administration within the School of Management; to introduce the students to the field of business and to the professional options or areas of specialization that would be open to them; and to begin to develop in these students the skills needed for both immediate and long-term success. These goals became an integral part of the structure and delivery of the course. They were communicated to the students in the objectives section of the course manual, which included the following statements:

> The course that evolved focuses on the prevailing management thrust towards skills required for effective conduct in the business world. You will see that attention is given to teamwork, oral presentation, writing, computer skills, and social skills that are connected with being part of a large institution. SOM 200 has the following learning objectives.

> When you have completed this course, you should be able to

> 1. Identify the skills that are necessary for success in business.
> 2. Understand how the skills necessary for success in business are applied in the "real world."
> 3. Create a plan for developing business skills while at Syracuse University.
> 4. Understand fundamental issues that arise when working in small teams.
> 5. Plan and carry out a project with a team.
> 6. Develop skills of analyzing an audience and tailoring written and oral reports to their interest and needs.
> 7. Use the S.U. online catalog to access library collections, services, and resources.
> 8. Research career information and become acquainted with relevant books, academic journals, and trade journals.
> 9. Cite sources in a written report, construct a bibliography, and discuss and evaluate the views of other authors.
> 10. Understand the concept of "computer system" as a means to an end in learning and in business.
> 11. Locate the essential computer facilities available to students on campus.
> 12. Use the two basic software application packages in the S.U. computer cluster: word processing and email.
> 13. Accomplish a smooth transition to college.
> 14. Build a strong identity with the School of Management and a solid direction for your future studies and career plans.

SOM 200 was designed to reach these objectives using a number of approaches (see Figure CS13.1):

• The text selected, *Who Is Going to Run General Motors?* by Green and Seymour, focuses directly on the essential competencies

Figure CS13.1.

Structure of Introductory School of Management Course

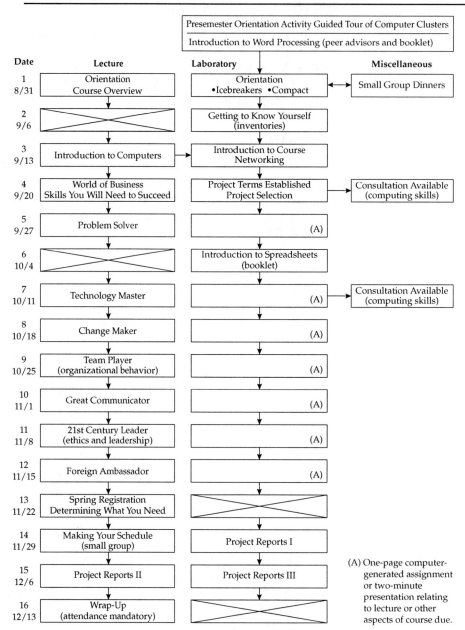

needed for success in business. The chapters of the book serve as the focus for the lecture portion of the course.

• Instead of faculty lectures, alumni and other business leaders describe their positions and explain why the specific competency under discussion is essential to them. Ample time is provided for discussion.

• Participation in course-related activities begins prior to the beginning of scheduled classes. At Syracuse, with the use of mail or online registration, over 90 percent of entering students have their complete schedules when they arrive on campus. During the time between final registration and the first class meeting, students are required to attend a brief orientation to the course. At this orientation, they are shown the computer clusters that they will be using. The few students not familiar with computer systems are required to complete an independent-learning sequence programmed to introduce them to word processing. This unit requires no additional faculty time.

The laboratory portion of the course focuses on team building, introduces the students to e-mail (which is used throughout the course for communication among students and between students and faculty), spreadsheets, and the use of the library.

A focused project requires all students to work in teams, to utilize computers, and to make an oral presentation.

Faculty, graduate assistants, and upper-division students all assist in the delivery of the course. Faculty teaching the laboratory portion of the course are assigned as advisers to the freshmen students in their section(s).

To improve long-term planning and course selection, formal advising for second-semester courses is built into the course.

As a result of this course, students' attitudes toward the school and the university have improved, as has their academic performance. Faculty teaching subsequent courses report that the skills and attitudes of students have improved. Although a number of changes have taken place in the course since its first offering—new text, new units on library research and on being part of a team—the basic concepts of the program have been maintained.

From the first time the course was offered, there has been a strong desire on the part of students to have the formal relationship with the school continue in the second semester. Although credit restrictions and accreditation requirements precluded having the course be a two-semester sequence, the school was able to initiate a successful second-semester internship program in which students have the opportunity to link with business and industries in the area. Offered through the university's Community Internship Program, the internship is a one-credit elective for those students who are interested in participating.

Distance Learning:
The Lessons Learned

Wallace Hannum and Robert King

Background

This online course on instructional design combined two courses from two institutions (The University of North Carolina at Chapel Hill and The University of North Carolina at Greensboro). It involved a community service organization, the Center for New North Carolinians, and was taught in the context of both service-learning and problem-based learning where students would focus on solving problems faced by the nonprofit organization. Students were working adults, geographically scattered.

The Course

Students, working in two interinstitutional design teams, followed a typical instructional design process which included the following steps: needs assessment, task analysis, educational goals, audience analysis, training methods determination, and evaluation. The approach evolved from the field of architecture, where different design teams are given identical problems by a client and then work independently to create a solution, which is then presented to the client. Resources provided to each design team were identical and each team had its own discussion forum and chat room with all members of both teams participating in a discussion forum and weekly chats. Faculty were available to answer questions.

Course Design and Planning _____

Assisted by an instructional design consultant or colleague, the two faculty met over a six-month period to design the course. The focus was on practical applications built around an agreed-upon instructional design model. Once learning outcomes were identified, the focus turned to determining the best approach to teaching that would allow us to reach these goals. Problem-based learning, where students would start with a problem and then work through a series of items to solve it, was chosen for three reasons: (1) it gave context and a framework for learning the specific knowledge required, (2) it was highly motivational, and (3) the approach also developed important team-building skills.

To further design the course around the specific needs and interests of the students, an assessment of students' backgrounds and knowledge of design were conducted before the course began. Changes in the content were made to address the findings of this survey.

To mimic real-world situations, weekly "work orders" guided the students through their assignments. Keyed to the tasks were a set of materials that provided the focus to their activities (see Figure CS14.1). Resources were chosen by the students to meet specific needs as they occurred.

Our work in designing and teaching this course was accomplished to a large extent online. The two instructors and the instructional design consultant or colleague lived in three different towns,

Figure C14.1.

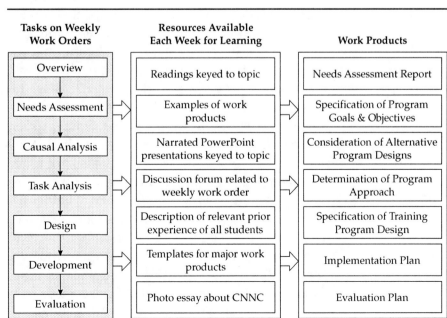

so our collaboration had to be supported through technology. We exchanged e-mails daily, often with attachments such as documents or presentations we were developing for our students, as well as talked by telephone and met as a group at several points during the course.

We started this course with an elaborate case study of a comprehensive instructional design project situated in a community development organization in Latin America. This showed how an organization following many of the precepts of instructional design, such as needs assessment, audience analysis, and consideration of alternatives, without specifically following a particular instructional design model, could be successful. The point of this case study was to show a real-world impact application of systems thinking and to demonstrate how a systematic approach can be applied in different situations to produce differing solutions that are appropriate in light of the context.

During the course the faculty spoke often, using VoIP (Skype) to discuss emerging issues or students' progress. Although we were active in the discussion forums, we did not dominate them in any way. The forums were for the voices of the students more than the faculty. We were constantly moving Word and PowerPoint files around among us for review and editing as well as modifying and updating the class Web site.

We also maintained a blog in which we, the design team, held running discussions regarding issues of pedagogy related to the design of this course. This blog started months before the course began when we were in the planning discussions. As an afterthought once the course was under way, we mentioned to the students that we were blogging about pedagogy, distance learning, and this course. They asked if they could read our blog, and we put a link to it for the students. This was an unexpected hit! Students enjoyed this blog to a great extent and reported being intrigued to see our thinking about teaching and about developing this course. The blog was also an entry point for them into some of the literature about teaching and learning, as we would discuss articles we had found that were relevant to what we were doing. We also held discussions about the best way to accomplish some instructional purposes—about the benefits and limitations of specific instructional strategies we were considering for parts of this class. They also got to read our debates and disagreements on topics, not just what we saw in common. At times the blog would be very specific about whether to introduce a certain example or reading related to some instructional design process. At other times the blog would be philosophical in which we discussed what learning was or argued about epistemology. As the three of us interacted, we were embarking on the use of Web 2.0 without having actually decided to do so. It just fit our needs as we worked collaboratively on developing and teaching this course.

Formative Evaluation and Course Modification _____

From the beginning we had planned to revisit the course design throughout the semester, making adjustments as necessary based on students' experiences, to ensure student learning. We recognized we would have to revisit the design, as we were experimenting with service-learning and problem-based learning in an online environment involving students and faculty at two different universities. In order to accomplish this, we held weekly team meetings to evaluate progress and make any needed revisions. We carefully followed the postings of our students and often asked where they were having difficulty and what we could do to help. Despite a considerable development effort to get this course up and going, we found we had to create additional materials when students experienced unanticipated problems. Through weekly chat sessions and ongoing discussion forums, we were also able to detect student problems. For example, when students had difficulty completing a needs assessment, we created a template for needs assessment, provided examples of needs assessment, and added more readings on the subject. Initially we had organized the course conceptually around the common steps in the instructional design process. For example, we had a folder labeled "evaluation" that contained all the readings and links to sites on evaluation. But several weeks into the course, students suggested they would rather have it organized on a weekly basis, so we created a folder for each week and placed all the related resources into that folder.

As the course unfolded students would ask us to identify key ideas about some topic or what we thought about the topic. In essence, they were asking us to give them our take on the topic—basically an introductory lecture on the subject. This was accomplished by creating PowerPoint presentations on each step in the instructional design process and then going back and adding narration. In the discussion forum and through some e-mail from students, we realized some students were feeling rather disconnected from their classmates. To counter this we created weekly chat sessions at a time they selected so that faculty and students could participate in a live discussion session. This gave students a feeling that others were out there and working together toward common goals. It was also a time to air concerns and frustrations as well as make adjustments when necessary.

A Focus on Course Revision

Often faculty members administer some form of a course evaluation on the last day of class. We were more interested in collecting systematic evaluation data while the course was under way so that we could make immediate modifications when they were called for. This was important to us because we were doing so many things that were new to us as faculty and we were not quite sure as to what would and would not work. Despite our extensive planning we knew some things would not work as well as we wished, so we did our first course evaluation several weeks into the semester when students had sufficient experience to evaluate it and we had sufficient time to make modifications to improve the course for them. We carefully analyzed the evaluation to identify problem areas. We then shared our findings with students to confirm what we learned and to see if the changes we proposed seemed sufficient to them. In essence, we renegotiated the course redesign with the students and made a number of changes to improve the course. We also conducted an evaluation at the end of the course to learn what we could via evaluations about teaching online courses in this manner.

Lessons Learned

Some students experienced difficulties likely resulting from their role in this course as compared to the role they had played in other courses. Undoubtedly some students arrived the first day of this course expecting that they would listen to some lectures, read some articles or a book, and write a final paper. Instead they became active participants in an environment that simulated a consulting company work team. In this role they had to deal with problems that involved uncertainty, outright confusion at times, time pressures, and the normal issues that arise when people have to work together in teams to accomplish a common goal. We as faculty also experienced frustration at times and were surprised by some of the problems and issues our students encountered. We had carefully explained how this class would be different from a traditional class and had explained the basis for using problem-based learning and service-learning rather than a more traditional approach to pedagogy. Students seemed genuinely excited about participating. Excited, that is, until things got under way and we were several weeks into the course. Then we saw a real push-back from some students. They were resisting the approach to pedagogy more than they were resisting distance learning per se. They were challenged by working at a distance in groups on real problems. This was new and different and they were uncomfortable. Some were asking in roundabout ways for us to just tell them what they needed to know, so that they could then memorize information and pass any quiz we might give. In short, they were reluctant to leave the comfortable world of the traditional classroom. As outlined in the previous section, when we sensed this we made some provisions to accommodate them and reduce their levels of stress. We believe the key point is that *students will experience some difficulty when comfortable modes of instruction are changed.*

Recommendations

Based on our experiences teaching this course, we have some recommendations for those teaching online courses, especially if their online course extends beyond typical lectures and readings, which we think a good course should. Our suggestions include:

Have clear expectations at the beginning. Don't assume students will figure everything out right away. Be explicit regarding what your students are expected to do during the course, what resources are available to assist them, what you expect them to produce, how you will evaluate them, and what your role will be.

Hold an initial meeting of the whole class so that they can begin to get to know each other and you as well. Have them discuss their backgrounds with regards to the subject matter of your course and with regards to any previous experience taking distance-learning courses. Ask them about any concerns and talk about how you will address these. Make sure they get any questions answered and that they understand how this course will operate and, especially, what they will have to do.

Talk with your students about the pedagogy of your course, especially features that may be new or different to some of them. Let them know why you are teaching the course in the manner you are so that they understand the rationale for the pedagogy. For example, if you are using problem-based learning for your course as we did, then be clear about what problem-based learning is, how it works, how this will be different from a traditional course, what you will be doing, what they will be doing, and why. We went so far as to review the research evidence on problem-based learning with our students at the beginning of the class and discussed the advantages people had found from using it, as well as its limitations. It is important to let your students know you are excited about using a different pedagogy because you expect it to help them learn better, and it is important to create the expectation within your students that they will do well following this approach. This is an opportunity to demonstrate your self-efficacy related to teaching via problem-based learning, or whatever approach you are using, and to enhance students' self-efficacy for learning in this way.

Help your students decide whether this course will be right for them and get their buy-in early on—the first day if possible. This serves two goals: you get students invested in the course and the distance-learning methodology you will be using, and you can use this to "encourage" those students who are not willing or not able to function well in this learning environment to look elsewhere for a course. Yes, we are suggesting that distance learning, especially distance learning that uses different pedagogy, is not for all students. A passive, dependent student who is not good at self-regulation may do fine in a traditional teacher-centered classroom but will flounder in a distance-learning course that requires more self-management and direction. We need to remember that at the post-secondary level we are getting students who have been successful in traditional classrooms. This approach has worked for them to some extent. They have figured out how to be a student in a traditional classroom or they couldn't have made it this far. This is even truer in a graduate level course. These students have been successful in four years of undergraduate school. They know how to "take" a traditional course. Those who weren't successful don't make it this far. So you may have some reluctant students when you tamper with the traditional approach to instruction, because you have students who have been successful to some extent with the traditional approach. Recognize that you are asking them to change and enter a less-familiar territory. When you explain this clearly, some students may see that this is not for them. It would be better for them to reach this conclusion early, preferably the first day, so that they can drop this course and add some other course.

Be sensitive to the students' experiences as they go through your course. Plan the course as carefully as you can—we spent six months planning our distance-learning course—but realize you can't get everything right ahead of time. Therefore pay close attention to your students as they go through your course. See where they stumble or get frustrated. See where they encounter problems or get confused. See where they are missing a key point or are developing misconceptions about some piece of content. As the instructor you need to have an active role in the distance-learning course—not as dispenser of information but as a monitor and guide who pays close attention to the students and intervenes to keep them on track.

Be responsive to students. One potential problem in a distance-learning course is that students don't "see" you like they do in a traditional class when they sit in front of you for three hours each week. It is important that you establish and maintain a "virtual presence" in your distance-learning course so that students know that you are there. You accomplish this by monitoring their progress as we suggested above and by being responsive when the situation calls for it. This does not mean you have to be online 24/7, but you do have to participate online on a regular basis, preferably daily. Sometimes, if you are up late one evening, you might go into the discussion forum or look at your e-mail and post a response at midnight or later. This will amaze your students who don't realize we old professors can stay up so late!

If there is complex content or you have a large assignment in your course, consider breaking this into more bite-sized chunks. Students might get overwhelmed when facing what appear to be awfully large projects, but can readily grasp these when they are presented in smaller, more manageable chunks. This will also help pace students through the course by having several, smaller assignments due at different times through the semester rather than a single large assignment due all at once. We ran into a problem with an assignment for our students to complete a needs assessment. This had them stumbling, and fussing, until we broke the assignment into four smaller, more focused assignments based on the four steps of doing a needs assessment. That allowed them to focus on step one and get it accomplished by the due date, then move on to step two.

An often-mentioned advantage of distance learning is that students can move through the course at their own pace. We recognize this as an important benefit of distance learning but caution you about giving too much free rein. Without interim due dates along the way, many students will postpone doing their work in a distance-learning course. When their other courses meet on a fixed schedule, they have some externally imposed pacing, such as having the reading done before Tuesday's class. If we leave all aspects of pacing up to students, they tend to let the assignments in their distance-learning course slide in order to meet deadlines in other courses or in their jobs. We suggest having a listing of due dates that you post at the beginning of the semester so they know up front what they have to get done when. We favor weekly assignments that are due on specific dates. That gives them some flexibility as to when to accomplish the work but does not allow them to let everything wait until the end of the class when they can't recover.

Conclusion

Teaching this course caused us to restructure our professional work as instructors, just as our students had to restructure their work as students. This was at times exhilarating, and at other times frustrating, but was overall well worth the effort. We learned how to work better collaboratively, often using technology in a cutting-edge "thin-client" way just because it enabled us to easily accomplish our collaborative work, not because we were seeking to make a statement of any sort. We learned that the skill set for problem-based teaching was much more about being able to think on one's feet and respond nimbly to changing circumstances than about having an unchanging set of best-laid plans. We learned that teaching using our approach works well as long as ample allowance is made for its newness compared with past experiences. We learned, or rather confirmed, that when teaching using distance learning, pedagogy matters much more than technology.

CASE STUDY 15

Revising an Existing Course
Music for the Non-Major

*State University of New York,
College at Fredonia*

Figures CS15.1 and CS15.2 are the field test and revised outlines of the first four-week module of a music course for non-majors at the State University of New York College at Fredonia. (Although this project was completed some time ago, the process that was used in its development and modification is almost identical to the model described in this book.)

The introductory module was designed to provide each student with an orientation to and framework for the entire course and with the prerequisites that were necessary for the units that follow. Because the student population was extremely diverse—some students had as many as eight years of formal music training while others had none—three tracks were used, with assignments based on the performance of the students on the pretest. Level One students had the most comprehensive music background; Level Two students had some musical experience or coursework; and students assigned to Level Three had little, if any, background in music.

The changes that were made as a result of the field test and the reasons for them are as follows (notice how these changes affected the operational sequence):

• **The course overview and the pretest were separated to improve the orientation session.** *Rationale:* the course was such

457

Figure CS15.1.

Fall Field-Test Version of Introductory Module for Music in the Western World

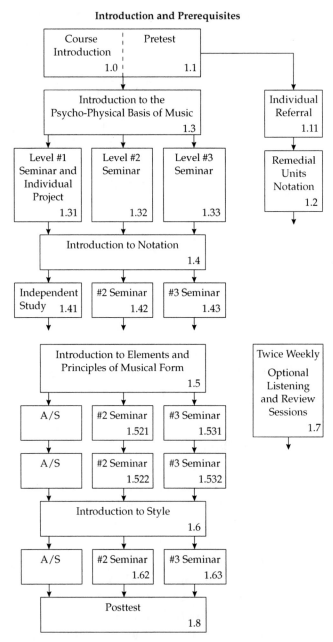

Source: Thomas Regelski and Robert Diamond.

a major departure from traditional courses, with its emphasis on independent study and options, that many students found the transition to it difficult. As a result, additional time had to be spent reviewing how to use the student manual as well as explaining to students how they could use the statements of instructional objectives to improve learning and increase the effectiveness of study time.

Figure CS15. 2.
Spring Revision of Introductory Module for Music in the Western World

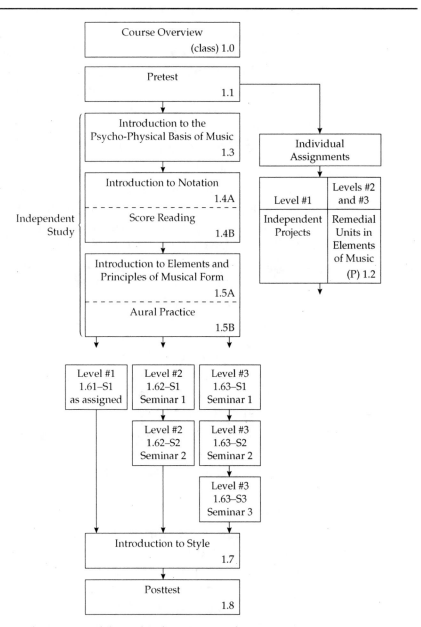

Source: Thomas Regelski and Robert Diamond.

• **The sequencing of seminars within the modules had to be substantially changed.** *Rationale:* for a seminar to be effective, a certain amount of background information is essential. The original sequence did not provide students with enough study time to complete the necessary units before they were discussed in the seminars. The seminars therefore were rescheduled later in the sequence.

- **New instructional units were required.** *Rationale:* on the posttest, students did not perform at the anticipated level in their ability either to read scores or to discriminate aurally. Two additional independent-study units on score reading were added. As a result, students' deficiencies were corrected.

- **One unit had to be completely redesigned.** *Rationale:* the original multiscreen presentation style proved to be instructionally ineffective and disliked (an understatement) by the students. This approach also proved cumbersome and inefficient as it forced all students to move at the same pace. It was replaced by a far more effective independent study sequence used in conjunction with written materials.

- **The number of seminars was reduced.** *Rationale:* as sometimes happens, the fall and spring semesters did not have the same amount of time available for instruction, forcing a modification in design. By placing the seminars later in the sequence and scheduling more seminars for the Level Three students and fewer for the well-prepared group, the number of seminars was reduced from fourteen (including three optional ones) to six. This decrease did not appear to have a negative effect on either attitudes or achievement. In addition, to permit maximum flexibility, this three-hour course was scheduled for an hour a day (five hours each week) so that every student could attend any session scheduled during that period. However, the maximum number of live meetings a student would attend during a four-week module was six.

- **The twice-weekly optional listening and review sessions were replaced by oral practice and optional audio recordings.** *Rationale:* because of a heavy assignment load, students did not attend the regularly scheduled, optional, faculty-led review sessions.

In addition, minor modifications were made in the pretest, in some of the independent learning sequences, and in the remedial units that were used. Several remedial assignments were also eliminated, and a more realistic time frame was established. The effectiveness of the new remedial module made it possible to eliminate grouping the students by entering levels of proficiency once this unit was completed.

REFERENCES

"Addressing the Challenges Facing American Undergraduate Education: A Letter to Our Members." American Council on Education, American Association of State Colleges and Universities, American Association of Community Colleges, Association of American Universities, National Association of Independent Colleges and Universities, and the National Association of State Colleges and Land-Grant Universities. Sept. 21, 2006.

Allen, L. R. "An Instructional Epiphany." *Change*, Mar.–Apr. 1996, *28*(2), J2.

American Council on Education and others. *Statement on Academic Rights and Responsibilities.* Washington, D.C.: American Council on Education, 1998.

Angelo, T. A., and Cross, K. P. *Classroom Assessment Techniques.* (2nd ed.) San Francisco: Jossey-Bass, 1993.

Angelo, T. A. *A Teacher's Dozen: Fourteen General, Research-Based Principles for Improving Higher Learning in Our Classrooms,* 1993. Retrieved from http://onlineaccess.shastacollege.edu/webct/Faculty/documents/angelo.pdf on July 27, 2007.

Association of American Colleges and Universities. *Integrity in the College Curriculum: A Report to the Academic Community.* Washington, D.C.: The Association of American Colleges and Universities, 1985.

Association of American Colleges and Universities. *Greater Expectations: A New Vision for Learning as a Nation Goes to College.* Washington, D.C.: The Association of American Colleges and Universities, 2002.

Association of American Colleges and Universities. "Engaged Learning and the Core Principles of Liberal Education." *Peer Review,* 2007, *93*(1). Washington, D.C.: Association of American Colleges and Universities. Available at http://ctl.stanford.edu/tomprof/postings.html.

Association of American Colleges and Universities. *College Learning for the New Global Century.* Washington, D.C.: Association of American Colleges and Universities, 2007.

Attewell, P., and Lavin, D. E. "Distorted Statistics on Graduation Rates." *The Chronicle of Higher Education,* July 6, 2007, p. B16.

Banta, T. J., and Associates. *Building a Scholarship of Assessment.* San Francisco: Jossey-Bass, 2002.

Banta, T. J., and Associates. *Assessment Update, Progress, Trends, and Practices in Higher Education, 19*(5). San Francisco: Jossey-Bass, Sept.-Oct. 2007.

Banta, T., Lund, J., Black, K., and Oblander, F. *Assessment in Practice: Putting Principles to Work on College Campuses.* San Francisco: Jossey-Bass, 1996.

Barr, R. B., and Tagg, J. "From Teaching to Learning: A New Paradigm for Undergraduate Education." *Change,* 1995, *27*(2), 24.

Bergquist, W. H., and Armstrong, J. L. *Planning Effectively for Educational Quality: An Outcomes-Based Approach for Colleges Committed to Excellence.* San Francisco: Jossey-Bass, 1986.

Beyond Dead Reckoning. National Center for Postsecondary Improvement. Stanford, Calif., 2002.

Boyer, E. L. *College: The Undergraduate Experience in America.* New York: Harper-Collins, 1987.

Boyer, E. L. *Scholarship Reconsidered: Priorities of the Professoriate.* San Francisco: Jossey-Bass, 1990.

Bransford, J. D., Brown, A. L., and Cocking, R. R. (eds.). *How People Learn: Brain, Mind, Experience, and School.* Washington, D.C.: National Academy Press, 1999. Available at www.nap.edu.

Burstyn, J., and Santa, C. "Complexity as an Impediment to Learning: A Study of Changes in Selected College Textbooks." *Journal of Higher Education,* 1977, *s*(5), 508–518.

Carey, K. *College Ranking Reformed: The Case for a New Order in Higher Education.* Washington, D.C.: Education Sector, 2006. Available at www.education sector.org.

Center for Institutional and International Initiatives. *New Times, New Strategies: Curricula Joint Ventures.* Washington, D.C.: American Council on Education, 2003.

Chickering, A. W., Gamson, Z., and Barsi, L. M. *The Seven Principles for Good Practice in Undergraduate Education: Faculty Inventor.* Milwaukee: Winona State University, 1989. Also available at www.johnson.Fdn.org/publica tions/ConferenceReports/Sevenprinciples/sevenprinciples-pdf.

Chickering, A., and Ehrmann, S. C. "Implementing the Seven Principles: Technology as Lever." *AAHE Bulletin,* Oct. 1996, pp. 3–6.

Chism, N.V.N. "Valuing Student Differences." In W. J. McKeachie, *Teaching Tips: Strategies, Research, and Theory for College and University Teachers.* (11th ed.) Boston: Houghton Mifflin, 2002.

Chism, N.V.N. "A tale of two classrooms." In N.V.N. Chism (ed.), *The Importance of Physical Space in Creating Supportive Learning Environments.* New Directions for Teaching and Learning, No. 92. San Francisco: Jossey-Bass, 2003.

Clinton, W. J. Commencement address at Morgan State University in Baltimore, MD. In 1997 *Public Papers of the Presidents of the United States, Books I and II.* Washington, D.C.: Government Printing Office, May 18, 1997. Available at www.gpoaccess.gov/pubpapers/wjclinton.html.

Crone, I., and Mackay, R. "Motivating Today's College Student." *Peer Review,* Winter 2007, *9*(1). Available at *Tomorrow's Professor* Web site at http://ctl. stanford.edu/tomprof/postings.html (TSP msg #795).

Cross, K. P., and Steadman, M. H. *Classroom Research: Implementing the Scholarship of Teaching.* San Francisco: Jossey-Bass, 1996.

Deci, E. L., and Ryan, R. M. *Intrinsic Motivation and Self-Determination in Human Behavior.* New York: Plenum, 1985.

Deci, E. L., and Ryan, R. M. "The 'What' and 'Why' of Goal Pursuits: Human Needs and the Self-Determination of Behavior." *Psychological Inquiry,* 2000, *11,* 227–268.

Diamond, R. M. *Designing and Assessing Courses and Curricula.* (2nd ed.) San Francisco: Jossey-Bass, 1998.

Diamond, R. M. "The Mission-Driven Faculty Reward System." In R. M. Diamond (ed.), *Field Guide to Academic Leadership.* San Francisco: Jossey-Bass, 2002.

Diamond, R. M. "Changing Higher Education: Realistic Goal or Wishful Thinking?" The National Academy, 2006. Available at www.thenationalacademy.org/ readings/hardtochange.html.

Diamond, R. M., and Adam, B. *Recognizing Faculty Work.* San Francisco: Jossey-Bass, 1993.

Diamond, R. M., and Allshouse, M. F. "Utilizing America's Most Useful Resource." *Inside Higher Ed,* Apr. 6, 2006. Available at http://insidehighered.com/ views/2007/04/06/diamond.

Diamond, R. M., and DeBlois, P. B. "Accountability and Academic Innovation: Don't Forget the Registrar." *Inside Higher Ed*, Jan. 20, 2007.

Donovan, M. S., Bransford, J. D., and Pellegrino, J. W. *How People Learn: Bridging Research and Practice.* Washington, D.C.: National Academy Press, 1999.

Dresser, D. L. "The Relationship Between Personality Needs, College Expectations, Environmental Press, and Undergraduate Attrition in a University College of Liberal Arts." Unpublished doctoral dissertation, College of Education, Syracuse University, 1987.

Englemann, D. "Assessment from the Ground Up." *Inside Higher Ed*, Aug. 14, 2007. Available at http://insidehighered.com/layout/set/print/views/2007/08/14/englemann.

Evensky, J. "Dealing with Skill Prerequisites: Extending the Margin of Success and Accomplishing Affirmative Action in Introductory Economics." Unpublished report, Syracuse University, 1991.

Ewell, P. Oral report to Board of Governors, Truman State University, Nov. 1991.

Facione, P. A. "Critical Thinking: What It Is and Why It Counts." *Insight Assessment and the California Academic Press*, 2007. Available at www.insight assessment.com.

Fink, L. D. *Creating Significant Learning Experiences: An Integrated Approach to Designing College Courses.* San Francisco: Jossey-Bass, 2003.

Gardiner, L. F. *Redesigning Higher Education: Producing Dramatic Gains in Student Learning. ASHE Higher Education Report, 23*(7). San Francisco: Jossey-Bass, 1996.

Gardiner, L. F. *Designing a College Curriculum.* St. Petersburg, Fla.: National Academy for Academic Leadership, 2006.

Glassick, C. E., Huber, M. T., and Maeroff, G. I. *Scholarship Assessed: Evaluating the Professoriate.* San Francisco: Jossey-Bass, 1997.

Gray, P. J., Diamond, R. M., and Adam, B. E. *A National Study on the Relative Importance of Research and Undergraduate Teaching at Colleges and Universities.* Syracuse, N.Y.: Syracuse University, 1996.

Gray, P. J., Froh, R. G., and Diamond, R. M. *A National Study of Research on the Balance Between Research and Undergraduate Teaching.* Syracuse, N.Y.: Syracuse University, 1992.

Green, C. *The Campus Computing Project.* 2000. Downloaded Aug. 31, 2007, from www.campuscomputing.net/summaries/2000/index.html.

Grunert-O'Brien, J., Millis, B. J., and Cohen, M. W. *The Course Syllabus: A Learning-Centered Approach.* (2nd ed.) San Francisco: Anker/Jossey-Bass, 2008.

Hannum, W. H., and Briggs, L. J. *How Does Instructional Systems Design Differ from Traditional Instruction?* Chapel Hill: School of Education, University of North Carolina, 1980.

Hardin, J. H. *Mathematics Prerequisites and Student Success in Introductory Courses: Final Report.* Syracuse, N.Y.: Center for Instructional Development, Syracuse University, 1992.

Hunter, M. S. "Fostering Student Learning and Success Through First-Year Programs." *Peer Review*, 2006, *8*(3).

Jaschik, S. "Bias Seen in Bias Studies." *Inside Higher Ed*, Jan. 22, 2007.

Jones, E. *Writing Goals Inventory.* U.S. Department of Education, 1994.

Jones, R. T. "Liberal Education for the Twenty-First Century: Business Expectations." *Liberal Education*, 2005, *91*(2), 32–39.

Keller, F. "Good-Bye Teacher." *Journal of Applied Behavior Analysis*, 1968, *1*, 79–89.

Knapper, C. "Research on College Teaching and Learning: Apply What We Know." Presentation at the 2004 Teaching Professor Conference. Retrieved July 27, 2007, from https://www.mcmaster.ca/stlhe/documents/Research%20on%20College%20Teaching%20and%20Learning.pdf.

Kotter, J. P. *Leading Change.* Boston: Harvard Business School Press, 1996, p. 4.

Krathwohl, D. R., Bloom, B. S., and Masia, B. B. *Taxonomy of Educational Objectives. The Classification of Education Goals: Handbook 2: Affective Domain.* New York: McKay, 1964.

Kreber, C. *Exploring Research-Based Teaching.* San Francisco: Jossey-Bass, 2006.

Kuh, G. D., Kinzie, J., Schuh, J., and Whitt, E. *Assessing Conditions to Enhance Educational Effectiveness.* San Francisco: Jossey-Bass, 2005.

Kuh, G. D. "How to Help Students Achieve." *The Chronicle of Higher Education,* June 15, 2007, pp. B12–B13.

Laufgraben, J. L., Shapiro, N. S., and Associates. *Sustaining and Improving Learning Communities.* San Francisco: Jossey-Bass, 2004.

Lee, J. B. *The "Faculty Bias" Studies: Science or Propaganda?* Washington, D.C.: JBL Associates, 2006.

Levesque, C. S., Sell, G. R., and Zimmerman, J. A. "A Theory-Based Integrative Model for Learning and Motivation in Higher Education." In S. Chadwick-Blossey (ed.), *To Improve the Academy,* 24, 86–103. Bolton, Mass.: Anker, 2006.

Loacker, G., and Mentkowski, M. "Creating a Culture Where Assessment Improves Learning." In T. W. Banta (ed.), *Making a Difference: Outcomes of a Decade of Assessment in Higher Education.* San Francisco: Jossey-Bass, 1993.

Lough, J. F. "Carnegie Professors of the Year: Models for Teaching Success." In J. K. Ross (ed.), *Inspiring Teaching: Carnegie Professors of the Year Speak.* Bolton, Mass.: Anker, 1996.

Mager, R. F. *Preparing Instructional Objectives.* Belmont, Calif.: Fearon, 1975.

Magruder, J., McManis, M., and Young, C. "The Right Idea at the Right Time: Development of a Transformational Assessment Culture." In P. J. Gray and T. W. Banta (eds.), *The Campus-Level Impact of Assessment: Progress, Problems, and Possibilities.* New Directions for Higher Education, No. 100. San Francisco: Jossey-Bass, 1997.

Marchese, T. "The Search for Next-Century Learning." *Wingspread Journal,* 1996, *8*(3). The Johnson Foundation, 4. Available at www.johnsonfdn.org/summer96/search.html.

Marchese, T. J. "Whatever Happened to Undergraduate Reform?" *Carnegie Perspectives, No. 26.* Stanford, Calif., 2006.

McGonigal, K. "Teaching for Transformation: From Learning Theory to Teaching Strategies." *Speaking of Teachers,* 2005, *14*(2), Center for Teaching and Learning, Stanford University.

McKeachie, W. J., and Svinicki, M. *McKeachie's Teaching Tips: Strategies, Research and Theory for College and University Teachers.* (12th ed.) Boston: Houghton Mifflin, 2006.

McKinney, M. "Setting Boundaries." Available at *Tomorrow's Professor* (#823) at http://cgi.stanford.edu/~dept-ctl/cgi-bin/tomprof/posting.php?ID=828.

Milton, O., and Associates. *On College Teaching: A Guide to Contemporary Practices.* San Francisco: Jossey-Bass, 1978.

Missouri State University. [Final report: President's Commission on Diversity.] Available at www.missouristate.edu/diversitycommission/10110.htm, 2005–06.

Missouri State University. "Imagining and Making Missouri's Future," Available at www.missouristate.edu/longrangeplan/modeling.htm, 2006.

Muffo, J. A. "Lessons Learned from a Decade of Assessment." *Assessment Update.* Sept.-Oct. 1996, *8*(5), 1–2, 11.

National Academy of Engineering. *The Engineer of 2020: Visions of Engineering in the New Century.* Washington, D.C.: National Academy Press, 2004.

National Academy of Sciences. *Rising Above the Gathering Storm.* National Academy of Sciences, National Academy of Engineering, and Institute of Medicine. Washington, D.C.: National Academy Press, 2007, p. 223.

O'Meara, K., and Rice, R. E. (eds.). *Faculty Priorities Reconsidered: Rewarding Multiple Forms of Scholarship.* San Francisco: Jossey-Bass, 2005.

Palomba, C. A., and Banta, T. W. *Assessment Essentials: Planning, Implementing, and Improving Assessment in Higher Education.* San Francisco: Jossey-Bass, 1999.

Pascarella, E. T., and Terenzini, P. T. *How College Affects Students: A Third Decade of Research.* Vol 2. San Francisco: Jossey-Bass, 2005.

Penny, J."Assessment for Us and Assessment for Them," *Inside Higher Ed,* June 26, 2007. Available at http://insidehighered.com/views/2007/06/26/penn.

Perry, W. G. *Forms of Intellectual/Ethical Development in the College Years: A Scheme.* Austin, Tex.: Holt, Rinehart and Winston, 1970.

Pervin, L., and Rubin, D. "Student Dissatisfaction with College and the College Dropout: A Transactional Approach." *Journal of Social Psychology,* 1967, *72,* 285–295.

Pieper, S. *Higher Learning Commission Self-Study.* Truman State University, 2005.

Powers, E. "Elephant Not in the Room." *Inside Higher Ed,* May 1, 2007.

Powers, E. "Introductory Course Makeover." *Inside Higher Ed,* Mar. 15, 2007. Available at http://insidehighered.com/news/2007/03/15/ncat.

Pusser, B., Breneman, D. W., Gansneder, B. M., Kohl, K. J., Levin, J. S., Milam, J. H., and Turner, S. E. *Returning to Learning: Adults' Success Is College in Key to America's Future.* Indianapolis, Ind.: Lumina Foundation for Education, 2007.

Putnam, R. D. "E Pluribus Unum: Diversity and Community in the Twenty-First Century." *Scandinavian Political Studies.* 2007, *30*(2), 137–174.

Radio-Television News Directors Association. *Future Trends in Broadcast Journalism.* Washington, D.C.: Radio-Television News Directors Association, 1984, p. 39.

Rehm, J. "The High Risk of Improving Teaching." *National Teaching and Learning Forum Newsletter,* 2006, *15*(6), National Teaching and Learning Forum.

Romer, R. *Making Quality Count in Undergraduate Education.* Denver: Education Commission of the States, 1995.

Rossett, A., Douglis, F., and Frazee, R. V. "Strategies for Building Blended Learning." *Learning Circuits,* American Society for Training and Development, 2003. Retrieved July 27, 2007, from http://www.learningcircuits.org/2003/jul2003/rossett.htm

Ruben, B. D. *Pursuing Excellence in Higher Education.* San Francisco: Jossey-Bass, 2003.

Rubin, S. "Professors, Students, and the Syllabus." *Chronicle of Higher Education,* 1985, *30*(23), 56.

Sell, G. R., and Lounsberry, B. "Supporting Curriculum Development." In J. G. Gaff, J. L. Ratcliff, and Associates (eds.), *Handbook of the Undergraduate Curriculum: A Comprehensive Guide to Purposes, Structures, Practices, and Change.* San Francisco: Jossey-Bass, 1996.

Shapiro, N. S., and Levine, J. H. *Creating Learning Communities: A Practical Guide to Winning Support, Organizing for Change, and Implementing Programs.* San Francisco: Jossey-Bass, 1999.

Shulman, L., and Hutchings, P. *Learning About Student Learning from Community Colleges.* Carnegie Perspectives, 2006. Available at http://www.carnegiefoundation.org/conversations/sub.asp?key=244&subkey=1548 (TP Msg. #716).

Singham, S., "Death to the Syllabus." *Liberal Education,* 2007, *93*(4). Available at *Tomorrow's Professor* (#834). http://amps-tools.mit.edu/tomprofblog.

Smith, B. L., MacGregor, J., Matthews, R., and Gabelnick, F. *Learning Communities: Reforming Undergraduate Education.* San Francisco: Jossey-Bass, 2004.

Springer, A. (2005). *Update on Affirmative Action in Higher Education: A Current Legal Overview.* Retrieved July 27, 2007, from http://www.aaup.org/AAUP/protect/legal/topics/aff-ac-update.htm.

Stanley, C. A., and Porter, M. E. (eds.). *Engaging Large Classes: Strategies and Techniques for College Faculty.* Bolton, Mass.: Anker, 2002.

Stark, J. S., and Lattuca, L. R. *Shaping the College Curriculum: Academic Plans in Action.* Needham Heights, Mass.: Allyn & Bacon, 1997.

Stim, R. *Getting Permission: How to License and Clear Copyrighted Material On-Line and Off.* Palo Alto, Calif.: Stanford University Libraries, 2004. Available at http://fairuse.stanford.edu.

Terenzini, P. T., and Pascarella, E. T. "Living with Myths: Undergraduate in America." *Change,* Jan.-Feb. 1994, *26*(1), 32.

The Task Force on the Student Experience. *Qualities of the Liberally Educated Person: A Description of Important Competencies.* Newark, N.J.: Rutgers University, 1986.

Tierney, W. G. "Academic Leadership and Globalization." *The Department Chair,* Spring 2007, *17*(4). Bolton, Mass.: Anker.

Tschinkel, W. R. "Just Scoring Points." *The Chronicle of Higher Education,* April 13, 2007, p. B13.

Turk, J. V. (ed.). *The Professional Bond—Public Relations Education and the Practice.* Washington, D.C.: The Commission on Public Relations Education, 2006.

U.S. Department of Education, Office of the Secretary. *Meeting the Challenge of a Changing World: Strengthening Education for the 21st Century.* Washington, D.C.: U.S. Department of Education, 2006.

U.S. Department of Education. *A Test of Leadership: Charting the Future of U.S. Higher Education.* Sept. 2006, (vii). Also available at http://fsuspc.fsu.edu/media/test_of_leadership.pdf.

Walker, C. J. "Assessing Group Process: Using Classroom Assessment to Build Autonomous Learning Teams." *Assessment Update,* Nov.–Dec. 1995, *7*(6), 4–5.

Watson, J. "What Psychology Can We Feel Sure About?" Teachers College Record 1960. Reprinted as a separate pamphlet, *What Psychology Can We Trust?* New York: Bureau of Publication, Teachers College, Columbia University, 1961.

INDEX

e denotes exhibit; *f* denotes figure; *t* denotes table.

A

AACU. *See* Association of American Colleges and Universities

Academic achievement: accreditation questions involving, 16; current lack of, 4–5; data collection about, 96–99; and math skills, 97; research related to, 194

Academic support centers, 26

Academy for Assessment of Student Learning, 334–336

Accountability: assessment for, 8; case studies related to, 417–418; increased demand for, x, 7–8; and instructional goals, 147–148; *U.S. News* rankings as, xiii

Accreditation: challenges of, xi; changes in, 15–16, 19; and content modification, 108; design considerations regarding, 130; for engineering programs, 330–333; faculty roles in, 15–20; guidelines for, 18–19; Higher Learning Commission's position on, 322; importance of, 15, 20; questions asked in, 16–17; timing of, 17

Accrediting agencies, 18, 20, 165

Accreditation Board for Engineering and Technology, 330–333

Achievement tests, 95

ACT College Outcomes Measurement Project, 389

Active learning: of adult learners, 263–264; effective technology uses for, 227; as instructional delivery method, 207–208; as principle of good practice, 195; research on, 115, 193; resources on, 214–216

"Active Learning: Creating Excitement in the Classroom" (Bonwell and Eison), 215–216

Adam, B., 28, 29, 32–33, 388

Adjunct faculty. *See* Part-time/adjunct faculty

Administrators: as barrier to change, xviii; communication with, 123; and continuous registration issues, 417; and decision to create new course, 70; input from, regarding design constraints, 131; as members of initial meetings, 76; and principles of reform, 314; priority-setting role of, 67; as reporting audience, 164–165; at Truman State, 390

Printed in the United States of America
03-14-13